FAMILY NEWSPAPERS?

Family Newspapers?

Sex, Private Life, and the British Popular Press 1918–1978

ADRIAN BINGHAM

OXFORD
UNIVERSITY PRESS

Great Clarendon Street, Oxford OX2 6DP

Oxford University Press is a department of the University of Oxford.
It furthers the University's objective of excellence in research, scholarship,
and education by publishing worldwide in

Oxford New York

Auckland Cape Town Dar es Salaam Hong Kong Karachi
Kuala Lumpur Madrid Melbourne Mexico City Nairobi
New Delhi Shanghai Taipei Toronto

With offices in

Argentina Austria Brazil Chile Czech Republic France Greece
Guatemala Hungary Italy Japan Poland Portugal Singapore
South Korea Switzerland Thailand Turkey Ukraine Vietnam

Published in the United States
by Oxford University Press Inc., New York

First published 2009

British Library Cataloguing in Publication Data
Data available

Library of Congress Cataloging in Publication Data
Bingham, Adrian.
Family newspapers? : sex, private life, and the British popular press 1918–1978 / Adrian Bingham.
p. cm.
Includes bibliographical references and index.
ISBN 978-0-19-927958-6
1. Sensationalism in journalism—Great Britain—History—20th century. I. Title.
PN5124.S45B56 2009
072'.0904—dc22 2008046058

Typeset by Laserwords Private Limited, Chennai, India
Printed in Great Britain
on acid-free paper by
MPG Books Group

ISBN 978-0-19-927958-6

1 3 5 7 9 10 8 6 4 2

For Dad

Acknowledgements

I would like to thank the Leverhulme Trust and the British Academy for funding the fellowships that enabled me to research this book. I held these fellowships at the Centre for Contemporary British History in the Institute of Historical Research, which provided a friendly and stimulating working environment. Pat Thane, in particular, offered useful advice and guidance. Conversations with Tanya Evans, Mark Hampton, Lesley Hall, Rebecca Loncraine, Alison Oram, and Chris Waters helped me to clarify my ideas. I finished the book at the University of Sheffield: thanks to all my colleagues for making the Department of History such an easy place to settle into. Martin Conboy has shown huge generosity in sharing his expertise in the popular press with me; he read the whole manuscript and offered typically perceptive comments. At OUP, Seth Cayley has been an unfailingly patient and supportive editor.

The publication of this book has been made possible by a grant from the Scouloudi Foundation in association with the Institute of Historical Research. I would like to thank the British Library, Express Newspapers, and Mirror Newspapers, for permission to reproduce those images for which they hold the copyright. The illustrations were supplied by Mirrorpix, the British Library Newspaper Library at Colindale, and the Centre for Cartoons and Caricature, University of Kent, Canterbury. Mel at Mirrorpix went beyond the call of duty in ensuring the digital images were in a suitable format.

On a personal note, thanks to Jane and Jon Legg, Andre Katz, Anita Aul, Rachel Mackie, Steve Dilley, Rhian Roberts, Graham Knight, Peter Smith, and Ellen Hughes—the book that you have followed with such amusement is finally ready! Thanks too to Mum, Nick and Birgit, and the Hay family. Most of all, I owe my happiness while writing this to Felicity's boundless love and warmth; and the arrival of Anna has made these last few months so much more enjoyable.

This book is dedicated to my much-loved and much-missed dad, Keith Bingham.

Contents

List of Illustrations

Introduction

One of the central tenets of modern popular journalism is that readers are interested in sex. 'Sex things' are 'always news', Lord Northcliffe, the founder of the *Daily Mail* and the *Daily Mirror*, told his staff in the first decade of the twentieth century, and few in Fleet Street disagreed.[1] Joining the *Mirror* as a young reporter in the late 1930s, Harry Procter found that the paper was 'perfectly honest' about what it sought from its employees. 'The *Mirror* wanted Sex . . . Sex, the *Mirror* discovered, sold papers—papers—papers by the million. Hard news was merely the third course.'[2] The editors of the *Daily Star*, Derek Jameson and Peter Grimsditch, were similarly honest when they outlined their policy shortly before the paper's launch in November 1978: 'Sex sells—that goes for pictures and words. So the *Star* will have its daily quota. Bigger and better than anyone else.'[3] Journalists tend to stick to what is successful, and sex, it seems, is a subject that has succeeded beyond all others.

Twentieth-century editors were certainly not the first to include sexual content in their newspapers, for there was a long tradition of prurient journalism dating back to the earliest news-sheets in the sixteenth century. They were the first, however, to grapple with the particular complexities of packaging sex for a mass audience. Not until 1896 did a British newspaper, *Lloyd's Weekly News*, break through the one million circulation barrier, and it was only after 1918 that the habit of daily newspaper reading spread throughout society.[4] This mass audience comprised precisely the sorts of people—the working classes, women, youths, the ill-educated—whom those in official and professional circles feared could be 'corrupted' by sexual knowledge and erotic images. In order to assuage the concerns of elite critics—and potential readers—popular newspapers presented themselves as family publications, retailing morally respectable material suitable for consumption by readers of both sexes and all ages. The 'family newspaper' label was a commercial necessity, and the public appetite for sex had to be satisfied within the constraints imposed by it. Editors were well aware that anything too explicit or 'indecent' would, in the long run, threaten circulation levels and

[1] N. Angell, *After All: The Autobiography of Norman Angell* (London: Hamish Hamilton, 1951), 120.

[2] H. Procter, *The Street of Disillusion* (London: Allan Wingate, 1958), 58.

[3] *UK Press Gazette*, 6 Nov. 1978, 3.

[4] R. Williams, *The Long Revolution* (Harmondsworth: Penguin, 1965), 215–36.

alienate advertisers. They had no way of restricting certain pages or columns to adults, nothing comparable to the age certificates or evening watersheds imposed on the cinema and the broadcast media. Journalists developed a range of different ways of covering sex—they sought at different times to titillate, to moralize, to advise, and to investigate—but in every case text and pictures were carefully crafted to remain within the bounds of acceptability as defined by their paper.

This book explores changing perceptions of what sexual content was deemed 'fit to print' in popular newspapers in the six decades after the First World War: from the start of the mass newspaper reading boom to the symbolic triumph of sexualized journalism in 1978. It was in March 1978 that Rupert Murdoch's *Sun*, which since its relaunch in 1969 had taken the coverage of sex to a new level of explicitness, finally overtook the *Daily Mirror* to become the country's most popular paper. The *Daily Star* was an attempt by one of Murdoch's rivals, Victor Matthews, to emulate this success with a paper based on a very similar editorial formula. Although its circulation fell well short of *The Sun*'s, the *Star* managed to remain commercially viable, and therefore became the first new popular daily paper to establish itself in the market for over half a century. The 'daily quota' envisaged by Jameson and Grimsditch for the *Star* in 1978—with photogaphs of topless models and unambiguous descriptions of sexual activity—would have been unthinkable in earlier decades, and vividly illustrated how far notions of acceptability had travelled over the century.

Yet while the greater sexual explicitness of the *Sun* and *Star* of the 1970s demonstrated how much had changed since the Great War, other aspects of their content betrayed significant continuities. Both maintained a vocal defence of 'family values' and vigorously denounced anyone who did not adhere to them with rhetoric that had been perfected by previous generations of journalists. While the *Sun* and the *Star* embraced certain aspects of modern 'permissiveness', they were keen to ensure that it did not go 'too far'. The social composition of their newsrooms was little different to those of their predecessors, and their discussions of sex continued to be shaped by ideas of class, gender, and race that had roots in earlier decades. If the reader of 1918 would have been shocked by the paper of 1978, the editorial voice would nonetheless have been familiar.

Fleet Street's preoccupation with sex meant that the press was a hugely significant source of knowledge and imagery about sexual behaviour, personal relationships, and moral codes. Between 1918 and 1978 newspapers were right at the heart of British popular culture, with the vast majority of adults regularly reading at least one national paper: at mid-century, indeed, Britons read more newspapers per capita than any other people.[5] The huge circulations achieved by the leading popular newspapers inevitably conferred political, social, and

[5] F. Williams, *Dangerous Estate: The Anatomy of Newspapers* (first pub. 1957; London: Longmans, Green, 1958), 1–2; Williams, *Long Revolution*, 232.

cultural authority on them, despite the elite disdain for their commercialism and sensationalism. They helped to set the tone of popular culture, and their contributions to public debate were closely monitored by politicians, policy-makers, campaign groups, as well as by other media. The popular press both reflected and shaped attitudes to sex and private life, and by examining the production, content, and reception of these papers we can obtain valuable insights into the sexual culture of modern Britain.

HISTORIOGRAPHICAL CONTEXT

In the past thirty years there has been a considerable amount of research on sexual discourses and representations of all kinds, much of it influenced by Michel Foucault's argument that sexuality should be understood as discursively produced.[6] Most of the work by historians of Britain has focused on the elite discourses of science, medicine, the law, and politics,[7] but there have been a number of illuminating studies of popular culture, especially of films, women's magazines, and best-selling fiction.[8] Some scholars have also examined the sexual content of the press. The 'new journalism' of the late-nineteenth century has been a popular field for such research, in particular W. T. Stead's notorious investigation of child prostitution in 1885, and the coverage of the 'Jack the Ripper' murders.[9] Various

[6] M. Foucault, *The Will to Knowledge: The History of Sexuality, Vol. 1*, trans. Robert Hurley (first pub. 1976; Harmondsworth: Penguin, 1990).

[7] For example, F. Mort, *Dangerous Sexualities: Medico-Moral Politics in England Since 1830* (London: Routledge & Kegan Paul, 1987); R. Porter and L. Hall, *The Facts of Life: The Creation of Sexual Knowledge in Britain 1650–1950* (New Haven: Yale University Press, 1995); A. McLaren, *The Trials of Manhood: Policing Sexual Boundaries 1870–1930* (Chicago: University of Chicago Press, 1997); L. Bland and L. Doan (eds.), *Sexology in Culture: Labelling Bodies and Desires* (Cambridge: Polity Press, 1998); G. Robb and N. Erber (eds.), *Disorder in the Court: Trials and Sexual Conflict at the Turn of the Century* (Basingstoke: Macmillan, 1999); H. Cocks, *Nameless Offences: Homosexual Desire in the Nineteenth Century* (London: IB Tauris, 2003); H. Cook, *The Long Sexual Revolution: English Women, Sex, and Contraception 1800–1975* (Oxford: Oxford University Press, 2004).

[8] For example, J. Hill, *Sex, Class and Realism: British Cinema, 1956–63* (London: BFI, 1986); B. Melman, *Flappers and Nymphs: Women and the Popular Imagination in the Twenties* (Basingstoke: Macmillan,1988); D. McGillivray, *Doing Rude Things: The History of the British Sex Film, 1957–81* (London: Sun Tavern Fields, 1992); J. Stacey, *Stargazing: Hollywood Cinema and Female Spectatorship* (London: Routledge, 1994); A. Aldgate, *Censorship and the Permissive Society: British Cinema and Theatre 1955–1965* (Oxford: Oxford University Press, 1995); M. Beetham, *A Magazine of Her Own? Domesticity and Desire in the Woman's Magazine* (London: Routledge, 1996); C. Gledhill and G. Swanson (eds.), *Nationalising Femininity: Culture, Sexuality and Cinema in Britain in World War Two* (Manchester: Manchester University Press, 1996); J. McAleer, *Passion's Fortune: The Story of Mills and Boon* (Oxford: Oxford University Press, 1999); M. Collins, 'The Pornography of Permissiveness: Men's Sexuality and Women's Emancipation in Mid-Twentieth Century Britain', *History Workshop Journal*, 47 (1999), 99–120.

[9] J. Walkowitz, *City of Dreadful Delight: Narratives of Sexual Danger in Late Victorian London* (Chicago: Chicago University Press, 1992); L. P. Curtis, Jr., *Jack the Ripper and the London Press* (New Haven: Yale University Press, 2001).

types of court reporting have been explored, notably cases involving divorce,[10] homosexual offences,[11] and gender-crossing.[12] The portrayal of homosexuality in the post-Second World War press has been discussed in some depth.[13] Journalism and cultural studies scholars have analysed several aspects of the contemporary press's coverage of sex, from page three pin-ups to the reporting of sex crimes, although much of this work has little or no historical dimension.[14] Editors and journalists themselves, while not necessarily sharing the same preoccupations as academic researchers, have also offered their reflections on the sexual content of newspapers.[15] Nevertheless, Roy Porter and Lesley's Hall's observation in 1995 that 'the role of the press in both reflecting and creating popular sexual knowledge and attitudes needs a good deal of further study' is still valid.[16] The literature produced so far, both scholarly and journalistic, tends to focus either on one particular campaign or case, or one particular newspaper, or at most on one particular theme, such as homosexuality. Although informative, it is difficult to make wider generalizations about the impact of the press on the basis of this work. What is lacking, and what this book aims to provide, is a broad historical overview of a whole range of sexual discourses across the spectrum of the popular daily and Sunday national press.

[10] On divorce cases see A. Humphries, 'Coming Apart: The British Newspaper Press and the Divorce Court', in L. Brake, B. Bell, and D. Finkelstein, (eds.), *Nineteenth-Century Media and the Construction of Identities* (Basingstoke: Palgrave, 2000); G. Savage, 'Erotic Stories and Public Decency: Newspaper Reporting of Divorce Proceedings in England', *The Historical Journal*, 41/2 (1998), 511–28.

[11] M. Vicinus, 'Lesbian Perversity and Victorian Marriage: The 1864 Codrington Divorce Trial', *The Journal of British Studies*, 36/1 (1997), 70–98; C. Upchurch, 'Forgetting the Unthinkable: Cross-Dressers and British Society in the Case of Queen vs. Boulton and Others', *Gender and History*, 12/1 (2000), 127–57; J. Vernon, '"For Some Queer Reason": The Trials and Tribulations of Colonel Barker's Masquerade in Interwar Britain', *Signs*, 26/1 (2000), 37–62; M. Houlbrook, '"Lady Austin's Camp Boys": Constituting the Queer Subject in 1930s London', *Gender and History*, 14/1 (2002), 21–61. For less celebrated cases, Cocks, *Nameless Offences*, ch. 3.

[12] A. Oram, *Her Husband Was A Woman! Women's Gender-Crossing in Modern British Popular Culture* (London: Routledge, 2007).

[13] F. Pearce, 'The British Press and the "Placing" of Male Homosexuality', in S. Cohen and J. Young (eds.), *The Manufacture of News: Social Problems, Deviance and the Mass Media* (rev. edn., London: Constable, 1981), 303–16; S. Jeffery-Poulter, *Peers, Queers and Commons: The Struggle for Gay Law Reform from 1950 to the Present* (London: Routledge, 1991); P. Higgins, *Heterosexual Dictatorship: Male Homosexuality in Postwar Britain* (London: Fourth Estate, 1996), ch. 13.

[14] Some of the best examples of this literature, which do have a historical perspective, include P. Holland, 'The Page Three Girl Speaks to Women, Too: A Sun-Sational Survey', *Screen*, 24/3 (1983), 84–102; ead., 'The Politics of the Smile: "Soft News" and the Sexualisation of the Popular Press', in C. Carter, G. Branston, and S. Allan (eds.), *News, Gender and Power* (London: Routledge, 1998), 17–32; K. Soothill and S. Walby, *Sex Crime in the News* (London: Routledge, 1991); M. Conboy, *Tabloid Britain: Constructing a Community Through Language* (London: Routledge, 2006), ch. 6.

[15] Examples include L. Lamb, *Sunrise: The Remarkable Rise of the Best-selling Soaraway Sun* (London: Papermac, 1989); A. Patmore, *Marge: The Guilt and the Gingerbread—The Authorized Biography* (London: Warner, 1993).

[16] Porter and Hall, *The Facts of Life*, 263.

The sexual content of popular newspapers has not received the attention it deserves partly because historians have tended to assume that it is entirely predictable, superficial, and socially conservative: a commercially-driven diet of cheap titillation, prurience, and hypocritical moralizing that is barely worth detailed scholarly investigation. Such assumptions are the legacy of a long tradition of critical commentary on the mass press, rooted in the belief that the true purpose of newspapers is to inform readers about politics and public life.[17] The development of 'human interest', lifestyle, and entertainment features, and the associated coverage of sex, is regarded as a deviation from this proper role, and has often been seen as marking a shift from an audience of enquiring, intelligent readers to a mass society of passive consumers. For writers in the Marxist tradition, newspapers were part of a 'culture industry' providing 'substitute gratification', which distracted working-class readers and prevented them from understanding the ways in which they were being exploited by capitalism.[18] The pioneering American sociologists of mass communication, Paul Lazarsfeld and Robert Merton, argued from a different perspective that the mass media had a 'narcotizing dysfunction', sedating their consumers into a self-satisfied apathy.[19] In Britain, Richard Hoggart's influential analysis of cultural change, *The Uses of Literacy*, suggested that the mass media were undermining an authentic working-class lifestyle by providing unhealthy entertainment that was 'full of a corrupt brightness, of improper appeals and moral evasions'.[20] Although more recent media and cultural studies work has challenged such interpretations, they continue to have a powerful resonance. The dominant historical framework for analysing the twentieth-century press remains the largely negative one of a gradual process of 'depoliticization' and commercialization. In his recent survey of modern journalism, for example, Jean Chalaby contends that after 1850 'triviality was a commercial strategy' dictated by the logic of the market, with the avoidance of 'controversial and serious material' deemed vital for attracting advertisers and a mass readership. The popular press has therefore increased the 'relative ignorance of the dominated classes'.[21]

These assumptions and arguments clearly have some foundation. Popular newspapers are highly formulaic products, put together at great speed to satisfy

[17] For the development of this ideal in the nineteenth century, see M. Hampton, *Visions of the Press in Britain, 1850–1950* (Urbana: University of Illinois Press, 2004), ch. 2.

[18] The classic exposition of this position is T. Adorno and M. Horkheimer, 'The Culture Industry: Enlightenment as Mass Deception', in id., *The Dialectic of Enlightenment*, trans. J. Cumming (London: Allan Lane, 1973).

[19] P. Lazarsfeld and R. Merton, 'Mass Communication, Popular Taste and Organized Social Action', in L. Bryson (ed.), *The Communication of Ideas* (New York: Harper & Bros., 1948), reprinted in P. Marris and S. Thornham (eds.), *Media Studies: A Reader*, 2nd edn. (Edinburgh: Edinburgh University Press, 1999), 18–30.

[20] R. Hoggart, *The Uses of Literacy* (first pub. 1957; London: Penguin, 1962) 339–40.

[21] J. Chalaby, *The Invention of Journalism* (Basingstoke: Macmillan, 1998), 104, 181. See also J. Curran and J. Seaton, *Power without Responsibility: The Press and Broadcasting in Britain*, 5th edn. (London: Routledge, 1997), pt. 1.

majority tastes. They are designed to make a profit, and the resulting commercial pressures mean that accuracy and reliability are often sacrificed for a good story, and entertainment is routinely prioritized over public service. Most newspapers are owned by wealthy individuals or corporations committed to consumer capitalism, and radical voices have often been marginalized. The press has often buttressed the social status quo by perpetuating and circulating negative stereotypes about women, sexual minorities, immigrants, and other groups lacking power. It is not difficult to understand why scholars have frequently voiced their frustration at the contents of popular newspapers.

Nevertheless, this book is based on the belief that it is inaccurate and unproductive to dismiss all popular journalism as cynical, trivial, and routine, or to reduce it to a tool for the maintenance of the existing social order. Many generalizations have been made about newspapers, but there has been far too little detailed investigation of their contents. Newspapers were more complex, diverse, and unpredictable than many critics have admitted, and they provided challenging, well-written, and informative material as well as undemanding entertainment. They were not invariably reactionary and negative, but could be progressive and generous; they did not merely pander to majority opinion, but sometimes provided a powerful voice for it against vested interests; they undermined stereotypes as well as consolidated them, and provided a platform for a wide range of contributors and causes. Different papers catered for different sections of society and strands of opinion, but all had to develop some form of connection with their audience if they were to survive in a competitive market. Readers recognized when they were being patronized or exploited, and would not buy a newspaper if it did not fulfil a genuine need for information or entertainment, especially when they had alternative sources of diversion such as radio and television. The sexual content of popular newspapers should be analysed seriously, rather than merely treated as a generic form of non-political mass culture.

METHODOLOGICAL APPROACH

This book embraces a catholic definition of what I have labelled for convenience 'sexual content' in order to explore the full range of sexual discourses in the press. Within the pages of a single copy of a newspaper, after all, the reader might be exposed to many types of material with a sexual dimension of some sort: an editorial imploring the government to amend one of the laws regulating sexuality; a report of a court case involving a sexual offence; a problem column dispensing advice on personal relationships; a pin-up photograph; revelations about the private life of a public figure; and an investigation into some aspect of contemporary sexual behaviour. These various features were produced by different journalists, with different intentions and styles, and often with different kinds of reader in mind. If titillating pictures were implicitly directed at the male reader, for example, the problem columnist usually wrote primarily for women; some journalists deliberately sought to shock and provoke, while others aimed to record and inform. Indeed, these can be seen as different genres of popular journalism, which conformed to particular rules and expectations.

This diversity of content was accepted—indeed, it was expected—by the reader, and it must also be accepted by any historian who seeks to produce a rounded study of the press's role in reflecting and creating sexual knowledge. This book examines the development of each of the main genres of sexual content, aiming in each case to answer three sets of questions. The first set relate to the editorial policies underlying the selection of material. Which subjects did newspapers highlight and which did they obscure? What new types of feature did they include, and what did they drop? How and why did these editorial priorities change over time? The second group address the newspaper content itself. What were the opinions of the main papers on the leading sexual issues, and to what extent did they alter across the period? What language and imagery did they use, how were different topics framed for the reader? The final set of questions, and the ones that are most difficult to answer, concern the impact of the press on public debate and on social attitudes. How did important groups such as politicians, policy-makers, the police, or campaign organizations respond to the output of journalists? In what ways are newspapers likely to have influenced the attitudes of ordinary readers? Of course it is not possible for one author, in a work of this size, to provide comprehensive answers to all these questions: the aim of this book is to draw out some of the main tendencies and encourage further research.

I have concentrated largely on the most popular national morning newspapers: the *Daily Mirror*, the *Daily Express*, the *Daily Mail*, the *Daily Herald* (and subsequently *The Sun*), and in the Sunday market the *News of the World*, *The Sunday Pictorial* (which in 1963 was renamed the *Sunday Mirror*), *The People*, and the *Sunday Express*. Where it provides a different perspective, I have used material from other popular papers, including the *News Chronicle*, the *Daily Sketch*, the *Sunday Dispatch*, and *Reynolds News*. Of course, it is possible only to examine a small fraction of these newspapers across such a wide period, but in a survey of this sort it is more useful to compare and contrast the approaches of a range of popular newspapers than to provide a more comprehensive coverage of just one or two publications. Different types of newspaper have been kept largely in the background. Elite papers, such as *The Times*, the *Daily Telegraph* and the (*Manchester*) *Guardian*,[22] evening papers, such as the *Evening Standard*, and local papers all had different editorial practices, different forms of content and very different readerships from the national morning press, and so deserve a separate treatment.

[22] The *Manchester Guardian* was renamed the *Guardian* in 1959.

There is a surfeit of newspaper content to analyse, but there is, unfortunately, a paucity of primary evidence relating to the production and reception of these newspapers. Whereas elite newspapers such as *The Times* and the *Guardian*, conscious of their historical importance, have maintained valuable editorial archives, most popular papers have not made record management a priority, and tend to be very reluctant to offer access to whatever archives they possess. The notable exception is Lord Beaverbrook's *Daily Express*: the vast collection of papers left by Beaverbrook is a goldmine for press historians of this period. It has by no means been fully exploited, having been used mainly in biographical studies.[23] These papers are used extensively in this work, as are those of Lord Northcliffe, Hugh Cudlipp, and other editors and journalists who have left useful archival material. There are, however, frustratingly large gaps in terms of primary evidence, which have to be filled by consulting published diaries, memoirs and recollections, and also the trade journals of the press industry. These sources have various limitations, but if employed carefully they can provide a fairly reliable picture of the editorial attitudes and practices that shaped the production of the newspapers.

Evidence regarding the reception of newspapers is also sketchy, especially for the earlier part of the period. Jonathan Rose has reminded historians of the importance of trying to discover how cultural products were understood by the individuals that consumed them, and has expressed his disappointment that 'even historical studies that promise to tell us something about the "impact" and "influence" of the press usually do not focus directly on audience response'.[24] This is a salutary warning, and Rose's own research demonstrates the variety and extent of the available evidence on reading patterns. The particular difficulty with newspapers, however, is that although there is a certain amount of material indicating the general response of readers to different newspapers, it is far harder to pin down their reaction to specific articles, or even to a series of articles. The autobiographical writing examined by Rose is far more likely to discuss memorable works of literature, read at length and perhaps reread many times, than newspapers which were bought and discarded each day and which had a more subtle, cumulative influence. The most obvious source of information regarding the reception of newspapers is the circulation figures, which are fairly reliable after 1918, especially once the Audit Bureau of Circulations was established in 1931. It is reasonable to assume that substantial rises or falls in the sales of a newspaper bear some connection to its success in appealing to its audience. To survive in the market a paper must in some way meet the needs of its readers, whether by representing their views, feeding their curiosity, or satisfying their

[23] The leading biographies are A. J. P. Taylor, *Beaverbrook* (London: Hamish Hamilton, 1972), and A. Chisholm and M. Davie, *Beaverbrook: A Life* (London: Hutchinson, 1992).

[24] J. Rose, *The Intellectual Life of the British Working Classes* (New Haven: Yale University Press, 2001), 9.

desire for entertainment and fantasy. Nevertheless, bald circulation figures do not indicate to which particular aspects of a newspaper readers are responding. It is not possible to tell from circulation figures alone whether the rising popularity of the *Sun* after 1969, for example, was due primarily to its bold sexual content or to its ability to capture the imagination of a new generation of readers in other ways.

There are, of course, more detailed surveys about newspaper readership patterns, both those commissioned by newspapers themselves, and investigations undertaken by independent research organizations such as Mass-Observation. Some of these are of great value, but they are by no means sufficiently numerous, comprehensive or reliable to answer all the historian's questions. In-depth surveys of readers' responses to particular articles or campaigns are also relatively rare: the most useful example for this study is the survey commissioned by the Ministry of Health in 1943 to investigate the success of its series of advertisements warning about the dangers of venereal diseases (see Chapter 2). Published letters from readers provide another potential source of evidence, but they must be treated with considerable caution. It is impossible to tell whether letters have been edited, altered, or even invented, nor can it be assumed that the balance of opinion on the letters page accurately reflects the balance of all letters received. Nevertheless, most published letters were probably genuine, and they can provide some useful insights; at the very least, they reveal the views that editors wanted to see voiced in the paper's columns. Furthermore, the very fact that national newspapers did receive hundreds of letters every week testifies to their importance in the lives of their readers, and editors recognized the importance of keeping in touch with the attitudes of the public. This was an important 'feedback' mechanism that helped to shape the way the newspapers were written and produced.

There was also an ongoing public debate about the content of the press in which politicians, campaigners, and the literary elite participated. This debate fluctuated in intensity, peaking in response to particularly controversial examples of journalistic practice—such as the sensationalized reporting of divorce court cases in the 1920s, or the lurid coverage of the Profumo affair in 1963—and was significant in determining the reputation of the press. It helped to shape how readers related to their newspapers, and the extent to which they trusted what they read. Public pronouncements about newspapers, and especially about sexual content, do not, of course, necessarily provide a clear guide to actual reading habits: condemnations of indecent material and intrusions into private lives did not usually prevent readers consuming such material with enthusiasm. Nevertheless, proprietors, editors, and journalists were often as conscious of the views of public figures as they were of the opinions of their readers, and this consciousness affected the newspapers they produced.

In order to assess the reception and 'impact' of the press, it is, of course, necessary to have a thorough knowledge of the broader social and cultural context. Some of this context is set out in Chapter 1. The key characteristics of the British newspaper market and the wider media environment are described. Some brief observations are offered about how rival media forms addressed sex and private life so that comparisons can be made with the press. The chapter also presents an overview of the main patterns of sexual behaviour in modern Britain in order that potential connections between changes in press content and shifts in sexual activity can be evaluated.

Peter Mandler has recently suggested that, if scholars are to avoid the many pitfalls associated with cultural history, they need to work harder to 'evaluate not only the meanings of a text but also its relations to other texts, its significance in wider discursive fields, its "throw", its dissemination and reception'.[25] By providing an integrated analysis of the production, content, and consumption of popular newspapers, this study hopes to provide sufficient context to reach a sensitive understanding of the complex role of the press in British society. Ultimately, however, there is no mechanical way of measuring the 'impact' or 'influence' of newspapers on society. Newspapers certainly did not wield an overwhelming coercive power over their audience. Readers do not necessarily believe, or even always understand, what they read. While newspaper articles, like any texts, usually contain a 'preferred' meaning, this meaning can be negotiated, resisted, or ignored by the reader.[26] Readers are always free to buy other newspapers if they dislike the content of the one they have chosen, or they can avoid buying one at all, and rely on other media. Nevertheless, newspapers clearly do have the power to shape opinions, and by circulating throughout the nation, they have an important role in the formation of what Benedict Anderson famously called 'an imagined community'.[27] Several scholars have argued plausibly that the influence of the media is greatest on those subjects outside the personal experience of the reader.[28] Sexual experience, of course, varied substantially across the population, but while most adults would have engaged in some form of sexual activity, their direct knowledge about the activities of others would usually have been very limited. In the first half of the twentieth century, moreover, information about sex remained fairly restricted, especially for women; sex education only gradually became available in some schools, and was often of poor quality. Most people had to rely on informal sources, such as family and friends, for their sexual knowledge. In this context newspapers made a significant contribution to attitudes about sex and sexuality.

[25] P. Mandler, 'The Problem with Cultural History', *Cultural and Social History*, 1/1 (2004), 96.

[26] S. Hall, 'Encoding/Decoding', reprinted in Marris and Thornham, *Media Studies: A Reader*, 51–61.

[27] B. Anderson, *Imagined Communities: Reflections on the Origin and Spread of Nationalism* (first pub. 1983; rev. edn. London: Verso, 1991).

[28] For an overview of recent research on the reception of media sexual content, see B. Gunter, *Media Sex: What Are The Issues?* (Mahwah: Lawrence Erlbaum Associates, 2002).

OVERVIEW

Running through the book is the desire to understand the ways in which the press defined sexuality in relation to ideas of *public* and *private* at different moments and in different contexts. Newspapers have played an important role in establishing and policing the boundaries between public and private. By providing a forum for the discussion of politics, business, and international diplomacy, the press helped to create what the social philosopher Jurgen Habermas called the 'public sphere'.[29] The news agenda of serious daily newspapers such as *The Times* was dominated in the eighteenth and nineteenth centuries by reports of the proceedings of public institutions such as Parliament, the law courts, the stock exchange, and professional associations. 'Private' life—the feminized sphere of home and family—was almost entirely absent from the newspaper columns, and sex was regarded as one of the most personal and intimate activities of this private world.[30] In the respectable Victorian press, sex tended to be mentioned only when it was an element of a court case, or when brave politicians or campaigners debated problems deemed to affect 'public' morality or 'public' health, such as prostitution and venereal disease. In general, though, sex was considered to be an inappropriate subject for general public discussion, and better left to the relevant (male) professional and official circles.

The rise of the popular Sunday and daily press gradually destabilized the boundaries between public and private. Aimed at the ordinary family reader rather than the urbane 'man of affairs', popular newspapers prioritized entertainment over information about public events. The sensation and titillation they sought was more commonly found not in the drama of politics or business, but by delving into the human interest of private lives. Reports on scandalous court cases assumed a new importance, particularly in the Sunday press, and gossipy columns about people in the public eye became more common. At the same time, popular newspapers sought to connect with the everyday experiences of their readers—women as well as men—by opening up the discussion of the domestic sphere. Northcliffe's *Daily Mail* led the way in providing features about cookery, fashion, furnishings, and housewifery.[31] These two impulses—to entertain, and to offer advice and information about the private sphere—paved the way for a significant rise in sexual content over the twentieth century as ideas about sex changed and sexuality came to be seen as the defining characteristic of the private self. Popular newspapers eventually took it as their role to provide both sexual

[29] J. Habermas, *The Structural Transformation of the Public Sphere: An Inquiry into a Category of Bourgeois Society*, trans. T. Burger (Cambridge: Polity, 1989).

[30] L. Brown, *Victorian News and Newspapers* (Oxford: Clarendon Press, 1985).

[31] A. Bingham, *Gender, Modernity, and the Popular Press in Inter-War Britain* (Oxford: Oxford University Press, 2004), ch. 1.

fantasy and sexual guidance—the former largely aimed at men, the latter largely at women—and to make public what had been regarded as private.

Many scholars have identified the 1960s as the decade in which the traditional definitions of public and private finally collapsed and the discussion of sex was transformed. This was the moment, it is argued, when the reticence that had traditionally marked British society started to disappear and sex was debated and represented more openly and explicitly than ever before. Simon Szreter has argued, for example, that Britain adhered to the Victorian code 'of euphemism, silence, ignorance and confusion on matters of sex and sexuality' until the early 1960s: only after 1963 did this code meet its 'public nemesis'.[32] Brian McNair agrees that it is 'since the 1960s' that 'sex has become a central part of mass, popular culture'.[33] It is to this sexualization of the public sphere that Philip Larkin was referring in his oft-quoted observation that sex began in 1963, 'Between the end of the Chatterley ban/And the Beatles' first L.P.'[34]

When examining television, cinema, magazines, and popular literature the 1960s does indeed seem a persuasive turning-point. There were very real shifts in the censorship regime in these years, and sexual imagery undoubtedly proliferated on screen and on the printed page.[35] If the focus switches to the popular press, however, a very different picture emerges. Exploring the output of Fleet Street it becomes clear that it was during the late 1940s and the 1950s that most significant changes occurred. After the Second World War the popular press's coverage of sex increased markedly and self-consciously 'modern' and 'scientific' approaches were adopted. The *Daily Mirror* and its sister paper the *Sunday Pictorial* campaigned for the democratization of sexual knowledge: in the Beveridgean Welfare State, they argued, it was the duty of the active citizen to be sexually informed. The popularization of sexual psychology encouraged journalists to label and define different types of sexual behaviour, and a new generation of advice columnists offered more detailed guidance for uncertain readers. In the 1950s, moreover, the consumer boom and the transition to a more affluent society significantly altered the environment in which sex was discussed. The press's increasing emphasis on sexual pleasure reflected a culture in which the horizons of the majority were no longer confined to the necessities. At the same time the competition posed by the rapid growth in the popularity of television, particularly after the launch of ITV in 1955, prompted the press to take risks and push back boundaries in a bid to retain the allegiance of young readers.

[32] S. Szreter, 'Victorian Britain, 1837–1963: Towards a Social History of Sexuality', *Journal of Victorian Culture*, 1.1 (Spring 1996), 142, 144.

[33] B. McNair, *Mediated Sex: Pornography and Postmodern Culture* (London: Arnold, 1996), 1.

[34] Philip Larkin, 'Annus Mirabilis', in *High Windows* (London: Faber, 1974).

[35] Aldgate, *Censorship and the Permissive Society*; Collins, 'The Pornography of Permissiveness'; A. Aldgate and J. Robertson, *Censorship in Theatre and Cinema* (Edinburgh: Edinburgh University Press, 2005), ch. 7; J. Sutherland, *Offensive Literature: Decensorship in Britain 1960–1982* (London: Junction Books, 1982); J. Green, *All Dressed Up: The Sixties and the Counterculture* (London: Pimlico, 1999), ch. 6.

The six chapters that follow the introductory section each examine a particular genre of sexual content and analyse how it developed over the six decades after 1918. The late 1940s and the 1950s are repeatedly highlighted as a period of notable change. Chapter 2 explores the press's attempts to inform readers about issues of sexual welfare, including contraception, abortion, and venereal disease. It suggests the *Mirror*'s decision in 1942 to provide information about the dangers of VD was the harbinger of a more general post-war shift in which the popular press adopted a more active role in informing and advising readers about sex. In so doing, the press made an important contribution to a climate of reform marked by the spread of public sex education programmes, the increasing respectability of contraception, and growing pressure to alter the laws governing abortion and marriage.

Chapter 3 examines the press's efforts to investigate the sexual attitudes and behaviour of 'ordinary people', endeavours which started in earnest in 1949 when the *Sunday Pictorial* paid for and serialized the first national sex survey in Britain, conducted by Mass-Observation. By the early 1950s such surveys had become firmly established on the popular press's news agenda: indeed, in 1953 Professor Kinsey's study *Sexual Behavior in the Human Female* was discussed in such detail that the Press Council was moved to criticize Fleet Street for its 'exploitation of sex'. As more information was gathered about the sexual habits of the public, however, complacent assumptions about the restraint and moral superiority of the British people became ever harder to defend.

The following two chapters study the press coverage of sexual transgression. Chapter 4 analyses court reporting, from the controversy over the coverage of divorce cases in the 1920s to the growth of 'chequebook journalism' in the 1960s and 1970s. Chapter 5 explores the moral crusade, notably those concerning prostitution and homosexuality. These forms of reporting enabled newspapers to display their adherence to family values, and to unite their diverse readerships against those who defied the law or respectable morality, while at the same time satisfying public curiosity by describing transgression and transgressors. The coverage of sex crimes became significantly more explicit in the 1950s, particularly with regard to homosexual offences, and public concern stimulated by the press was one of the reasons why the Wolfenden Committee was established to examine the laws on prostitution and homosexuality in 1954. Prejudice against gay men and women was very slow to die in Fleet Street, although a number of popular newspapers did contribute to the pressure for legal reform by supporting Wolfenden's proposals to decriminalize adult male homosexuality. By the 1970s the press hostility to sexual 'deviants' was beginning to crystallize on the paedophile.

The final two substantive chapters address press attempts to entertain and titillate. Chapter 6 focuses on the rise of the pin-up from the 'bathing belle' photos of the 1920s to the *Sun*'s introduction of the topless 'page three girl' in the 1970s. Chapter 7 examines the coverage of the 'private lives' of public figures, including film stars, politicians, and members of the royal family. Once again the 1950s emerge as a pivotal decade: it was then that the pin-up became a staple feature throughout the popular press, that Sunday papers started to compete to secure celebrity sexual revelations, and that the royal 'soap opera' reached full swing with the intense scrutiny of Princess Margaret's affair with Peter Townsend. In Murdoch's *Sun* these two genres of journalism came gradually to dominate. In the 'permissive society' of the 1970s, when children seemed to become sexually knowledgeable at ever younger ages, seeking to educate and inform readers on sexual issues appeared somewhat outdated and idealistic. The *Sun*'s editorial team were trying to build circulation quickly, moreover, and eye-catching photos and 'sensational' revelations were deemed the most reliable tools to use. As the *Sun*'s rivals moved to compete with the young upstart, pleasure (or at least particular male-defined versions of pleasure) came to dominate the press agenda.

Ultimately, though, the sexual content of the press resists neat generalizations. In their bid to cater for a vast and diverse audience, popular newspapers offered a miscellany embracing a wide range of different types of material. The press sought to disguise the tensions imposed by the need to entice readers with sex while defending particular versions of family morality, but intellectual coherence was never a priority, and editors did not hesitate to play on the insecurity, confusion, or downright hypocrisy of readers. The result was a spectacular heterogeneity. Critics from all kinds of political and social viewpoints highlighted the incongruities and absurdities of this approach, but millions of consumers were prepared to accept or overlook them so long as they could find material that interested them. And as long as sex continued to sell, journalists were happy to exploit it in whatever ways they could.

1

Contexts: The Media and British Sexual Culture

Like any other historical evidence, newspapers must be placed in the appropriate political, social, and cultural contexts if their content is to be properly understood. This chapter describes the environment in which the popular press was produced and consumed. It begins by outlining the main characteristics of British newspapers, including the structure of the market, circulation trends, patterns of ownership and control, economic organization, basic editorial practices, and the background and training of journalists. The second section describes the wider media landscape, of which the press was merely one, albeit prominent, feature. In particular, it describes how other media forms, including the cinema, radio and television broadcasting, magazines and popular literature, approached sex and private life. The final part provides a broad overview of the patterns of change in British sexual culture over the twentieth century. It includes information about fluctuating rates of marriage, fertility and divorce, and the use of contraception and abortion. It examines the impact of intellectual developments such as feminism, sexology, and psychoanalysis on the understanding of sexuality; the role of the state and changes in the law; the effects of increasing affluence; and medical and scientific advances.

NEWSPAPERS IN BRITAIN

Circulation Patterns

A favourable geographical, political, social, and cultural environment enabled the emergence of a powerful national press in Britain. By the second half of the nineteenth century the ingredients were in place for London-based newspapers to flourish. Britain was a relatively small nation with a centralized political system, was dominated by a single language, covered by an extensive rail network, and contained a heavily urbanized, comparatively prosperous and increasingly literate population. Sunday newspapers such as *Lloyd's Weekly News* (1842) and the *News of the World* (1843) first demonstrated the commercial potential of the national market. By providing a cheap and entertaining miscellany of stories about unusual events, sensational court cases, and the latest political dramas, the Sunday press enticed working-class readers seeking diversion on their day of leisure.[1] Northcliffe's *Daily Mail*, launched in 1896 and targeted initially at the burgeoning lower middle classes, offered a brighter and more accessible version of the respectable daily, with feature material and serial stories designed to appeal to women and children.[2] Its success indicated that a mass audience existed for dailies as well as weeklies, and a number of competitors soon entered the new market, including the *Daily Express* (1900), the *Daily Mirror* (1903) and the *Daily Sketch* (1908).

Despite the flurry of activity in Fleet Street at the turn of the century, it was only after 1918 that the national press eclipsed the provincial press. The combined circulation of the nationals finally passed that of the provincials in 1923, and many provincial papers were forced to close or become part of national chains. During the inter-war period, the practice of reading daily newspapers extended beyond the lower middle-classes and became a normal feature of working-class life. By 1939 some two-thirds of all adults regularly saw a national daily paper, and almost everyone saw a Sunday paper. Circulations continued to rise during the Second World War, and reached a peak in 1950–1, with national dailies achieving a combined circulation of 16.6 million copies per day, and Sundays selling just over 30 million copies per week.[3]

At mid-century the market was close to saturation point, with over 85 per cent of the population reading a paper every day. Reading and talking about the stories in London-based newspapers seems to have fostered a feeling of engagement in a national, rather than merely local, community.[4] Newspapers permeated society to such an extent that they demanded attention. Anyone going about their normal business would have found them almost impossible to avoid. Vendors bellowed the names of the papers they were trying to sell from street corners in towns and cities across the country; pavements were furnished with branded sandwich boards that offered a tantalizing glimpse of the latest headlines; trains,

[1] V. Berridge, 'Popular Sunday Papers and Mid-Victorian Society', in G. Boyce, J. Curran, and P. Wingate (eds.), *Newspaper History from the Seventeenth Century to the Present Day* (London: Constable, 1978), 247–64.

[2] A. Bingham, *Gender, Modernity and the Popular Press in Inter-War Britain* (Oxford: Oxford University Press, 2004), ch. 1.

[3] G. Harrison, F. Mitchell, and M. Abrams, *The Home Market*, rev. edn. (London: G. Allen & Unwin, 1939), ch. 21; A. P. Wadsworth, 'Newspaper Circulations 1800–1954', *Manchester Statistical Society Transactions*, 4, Session 1954–55; A. Jones, 'The British Press 1919–1945', in D. Griffiths (ed.), *The Encyclopedia of the British Press 1422–1992* (London: Macmillan, 1992); J. Tunstall, *Newspaper Power: The New National Press in Britain* (Oxford: Clarendon Press, 1996), ch. 3; C. Seymour-Ure, *The British Press and Broadcasting since 1945*, 2nd edn. (Oxford: Blackwell, 1996), ch. 3.

[4] B. Anderson, *Imagined Communities: Reflections on the Origin and Spread of Nationalism*, rev. edn. (London: Verso, 1991), 35. For examples of this feeling of engagement, see J. Rose, *The Intellectual Life of the British Working Classes* (New Haven: Yale University Press, 2001), 10, 28–9; R. Roberts, *The Classic Slum: Salford Life in the First Quarter of the Century* (Harmondsworth: Penguin, 1973), 162–3, 228–9.

buses, and trams were filled with people consuming that day's issue; countless sporting and cultural events were decorated with banners of newspapers that were sponsoring them; even those staying at home might be disturbed by the knock of canvassers selling subscriptions. There were countless invitations to participate in this shared experience, and it would have been easy to feel that not joining in would have been to forfeit something important. One did not even need to purchase a copy to be drawn in. Of those who did not buy a paper regularly, many must have been like the 'young Londoner' who told Mass-Observation that when he passed a news-stand in the morning he would 'glance at all the papers displayed there [and] read the big headlines'; he also 'read bits' over the shoulders of passengers on the bus.[5] Hugh Cudlipp[6] recognized that newspapers could make an impact on these passers-by: he used 'strong words and compelling type' to deliver the *Mirror*'s message 'not only to the millions who bought the paper regularly but to the millions who would catch a glimpse of the headlines on the shop counters, the railway bookstalls, the street corners, the trains and buses.'[7]

Circulation managers chartered trains and devised elaborate delivery systems to ensure that newspapers produced in London circulated as widely as possible throughout Britain. The task was considerably easier when there were multiple production sites. The *Mail* led the way in 1900 by opening a printing plant in Manchester that produced an edition for northern England and Scotland. Many other nationals followed suit in the 1920s, while Beaverbrook's *Express* went a step further by opening a plant in Glasgow as well as Manchester.[8] But not everyone participated equally in this national culture. Scotland provided the greatest resistance to the London-based press. In 1935 only 43 per cent of the population read a Fleet Street daily, whereas 60 per cent read a Scottish morning paper.[9] Scottish Sunday papers were even more successful than the dailies: the popularity of Glasgow's *Sunday Mail* and the Dundee-based *Sunday Post* ensured that titles from the south struggled.[10]

Outside Scotland, the most significant regional variations were found in the north-west of England. In Lancashire, the Manchester-based *Daily Dispatch* and *Empire News* circulated widely until they were absorbed by other

[5] Mass-Observation, *The Press and Its Readers: A Report Prepared By Mass-Observation for the Advertising Service Guild* (London: Arts and Technics, 1949), 25.

[6] Hugh Cudlipp (1913–1998) joined the *Daily Mirror* as features editor in 1935, moving on to edit the *Sunday Pictorial* from 1937 to 1940 and (after war service) 1946 to 1949. Following a brief spell at the *Sunday Express*, he served as editorial director for both the *Mirror* and *Pictorial* from 1953 to 1968, and chairman of parent company IPC until his retirement in 1973. See R. Edwards, *Newspapermen: Hugh Cudlipp, Cecil Harmsworth King and the Glory Days of Fleet Street* (London: Secker & Warburg, 2003).

[7] H. Cudlipp, *Walking on Water* (London: Bodley Head, 1976), 96.

[8] Griffiths, *Encylopedia*, 183–4; Tunstall, *Newspaper Power*, 63.

[9] Political and Economic Planning, *Report on the British Press* (London: PEP, 1938), 148–9.

[10] Tunstall, *Newspaper Power*, 62–4.

papers in 1955 and 1960 respectively. Some differences in the readership of the national press were based on disparities in prosperity across the country: throughout the period, people living in the wealthy regions of London and south-east England tended to buy more newspapers than those in other areas. Yet beyond the issue of relative affluence, there were also those who disliked the metropolitan bias of the 'national' press, which could not be disguised by the provision of different editions with some locally relevant news. Whereas fewer than one in ten people in the south-east did not read a national daily, in northern areas of England about one in three did not. On Sundays, though, competition from local papers was much weaker, and throughout England and Wales fewer than one person in ten did not read a national paper.[11]

Patterns of readership also varied according to sex and age. Women were slightly less avid newspaper readers than men, although there were significant differences between publications. A survey in 1934 suggested that the ratio of male to female newspaper readers was about eleven to nine, and a number of subsequent surveys produced similar results.[12] Newspaper readership levels also tended to be slightly lower among the younger and older age groups than among people aged between 25 and 65.[13]

Inevitably, the extraordinary sales growth of the national press in the first half of the century could not be sustained. In the face of increasing competition from television and radio, national newspaper circulations declined from the 1950s. The popular Sundays were the hardest hit, with combined sales dropping by almost 40 per cent between 1950 and 1975. The dailies fared rather better, losing only about 15 per cent of circulation in the same period. The number of provincial morning papers continued to fall, and in the 1970s provincial weeklies were affected badly by the emergence of free local papers dominated by advertising. The only papers to prosper were those aimed at the social elites. With demand stimulated by the expansion of higher education, upmarket dailies increased their circulation by 42 per cent in the two decades after 1955, while the launch of *Sunday Telegraph* in 1962 helped the upmarket Sundays to more than double their sales.[14]

[11] J. Hobson, H. Henry, and M. Abrams, *The Hulton Readership Survey 1949* (London: Hulton Press, 1949), 31.

[12] Political and Economic Planning, *Report on the British Press*, 28; Harrison et al., *The Home Market*, 109; T. Jeffery and K. McClelland, 'A World Fit to Live in: The *Daily Mail* and the Middle Classes 1918–39', in J. Curran, A. Smith, and P. Wingate (eds.), *Impacts and Influences: Essays on Media Power in the Twentieth Century* (London: Methuen, 1987), 39; Hobson et al., *Hulton Readership Survey 1949*, 32–3.

[13] M-O File Report 1339, June 1942, 'Report on *Daily Express* Readership', 7–8; File Report 1420, 15; *Hulton Readership Survey 1949*, 32–3; Royal Commission 1974–7, *Attitudes to the Press*, (London: HMSO, 1977), Cmd. 6810–419.

[14] Tunstall, *Newspaper Power*, ch. 3; Seymour-Ure, *British Press and Broadcasting*, ch. 3.

Market Structure

The national market was characterized by fierce competition between a small number of newspapers, with the leaders obtaining mammoth circulations. Sunday newspapers were the most popular, as they had been since the early nineteenth century. The *News of the World* was the most widely read newspaper throughout the period, with a circulation of around 1.5 million in 1910, rising to 3.4 million in 1930 and reaching a peak of 8.44 million copies per issue in June 1950, at which time it was read by more than half of all adults in Britain.[15] *The People*, the *Sunday Pictorial/Sunday Mirror* and the *Sunday Express* competed aggressively for second place. In the mid-1950s the *People* and the *Pictorial* had circulations of over 5 million copies, and the *Sunday Express* over 3 million. The *News of the World*'s circulation declined more rapidly than its three rivals: by the mid-1970s it sold about 5.5 million copies, while the others were just above or just below the four million mark.[16]

The leadership of the national daily market was more volatile. From its foundation in 1896 until the late 1920s, the *Daily Mail* led the field, reaching a circulation of around 1 million copies during the First World War and 1.96 million by 1930. The *Daily Mirror*, launched by Northcliffe as a newspaper for women in 1903 before being turned into a successful picture paper, competed with the *Mail* until 1918, when it slipped into decline. In the ferocious battle for sales in the early 1930s, which saw millions of pounds being spent on free gifts and insurance schemes in return for subscriptions, the *Daily Herald* and the *Daily Express* overtook the *Mail* and broke through the two million circulation barrier. While the *Herald* was unable to maintain its success, the sales of Lord Beaverbrook's *Express* continued to rise, and passed the four million mark in the early 1950s. By that time, however, it had already been surpassed by a resurgent *Daily Mirror*, which had been reinvented in the mid-1930s as an explicitly working-class tabloid. The *Mirror* picked up readers at a spectacular rate during and after the Second World War, and overtook the *Express* to become the most popular daily in 1949; in 1967 it reached the unprecedented circulation peak of 5.25 million copies.[17] At the end of the decade, however, a new challenger emerged in the form of *The Sun*, a paper launched by the Mirror Group in 1964 to replace the faltering *Daily Herald* and then bought and relaunched by Rupert Murdoch in 1969. The *Sun*'s rise was meteoric: within five years it was selling over three million copies and

[15] D. Butler and G. Butler, *Twentieth-Century British Political Facts 1900–2000*, 8th edn. (Basingstoke: Macmillan, 2000), 538; Tunstall, *Newspaper Power*, 13; Hulton Press Survey 1952, as summarized in *World Press News*, 19 September 1952, 3.

[16] Seymour-Ure, *British Press and Broadcasting*, 30–1.

[17] Tunstall, *Newspaper Power*, 43–5.

in 1978 it surpassed the *Mirror* to become Britain's most popular national daily.[18] At the time of writing, the *Sun*'s circulation remains far higher than any of its daily rivals.

In this highly competitive market, newspapers were under heavy pressure to maximize their circulation not only to increase sales revenue but also to attract advertisers. Successful papers obtained considerable advantages over less popular rivals: they could realize substantial benefits through economies of scale and by offering more enticing terms to advertisers.[19] With production costs rising significantly after 1945, weaker publications found themselves struggling for survival. Even circulations well above one million were not necessarily sufficient for popular papers if they did not reach enough of the prosperous, young readers that were most attractive to advertisers. The *News Chronicle*, the *Daily Sketch*, the *Empire News*, and the *Sunday Dispatch* all found this to their cost and were either forced to close or were merged with other papers between 1960 and 1971.[20]

On the other hand, elite newspapers such as *The Times* and the *Daily Telegraph* could survive with far smaller circulations because their educated and affluent readership generated much more advertising revenue per copy. These publications had a markedly different set of news values to the popular newspapers, and covered politics, foreign affairs, and business in far greater detail. The newspaper market in Britain was therefore clearly stratified by class and education. Among the elite papers the *Daily Telegraph* and the *Sunday Times* dominated, each achieving sales of around 1.3 million in the mid-1960s; their competitors lagged far behind, with *The Times* and the *Guardian* selling around a quarter of a million copies each in the mid-1960s. In contrast to the popular papers, however, the sales of elite dailies increased in the second half of the twentieth century.[21]

National newspapers were—and are—more widely read and more competitive in Britain than in comparable countries. During the period of circulation expansion in the middle decades of the twentieth century, surveys revealed that the British read more newspapers per capita than any other people in the world—almost twice as many as Americans in the mid-1950s, and nearly three times as many as the French.[22] In the United States, as well as in France, Italy, and Spain, local and regional newspapers had a far stronger position than in Britain, and by the 1950s no individual paper in these countries could match

[18] Tunstall, *Newspaper Power*, 43.

[19] See Royal Commission on the Press 1961–62, *Report* (London: HMSO, 1962), Cmd. 1811, 67–72; Royal Commission on the Press 1974–77, *Final Report* (London: HMSO, 1977), Cmd. 6810, ch. 6.

[20] J. Curran, 'The Impact of Advertising on the British Mass Media', *Media, Culture and Society*, 3/1 (1981), 43–69.

[21] Seymour-Ure, *British Press and Broadcasting*, 26–32; Tunstall, *Newspaper Power*, 46–56.

[22] F. Williams, *Dangerous Estate: The Anatomy of Newspapers* (first pub. 1957; London: Longmans, Green, 1958), 1–2. See also Royal Commission on the Press 1974–77, *Final Report*, Appendix C, 105.

the huge circulations achieved in Britain. In the United States, there was a long tradition of city newspapers using populist techniques—derided by critics as 'yellow journalism'—to build up large circulations, but after 1945 sensational journalism and celebrity coverage were largely confined to a separate section of the market, namely the weekly 'supermarket tabloids' such as the *National Enquirer*. These publications deliberately blurred the boundaries between 'fact' and 'fiction' and hence were not considered to be 'newspapers'.[23] In France, Italy, and Spain, the habit of daily newspaper readership did not spread to the working classes as widely as it did in Britain, and a popular press did not emerge in the same way. Post-war (West) Germany did produce a popular tabloid of comparable reach to those in Britain in the form of Axel Springer's *Bild Zeitung*, but it was alone in the market and had no national rivals which could even come close to matching its circulation. In Scandinavia, meanwhile, readership levels were, by the 1970s, similar to, or greater than, those in Britain, but again this readership was dispersed among a wide selection of local and provincial papers.[24] The press in Britain, then, was unusually centralized and vigorous, and popular newspapers in particular had a far greater cultural significance than in other countries.

If the structure of the various national newspaper markets were very different, however, editors and journalists in Britain were still influenced by foreign newspapers, and particularly those from the United States. Northcliffe learned much from the clear, concise writing style, bright layout, and spirited campaigning of papers such as Dana's *New York Sun*, Pulitzer's *New York World*, and Hearst's *New York Journal*.[25] The dramatic changes in the style of the *Daily Mirror* in the mid-1930s were made in consultation with the British arm of the American advertising agency, J. Walter Thompson, and imitated the models provided by the *New York Daily Mirror* and the *New York Daily News*. The decision to introduce several strip cartoons, for example, was taken on the basis of their popularity the United States.[26] These moves in a populist direction were often criticized by cultural conservatives as a further step in the 'Americanization' of Britain, a fear which gathered pace in this period as the political, economic, and cultural power of the United States grew.[27] The sensationalism and intrusiveness for which the British press were criticized

[23] On the American press see M. Emery, E. Emery, and N. Roberts, *The Press and America: An Interpretive History of the Mass Media*, 9th edn. (Boston: Allyn and Bacon, 2000); on the 'supermarket tabloids', B. Sloan, *"I Watched a Wild Hog Eat my Baby!" A Colorful History of Tabloids and Their Cultural Impact* (New York: Prometheus Books, 2001).

[24] On the European press, see Euromedia Research Group, *The Media in Western Europe: The Euromedia Handbook* (London: Sage, 1997).

[25] For an overview of American popular journalism, see M. Conboy, *The Press and Popular Culture* (London: Sage, 2002), ch. 3.

[26] M. Edelman, *The Mirror: A Political History* (London: Hamish Hamilton, 1966), 40–1.

[27] On fears of 'Americanization' see R. McKibbin, *Classes and Cultures: England 1918–1951* (Oxford: Oxford University Press, 1998), ch. XI and XIII.

were often considered to be American traits, which sat ill with 'traditional' British characteristics of reserve and respect—even though American journalists acknowledged that the cultural traffic across the Atlantic was not one way, and that they were influenced by their London counterparts.[28]

Political and Social Influence

The dominance of a small number of national newspapers generated anxiety about the power of wealthy proprietors to wield a disproportionate influence on public life, especially as some 'press barons' owned more than one newspaper. Before 1914, for example, Lord Northcliffe owned the two most popular daily newspapers, the *Mail* and the *Mirror*, as well as the elite 'paper of record', *The Times*. After Northcliffe's death in 1922, his brother, Lord Rothermere, not only had control of the *Mail* and the *Mirror*, he also held a stake in the *Daily Express* and the *Sunday Express*, and built up a substantial portfolio of local newspapers. Fears about the concentration of newspaper ownership restricting healthy democratic debate led to the formation of a Royal Commission on the Press in 1947–9 under the chairmanship of Sir William Ross.[29] The commission could not, however, find a feasible solution to the problem, and market concentration increased further in the post-war period when the Mirror Group absorbed the *Daily Herald* and the *People*. A second Royal Commission found that in 1961 the three leading press corporations controlled 89 per cent of national daily circulation and 84 per cent of national Sunday circulation. Levels of concentration diminished slightly in the final third of the century, but the influence of leading proprietors continued to cause concern, with Rupert Murdoch becoming the most controversial of the next generation of press magnates.[30]

Such concentrations of ownership were particularly controversial due to the partisan nature of the British press. Although the direct ties between political parties and individual newspapers loosened in some respects during the twentieth century,[31] and overtly political content declined in quantity in the popular press, newspaper journalists were not restricted by the duty of impartiality laid on

[28] J. Wiener and M. Hampton (eds.), *Anglo-American Media Interactions, 1850–2000* (Basingstoke: Palgrave Macmillan, 2007).

[29] T. O'Malley, 'Labour and the 1947–9 Royal Commission on the Press', in M. Bromley and T. O'Malley (eds.), *A Journalism Reader* (London: Routledge, 1997).

[30] Having built up a media empire in Australia, Murdoch entered the UK market in 1969 by buying both the *News of the World* and *The Sun*. News International (the UK subsidiary of Murdoch's company News Corporation) complemented this with the purchase in 1980–1 of *The Times* and the *Sunday Times*, thereby giving Murdoch control of key titles in the popular and elite markets. The Murdoch empire continued to expand, adding substantial interests in the United States and China, including Fox TV, the *New York Post* and the *South China Morning Post*. In 1989 News Corporation launched the satellite broadcasting company Sky Television in the UK. See W. Shawcross, *Murdoch* (London: Simon and Schuster, 1993).

[31] For details of this process, see S. Koss, *The Rise and Fall of the Political Press in Britain, Vol. 2, The Twentieth Century* (London: Hamish Hamilton, 1984).

broadcasters, and they continued to engage vigorously in political debate. In the inter-war period Lords Beaverbrook and Rothermere often behaved as if they could dictate policy to leading politicians by mobilizing the support of their many readers.[32] After the Second World War such hubristic behaviour was regarded with disdain: when Cecil King used the front page of the *Daily Mirror* to launch a vicious attack on Harold Wilson in 1968, he was swiftly deposed as chairman.[33] Nevertheless, politicians could by no means expect an easy ride from the press, and newspapers continued to campaign energetically against policies they disliked. Left-wing politicians argued that they received particularly rough treatment. The balance of the press was generally weighted in favour of the Conservative party, particularly during the inter-war period (when the *Mirror* had yet to cross to the left) and in the 1970s and 1980s (when the Tories obtained the support of the *Sun*).[34] The closure of the liberal *News Chronicle* in 1960, and the sale of the previously Labour-supporting *Sun* to Rupert Murdoch, removed important counterweights to the conservatism of the *Mail* and the *Express*.

The historian James Curran has argued that the press's reliance on advertising revenue played a substantial role in maintaining this right-wing predominance. The newspaper market is not 'free', as is often claimed: advertising operates as a 'concealed subsidy' that favours papers with affluent readerships and discriminates against 'alternative' and anti-business voices.[35] This is a powerful argument and there are, indeed, numerous examples of advertisers' hostility to left-wing publications. Nevertheless, the limits to the influence of advertisers must also be recognized. Ultimately advertisers are attracted to newspapers with large circulations, and individual companies are not usually in a position to dictate to popular papers that have won the public's support. Indeed, the most successful daily newspaper in this period, the *Mirror*, transformed its fortunes from the mid-1930s by moving 'downmarket' and towards the left of political debate. By the 1970s, moreover, popular papers were only obtaining between a third and a quarter of their revenue from advertising.[36]

More persuasive is the argument that the reliance on advertising encouraged a general ethos of consumerism. In certain instances, this inhibited the investigation of dubious or damaging products, although, again, the power of advertisers remained limited. The research organization Political and Economic Planning observed in 1938 that there was a 'tendency to soft-pedal problems that ought

[32] A. Chisholm and M. Davie, *Beaverbrook: A Life* (London: Hutchinson, 1992), chs. 14–15.

[33] On King see Edwards, *Newspapermen*. On political influence more generally see D. G. Boyce, 'Crusaders without Chains: Power and the Press Barons 1896–1951' in, Curran, Smith, and Wingate (eds.), *Impacts and Influences*.

[34] Seymour-Ure, *British Press and Broadcasting*, 214–24; R. Negrine, *Politics and the Mass Media in Britain*, 2nd edn. (London: Routledge, 1994).

[35] Curran, 'The Impact of Advertising'; J. Curran and J. Seaton, *Power without Responsibility: The Press and Broadcasting in Britain*, 5th edn. (London: Routledge, 1997), pt. 1.

[36] Royal Commission on the Press 1977, *Final Report*, 47.

to be widely discussed, but which are inconvenient to advertising interests', such as the value of patent medicines or the damaging effects of alcohol or tobacco; nevertheless it concluded that 'if a big issue burst into prominence, no amount of advertising influence could induce a newspaper to suppress it, or even write it down'.[37] The case of tobacco, in fact, would subsequently provide evidence to confirm this judgement. Tobacco firms, very important advertisers in the press, were unable to prevent the health risks of cigarette smoking becoming a major news issue story in the early 1950s.[38]

The vigour of the press's engagement in politics was in part a reflection of its self-perception of being a 'Fourth Estate'[39] in the nation, scrutinizing the workings of Parliament for the benefit of public. Once the 'taxes on knowledge' were removed in the mid-nineteenth century the press jealously guarded its independence from the state and resisted any special laws regulating its activities. Nevertheless, the press was never entirely 'free'. It was subject to a strict libel law, the obscenity regime, contempt of court restrictions, and, from 1889, the Official Secrets Act.[40] During wartime, moreover, the Defence of the Realm regulations gave the government sweeping powers of censorship. In 1941, the *Daily Worker*, a Communist newspaper, was suppressed; the following year the *Daily Mirror* was threatened with closure after printing what Churchill's government regarded as damaging criticism of the war effort.[41]

The paper rationing implemented during the war also had serious repercussions for the press. Popular newspapers that in the 1930s had consisted of twenty or twenty-four broadsheet pages were after 1940 restricted to producing four or six page issues. This rationing continued until well after the war had ended: statutory controls remained until the end of 1956, and a loose voluntary system ran for a further two years.[42] In the meantime, newsprint prices and production costs rose significantly, and in some cases pagination levels did not return to pre-war levels until the 1970s or even later. The *Daily Express*, for example, averaged fifteen broadsheet pages in 1966, compared with twenty in 1937.[43] Reduced pagination levels did temporarily diminish some of the economic pressures on weaker papers however, for advertisers were forced to take space where they

[37] Political and Economic Planning, *Report on the British Press*, 21–2.

[38] This was a point made by the Press Council in its first Annual Report: General Council of the Press, *The Press and the People* (London: Press Council, 1954), 11.

[39] Edward Burke (1729–97) is credited as the originator of the phrase 'fourth estate', although it was brought into more general circulation by Thomas Carlyle in the 1830s; J. Watson and A. Hill, *Dictionary of Media and Communication Studies*, 5th edn. (London: Arnold, 2000), 116.

[40] T. O'Malley and C. Soley, *Regulating the Press* (London: Pluto Press, 2000), chs. 1, 3.

[41] N. Pronay, 'The News Media at War', in N. Pronay and D. Spring (eds.), *Propaganda, Politics and Film, 1918–45* (London: Macmillan, 1982); H. Cudlipp, *Publish and Be Damned! The Astonishing Story of the Daily Mirror* (London: Andrew Dakers, 1953), chs. 20–8.

[42] On rationing, see I. McDonald, *The History of the Times, Volume V: Struggles in War and Peace 1939–66* (London: Times Books, 1984), 295–9.

[43] Tunstall, *Newspaper Power*, 32.

could find it. It was no coincidence that a wave of closures and amalgamations followed the removal of controls in the mid-1950s.

The Culture of Journalism

Run by private companies, politically partisan and free from close regulation, the culture of newspaper journalism was very different from the 'public service' ethos that developed in broadcasting. In contrast to the United States, where university courses in journalism developed in considerable numbers at the beginning of the twentieth century, journalism in Britain remained an open trade resistant to professionalization. Only one diploma course in journalism was offered in the inter-war period, at King's College, London, and that was not restarted after 1945. Most journalists learned 'on-the-job', usually serving an apprenticeship in provincial newspapers before joining a national.[44] The report of the first Royal Commission on the Press in 1949 criticized the lack of training and the 'inadequate standard of education in the profession of journalism', and recommended measures to rectify the situation.[45] A National Council for the Training of Journalists was eventually established in 1955, but its impact was, initially at least, limited. Postgraduate qualifications in journalism were not offered until 1970 when University College Cardiff introduced a new course, and it was only in the 1990s that undergraduate degrees were established.[46] The two main organizations for journalists, the National Union of Journalists (NUJ) and the Institute of Journalists, made some efforts to raise the standards and prestige of journalism—in 1936, for example, the NUJ introduced a code of conduct for journalists—but most of their energy was expended trying to improve pay and working conditions.[47] Critics of the press's triviality would frequently return to the comments of the Royal Commission and accuse journalists of being ill-educated and poorly trained.

National newspapers were dominated by men at almost all levels. There was, in fact, a long history of notable female journalists, from Harriet Martineau at the *Daily News* in the mid-nineteenth century, via Flora Shaw, the first woman on the permanent staff of *The Times* in the 1890s, to inter-war reporters such as Margaret Lane at the *Daily Mail* and Hilde Marchant at the *Daily Express*. Nevertheless, the number of such women remained small. In 1927, for example, an International Labour Organization survey estimated that there were only around 400 women out of a total of 7,000 journalists in Britain.[48] Those women who managed to gain a position in national newspapers were generally restricted

[44] D. Chambers, L. Steiner, and C. Fleming, *Women and Journalism* (London: Routledge, 2004), ch. 3.

[45] Royal Commission on the Press 1947–9, *Report* (London: HMSO, 1949), Cmd. 7700, 153.

[46] Chambers et al., *Women and Journalism*, 69–70.

[47] O'Malley and Soley, *Regulating the Press*, 42–3.

[48] F. Hunter, 'Women in British Journalism', in Griffiths (ed.), *Encyclopedia*, 689.

to the women's pages or the feature sections; politics, economics, foreign affairs, and sports reporting in particular were considered to be male domains. Women also struggled to reach positions of authority: only 2 per cent of senior positions on British newspapers were held by women in 1965.[49] It was not until 1987, when Wendy Henry was given the top role at the *News of the World*, that a woman became editor of a national paper.[50]

The newsrooms were marked by an aggressively masculine culture of heavy-drinking, boisterous behaviour, and long hours. Women were excluded from the Press Clubs in London and Manchester, and were forced to remain in the back room of Fleet Street's most famous bar, El Vino's. Ann Leslie, then working for the *Daily Express*, observed in 1966 that 'Fleet Street remains ineradicably male—from a practical point of view right down to its set of basic standards and attitudes'.[51] Felicity Green, who gradually climbed up the *Mirror* hierarchy to become in 1973 the first woman on the executive board of a national newspaper, experienced 'a wall of opposition and hostility' from the older men and found that 'the macho male was in evidence everywhere'.[52] Green's rise was one sign that attitudes were gradually shifting by the 1970s, but the process was painfully slow. A TUC survey found that the proportion of women journalists in national newspapers rose by 3 per cent between 1972 and 1977, from 9.6 to 12.6 per cent, but this was largely the result of more men than women leaving the industry as it contracted.[53] Women remained very isolated in the newsrooms. When Anne Robinson was appointed assistant editor of the *Mirror* in 1982, she found that only 22 female journalists worked in the paper's London office, alongside 496 men; the Manchester office, employing 123 journalists, did not employ a single woman.[54] The pace of change increased in the 1990s, by which time women made up 22.6 per cent of newspaper journalists. Even in that decade, though, over 50 per cent of female journalists claimed to have either experienced discrimination or to have witnessed it against other women.[55]

Women were not the only people to feel marginalized in Fleet Street. When he was arrested with Lord Montagu for homosexual offences in 1954, Peter Wildeblood, diplomatic correspondent of the *Daily Mail*, revealed how difficult it was for those who did not share the assertive heterosexuality displayed by most journalists. 'I could hardly have chosen a profession in which being a homosexual

[49] Tunstall, *Newspaper Power*, 138.

[50] Excepting Mary Howarth, who edited the *Daily Mirror* in 1903 in the few short months in which it remained a paper for women.

[51] A. Leslie, 'Women in Fleet Street', in V. Brodzky (ed.), *Fleet Street: The Inside Story of Journalism* (London: MacDonald & Co., 1966), 86.

[52] R. Greenslade, *Press Gang: How Newspapers Make Profits from Propaganda* (London: Macmillan, 2003), 367; B. Hagerty, *Read All About It! 100 Sensational Years of the Daily Mirror* (Lydney, Glos.: First Stone, 2003), 105.

[53] TUC, *Images of Inequality: The Portrayal of Women in the Media and Advertising* (London: TUC, 1984), 12.

[54] Greenslade, *Press Gang*, 370.

[55] Chambers et al., *Women and Journalism*, 93, 100.

was more of a handicap than it was in Fleet Street,' he wrote in 1955. 'Its morality was that of the saloon bar: every sexual excess was talked about and tolerated, provided it was "normal".'[56] Wildeblood successfully concealed his homosexuality until his arrest, but some gay journalists, such as Godfrey Winn, were more open, and faced being ridiculed.[57] Nancy Spain, who joined the *Daily Express* in 1952 as a book reviewer, certainly experienced some hostility due to her sexual orientation. The *Express* editor, Arthur Christiansen, described her to Lord Beaverbrook as 'a raging Lesbian' who looked like a 'circus freak' due to her masculine clothing; another journalist complained that the paper would become a 'laughing-stock by employing her because of her reputation'.[58] Both Winn and Spain were recognized as being talented writers, however, and so they were tolerated by their editors.

Black and Asian journalists also found it very difficult to enter the national press. In the mid-1970s fewer than a dozen had positions on mainstream newspapers and magazines.[59] Many were restricted to working on local West Indian and Asian papers, or the national versions that were being opened at the end of this period, such as the *Caribbean Times* (1977) and the *Voice* (1982).[60] South African journalist Lionel Morrison—who became the first black president of the NUJ—exposed the racism he encountered when applying for jobs in Fleet Street in the late 1960s and early 1970s: despite his considerable experience he was forced to carve out a career as a freelance.[61] Even as issues of race and integration rose up the political agenda national newspapers gave very little space to ethnic minority voices.[62]

One group of Fleet Street employees that became increasingly significant after 1945 was the heavily unionized body of printing, production, and distribution workers. Products with a one day shelf-life, newspapers were particularly susceptible to the threat of strikes, and in the absence of any concerted resistance from proprietors, unions were able to extract very favourable pay and conditions. The second Royal Commission on the Press revealed in 1962 that the average earnings of manual workers in the newspaper industry were 'the highest of any paid to manual workers in this country'. Over-manning and inefficiencies meant that production costs were hugely inflated: the commission argued that 'In some national newspaper offices it would not be unreasonable to look for a reduction

56 P. Wildeblood, *Against The Law* (first pub. 1955; Harmonsdsworth: Penguin, 1957), 36.

57 Cudlipp, *Walking on Water*, 144.

58 House of Lords Record Office, London, Beaverbrook Papers, H/155, Arthur Christiansen to Lord Beaverbrook, 6 Mar. 1952.

59 L. Morrison, 'A Black Journalist's Experience of British Journalism', in C. Husband (ed.), *White Media & Black Britain: A Critical Look at the Role of the Media In Race Relations Today* (London: Arrow, 1975), 167.

60 I. Benjamin, *The Black Press in Britain* (Stoke: Trentham Books, 1995).

61 Morrison, 'A Black Journalist's Experience of British Journalism'.

62 P. Gordon and D. Rosenberg, *Daily Racism: The Press and Black People in Britain* (London: Runnymede Trust, 1989).

of about one third in the wages bill.'[63] These costs inhibited the growth of pagination levels after the end of newsprint rationing. Yet throughout the 1960s and 1970s little action was taken to remedy the situation. Substantial cuts were not made, printing plants remained unmodernized, and the potential benefits of computer technology were not realized. Articles criticizing unions provoked clashes that sometimes resulted in impromptu printing strikes. The failure of the management and unions to reach agreement ensured that by the late 1970s the industry seemed to be in crisis—the most visible sign of which was the stoppage of *The Times* for eleven months due to an industrial dispute. This situation eventually altered in the 1980s, when the new legal environment created by Margaret Thatcher's Conservative government enabled proprietors, led by Eddie Shah and Rupert Murdoch, to challenge the unions. Murdoch's clandestine transfer in 1986 of the production of his papers to a plant in Wapping, east London, marked the beginning of a period in which the economics of the press would be transformed.[64]

In conclusion, national popular newspapers held a very significant place in British society. They were widely read across the country, and made a major contribution to public debate. The newspaper market was very competitive, and editors were constantly seeking new ways of attracting readers. Unlike broadcasters, journalists did not have to subscribe to a public service ethos, and they were free instead to be partisan and irreverent. The press did not reflect the diversity of society it reported on: women and individuals from sexual and ethnic minorities found it difficult to progress in journalism. By the 1960s, the long period of circulation growth had ended, and newspapers faced the twin problems of rising production costs and increasing competition from other media.

MEDIA ENVIRONMENT

Newspapers were only one of a number of media forms competing for the attention of the public. Magazines and books offered alternative types of reading material, as they had long done, but in the twentieth century other media emerged to inform and entertain a popular audience. The film industry developed very rapidly after the Lumière brothers demonstrated their moving picture technology in London in 1896. In 1922, while cinemas were being constructed apace, regular radio broadcasting began under the monopoly of the BBC; fourteen years later the corporation took its pioneering steps in television broadcasting. The BBC's monopoly was finally broken with the launch of ITV in 1955, and in the years that followed broadcasting output steadily increased as new channels were introduced and broadcasting hours were extended. In the six decades after 1918,

63 Royal Commission on the Press 1961–62, *Report*, 31–2.

64 Tunstall, *Newspaper Power*, chs. 2–3.

therefore, the media landscape was completely transformed, and newspapers had to adapt accordingly. This section provides a brief overview of these competing media and the way they covered sex and private life, beginning with the print media and then exploring the newer media forms.

Popular Fiction

Books of all kinds circulated more widely after 1918 than ever before. Demand was stimulated by the extension of the public library network, the rise of book clubs, and, from the mid-1930s, the increasing availability of cheap paperback editions produced by publishers such as Penguin.[65] The best-selling books were generally popular romantic fiction, especially novels from the Mills and Boon publishing house, or by rival authors Barbara Cartland, Ruby Ayres, and later Catherine Cookson.[66] While love and passion were at the forefront of these novels, sexual activity itself remained in the background. Mills and Boon 'insisted on sexual propriety in their publications at all times' and adhered to the ideal of virginity for its unmarried heroines. Notions of acceptable content did change across the period, but the company ensured that its fiction steered well clear of controversy.[67] Barbara Cartland was similarly conventional in her morality, insisting even in 1975 that 'All my heroines are virgins—I don't think sleeping together is romantic'.[68]

Not all popular literature was quite so chaste, however. During the inter-war decades there emerged a body of popular erotic fiction that explored sexual themes for a largely female audience.[69] The most notable example of this genre was E. M. Hull's *The Sheik*, which was published in 1919 and went through no fewer than 108 editions in Britain by 1923; it was also made into a popular Hollywood film starring Rudolph Valentino.[70] The novel was not particularly graphic, lapsing into euphemism in the relevant scenes, but it had an unmistakably sado-masochistic scenario, in which the heroine gradually falls in love with the Arab Sheikh who captures and repeatedly rapes her. This escapist fantasy, argues the historian Billie Melman, was pornography for women, and it spawned a number of imitations, written by the likes of Ethel Dell and the pseudonymous authors Kathlyn Rhodes and Joan Conquest. More 'middlebrow' fiction, such as Michael Arlen's *The Green Hat* (1924) and Margaret Kennedy's *The Constant Nymph* (1924), also addressed sexual themes more openly than

[65] J. McAleer, *Popular Reading and Publishing 1914–50* (Oxford: Clarendon Press, 1992); McKibbin, *Classes and Cultures*, ch. XIII.

[66] J. McAleer, *Passion's Fortune: The Story of Mills and Boon* (Oxford: Oxford University Press, 1999).

[67] McAleer, *Popular Reading and Publishing*, 244.

[68] N. Beauman, *A Very Great Profession: The Woman's Novel 1914–39* (London: Virago, 1983), 185.

[69] B. Melman, *Women and the Popular Imagination in the Twenties: Flappers and Nymphs* (Basingstoke: Macmillan, 1988).

[70] Ibid., 46, ch. 6.

previously.[71] Nevertheless, there were still significant restrictions on the fictional discussion of sexuality. Novels which were too explicit in their descriptions or dialogue—such as D. H. Lawrence's *Lady Chatterley's Lover* (1928) or Norah James's *Sleeveless Errand* (1929)—or which addressed what were regarded as 'distasteful' issues—such as Radclyffe Hall's exploration of lesbian relationships, *The Well of Loneliness* (1929)—were banned or withdrawn.[72] Even if not banned, some libraries and bookshops refused to stock controversial novels. As a result, many sexual themes—in particular homosexuality—were not explored in fiction in any real detail.

These restrictions survived until well after the Second World War—indeed, there was a fresh bout of concern about 'obscene' literature in official circles in the early 1950s. The Home Office issued a secret *Blue Book* to chief constables listing works that were to be suppressed, focusing in particular on pulp fiction books imported from America.[73] In 1954 there were 132 separate prosecutions under the Obscene Publications Act, compared to 39 in 1935.[74] A number of the obscenity cases in these years involved high-profile publishers such as Secker & Warburg, Heinemann, and Hutchinson, much to the consternation of the literary elite. The response was a campaign to reform the obscenity laws, which in 1959 resulted in the successful passage of a new Obscene Publications Act. This Act introduced a new 'public good' defence and ensured that when determining obscenity the jury was obliged to consider the work as a whole. It was under this new legislation that the Director of Public Prosecutions in 1960 prosecuted Penguin Books for its publication of *Lady Chatterley's Lover*. The acquittal of Penguin—and the unparalleled commercial success of the paperback edition of Lawrence's novel—paved the way for far greater permissiveness in popular literature.[75] Descriptions of sexual activities became far more explicit, and racy fiction by authors such as Harold Robbins, Jacqueline Susann, and Jackie Collins became a staple of popular culture. The novelists Kingsley Amis and Elizabeth Jane Howard lamented in 1972 that 'Today, more than at any other time easily recalled, there is pressure on the writer to introduce overt sex into his book', because of the publishers' belief that 'sex sells'.[76] Different forms of sexuality could now be explored, and a number of books describing the experience of gay men and women emerged. The momentum behind this process of liberalization was sufficiently strong that in 1979 the Williams Committee on Pornography

[71] N. Humble, *The Feminine Middlebrow Novel 1920s to 1950s: Class, Domesticity, and Bohemianism* (Oxford: Oxford University Press, 2001).

[72] C. Baldick, *The Oxford English Literary History, Vol. 10, 1910–1940: The Modern Age* (Oxford: Oxford University Press, 2004), ch. 17.

[73] A. Travis, *Bound and Gagged: A Secret History of Obscenity in Britain* (London: Profile Books, 2000), ch. 5.

[74] Ibid., 94.

[75] J. Sutherland, *Offensive Literature: Decensorship in Britain 1960–82* (London: Junction Books, 1982).

[76] Longford Committee, *Pornography: The Longford Report* (London: Coronet, 1972), 153.

argued that only photographic images, rather than written representations, should ordinarily be considered pornographic.[77]

Magazines

The first publications to demonstrate the potential of the mass magazine market were George Newnes's *Tit-bits* (1881) and Alfred Harmsworth's *Answers* (1888). They provided readers with a miscellany of curious facts, serialized fiction, jokes, puzzles, and competitions; they were family-oriented and generally steered clear of contentious subjects.[78] Although their circulations declined in the first quarter of the twentieth century, they both remained among the market leaders, selling over 400,000 copies per week in the early 1920s.[79] Very different, and far more rumbustious, was *John Bull*. Established in 1906 by the controversial MP Horatio Bottomley, during the First World War it became the first British magazine to sell more than one million copies. *John Bull* combined a raucous patriotism with an irreverent attitude to authority, exposing corruption, favouritism, and bureaucratic incompetence, and seeking redress for victims of injustice. Its crusades frequently addressed moral topics: in April 1920, for example, it attacked the rise of 'massage parlours' in London.[80] In the 1920s *John Bull* introduced a women's page—as did *Tit-bits* and *Answers*—and this occasionally provided a forum in which to explore sexual issues. In 1925, when the magazine was still selling around one million copies a week, Marie Stopes was invited to answer letters from correspondents; for almost half a year she wrote about sex, birth control, and abortion. The letters that Stopes received suggest that these articles provided an important source of information for her readers, and they certainly helped to consolidate Stopes's growing reputation as the leading popular authority on sex.[81]

Many other successful general interest magazines emerged in the inter-war period. The *Radio Times*, launched in 1923, pioneered the listings format that would produce the century's most widely-circulated magazines. The *Radio Times*'s peak circulation of 8.1 million copies at the end of the 1940s is unlikely ever to be surpassed by a British magazine; after 1955 its dominance was challenged by *TV Times*.[82] From the mid-1930s a string of popular illustrated

[77] L. Nead, *The Female Nude: Art, Obscenity and Sexuality* (London: Routledge, 1992), 96–7; G. Hawkins and F. E. Zimring, *Pornography in a Free Society* (Cambridge: Cambridge University Press, 1991).

[78] K. Jackson, *George Newnes and the New Journalism in Britain, 1880–1910: Culture and Profit* (Aldershot: Ashgate, 2001).

[79] D. Reed, *The Popular Magazine in Britain and the United States 1880–1960* (London: The British Library, 1997), 129, 141.

[80] *John Bull*, 17 April 1920, cited Reed, *The Popular Magazine*, 139.

[81] C. Davey, 'Birth Control in Britain during the Interwar Years: Evidence from the Stopes Correspondence', *Journal of Family History*, 13/3 (1988), 335–6.

[82] Reed, *The Popular Magazine*, 209.

magazines were launched to great success, including *Weekly Illustrated* (1934, becoming *Illustrated* in 1939), *Picture Post* (1938), *Reveille* (1940), and *Week-end* (an offshoot of the *Overseas Daily Mail*, and originally launched as *Weekend Mail* in 1953). These publications provided informative and entertaining articles on a broad range of social and cultural topics, illustrated throughout with the vivid photography that had been made possible by improvements in printing technology. *Picture Post*, selling 1.2 million copies a week by 1940, made a particular cultural impact at time when popular newspapers were very restricted in size; its 'Plan for Britain', published in January 1941, was widely admired.[83]

As competition intensified in an increasingly crowded magazine market, titillating features became more prominent. Analysing the success of *Reveille* (published by the Mirror Group) in 1949, E. J. Robertson, the chairman of Express Newspapers, told Beaverbrook that it was largely due to the magazine's sexual content. It contained 'all the worst features of the *Mirror* and the *Pictorial*: a very plentiful supply of pictures of nude and semi-nude women, supported by letterpress of which sex is the predominating interest'.[84] *Picture Post*, which had traditionally been more serious in content than its rivals, was soon under pressure to go down a similar avenue. Arthur Christiansen, the *Daily Express* editor, discussed the magazine's position with James Cameron, one of its most famous contributors, in June 1951, and was told that 'in an endeavour to stop the circulation rot, the paper had gone in for "cheesecake" and cut out foreign affairs'.[85] A few months later the Archbishop of Canterbury condemned a *Picture Post* series for its unsuitable sexual content.[86]

By the end of the 1950s, the challenge from television started to take its toll. British magazine circulations peaked in 1956–7 and gradually declined thereafter.[87] As newspapers grew in size and expanded their feature coverage, the general magazine was particularly badly hit. *Picture Post* closed in 1957, and by 1964 both *Illustrated* and *John Bull* had merged with other titles. Magazines would increasingly have to target a more specific audience to prosper. After all, newspapers were beginning to launch their own magazines for the general market: the *Sunday Times* led the way in February 1962 and was soon followed by the *Observer*, the *Daily Telegraph*, and (briefly) the *Daily Mirror*.

Women's magazines had been a prosperous sector of the magazine market since the eighteenth century.[88] Most publications for women were dominated by fashion advice, features about housewifery and domestic life, and romantic

[83] T. Hopkinson (ed.), *Picture Post 1938–50* (London: Penguin, 1970). On the 'Plan for Britain', see 90–9.

[84] Beaverbrook Papers, H/136, Robertson to Beaverbrook, 25 Nov. 1949.

[85] Beaverbrook Papers, H/148, Christiansen to Beaverbrook, 6 June 1951.

[86] Beaverbrook Papers, H/151, Robertson to Beaverbrook, 12 Dec. 1951.

[87] Reed, *The Popular Magazine*, 224.

[88] C. White, *Women's Magazines 1693–1968* (London: Michael Joseph, 1971); M. Beetham, *A Magazine of Her Own? Domesticity and Desire in the Woman's Magazine 1800–1914* (London: Routledge, 1996).

fiction; the inclusion of 'problem pages' also opened up the realm of personal relationships. The sector was highly fragmented by age and class. In the early twentieth century, the reading of working-class girls and young women was dominated by the fiction papers such as *Girls' Friend* (1899), *Red Letter* (1899) *Peg's Paper* (1919), and *Red Star Weekly* (1929).[89] These magazines provided melodramatic stories involving love, passion, and revenge. Nevertheless the leading publishers, such as Dundee-based D. C. Thomson, were careful to ensure that nothing too explicit was included and that inappropriate elements did not creep in: *Red Letter* and *Red Star Weekly* were both prominently labelled 'For the Family Circle'.[90] For the older working-class woman, magazines such as *Home Chat* (1895), *My Weekly* (1910), and *Woman's Weekly* (1911) provided entertaining miscellanies focused on the domestic sphere, while middle-class women were served by publications such as *Queen* (1861), *The Gentlewoman* (1890) and the amazingly successful *Good Housekeeping* (1922), which treated housewifery as a profession. The 1930s saw the introduction of a number of new weekly titles, notably *Woman's Own* (1932) and *Woman* (1937), which marked the beginning of a boom in women's magazines. *Woman* soon led the market, reaching a circulation of one million by 1940 and peaking at just under 3.5 million copies a week in 1957.[91] By the late 1950s, the market was almost saturated: five out of every six women read at least one women's magazine a week, and many were reading several.[92] From that point the circulation of women's weeklies declined steadily, although the readership of monthlies held up.

Women's magazines generally promoted domestic contentment and an ethos of consumption, while providing a safety-valve of escapism with romantic serials. Women were told how to look beautiful, succeed in the roles of wife and mother, and enjoy their new affluence. With a healthy sexual relationship increasingly regarded as an essential element in a happy marriage, sex also became a topic of discussion. Soon after its launch, for example, *Woman* published a series on the 'Psychology of Sex' and included a test for frigidity.[93] Nevertheless, the amount of explicit information given was generally limited, and there was little discussion of extra-marital sexuality. Editors such as Mary Grieve, in charge of *Woman* between 1940 and 1962, maintained a cautious approach to subjects such as birth control, marital infidelity, and homosexuality, and ensured that the advice given by their agony aunts was 'respectable'.[94] Only with a new generation of

[89] Melman, *Women and the Popular Imagination*, ch. 7 and 8.

[90] McKibbin, *Classes and Cultures*, 493–4.

[91] Reed, *The Popular Magazine*, 221.

[92] M. Pugh, *Women and the Women's Movement in Britain 1914–59* (Basingstoke: Macmillan, 1992), 209–10.

[93] J. Weeks, *Sex, Politics and Society: The Regulation of Sexuality since 1800* (London: Longman, 1981), 206.

[94] White, *Women's Magazines*, 107–10; R. Kent, *Agony: Problem Pages Through The Ages* (London: Star, 1987), 27; R. Porter and L. Hall, *The Facts of Life: The Creation of Sexual Knowledge in Britain, 1650–1950* (New Haven: Yale University Press, 1995), 265; Pugh, *Women and the Women's Movement*, 216.

magazines such as *Nova* (1965) and in particular *Cosmopolitan* (1972) did the coverage of sex become more detailed and wide-ranging. *Cosmopolitan* celebrated a liberated female sexuality that was not confined to the institution of marriage, and included photographs of male pin-ups and guides on sexual technique.

There were far fewer magazines directed specifically at men: it was generally assumed that they were sufficiently catered for by newspapers and by more specialized sports, motoring, or hobby publications. Many men read fiction magazines, several of which were imported from America, filled with crime, Western, or sports stories. These publications—especially the American versions—were frequently violent and often included sexually titillating elements.[95] The first successful men's lifestyle magazine in the twentieth century was *Men Only*, which launched in 1935 and by 1947 claimed a readership of approaching two million. To its features on topics such as travel, exploration, sport, literature, and consumption were added 'artistic' nudes, which probably attracted much of its readership.[96] Less popular imitators included *Lilliput* and *Parade*. Bolder in its content was *Playboy*, launched in the United States in 1953 and soon selling well in Britain. *Playboy* targeted an idealized readership of wealthy, sophisticated, and sexually liberated men, and paved the way for an explosion of glossy pornographic magazines in the 1960s. Publications such as *King* (1964), *Penthouse* (1965), and *Mayfair* (1966) differed from their British predecessors in being unapologetic about providing erotic content designed to arouse sexual feeling.[97] Their content was also far more explicit, with *Penthouse* pushing back the boundaries of acceptability from 1970 by displaying pubic hair. Existing magazines had to adapt to the new environment if they were to survive, as did *Men Only* after being taken over by Paul Raymond. This 'modern pornography' was a publishing phenomenon. *Penthouse*, which had already attracted a monthly circulation of 150,000 by 1966, achieved sales of 429,000 by 1976; by then it had been surpassed by *Mayfair* (461,000) and the relaunched *Men Only* (434,000), while *Club International* was not far behind (324,000).[98] Pornography had entered mainstream culture, and explicit sexualized imagery was more accessible than ever before.

Cinema

In the first quarter of the twentieth century, the cinema industry expanded rapidly and assumed a central place in British popular culture. The first purpose-built cinema was opened in 1906, and by 1916 some 3,500 picture houses had been

[95] McKibbin, *Classes and Cultures*, 496.

[96] J. Greenfield, S. O'Connell, and C. Reid, 'Fashioning Masculinity: *Men Only*, Consumption and the Development of Marketing in the 1930s', *Twentieth Century British History*, 10/4 (1999), 457–76.

[97] M. Collins, *Modern Love: An Intimate History of Men and Women in Twentieth-Century Britain* (London: Atlantic, 2003), ch. 5.

[98] Ibid., 141.

built.[99] By the 1930s there were 18–19 million attendances at British cinemas every week; audiences peaked in 1946 when there were 31.4 million weekly attendances. In this period, the British went to the cinema more than any other people, including Americans. All sections of the population were lured into the cinema, but, on average, the young went more frequently than the elderly, the working-class more than the middle and upper-classes, and women more than men.[100] The rise of television ended cinema's golden age, dramatically reducing the size of the audiences in the second half of the century. In 1970 there were only 3.71 million weekly admissions, barely a tenth of the figure twenty-four years earlier. Between 1950 and 1970 the number of cinemas fell from 4,584 to 1,529.[101]

Film production was dominated by the large studios of Hollywood, which powerfully stimulated fears of the 'Americanization' of British culture. Attempts were made to restrict this dominance—the Cinematograph Films Act of 1927 introduced a quota system whereby a certain proportion of films shown in Britain had to be British-made, and quotas remained in place in some form until 1983[102]—but ultimately the popularity of the exciting and stylish big-budget Hollywood films could not be denied. Film stars became the new heroes of popular culture: figures such as Rudolph Valentino, Jean Harlow, Clark Gable, Greta Garbo, James Dean, Marilyn Monroe, Clint Eastwood, and Elizabeth Taylor were portrayed as the epitomes of glamour and 'sex appeal'. As George Orwell observed in 1937, many working-class people sought escape from the drabness of their everyday lives by 'indulging in a private daydream' of being one of these stars.[103] Women, in particular, were influenced by the fashions and styles of the leading actresses: movies were an important stimulus to the rapid take-up of cosmetics in this period, for example.[104] The cinema provided new opportunities for fantasy for many women, and, as Jackie Stacey has shown, identification with confident and sophisticated female stars could inspire spectators to demonstrate independence and express their sexuality.[105] On the other hand, the Hollywood emphasis on 'sex appeal' could encourage young women to be judged by increasingly demanding standards of appearance.

The potency and popularity of this new medium ensured that parliament and local authorities were very quick to demand measures to regulate it. The

[99] J. Robertson, *The British Board of Film Censors: Film Censorship in Britain, 1896–1950* (Beckenham: Croom Helm, 1985), 1, 3.

[100] McKibbin, *Classes and Cultures*, 419–22.

[101] M. Garnett and R. Weight, *The A-Z Guide to Modern British History* (London: Jonathan Cape), 96.

[102] S. Street, *British National Cinema* (London: Routledge, 1997), ch. 1.

[103] G. Orwell, *The Road to Wigan Pier* (first pub. 1937; Harmondsworth: Penguin, 1978), 79.

[104] I. Zweiniger-Bargielowska, 'The Body and Consumer Culture', in ead. (ed.) *Women in Twentieth Century Britain* (Harlow: Longman, 2001), 187–88.

[105] J. Stacey, *Stargazing: Hollywood Cinema and Female Spectatorship* (London: Routledge, 1994). See also S. Alexander, 'Becoming a Woman in London in the 1920s and 1930s', in ead., *Becoming a Woman and Other Essays* (New York: New York University Press, 1995).

1909 Cinematograph Act gave local authorities the power to licence cinema performances, initially for safety reasons, but the scope of the act was soon found to extend to the content of films. The industry responded by establishing the British Board of Film Censors (BBFC), which began operation in 1913.[106] This body awarded films certificates of either 'U' (universal) or 'A' (adults), but children were allowed into 'A' films if accompanied by an adult. This system effectively meant that all films had to be suitable for a family audience; those that were not faced a ban. It was clear from the outset that the BBFC considered sexual themes or erotic material to be unsuitable for such an audience. Its first annual report, published in 1914, listed twenty-two grounds on which it had cut or banned films, several of which related to sexual content. Among the prohibitions were 'vulgarity and impropriety in conduct and dress', 'indelicate sexual situations' and 'scenes suggestive of immorality'.[107] In 1926, these objectionable elements were codified more thoroughly. Reasons for cuts or a ban now included any form of visual titillation ('nude and semi-nude figures', 'girls' clothes pulled off, leaving them in scanty undergarments', 'women in alluring or provocative attitudes'), the simulation of sexual activity ('degrading exhibitions of animal passion', 'passionate and unrestrained embraces', 'men and women in bed together'), suggestions of promiscuity ('themes indicative of habitual morality', 'marital infidelity and collusive divorce'), and all types of crime relating to sex ('abortion', 'criminal assault on girls', 'scenes in and connected with houses of ill repute', 'procuration', 'white slave traffic'). 'Subjects dealing with venereal disease' were forbidden, as were 'equivocal situations between white girls and men of other races'; even the use of the phrase 'sex appeal' in inter-titles was expressly rejected.[108] The BBFC, in short, sought to ensure that middle-class morality and the institution of marriage were not threatened by this powerful new industry. This was part of a wider conservatism among the film censors which ensured that the inter-war cinema would be unable to tackle any topic that had the potential to be politically or socially 'controversial'.[109]

Directors continually tested the limits of censorship and tried to smuggle in sexual content. In the early 1930s, American films such as the Mae West vehicles *She Done Him Wrong* and *I'm No Angel*, and *Blonde Bombshell* starring Jean Harlow, exploited the opportunities for suggestiveness and innuendo to the full. These films soon brought an official response, however: in 1934, censorship was tightened in the United States with the adoption of the 'Hays' Code', and such innuendo largely disappeared from view for several years. There were some minor relaxations of BBFC policy during the war and immediate post-war years but it was only in 1951 that the regulatory system itself was modified with the introduction of the 'X' certificate preventing admission of children under

[106] Robertson, *British Board of Film Censors.* [107] Ibid., 7. [108] Ibid, 180–2.

[109] J. Richards, *The Age of the Dream Palace: Cinema and Society in Britain 1930–1939* (London: Routledge & Kegan Paul, 1984).

sixteen.[110] For the first time the board recognized that it was legitimate to produce a film aimed at adults. This did not, by any means, lead to an immediate dropping of restrictions on sexual content. The full implications of the new system were only realized under John Trevelyan, who was responsible for a substantial, if gradual, liberalization of policy, as head of the BBFC from 1958 to 1971. British films addressing sexual themes, with more realistic scenarios and dialogue, began to emerge. The 'new wave' films *Room at the Top* (1958), *Saturday Night Sunday Morning* (1960), *A Taste of Honey* (1961), *A Kind of Loving* (1962), and the *L-Shaped Room* (1962) tackled a range of 'controversial' issues, including extra-marital sex, inter-racial relationships, abortion, and unmarried motherhood.[111] Censors remained particularly sensitive about homosexuality—*A Taste of Honey* had to be toned down for that reason—but they slowly came to recognize it as a legitimate subject. In 1961 the BBFC accepted *Victim*, starring Dirk Bogarde as a barrister who, in the face of considerable personal risk, reveals that he is gay in order to expose a team of blackmailers; at the end of the decade it passed *The Killing of Sister George* which prominently featured a lesbian relationship. Both films were highly sanitized and judgemental, but they did illustrate an increasing openness about homosexuality.[112]

From the mid-1960s, the moral guidelines that had formed that basis of BBFC policy since its foundation were finally abandoned. The board became far more relaxed about nudity, swearing, and violence in films directed at adults. The definition of 'adult' was tightened in 1970—admission to X films was now permitted only to those over 18—but this paved the way for more explicit content. The portrayal of sexual activity became far more graphic in films such as *The Devils* (1970), *Last Tango in Paris* (1972), and *Emmanuelle* (1974). This greater permissiveness inevitably caused controversy. Some local authorities refused to accept the recommendations of the BBFC, often prompted by the protests of pressure groups such as Mary Whitehouse's National Viewers' and Listeners' Association (NVLA) and the Festival of Light. The fiercest arguments centred on films combining sex and violence, such as *A Clockwork Orange* (1971) and *Straw Dogs* (1971), both of which contained rape scenes. Declining audiences had not reduced cinema's ability to generate heated debate about sex and morality.

Broadcasting

Newspapers were quick to appreciate the popularity of the cinema and believed that the two media could have a beneficial relationship. Film lovers turned to

110 Robertson, *British Board of Film Censors*, 139–43, 167–8, 174–5.

111 J. Hill, *Sex, Class and Realism: British Cinema 1956–1963* (London: BFI 1986). A. Aldgate, *Censorship and the Permissive Society: British Cinema and Theatre, 1955–1965* (Oxford: Oxford University Press, 1995).

112 K. Howes, *Broadcasting It: An Encyclopaedia of Homosexuality on Film, Radio and TV in the UK 1923–1993* (London: Cassells, 1993).

the press to find out the latest news about the industry: as one critic observed in 1936, 'newspaper reviews of films are read with interest and play a large part in influencing people of all classes in their appreciation of the films shown'.[113] Cinema showings generally included a short newsreel covering the main stories of the week, but such footage was not regarded as offering serious competition to the press. Fleet Street recognized immediately that radio and television broadcasting posed a far greater threat to the press. When the BBC was founded in 1922, the Newspaper Proprietors' Association persuaded the government to prohibit news broadcasts before 7 p.m., so as not to damage sales of newspapers. The company was initially forced to rely on news supplied by outside agencies such as Reuters rather than develop its own newsgathering apparatus; concern about the potential political impact of this new medium also led to a ban on political commentary and controversy on the radio.[114] Such was the narrow definition of news adopted by the BBC that in one famous bulletin on Good Friday 1930, the announcer declared 'there is no news tonight'.[115]

Yet as broadcasting became more popular—and by the end of the 1930s, over 70 per cent of households had a radio licence—it was increasingly clear that the press lobby, powerful as it was, could not prevent the eventual realization of radio's potential as a news medium. The BBC steadily built up its news department during the late 1930s, and the Second World War provided the opportunity for the department to throw off many of the shackles that had constrained its earlier development. News bulletins were finally broadcast throughout the day, and they were complemented with extended news programmes such as *Radio Newsreel*, introduced in 1940. The newsgathering operation was extended significantly, and in 1944 the BBC started to appoint its own correspondents.[116] It has been estimated that up to 80 per cent of the population heard about the D-Day invasion on the radio.[117] Cecil King recognized the portents for the press. Writing to his colleague Hugh Cudlipp in December 1943, he predicted that there was 'clearly going to be more and better radio after the war', which would 'entirely and obviously kill the function of the newspaper in purveying hot news'. Newspapers would have to offer something different from the radio, he concluded, making 'all the more important the organising of a good service of the simple human kind of story which is meat and drink to the tabloid newspaper'.[118]

[113] Winifred Holmes in *World Film News*, 1, no. 9 (Dec. 1936), cited in Richards, *Age of the Dream Palace*, 8.

[114] S. Nicholas, 'All the News that's Fit to Broadcast: The Popular Press versus the BBC, 1922–45', in P. Catterall, C. Seymour-Ure, and A. Smith (eds.), *Northcliffe's Legacy: Aspects of the British Popular Press 1896–1996* (Basingstoke: Macmillan, 2000).

[115] Ibid., 130.

[116] A. Crisell, *An Introductory History of British Broadcasting* (London: Routledge, 1997), 56.

[117] Seymore-Ure, *British Press and Broadcasting*, 151.

[118] Bute Library, University of Cardiff, Cudlipp Papers, H.C.2/1, Cecil King to Hugh Cudlipp, 16 Dec. 1943.

Although an undoubted competitor for the press as a supplier of news, BBC broadcasting was nevertheless a very different sort of cultural experience than that offered by popular newspapers. John Reith, general manager and then director-general of the BBC from 1922 until 1938, developed a high-minded ideal of public-service broadcasting for the organization, which laid great emphasis on its duty to inform and educate listeners, as well as entertain them. 'Our responsibility is to carry into the greatest possible number of homes everything that is best in every department of human knowledge, endeavour, and achievement', he wrote in 1924; this was the best as defined by the educated elite, with the belief that such a diet would serve to elevate the tastes of the public.[119] Popular programming, such as variety and light entertainment shows, was included, but it was mixed in with more challenging and highbrow broadcasts. The BBC also laid down very strict rules about decency and vulgarity. Reith had strong Calvinist beliefs and he ensured that a rigorous Christian morality pervaded the corporation. C. A. Lewis, the first organizer of programmes, declared that the organization should aim 'to keep programming on the "upper side" of public taste and to avoid giving "offence"'; it should set itself apart from the popular press by refusing to pander to the interest in 'sensational murder details, or unsavoury divorce cases'.[120] These general principles were gradually codified into more specific instructions. The *Variety Programme and Policy Guide for Writers and Producers* (informally known as the 'Green Book'), composed in the 1930s, declared that:

> Programmes must at all costs be kept free of crudities. There can be no compromise with doubtful material. It must be cut. There is an absolute ban upon the following: jokes about lavatories, effeminacy in men, immorality of any kind, suggestive references to honeymooning couples, chambermaids, fig leaves, ladies' underwear (e.g. winter draws on), animal habits (e.g. rabbits), lodgers, commercial travellers. When in doubt—cut it out.[121]

The innuendo and 'vulgar' humour that had long been a staple of the working-class music hall was entirely prohibited, therefore, and performers such as George Formby were treated with great caution: Formby's saucy song 'When I'm Cleaning Windows' was banned for a time. This concern for propriety even extended to the private conduct of the employees. In 1929, for example, Reith dismissed the BBC's talented chief engineer, Peter Eckersley, when he was cited in a divorce case.[122]

In this context, there was very little discussion of sexual issues, although the reticence did gradually break down after Reith's departure. From the early 1930s

[119] J. Reith, *Broadcast Over Britain* (1924), cited in J. McDonnell, *Public Service Broadcasting: A Reader* (London: Routledge, 1991), 11–12.

[120] C. A. Lewis, *Broadcasting from Within* (1924), cited in McDonnell, *Public Service Broadcasting*, 12.

[121] J. Green, *All Dressed Up: The Sixties and the Counterculture* (London: Pimlico, 1999), 64.

[122] McKibbin, *Classes and Cultures*, 461–2.

health talks were broadcast, usually given by Dr Charles Hill, the 'radio doctor', and covering a variety of topics including childcare. During the war, these were extended to include the pressing problem of venereal disease, starting with the Chief Medical Officer's broadcast on the subject in October 1942. In April 1943, the BBC made VD an official campaign, aiming to produce a relevant broadcast every month.[123] *Woman's Hour*, launched on the Light Programme in 1946, discussed sexual issues and personal relationships, despite the disapproval of some controllers: in 1948 one complained that it was 'acutely embarrassing' to hear a discussion of the menopause in the early afternoon.[124] The stratification of the BBC radio output into Light, Home, and Third Programmes (and in 1967 into Radios 1–4) enabled an expansion of populist programming, and comedy, drama, and light entertainment producers benefited from an increasingly flexible interpretation of the rules on decency.

During the post-war decades, however, radio was gradually overtaken in importance by television broadcasting. The BBC's television service, which began in November 1936, was suspended during the war, and resumed only in 1946. At first television was regarded with some suspicion and scepticism by the corporation's hierarchy: in 1950 the budget for television was only half that of the Home Service.[125] The potential value—and popularity—of television was first truly demonstrated by the live coverage of Queen Elizabeth's coronation on 2 June 1953. An estimated 56 per cent of the population watched the proceedings in Westminster Abbey, and as *The People* observed, 'they were able to see the ceremony on the screen at the exact moment of its happening and with greater intimacy and detail than was possible for anyone in the Abbey.'[126]

In 1955 television viewing began to exceed radio listening for the first time, partly encouraged by the introduction in September of a second channel, ITV, funded by advertising. ITV quickly established itself as a populist alternative to BBC, offering game shows, variety spectaculars, and soap operas of a type unseen on the public service channel.[127] Here was a powerful double threat to the press: not only was there a new rival for advertising expenditure, but one that provided a form of entertainment unashamedly aimed at a popular audience. Some newspapers groups, such as Associated Newspapers (owner of the *Daily Mail*) and the Mirror Group, tried to protect themselves by investing in commercial television, but there was no doubting the anxiety in Fleet Street. In 1959, for example, Edward Pickering, the editor of the *Daily Express*, told Beaverbrook that he preferred the paper to comment on the previous night's television programmes rather than preview that day's 'because I think we are then

[123] S. Nicholas, *The Echo of War: Home Front Propaganda and the Wartime BBC, 1939–45* (Manchester: Manchester University Press, 1996), 95–8.

[124] Chambers et al., *Women and Journalism*, 50.

[125] Crisell, *British Broadcasting*, ch. 4.

[126] Ibid., 75; *The People*, 7 June 1953, 8.

[127] C. Johnson and R. Turnock (eds.), *ITV Cultures: Independent Television over Fifty Years* (Maidenhead: Open University Press, 2005).

merely inviting more people to look at TV'. John Junor, Pickering's counterpart at the *Sunday Express*, similarly admitted that he deliberately gave preference to the cinema over television in the paper's entertainment coverage because it was more 'readable' and because the film industry 'spends so much money in advertising'.[128] But such resistance was futile. Television became ever more popular: by 1960 some two-thirds of households had a television set, and ten years later there were very few without one.[129]

In the 1960s and 1970s, as the BBC and ITV settled into a duopoly, television gradually became the dominant form of popular culture. ITV, stung by the criticisms of the Pilkington committee in 1962, gradually increased its serious content and took up some of the characteristics of a public service broadcaster. Meanwhile the BBC, which launched a second channel in April 1964, began to interpret its role more flexibly, and, under the leadership of Hugh Carleton Greene, liberalized its outlook. Greene was determined to respond to the social and cultural shifts of the 1960s and encouraged the BBC to reflect the pluralism of British life. 'A broadcasting organisation must recognise an obligation towards tolerance and towards the maximum liberty of expression,' he declared; '. . . I believe we have a duty to take account of the changes in society, to be ahead of public opinion rather than always to wait upon it . . . it is better to err on the side of freedom than of restriction.'[130] Programmes broadcast after the 9 p.m. watershed increasingly included adult material for an adult audience. Greene relaxed the rules on morality and vulgarity, allowing modest amounts of swearing and nudity, and producers were given greater licence to tackle contemporary issues in a challenging and often controversial fashion. *That Was The Week That Was*, shown in 1962–63, irreverently satirized politicians and the establishment, while the series of Wednesday Plays provided a platform for writers such as Dennis Potter and Ken Loach to examine social problems, including family breakdown, abortion, and homelessness, with a new realism. Discussion shows also debated topics such as pre-marital sex, homosexuality, and prostitution.[131]

This liberalization of policy inevitably produced a reaction, which crystallized in the form of Mary Whitehouse's Clean-Up TV (CUTV), launched in 1964 (and relaunched in November 1965 as the National Viewers' and Listeners' Association). CUTV's manifesto accused the BBC of employing 'people whose ideas and advice pander to the lowest human nature' and broadcasting 'a stream of suggestive and erotic plays which present promiscuity, infidelity and drinking as normal and inevitable'.[132] Whitehouse correctly observed that the strict Christian morality that had typified the Reithian BBC was being abandoned;

[128] Beaverbrook Papers, H/205 Pickering to Beaverbrook, 29 April 1959; John Junor to Beaverbrook, 24 April 1959.

[129] Crisell, *British Broadcasting*, chs. 5–6.

[130] Green, *All Dressed Up*, 61.

[131] Ibid., ch. 6; Crisell, *British Broadcasting*, ch. 6.

[132] M. Whitehouse, *Cleaning-Up TV: From Protest to Participation* (London: Blandford, 1967), 23.

more controversial was her claim that a 'silent majority' of the population shared her disgust.[133] What was undeniable, however, was that sex had become an important element of both fictional and non-fictional programming.

Commercial television further extended the already considerable reach of advertising in British culture. Advertising was an important source of imagery and information about sex throughout the period. Perhaps most significant has been the use of the female body to sell products. Even in 1933 A. P. Braddock, a publicity expert, observed in his handbook that 'Pictures of girls and women form a large percentage of the principal studies for [advertising] posters . . . . A sex appeal is often thus made.'[134] This 'sex appeal' became far more frequent from the 1950s, and by the 1970s nudity was not unusual in advertising pictures.[135] In March 1971, for example, *The Times* caused some controversy among its readers by including an advert for the chemicals firm Fisons that was a full page nude shot of the model Vivien Neves.[136] Such images were frequently accompanied by heavy innuendo: an advert for Thames Showers consisted of a titillating photo of a woman in a transparent wet top declaring that 'If we had a shower I'd get fresh a lot more often'.[137] Television advertising was not allowed to be so explicit—before 1971, for example, women could not be shown modelling underwear except in silhouette[138]—but scantily-clad women were a standard feature in many campaigns, especially for high-value products such as cars. Such obvious exploitation of the female body became a prime target of the feminist movement in the 1970s, with organizations such as the Women's Media Action group trying to put pressure on the Advertising Standards Association (ASA) to take a tougher line on the use of sexual imagery. The ASA remained unconvinced by feminist arguments, however, and only intervened in cases where it believed that a 'high proportion' of viewers were likely to be offended by an advertisement.[139]

Yet if titillating imagery was considered to be acceptable, there was a greater caution about advertising products for intimate bodily use. Most daily newspapers refused to accept advertisements for contraception until well after the Second World War,[140] and commercial television was forbidden from advertising condoms throughout this period. Adverts for female sanitary products appeared in the press from the 1930s, but again, they were prohibited on television until the

[133] T. Newburn, *Permission and Regulation: Laws and Morals in Post-War Britain* (London: Routledge, 1992), ch. 2.

[134] A. P. Braddock, *Applied Psychology for Advertisers* (London: Butterworth, 1933), 101; see also 106.

[135] B. Gunter, *Media Sex: What Are The Issues?* (Mahwah: Lawrence Erlbaum Associates, 2002), ch. 9.

[136] *The Times*, 17 Mar. 1971, 7; reader reaction 19 Mar. 1971, 21.

[137] *Daily Express*, 20 June 1977, 15.

[138] Crisell, *British Broadcasting*, 102.

[139] Women's Library, Women's Media Action Group Papers, 5/WMA/1/5, Correspondence; ASA Case Report 15 June 1978; Women's Media Action Group Bulletin, No. 1 (1979).

[140] Bingham, *Gender, Modernity, and the Popular Press*, 156.

late 1970s.[141] Such restrictions reflected the outlook that sexual display, within carefully maintained limits, was 'just a bit of fun', while reference to subjects such as contraception and menstruation could cause 'offence' and should be avoided where possible. As a result, information about legitimate goods of genuine value could not be provided to those that needed it.

By the final quarter of the twentieth century, then, newspapers were operating in a very different media environment to that existing in the first quarter. They had lost their position as the main source of information about society to television, and were forced to find new ways to appeal to a public that had a far greater range of media forms at their disposal. Throughout popular culture sex was discussed and portrayed far more prominently and explicitly than before. There were many more opportunities for authors, publishers, and film and television producers, to tackle adult themes for an adult audience. The challenge for Fleet Street was how to respond to this changed climate while ensuring that newspapers remained acceptable for a family readership.

SEXUAL BEHAVIOUR AND ATTITUDES

Sexual behaviour and attitudes altered significantly over the course of the twentieth century. The causes of these changes are complex and multi-faceted, ranging from broad social and cultural trends, such as the shifts in class and gender relations, and the emergence of a consumer society, via intellectual developments such as feminism, sexology, and psychology, to far more specific medical and scientific advances, such as the invention of the contraceptive pill. This study is focused on how popular newspapers mediated and contributed to these changes, but the press's role can only be appreciated in the context of a wider understanding of the nature and extent of the transformation of British sexual culture.

The early decades of the twentieth century were marked by widespread ignorance about sex and sexuality. The state, churches, and schools all sought to contain sex within marriage, and there was a widespread fear in official and professional circles that exposure to sexual knowledge and erotic imagery might lead those without sufficient discipline and restraint into irresponsible experimentation and 'immorality'. As a result of these attitudes, children and young people were provided with little information about their bodies or their sexual development.[142] Formal sexual education was unusual in schools before the

[141] Crisell, *British Broadcasting*, 102.

[142] On this climate of ignorance, see H. Cook, *The Long Sexual Revolution: English Women, Sex, and Contraception 1800–1975* (Oxford: Oxford University Press, 2004), ch. 7; K. Fisher, *Birth Control, Sex, and Marriage in Britain 1918–60* (Oxford: Oxford University Press, 2006); E. Roberts, *A Woman's Place: An Oral History of Working-Class Women 1890–1940* (Oxford: Blackwell, 1984), ch. 3; S. Humphries, *A Secret World of Sex—Forbidden Fruit: The British Experience 1900–1950* (London: Sidgwick & Jackson, 1988).

Second World War, and despite improvements after 1945, provision remained very patchy: a series of reports in the 1960s criticized the lack of a coordinated strategy on sex education.[143] The public discussion of sex remained subject to various restrictions and inhibitions: indeed, even in June 1942, *Love without Fear*, a serious 'guide to sex technique for every married adult' written by the Harley Street gynaecologist Eustace Chesser, was prosecuted for obscenity.[144]

Women generally suffered more than men from these silences. Men were 'trusted' with more sexual knowledge, had access to a wider range of sources of sexual information, and were exposed to more conversations about sex at their workplace or in the course of their social interaction. One of the most consistent themes of the testimony of women of all classes, Simon Szreter has observed, is 'the profound ignorance of reproductive biology at marriage, absence of the most rudimentary instruction from their own mothers, and often innocence of, fear and distaste at their own bodies' sexual functionings.'[145] For many women, this sexual innocence seems to have been an important aspect of their identity.[146]

In this climate of ignorance and secrecy, many women viewed sex in negative terms as something to be endured when their husbands insisted. Men were generally expected to initiate and dominate proceedings, and women rarely expected sexual gratification: many were more concerned about becoming pregnant, with the consequent impact that had both on their health and on family finances. 'Sex is duty, and women are not trained to expect any particular pleasure', one survey found in the mid-1940s.[147] The pleasure that was achieved was often threatened by feelings of guilt and shame brought on by religious and societal injunctions against sexual indulgence. Sex was commonly regarded as 'dirty' and respectable people were expected to control carefully their sexual desires.

The anxieties surrounding sex were exacerbated by the fear of venereal diseases, which posed a serious danger to public health in the early twentieth century. Some officials regarded this fear as having a useful function in inhibiting promiscuous behaviour.[148] The extent of the problem was highlighted in 1916 by the Royal Commission on Venereal Diseases, whose report suggested that

[143] L. Hall, 'Birds, Bees and General Embarrassment: Sex Education in Britain, From Social Purity To Section 28', in R. Aldrich (ed.), *Public or Private Education? Lessons From History* (London: Woburn Press, 2004); J. Hampshire and J. Lewis, ' "The Ravages of Permissiveness": Sex Education and the Permissive Society', *Twentieth Century British History*, 15/3 (2004), 294–5.

[144] L. Hall, *Sex, Gender and Social Change in Britain since 1880* (Basingstoke: Macmillan, 2000), 136–7.

[145] S. Szreter, *Fertility, Class and Gender 1860–1940* (Cambridge: Cambridge University Press, 1996), 425.

[146] Fisher, *Birth Control, Sex, and Marriage.*

[147] E. Slater and M. Woodside, *Patterns of Marriage: A Study of Marriage Relationships in the Urban Working Classes* (London: Cassell and Company Ltd., 1951), 167; Cook, *Long Sexual Revolution*, ch. 4.

[148] R. Davenport-Hines, *Sex, Death and Punishment: Attitudes to Sex and Sexuality in Britain since the Renaissance* (London: Fontana, 1991), 274.

some 10 per cent of the urban population had been affected by syphilis, and more had been affected by gonorrhoea.[149] Syphilis was one of the main 'killing diseases' and was responsible for thousands of deaths every year: in 1924 it caused over 60,000 deaths, which was more than cancer or tuberculosis.[150] Treatment improved considerably in the inter-war period following Paul Ehrlich's discovery of Salvarsan, and was further enhanced by the introduction of penicillin from 1944, but the fears associated with the diseases remained potent well beyond the Second World War.

Nevertheless, opportunities for the serious public discussion of sex—and the encouragement of sexual pleasure—were growing. During and after the First World War the social purity movement, which had viewed sexuality in overwhelmingly negative terms as something to be controlled, increasingly came to be seen as outdated and repressive. Instead, the arguments of 'social hygienists'—who emphasized the importance of educating the public to express their sexuality in a 'healthy' and racially beneficial manner—gained influence in official and professional circles.[151] Symbolic of the new era were Marie Stopes's two landmark books, *Married Love* and *Wise Parenthood*, both published in 1918. *Married Love* was the first sex manual aimed at a respectable, mixed-sex audience, and it quickly became a bestseller: it had sold 820,000 copies worldwide by 1937.[152] The book was notable for providing a positive description of female sexual desire, an emphasis that feminists such as Dora Russell and Stella Browne were keen to reinforce. Its success paved the way for a wave of similar manuals and significantly raised the profile of the discourse on heterosexual, married sexuality.

Wise Parenthood was comparably influential in opening up the discussion of birth control. Newly-formed organizations such as Stopes's Society for Constructive Birth Control (established in 1921), the National Birth Control Council (1930, in 1939 renamed the Family Planning Association), the Abortion Law Reform Association (1936), and the Marriage Guidance Council (1938) all encouraged this public debate about sex and produced informative literature to guide opinion. Pressure was exerted on politicians to consider changes to the law, and the churches were forced to rethink their teachings on sexual relationships. The public were urged to be more self-conscious about their sexual activities, in order to develop loving relationships, 'plan' pregnancies, and protect their health. Middle-class reformers would, however, continue to find it difficult to persuade working-class couples to think 'rationally' about sex.[153]

Sex was increasingly discussed in medical and psychological terms rather than moral and religious ones. The work of sexologists such as Havelock Ellis, who produced his monumental seven-volume *Studies in the Psychology of Sex* between

[149] Royal Commission on Venereal Diseases, *Final Report* (London: HMSO, 1916), Cmd. 8189.

[150] Davenport-Hines, *Sex, Death and Punishment*, 246.

[151] F. Mort, *Dangerous Sexualities: Medico-Moral Politics in England since 1830*, 2nd edn. (London: Routledge, 2000), ch. IV.

[152] Cook, *Long Sexual Revolution*, 194.

[153] Fisher, *Birth Control, Sex, and Marriage.*

1897 and 1928, came to have significant influence in official and professional circles. Sexologists argued that what had previously been regarded as 'immoral acts' were, in fact, sexual 'deviations' rooted in the character of the individual, which needed to be analysed scientifically.[154] Ellis's *Sexual Inversion* (1898), for example, argued that, 'inversion' was generally a congenital condition, even if some homosexual tendencies could be acquired.[155] By the 1920s, Sigmund Freud's writings on psychoanalysis were becoming widely known in Britain, and they inspired many followers. Freud encouraged the scientific study of normal sexuality, rather than just 'perversions', and developed a model of psychology in which sexual drives were at the centre. Freudians frequently diagnosed neuroses as being the result of sexual repression. During the inter-war period, medical and psychological perspectives gradually became a feature of court cases. One notable British Freudian, Dr Edward Glover, established the Institute for the Scientific Treatment of Delinquency in 1932, which examined numerous sex offenders referred by magistrates and probation officers.[156] The Tavistock Clinic also provided psychiatric treatment for sex offenders, and developed pathological models to explain sexual deviancy.[157] Some of these scientific understandings of sexuality were disseminated to a wider audience through the sexual manuals and the work of the reform organizations.

Yet if there were many new ways of thinking about sex, almost all writers continued to assume that marriage provided the bedrock of society and should remain the proper place for the expression of sexuality. Indeed, sexual compatibility was increasingly seen as being a vital ingredient in ensuring a healthy marital relationship. The institution of marriage was actually becoming more popular: there was a rise in the marriage rate from the late 1930s to a peak in 1972.[158] The average age at first marriage also declined significantly: in the period 1921–5 it was 27.4 years for men and 25.6 years for women, whereas by 1970 it was some three years earlier, at 24.4 years and 22.7 years respectively.[159] Although the divorce laws were liberalized in 1923 (providing equality between women and men) and again in 1937 (extending the grounds), divorce continued to be rare until the 1960s. Only 6 per cent of the marriages of 1936 had ended in divorce twenty years later, and only 7 per cent of those of 1951.[160] Indeed, as life expectancy lengthened and widowhood became less frequent, the average duration of marriages increased.

154 L. Bland and L. Doan (eds.), *Sexology in Culture: Labelling Bodies and Desires* (Cambridge: Polity Press, 1998); C. Waters, 'Sexology', in H. Cocks and M. Houlbrook (eds.), *Palgrave Advances in the Modern History of Sexuality* (Basingstoke: Palgrave Macmillan, 2006).

155 J. Weeks, *Coming Out: Homosexual Politics In Britain from the Nineteenth Century to the Present*, rev. edn. (London: Quartet Books, 1990), ch. 2.

156 C. Waters, 'Havelock Ellis, Sigmund Freud and the State: Discourse of Homosexual Identity in Interwar Britain', in Bland and Doan, *Sexology in Culture*, 174–6.

157 A. MacLaren, *The Trials of Masculinity* (Chicago: Chicago University Press, 1997), ch. 9.

158 A. H. Halsey (ed.), *British Social Trends Since 1900* (Basingstoke: Macmillan, 1988), 70–5.

159 Butler, *British Political Facts*, 350.

160 Halsey, *British Social Trends*, 75.

The nature of marriage was changing because families were becoming smaller and women were spending less of their lives in pregnancy and child rearing. The marked decline in the birth rate from the 1870s had at first been largely restricted to middle-class couples, but by the inter-war period fertility rates were declining among the working classes as well, with a low point reached in 1934. There was a determination among many working-class couples to follow a different pattern of life from their parents, and with infant mortality becoming less common, that meant having smaller families. Families of two or three children gradually became the norm. Nevertheless, much of this decline seems to have been achieved by abstinence and the 'withdrawal method', rather than by the new modern methods of contraception advocated by Stopes and others. There was a resistance to intrusive devices that seemed 'unnatural' and reduced the 'spontaneity' of intercourse.[161] As the sexual climate altered and sexual restraint relaxed slightly, the historian Hera Cook argues, these low fertility levels could not be maintained. From the mid-1930s fertility levels rose gently, followed by a post-war 'baby boom' peaking in 1964, although family sizes remained far lower than they had been before the First World War.

The real advances in contraceptive technology occurred in the 1950s and 1960s, firstly with the introduction of the modern condom, thin and pre-lubricated, and then with the development of the contraceptive pill. The pill was first issued in Britain in 1961, and by 1964 was being used by some 480,000 women.[162] Effective, controlled by women, and not interfering with the spontaneity of sexual activity, the pill had a major impact on sexual culture and further undermined attempts to contain sex within marriage. In 1964, Helen Brook opened the first birth control clinic in London to cater for unmarried women, and the Family Planning Act of 1967 enabled local authorities to provide contraception without reference to age or marital status. By 1975, family planning services and supplies were provided by the NHS free of charge. As a result of this expansion of contraceptive provision, young women gained the confidence of being able to engage in intercourse without fear of pregnancy. Intermittent scares about the long-term health risks of taking the pill did little to reduce its popularity. By 1989, over 80 per cent of women born in 1950–9 had used the pill as a contraceptive method.[163] The greater efficiency of the new contraceptive technologies assisted a fall in the fertility rate, which by the late 1970s had dropped almost to the low point reached in 1934.

The introduction of the pill was only one, albeit highly significant, factor in a broader transformation of British sexual culture in the second half of the century. The establishment of the National Health Service and medical advances

[161] Cook, *Long Sexual Revolution*, chs. 4–5; Fisher, *Birth Control, Sex, and Marriage*; K. Fisher and S. Szreter, '"They Prefer Withdrawal": The Choice of Birth Control in Britain, 1918–1950', *Journal of Interdisciplinary History*, 34/2 (2003), 263–91.

[162] Cook, *Long Sexual Revolution*, 268.

[163] Ibid.

such as the development of antibiotics produced notable improvements in physical and sexual health, especially for women who had often been reluctant to spend money on treatment for themselves. Of the women surveyed in the *Working Class Wives* study of 1939, 15 per cent suffered from gynaecological ailments, for example, and many of these had received no treatment.[164] After the war childbirth became far safer, and venereal diseases could be cured more effectively. Improvements in health and nutrition also resulted in a lowering of the average age of puberty. Increasing affluence from the mid-1950s, and particularly improvements in housing, which reduced overcrowding and gave many people easy access to indoor toilets and hot water for the first time, provided a more conducive environment in which to focus on intimate relationships—working-class couples had previously struggled to find the privacy required for frequent sexual indulgence. The self-denial and discipline associated with times of unemployment and austerity were gradually replaced in this more prosperous society by an emphasis on pleasure and consumption; at the same time the teaching of the Christian churches increasingly lost authority and church attendance declined.[165] These various changes inevitably affected attitudes to sex, and the available evidence—including a dramatic rise in the illegitimacy rate from the early 1960s—suggests that sexual activity increased significantly among young, unmarried people.

These trends helped to generate pressure to reform the laws governing sexual morality. New, more individualistic ways of thinking about personal relationships encouraged a revision of the divorce laws, which resulted in the Divorce Act of 1969.[166] This replaced the old system of 'matrimonial offences', by which one spouse was deemed to be guilty of undermining the marriage, with the requirement that the 'irretrievable breakdown' of the marriage be demonstrated. Divorce rates rose substantially: 19 per cent of the marriages of 1974 ended within ten years.[167] The Abortion Act of 1967 significantly extended the conditions under which an abortion could be obtained by allowing doctors to take account of the psychological health of the mother. Thousands of women no longer had to resort to illegal and often unhygienic 'back-street' abortions.[168] Perhaps most notable of all, in 1967 homosexual activities between consenting adult males in private were decriminalized in England. The Wolfenden Report of 1957 had recommended this move on the grounds that the state should not intervene in the private lives of its citizens if others were not being harmed, but governments had been reluctant to support the measure. Like the divorce

[164] Cook, *Long Sexual Revolution*, 133.

[165] C. Brown, *The Death of Christian Britain: Understanding Secularisation 1800–2000* (London: Routledge, 2001), ch. 8.

[166] Jane Lewis, 'Public Institution and Private Relationship: Marriage and Marriage Guidance, 1920–68', *Twentieth Century British History*, 1/3 (1990), 233–63.

[167] Halsey, *British Social Trends*, 75.

[168] B. Brookes, *Abortion in England 1900–67* (London: Croom Helm, 1967), ch. 6.

and the abortion legislation, the eventual act was a successful Private Member's Bill. Nevertheless, the reform was accompanied by a tightening of related laws: penalties for offences involving minors or male importuning were increased, and there were actually many more prosecutions for homosexual offences in the 1970s than in the 1950s. Nor did the legislation apply to Scotland or Northern Ireland, where opposition was far stronger. In these countries, homosexuality was only decriminalized in 1980 and 1982 respectively.[169]

Individually, these reforms were cautious and pragmatic, but viewed together (and alongside the relaxation of obscenity laws and censorship powers, examined above) they represented a significant rethinking of the state's role in enforcing sexual morality.[170] They did much to contribute to the growing notion that Britain was becoming a pluralistic and 'permissive' society. Nevertheless, these legal and social changes were occurring far too slowly for those who were heady on the Sixties spirit of revolutionary transformation. Tapping this dissatisfaction was the reinvigorated women's movement, in which a new generation of feminists demanded a wide-ranging liberation for women. Altering society's attitudes to women's sexuality was one of the central aims of this feminist activity, and leading figures such as Sheila Rowbotham, Kate Millet, and Germaine Greer encouraged women to reject conventional expectations of femininity and to claim sexual independence and freedom. The assumptions of Freudian psychology about women's sexuality were much criticized, especially the insistence on the vaginal orgasm as the proper source of female sexual pleasure.[171] Feminists sought to highlight and counter the sexual objectification of women. Some of the most high-profile protests occurred at beauty contests. In 1968 women demonstrated outside the Miss America pageant at Atlantic City, and in November 1970 activists disrupted the televized Miss World show in London. Feminist discontent at the sexism of the mainstream media led both to the formation of organizations to monitor and criticize media output, such as Women in Media and the Women's Media Action Group, and the production of a plethora of 'alternative' publications, the most famous of which was the magazine *Spare Rib* (1972). Others worked to ensure that sexual violence and rape were taken more seriously, and called for a further liberalization of the abortion laws and an extension of nursery provision. The women's movement was diverse and often divided, and its ideas were frequently resisted and condemned: there can be little doubt, however, that it succeeded in shifting the parameters of public debate about sex and sexuality.[172]

The gay rights movement that emerged in Britain in the early 1970s was similarly controversial and similarly influential, at least in the long term. The

[169] Weeks, *Coming Out*; P. Higgins, *Heterosexual Dictatorship: Male Homosexuality in Postwar Britain* (London: Fourth Estate, 1996).

[170] Weeks, *Sex, Politics and Society*, ch. 13.

[171] Cook, *Long Sexual Revolution*, ch. 11.

[172] A. Coote and B. Campbell, *Sweet Freedom: The Struggle for Women's Liberation* (London: Pan, 1982); M. Wandor, *Once A Feminist: Stories of a Generation* (London: Virago, 1990).

movement developed from the sense of frustration at the limits of the 1967 reform and the slowness with which public attitudes to homosexuality were changing. In November 1970 Bob Mellors and Aubrey Walter, two LSE students inspired by the emergence of a militant movement in America following the Stonewall riots of the previous summer, established a British Gay Liberation Front. The new movement did not want gay men and women merely to assimilate quietly into society, but rather to be open and unapologetic about their sexuality: the emphasis was on 'coming out', on both an individual and a collective basis. Considerable effort was expended in developing self-help organizations and in expanding the gay subculture.[173] The growing self-confidence of the movement was demonstrated in the first Gay Pride march in Hyde Park in July 1972, and by the establishment at the same time of the paper *Gay News*. By 1976, *Gay News* had a circulation of over 20,000 and was stocked by WH Smiths; it was able to fill several pages with advertising and listings of events for the gay community.[174] There were tensions within the movement, with women in particular feeling marginalized. Many lesbians found that feminist organizations provided a more sympathetic environment. The Gay Liberation Front itself soon collapsed under the strain of these divisions. Like the women's movement, dreams of a swift and far-reaching revolution were not realized, but the campaign had a substantial longer-term impact on social attitudes. By the late 1970s the voices of gay men and women had obtained a new visibility in the public sphere, and the gay subculture had been considerably strengthened.

British sexual culture, then, changed significantly between 1918 and 1978. By the end of the period, most individuals were far more self-conscious and informed about sex. The development of contraceptive technologies and the legalization of abortion allowed family size to be controlled more effectively and with fewer restrictions on sexual activity, and attempts to contain sex within marriage were increasingly undermined. Marriage remained popular, but became easier to dissolve. Traditional views of sex and sexuality were gradually eroded by the rise of scientific and psychological modes of thought, and by the challenges of the feminist and gay movements. As we will see, newspapers both reflected and shaped these changes.

[173] A. Walter (ed.), *Come Together: The Years of Gay Liberation 1970–73* (London: Gay Men's Press, 1980); Weeks, *Coming Out*, chs. 16–17; S. Jeffery-Poulter, *Peers, Queers and Commons: The Struggle for Gay Law Reform from 1950 to the Present* (London: Routledge, 1991), ch. 5.

[174] Weeks, *Coming Out*, 220–2.

2

Informing and Advising: Sexual Welfare

One of the defining characteristics of the popular journalism that developed in the early twentieth century was its concern with the health and well-being of its readers. Northcliffe believed that his newspapers needed to explore the sphere of private life if they were to engage a mass audience, and he considered health to be a topic rivalled only by sex and money in terms of stimulating curiosity.[1] Doctors and medical professionals became a familiar presence in newspaper columns, offering information and advice on diet, avoiding illness, and maintaining peak physical condition. The interest in public health—which was partially motivated by contemporary anxieties about national degeneracy—stimulated some high-profile campaigns, such as the *Daily Mail*'s crusade in 1911 to promote the nutritional benefits of wholemeal 'standard bread'.[2] But there were distinct limits to the coverage of medical matters. Despite the widespread sexual ignorance in Britain, and the prevalence of venereal diseases, the popular press remained very reluctant to address any health issues associated with sex, pregnancy, or childbirth. Wary of causing 'offence', editors regarded this particular area of private life as being unsuitable for discussion in mainstream, mixed-sex publications.

After 1918 these silences became harder to sustain as the problems associated with sexual ignorance were increasingly recognized. The First World War brought into focus the damage inflicted by venereal diseases on public health, and encouraged an emerging consensus in official circles that a more effective information campaign was essential to reduce the level of infection in the long-term.[3] A broad coalition of educationalists, sexologists, eugenicists, and psychologists argued that lack of knowledge was associated with marital breakdown, uncontrolled fertility, sexual deviance, and crime. If Britain was to ensure social stability and maintain or improve the 'quality' of its population, they suggested, the public

[1] N. Angell, *After All: The Autobiography of Norman Angell* (London: Hamish Hamilton, 1951), 120.

[2] The *Mail* published no fewer than 202 articles in its standard bread campaign in 1911; S. J. Taylor, *The Great Outsiders: Northcliffe, Rothermere and The Daily Mail* (London: Weidenfeld & Nicolson, 1996), 136; R. Pound and G. Harmsworth, *Northcliffe* (London: Cassell, 1959), 404–5.

[3] See for example the recommendations of the Royal Commission on Venereal Diseases, *Final Report* (London: HMSO, 1916), Cmd. 8189.

needed to be properly advised on how to channel their sexuality in a healthy and responsible fashion.[4] But although post-war governments were prepared to fund the propaganda efforts of independent bodies such as the National Council for the Combating Venereal Diseases (NCCVD), they had little desire to invest the resources required to develop a coordinated national programme of sex education, or to overcome the inevitable opposition that such a programme would have entailed.[5] Enterprising individuals such as Marie Stopes attempted to fill this information vacuum by producing advice literature commercially. Stopes's sex manual *Married Love*, published in March 1918, was an unexpected bestseller and paved the way for a new genre of books about sex designed for a broad, non-specialist, mixed-sex audience.[6] Campaigning organizations such as the Society for Constructive Birth Control and the Family Planning Association also established clinics and provided information about contraception and sexual welfare. Important as these endeavours were, however, they could not by themselves eradicate the ignorance that pervaded society.

With so few reliable sources of information about sexual welfare accessible to the majority of the population, anything printed in the popular press inevitably carried considerable influence. For all the success of her books, Stopes knew that she could reach many more people through articles in popular newspapers and magazines. Whenever she contributed a piece to a mass market publication she was invariably deluged with letters from readers desperately seeking more information. But Stopes quickly became frustrated at how reluctant the media were to realize their educational potential. In the inter-war period the popular press did report the fierce public debates about contraception, sex education, and the birth rate—frequently at some length—but journalists concentrated on the social, rather than the personal, implications of the issues, and refused to enter into specifics and practicalities. Reporters were usually so keen to show off their descriptive powers, but when writing about sex their prose dissolved into imprecision, euphemism, and suggestion. Newspapers resisted the idea that they could play a direct role in combating sexual ignorance.

It was only during the Second World War that certain popular newspapers challenged this evasiveness and started to adopt an explicitly educational role. The *Daily Mirror* ushered in the new era with a high profile campaign warning the public about the dangers of venereal diseases. The campaign was couched in

[4] On the rise of social hygiene in this period, see F. Mort, *Dangerous Sexualities: Medico-Moral Politics in England Since 1830*, 2nd edn. (London: Routledge, 2000), ch. IV; S. Kent, *Making Peace: The Reconstruction of Gender in Inter-War Britain* (Princeton: Princeton University Press, 1993).

[5] The NCCVD, founded in 1914, was renamed the British Social Hygiene Council in 1925; its direct grant from the Treasury ended in 1929, to be replaced by discretionary funding from local authorities. On sex education, see L. Hall, 'Birds, Bees and General Embarrassment: Sex Education in Britain, From Social Purity To Section 28', in R. Aldrich (ed.), *Public or Private Education? Lessons From History* (London: Woburn Press, 2004), 102–3.

[6] H. Cook, *The Long Sexual Revolution: English Women, Sex, and Contraception 1800–1975* (Oxford: Oxford University Press, 2004), ch. 8.

the populist and democratic rhetoric that the paper had been developing since the late 1930s. At a time when the rights and obligations of citizenship were being widely discussed, the *Mirror* argued that ordinary people could only fulfil their social responsibilities if they were properly informed and educated. It claimed that being sexually informed was an essential element of modern citizenship, and that therefore popular papers had a duty to play their part in the fight against ignorance. The controversy in Fleet Street over the *Mirror*'s stance turned to crisis in February 1943 when the government asked all national newspapers to carry public health advertisements about VD. The *Daily Express*, the highest-selling national daily, refused outright to carry the advertisements, adhering to its belief that such material was inappropriate in a 'family newspaper'; several other papers accepted them only when some of the more explicit language had been removed. Even in the special circumstances of a wartime health emergency, many editors were determined to maintain the silences and euphemisms that surrounded sex.

Emboldened by the success of the VD campaign, the *Mirror* and the *Sunday Pictorial* sought to open up the public discussion of sexual welfare in the post-war years. They targeted a younger generation eager for a more candid treatment of sex and perfected an idealistic, modern language which assuaged concerns that such material was inappropriate or indecent. The circulation success of these papers encouraged rivals to move away from their evasive policies, and by the mid-1950s issues such as contraception, abortion, and divorce were covered far more extensively than before the war. Pressure groups received more space, journalists learned the terminology of sexual psychology, and advice columns became common features. 'Agony aunts' strove to counter the widespread view of sex as the satisfaction of male appetites, and encouraged women to explore their own sexualities. Popular newspapers challenged traditional beliefs and made an important contribution to the climate of reform that produced the legislative changes of the late 1960s—although the spread of knowledge brought with it greater pressure to conform to contemporary wisdom.

By the mid-1960s it was becoming increasingly difficult for the popular newspapers to present themselves as educators battling sexual ignorance. Television, cinema, the theatre, and fiction were all now enthusiastically exploring sexual themes and popular culture was becoming ever more sexualized. The curious or ill-informed had at their disposal many accessible sources of information about most aspects of sexual behaviour. The press's idealistic rhetoric of sexual reform gradually faded, and was slowly superseded by a more hedonistic and consumerist discourse of sexual liberation. This reached its fullest expression in Rupert Murdoch's *Sun*, which provided countless articles explaining how to maximize sexual pleasure, improve sexual technique, and achieve a sexy and seductive appearance. For the *Sun* heterosexual sex was a form of entertainment and a set of lifestyle choices, and it tried hard to avoid the serious, overtly instructional tone that other papers had tended to employ. It refused to apologize for or elaborately justify its sexual content; the excuses and alibis that had become so familiar over the decades were gradually retired.

THE INTER-WAR DEBATES ABOUT BIRTH CONTROL

The nature of the popular press's coverage of sexual welfare issues at the start of the period is exemplified by the reporting of the fierce post-First World War debates about contraception. Marie Stopes and Lord Dawson of Penn did much to propel the subject of birth control into the public domain during the 1920s and their activities received considerable space in newspapers. But journalists discussed the topic within well-defined limits, and most remained wary of offering an opinion on the merits or otherwise of using contraceptive methods. Readers searching for practical information had to look elsewhere.

Stopes's *Married Love*, published at the end of March 1918, initially received little attention in the national press—unsurprisingly for a book published by a small firm, with limited advertising, at a time when newspapers were reduced in size due to paper rationing and were filled with war news.[7] But once the public interest in the work became evident, it did not take long for a popular newspaper to offer Stopes a platform for her views. The *Sunday Chronicle*, a moderately successful liberal popular weekly, invited her in the summer of 1918 to write a series of articles, for what she thought a 'rather low' payment, on the problems caused by widespread ignorance about sex.[8] Stopes was well aware that she would have to adapt her approach to the euphemistic style of the popular press. After submitting her first piece to the editor, she told him that he could replace her phrase 'pregnant mother' with 'expectant mother': 'I, of course, use the scientific term, but you might prefer to think of your squeamish readers'.[9] In fact, the editor was happy to accept the original phrase, probably because the rest of the article remained within acceptable boundaries. For Stopes took great care not just with her use of language, but in the selection of arguments to make her case. She focused squarely on the eugenic and public health benefits of providing access to contraception, rather than on the greater freedom and control that it would offer the individual. The issue of female sexual pleasure, broached so boldly in her bestseller, was not mentioned at all.

In the first article, headlined 'The Only Real Chance For The Babies—Motherhood and Knowledge: A Plea for the Cure of Ignorance', Stopes applauded

[7] The book was published by Fifield & Co and sold over two thousand copies within a fortnight of its release. There were some positive reviews in specialist periodicals, such as the *Medical Times*, the *Lancet* and the *English Review*; J. Rose, *Marie Stopes and the Sexual Revolution* (London: Faber and Faber, 1993), 108, 118.

[8] Wellcome Library, London, Marie Stopes Papers, Box 64, PP/MCS/G2, Stopes to A. W. Woodbridge, 24 July 1918.

[9] Ibid., Stopes to Woodbridge, 27 July 1918.

the increasing attention being paid in recent years to the health of the nation, and in particular to the welfare of mothers and their babies; yet, she feared, Britain remained far from an ideal where 'no child is conceived unless there is a good chance that it will grow to health and happiness'. The only way to 'weed out unhealth' and combat 'racial disease' amongst Britain's 'miserably deteriorated stock' was to ensure that women knew about birth control and were aware of their responsibilities to the community:

> The wife, then, is the one who must think of the race and who must bear the great national ideal before her into the practical details of her daily life. Hence the wife must have knowledge—detailed, specific, scientific knowledge of how to control, for the benefit of the whole race, the greatest force with which the race is endowed.[10]

Stopes's progressive demand for the 'cure of ignorance' was tempered by her punitive attitude to the 'incorrigible residuum of individuals incapable of being stirred by ideals or strengthened by knowledge'. She suggested that such people 'must be treated as criminals' or at least prevented from reproducing and thereby 'creating misery'.[11] Here was an unusually open acknowledgement that conditions were attached to the spread of sexual knowledge: those not using it in socially approved ways would render themselves liable to disciplinary measures.

Her second article the following week addressed similar themes, albeit in rather more human terms. She described the pitiful life of a poor mother giving birth to a syphilitic baby because she did not know how to control her fertility. Stopes lambasted the medical profession for doing so little to enlighten such women, and thereby leaving them at the mercy of the 'gossip of the slum alley and the street corner'. 'There is,' she concluded, 'enough knowledge now in the world for the race to transform itself in a couple of generations. All now depends on an intelligent organisation for the spread of true knowledge, so that it shall be at hand when the very poorest need it.'[12] Stopes's final article ranged more broadly and discussed the 'Hideous Squalor of Our Commercial Cities', before returning to her essential message that 'No child must be born of neglect, or accident, or stupidity, nor of hideous rape, in marriage or out of it. If mothers knew their power every child would be conceived in the beauty of love'.[13]

The articles demonstrated Stopes's ability to tailor her message for different audiences. Her sensitivity to demands of the mass market, combined with her obvious idealism, made her attractive to editors afraid of upsetting readers. The popularity of her books and her participation in the National Birth Rate Commission kept her in the public eye in 1919–20, and she accepted further invitations to write for the *Sunday Chronicle* (at a rather higher rate) as well as contributing articles to other papers, including the *Daily Mail*.[14] Yet as her

[10] *Sunday Chronicle*, 11 Aug. 1918, 2. [11] Ibid.
[12] *Sunday Chronicle*, 18 Aug. 1918, 2. [13] *Sunday Chronicle*, 25 Aug. 1918, 2.
[14] Stopes Papers, Box 64; Rose, *Marie Stopes*, 124, 132.

profile rose and she started campaigning more actively for reform, she became increasingly frustrated by the limits the press imposed on the discussion of birth control. When she opened Britain's first birth control clinic in Holloway, north London in 17 March 1921, the event was ignored by many of the leading national papers, including the *Daily Mail*, the *Daily Express*, and the *Daily Mirror*. The *Mirror* admitted in a letter to Stopes that it considered the subject 'inappropriate for discussion or publicity'.[15] It was only through press publicity, however, that Stopes could reach many of the women most needing her help, and letters poured in whenever her work was mentioned in mass-circulation newspapers. 'I was reading *Lloyd's News* on Sunday', wrote a working-class housewife from South Wales on 22 March 1921, 'and I read about what you were going to do and about the Mothers Clinic that you have opened what I would like to know is how I can save having any more children as I think that I have done my duty to my Country having had 13 children'.[16] For women with no access to reliable information about sex and contraception, even brief articles in the press could have a real impact by raising the possibility that it was possible to control fertility with the correct knowledge.

Stopes's efforts to give the birth control campaign momentum by holding public events were handicapped by the lukewarm press response. A meeting held at the Queen's Hall in London at the end of May 1921 drew an audience of over 2,000 and led to the establishment of the Society for Constructive Birth Control (SCBC), but it was ignored by many papers. In September she complained to Beaverbrook that the *Daily Mail* had denied 'us all legitimate publicity for the huge Q. Hall meeting' and was now refusing 'advertisement announcements of the CBC regular meetings'. She asked whether the *Express* would be prepared to publicize the campaign, suggesting boldly that an association with her would 'very materially extend' the *Express*'s 'influence and circulation'—after all she had 'sold over a quarter of a million copies' of her recent books 'with very little advertising'.[17] Beaverbrook was completely unsympathetic, and his paper remained hostile to her campaign for many years. (She was obviously unaware of Beaverbrook's views on this issue: in 1933, returning a book that she had sent him, he claimed to 'know nothing about Birth Control' and observed that he was 'very much attached to the Roman Catholics—like many another Presbyterian'.)[18] Of the national dailies, it was the *Daily Herald* that was most consistently willing to publicize Stopes's campaign in the early 1920s, but the paper certainly did not commit itself fully.[19]

[15] M. Jennings, *Daily Mirror* to Stopes, 14 Mar. 1921, cited in Rose, *Marie Stopes*, 144.

[16] Mrs R.G.H. to Marie Stopes, 22 Mar. 1921, cited in R. Hall (ed.), *Dear Dr Stopes: Sex in the 1920s* (Harmondsworth: Penguin, 1981), 14.

[17] British Library, Stopes Papers, Add. MS, 58555, Stopes to Beaverbrook, 30 Sept. 1921.

[18] Ibid., Beaverbrook to Stopes, 18 May 1933.

[19] As can be seen, for example, by the paper's hesitant reaction to the Stopes libel trial, discussed below.

It was not Marie Stopes but Lord Dawson of Penn who propelled the subject of birth control onto the front pages. Dawson was King George V's physician, an establishment figure who could attract the attention of the press far more effectively than Stopes. In October 1921 he gave an address to the Anglican congress in Birmingham calling for the Church to adopt more positive views on sexual love—'natural passion in wedlock is not a thing to be ashamed of or unduly repressed'—and to accept that 'birth control is here to stay'. The *Daily Express* described the speech as 'sensational' and suggested that the congress had never 'experienced any single shock so great'.[20] The extensive publicity the speech received in the press ensured that it reverberated far beyond the conference hall, particularly the section on contraception. But Fleet Street's caution was once again evident in the reluctance of papers to offer their own opinions on the controversial issues that had been raised. The *Mail* described Dawson's words as 'frank' and 'emphatic' but it did not comment in its editorial column.[21] The *Mirror*'s leader-writers were also silent.[22] The *Express* produced a carefully-written leading article under the headline 'Wholesome Shocks', arguing that 'the Church must be prepared to discuss sex questions with this generation as frankly as this generation discusses them outside the Church'. But on the question of birth control, the paper was hardly frank itself, appearing broadly supportive without stating its views explicitly.[23] Several of the Sunday papers also adopted a relatively neutral position. The *News of the World* printed the full text of Dawson's speech, but it made no editorial comment.[24] The *Weekly Dispatch* collated the responses of a number of churchmen and public figures, ranging from the Bishop of Truro's comment that the 'The presence of contraceptives simply means the danger of sexual promiscuity' to the vice-president of the BMA's insistence that birth control could help to produce a 'healthy and industrially active population'.[25] Such reports underlined the diversity of opinion on the issue. Acutely conscious of this lack of consensus, and the powerful reactions that it generated, many editors did not wish to run the risk of alienating large sections of the readership by choosing one side or the other.

One paper was prepared to commit itself, however, and managed to fan the flames of the controversy in the process. Beaverbrook and his editorial team at the *Sunday Express* believed that the 'press and pulpit' had been far too generous in their coverage of Dawson's speech and decided to 'strike hard to gain a hearing'.[26] The result was the infamous front-page headline 'Lord Dawson Must Go!', with sub-headings outlining the *Sunday Express*'s views in no uncertain terms: 'Perilous Advice From The King's Physician—Birth Control

[20] *Daily Express*, 14 Oct. 1921, 1, 6.
[21] *Daily Mail*, 13 Oct. 1921, 5.
[22] *Daily Mirror*, 13 Oct. 1921.
[23] *Daily Express*, 14 Oct. 1921, 6.
[24] *News of the World*, 16 Oct. 1921, 4.
[25] *Weekly Dispatch*, 16 Oct. 1921, 8.
[26] *Sunday Express*, 23 Oct. 1921, 9.

Menace—Britain Counselled To Join The Dying Nations'.[27] The paper insisted that this was an unprecedented threat which demanded an immediate rebuttal. The 'stealthy and furtive cult' of Malthusianism, which had previously 'never dared to show itself openly and shamelessly in the light of day' had 'for the first time in our national life' appeared on the public stage, expounded by an eminent physician. The *Sunday Express*'s counter-arguments were based squarely on the need to protect British virility in an unstable international climate in which only the fittest nations survived:

> England needs more children, not fewer. The Great War has deprived her of nearly a million of her bravest and best men. How can she hold her own if birth-control robs her of the men who will guard her heritage and keep inviolate her freedom? . . . Nations that lack men to resist aggression are doomed to perish. The British Empire and all its traditions will decline and fall if the motherland is faithless to motherhood.[28]

This article was reprinted the next morning in the *Daily Express*, which abruptly abandoned its supportive position: it now invoked biblical teaching to claim that 'race suicide' contravened God's first injunction to 'be fruitful and multiply'.[29] By intervening in such a prominent manner, the *Express* provoked those on either side of the debate either to defend or to condemn Dawson. As the historian Richard Soloway notes, 'Birth control in a matter of weeks became a respectable subject for public discussion'.[30]

This attempt to whip up moral outrage in defence of conservative notions of sexual propriety was an early example of a tactic that would become very familiar in the *Sunday Express*. James Douglas's denunciation of the *Well of Loneliness* in 1928, and John Gordon's attacks on 'perversion' in the early 1950s were further notable examples of this tradition (see Chapter 5). But such outspokenness remained untypical in the popular press's coverage of birth control. Indeed, the *Sunday Express* itself actually provided space for alternative viewpoints. In the same issue as the 'Lord Dawson Must Go!' diatribe, the female physician and medical journalist Elizabeth Sloan Chesser was given the opportunity to write about marriage, sex, and birth control. Chesser certainly shared some of the *Express*'s anxieties about contraception, arguing that 'any serious limitation of family is socially undesirable in a properly regulated State' and suggesting that ideally women should be encouraged to have between six and eight children. Yet she insisted that 'Every physician knows that in some marriages the birth of children is not always desirable, and that at certain periods the family must be curtailed, and yet sex union cannot reasonably be denied'. She therefore believed in birth control 'with proper safeguards'. Moreover, these comments were part of a wider argument in favour of a positive embrace of sexuality. 'There is nothing necessarily unworthy or indecent in gratification of sex desire', she

[27] *Sunday Express*, 16 Oct. 1921, 1. [28] Ibid. [29] *Daily Express*, 17 Oct. 1921, 6–7.

[30] R. Soloway, *Birth Control and the Population Question in England, 1877–1930* (Chapel Hill: University of North Carolina Press, 1982), 187.

contended, adding that proper sex education was an essential prerequisite of a stable relationship: 'Ignorance of simple sex psychology mars nine marriages out of ten; its better understanding would raise the standard of human happiness and prevent 80 per cent of divorce'.[31] The inclusion of this different voice was a sign of an editorial awareness that it was not prudent to ignore other perspectives on such a controversial topic.

There were certainly commercial risks in taking such a forthright stance. The following week the *Sunday Express* was forced to admit that its censure of Lord Dawson had not been well received by readers. Letters had 'poured in' to the *Express* office, but only a minority were sympathetic to the editorial line. The paper protested that 'The thinkers are never so clamorous as the mob', and that it would not be diverted from its cause—but the campaign clearly shifted into a more minor key, and the ringing denunciations were toned down.[32] Elsewhere in Fleet Street, the hostile public response to the *Express* articles was likely to have reinforced the perception that birth control was an issue that should be approached with great care. Hamilton Fyfe, an experienced journalist who edited both the *Daily Mirror* and the *Daily Herald* in his long career, bracketed birth control with religion and the 'folly of gambling' as subjects that journalists sought to avoid as far as possible, as to discuss them 'would be sure to irritate some readers'.[33] It was becoming acceptable to report the debate about contraception—but articles that were too detailed, or sought to campaign for one side or the other, were still regarded as being very risky.

The Dawson controversy established the birth control debate as an important news story, albeit one that required careful handling. The press's interest in the subject was confirmed by the extensive coverage given to the libel suit brought by Marie Stopes against Dr Halliday Sutherland, which came to court in February 1923. Stopes sued Dr Sutherland, a Roman Catholic physician, for claiming in his book *Birth Control* that she was dangerously and immorally experimenting on the bodies of working-class women.[34] The publicity surrounding this case finally propelled Stopes onto the front pages of the popular press and gave her a truly national profile.[35] Articles discussed her 'Remarkable Career' including details of her disastrous first marriage to Reginald Ruggles Gates, which gave her the initial motivation to learn about sex and instruct others on how to enjoy it.[36] Every paper produced daily summaries of the frequently heated courtroom cross-examinations, omitting, of course, the most explicit references to sex and

[31] *Sunday Express*, 16 Oct. 1921, 8.

[32] *Sunday Express*, 23 Oct. 1921, 9. The language of the next editorial on the subject, a week later, was conspicuously less strident and the focus shifted to the dangers posed to family life—an attempt to retreat to safer, less controversial ground: *Sunday Express*, 30 Oct. 1921, 8.

[33] H. Fyfe, *Sixty Years of Fleet Street* (London: W. H. Allen, 1926), 217.

[34] Rose, *Marie Stopes*, 163–75.

[35] Front page coverage of the case included *Daily Mirror*, 22, 24, 28 Feb. 1923; *People*, 25 Feb. 1923; *Daily Express*, 1 Mar. 1923.

[36] For example, *News of the World*, 25 Feb. 1923, 4.

contraception. The trial ended with a partial defeat for Stopes, although the publicity continued as the legal proceedings continued for over a year, with the verdict being overturned by the Court of Appeal before being reinstated by the House of Lords in November 1924.

But while the press reported the case with enthusiasm, most papers once again refused to offer their own opinions on the subject. The *Daily Herald* and the *News of the World* were among those that offered no editorial comment. A leading article in the *Daily News* stated that it had 'nothing to say here as to the rightness or wrongness of birth control', insisting only that Stopes had the right to advocate her cause without being unfairly attacked. The paper did, however, print a feature article claiming that 'constructive birth control gives a new ray of hope for humanity'.[37] *The People* went one better by inviting Stopes herself to write an article outlining her 'policy of birth control for all', but it underlined that 'Dr Stopes expresses here her own views'—like the *News*, it was not prepared to divulge its own opinions.[38] It was left to the *Express* and the *Mirror* to stir up the debate in Fleet Street. The *Express* returned to the themes that it had set out two years earlier, protesting that 'To rob parenthood of its essential sacredness and to reduce it to the level of a semi-scientific formula is an unworthy doctrine whether propounded by Dr Marie Stopes or Lord Dawson of Penn. We do not want race suicide in England.' The paper urged those who could afford it, to have more children.[39] The *Mirror*, by contrast, adopted the gloomy Malthusian stance that it would maintain over the next decade. 'The burden of numbers presses horribly on this generation,' it claimed, resulting in a housing shortage, unemployment and 'grievous taxation'. Even worse, 'the incidence of the birth rate is fatally wrong, the ignorant and unthrifty increasing at the expense of the prudent and the fit'. To prevent a eugenic disaster, the community had to be able to regulate its numbers.[40] The national dimension remained very much at the forefront: neither addressed the potential impact of contraception on personal and sexual relationships.

The significance of the press coverage of the libel trial in awakening public interest in birth control is indicated by the enormous increase in the correspondence received by Stopes. She was soon forced to hire extra staff to manage it all.[41] 'I have followed your action in the Courts with great interest', read one typical letter from a working-class woman in Birmingham; another specifically mentioned seeing the article in the *People* written after the trial. The frustrating lack of detail in the newspapers led these women to ask for more information about Stopes's work—the Birmingham correspondent sought to be 'one of the fortunate ones who have the superior knowledge of contraception'.[42] The interest in the topic was certainly noted in newspaper offices. The *Daily Herald* observed that it had received 'very heavy correspondence on the subject: Should

[37] *Daily News*, 2 Mar. 1923, 4.
[38] *The People*, 11 Mar. 1923, 6.
[39] *Daily Express*, 2 Mar. 1923, 6.
[40] *Daily Mirror*, 2 Mar. 1923, 5.
[41] Hall, *Dear Dr Stopes*, 12.
[42] Ibid., 12, 21.

Families Be Limited?', and printed a balanced selection over two days.[43] The *Mirror* discerned 'an immense amount of interest' in the libel suit.[44] With the appeal proceedings receiving further publicity over the coming months, the trial can be seen as a key-turning point in the campaign to spread information about birth control. Stopes herself achieved celebrity status as the public face of the birth control campaign, and came to feature frequently in photo pages and gossip columns; news of the birth of her son, Harry, in March 1924 reached the front page of the *Daily Express*.[45] A prominent series of articles for the popular magazine *John Bull* in 1925 consolidated her fame.[46] She still believed that some media outlets were not giving her work due attention—she became embroiled in disputes with *The Times* and the *Morning Post*, and resented the BBC's reluctance to invite her to broadcast—but her opponents could not stifle her campaign now.

By the mid-1920s, therefore, the controversies sparked by Dawson and Stopes had placed the issues of fertility, contraception, and sexual health firmly on the press agenda. Over the following decade, significant shifts in public policy and notable polemical interventions on these topics received widespread coverage. In August 1930, for example, the Lambeth Conference's decision to break with previous Church of England doctrine and offer a qualified acceptance of birth control within marriage was discussed in detail on front pages and editorial columns.[47] A request from the *Daily Herald* in the same month prompted a reluctant Ministry of Health to publicize memorandum 153/MCW, which established that local authorities could provide advice on birth control in clinics.[48] Repeated pleas from the bench by the eminent judge Mr Justice McCardie to spread contraceptive knowledge and hence reduce the number of cases of abortion also generated prominent headlines.[49] During the 1930s, indeed, abortion was increasingly identified as a separate subject from birth control, raising a different set of questions.[50] The phrase 'birth control' had often been used broadly: in 1922 Stopes complained to the *Daily Express* when an article reporting on the trial of 84 German women for 'allowing illegal operations to be performed' was given the headline 'Birth Control Crime'.[51] By the late 1930s the distinctions were clearer, and the heavy coverage in July 1938 of the trial of the London surgeon Aleck Bourne for conducting an abortion on a 14-year-old girl who had been raped by guardsmen showed a new press interest in the topic. Several papers

[43] *Daily Herald*, 3 Mar. 1923, 2; 5 Mar. 1923, 2.

[44] *Daily Mirror*, 2 Mar. 1923, 5.

[45] *Daily Express*, 27 Mar. 1924, 1.

[46] C. Davey, 'Birth Control in Britain during the Interwar Years', *Journal of Family History*, 13/3 (1988), 335–6.

[47] *Daily Express*, 15 Aug. 1930, 1, 2, 8; *Daily Mail*, 15 Aug. 1930, 8–10.

[48] Soloway, *Birth Control*, 311–12.

[49] *Daily Herald*, 1 December 1931, 1; 12 Dec. 1931, 3; *Daily Express*, 12 Dec. 1931, 7; 19 Dec.1931, 7; B. Brookes, *Abortion in England 1900–67* (London: Croom Helm, 1988), 37–40.

[50] Brookes, *Abortion in England*, 2–3.

[51] *Daily Express*, 26 Jan. 1922, 1; Stopes papers PP/MCS/E3, Stopes to Daily Express, 27 Jan. 1922.

used the occasion to highlight the prevalence of illegal abortions and to call for greater legal clarity: 'The country demands that the subject be now thrashed out once and for all', wrote an unnamed lawyer in an article for the *Mirror*, 'and that secret abortions, with all their attendant misery, be abolished'.[52]

Despite this coverage, though, the caution and evasiveness of the press on these issues remained conspicuous. Popular papers remained reluctant to risk alienating readers by openly supporting or advertising birth control, instead seeking to maintain 'balance' by inviting supporters and opponents to put their cases. The articles that were published were euphemistic and provided little detail for those readers seeking to learn more. Richard Soloway has suggested that the left-wing *Herald* was the most sympathetic national newspaper to the birth control campaign in the inter-war period, but even its support was far from solid. In 1926 it acceded to the demands of the Labour party leadership and refused to print a letter from Dorothy Jewson on the subject so as not to stir up divisive debate.[53] Once the paper was taken over by commercial publisher Odhams Press in 1929, moreover, the paper's policy of accepting advertisements for birth control clinics and products was reversed. In March 1932, the *Herald*'s advertising manager told the Society for Constructive Birth Control (SCBC) that he 'had definite instructions that NO birth control advertisements were to be accepted in any circumstances. . . . He said that they would lose readers by letting in such advertisements'.[54] The *Daily Sketch* informed the SCBC that 'no papers will take any Birth Control advertisements where the paper is circularised in Ireland, as that paper would be barred'.[55] This was certainly a consideration, but the Irish ban was often used to justify a wider conservatism. In reality, this sort of content was defined as being unsuitable for a 'family newspaper'.

EDUCATING THE PUBLIC: THE VD INFORMATION CAMPAIGN

It took the pressures of a national health crisis to provoke a decisive challenge to this evasive culture. In 1942 the *Daily Mirror* led a press campaign to highlight the dangers of venereal diseases during wartime, and in so doing it paved the way for popular newspapers to assume an educational role on issues of sexual welfare.[56] The significance of the campaign is perhaps most clearly illustrated by making a comparison with the timid press coverage of the VD problem during the First

[52] *Daily Mirror*, 20 July 1938, 12; *News Chronicle*, 20 July 1938, 1, 10; *News of the World*, 23 July 1938, 13.

[53] Soloway, *Birth Control*, 196, 294.

[54] Marie Stopes Papers, Add. MS 58598, fo. 76, M. Poyser to G. B. Higgs, 8 Mar. 1932.

[55] Ibid. fo. 179, EB to Marie Stopes, 4 Aug. 1933.

[56] For a more detailed account of the controversy, see A. Bingham, 'The British Popular Press and Venereal Disease during the Second World War', *Historical Journal*, 48/4 (2005), 1055–76.

World War, when official concern was just as intense. In 1916, for example, the *Mirror* did not consider the publication of the Royal Commission on Venereal Disease's final report worthy of any coverage.[57] For most popular papers this was still the 'hidden plague'. The diseases were often referred to euphemistically as 'social' or 'contagious' rather than sexual or venereal, and proper scientific names were used very rarely.[58] They stirred up strong feelings because of their powerful associations with prostitution, sin, and punishment, and victims were often seen, subconsciously if not consciously, as being penalized for their immorality or promiscuity.[59] The campaign to control the diseases and educate the public was reported intermittently in papers such as the *Daily Mail* and the *Daily Herald*, and the wartime legislation aimed at containing the problem—Defence of the Realm Regulation 40D, passed in March 1918, making it illegal for a woman with communicable VD to solicit or to have intercourse with a serviceman—also generated some debate.[60] As with birth control, however, press coverage tended to focus on the generalities of the national interest or public health, and very little specific information was provided. Newspapers left the task of educating the public to the local authorities and the NCCVD, and did not maintain much interest in the issue once the incidence of both syphilis and gonorrhoea started to decline in the inter-war period. This continuing reticence was noted by Robert Graves and Alan Hodge, who observed that that 'although the general taboo against the mention of venereal disease weakened' in these decades, it remained 'a tabooed subject in the press'.[61]

By the time the incidence of venereal diseases rose sharply again in the early years of the Second World War, views about combating them had shifted, both inside and outside of Fleet Street. The Chief Medical Officer, Sir Wilson Jameson, shared the growing emphasis in medical circles on prevention: only by keeping the public informed about illness and disease could individuals successfully maintain their health.[62] This reflected wider debates about citizenship in these years, especially in the context of the 'People's War': rather than simply defer to authorities, citizens should be encouraged to participate actively and responsibly in the war effort and the reconstruction of democracy.[63] In the

[57] *Daily Mirror*, 3–10 Mar. 1916.

[58] Bingham, 'The British Popular Press and Venereal Disease', 1059–61.

[59] R. Davenport-Hines, *Sex, Death and Punishment: Attitudes to Sex and Sexuality in Britain since the Renaissance* (London: Fontana, 1991), ch. 5.

[60] P. Levine, *Prostitution, Race and Politics: Policing Venereal Disease in the British Empire* (New York: Routledge, 2003), 163–5.

[61] R. Graves and A. Hodge, *The Long Week-end: A Social History of Great Britain 1918–39* (first pub. 1940; Harmondsworth: Penguin, 1971), 109.

[62] V. Berridge, *Health and Society in Britain since 1939* (Cambridge: Cambridge University Press, 1999), 21, 50–1; N. Goodman, *Wilson Jameson* (London: George Allen & Unwin, 1970), 86–90, 190–4.

[63] S. Rose, *Which People's War? National Identity and Citizenship in Wartime Britain 1939–1945* (Oxford: Oxford University Press, 2003); P. Addison, *The Road to 1945: British Politics and The Second World War* (London: Jonathan Cape, 1975).

field of sexual health, this entailed a greater confidence in the merits of sex education, overcoming the fear that informing working-class men and women about sex, and in particular prophylaxis, might simply encourage promiscuity. The inter-war debates about birth control had helped to extend knowledge about sex, and falling birth rates and rising condom sales suggested that many people were managing their sexual activity more carefully. Despite this, ignorance about sex and human biology remained very common and much work remained to be done to surmount the reluctance to speak directly about problems such as VD. 'With the co-operation of the public we could reduce the incidence of these diseases enormously', observed Sir Wilson Jameson in 1943, 'but the public have difficulty in co-operating because of the extraordinary policy of secrecy that has been maintained regarding this particular subject'.[64]

Since its reinvention as a working-class tabloid in the mid-1930s, the *Daily Mirror* had placed considerable emphasis on sexual content to entertain and titillate readers. Another aspect of the editorial repositioning was the development of a populist social democratic rhetoric, a rhetoric that became more prominent and strident after the outbreak of the war. The VD campaign enabled the *Mirror* to weave together these two distinctive strands of its new identity, and to demonstrate that its sexual frankness could provide something more substantial than the fleeting thrills offered by the *Jane* cartoon. The paper argued that Fleet Street's reticence about sex not only denied a source of pleasure, it maintained an ignorance that could damage the nation's health and its wartime strength. By the time the *Daily Mirror* launched its campaign in August 1942, action to combat the rising incidence of venereal diseases was becoming an increasing priority at the Ministry of Health and the Central Committee of Health Education (CCHE). But the *Mirror* took the initiative before the Ministry had developed its own propaganda strategy—indeed, the paper's directors, Cecil King and Harry Bartholomew, believed it was their efforts that stirred the Ministry into action.[65]

The *Mirror*'s first intervention on the subject, an article written by regular contributor Elizabeth Rowley, suggested that the spread of venereal diseases was largely due to prostitution, and that to combat the problem the police should clamp down on the 'white slave traffic' in London.[66] This was a rather old-fashioned analysis which exaggerated the importance of prostitution and underestimated the increasing significance of other forms of extra-marital sexual contact. But when the *Mirror* returned to what it described as 'the forbidden topic' in an editorial two days later, the leader-writer wisely narrowed the focus and made no reference to prostitution. Observing

[64] Goodman, *Wilson Jameson*, 193.

[65] Cudlipp Papers, H.C.2/1 Cecil King to Hugh Cudlipp, 25 Nov. 1942; 25 Feb. 1943; Royal Commission on the Press 1947–49, *Minutes of Evidence*, Day 22 (London: HMSO, 1948), Cmd. 7398, 12.

[66] *Daily Mirror*, 8 Aug. 1942, 4.

that the earlier article 'has achieved a good deal of attention', the author used the crusading rhetoric that would be repeated frequently over coming weeks:

> Nice people may have been shocked by it. We hope they were. We are convinced that a dangerous situation in regard to the health of our people and the future of our race has arisen, and that the remedy can only be found in the utmost frankness. The veil of prudery and so-called good taste must be torn aside from this subject. It is imperative that the facts be made known, and the public called upon to assist in a campaign of systematic eradication.[67]

Yet for all its rhetoric of shocking the 'nice' sections of society, the *Mirror* was far from challenging conventional notions of respectable sexual behaviour. The editorial concluded by condemning the promiscuity it blamed for the spread of the diseases. 'Let no one be afraid to speak out boldly on the spiritual side,' the editorial concluded. 'Moral values have been falling rapidly of recent years, and it is time that the real cause of the "social evil" should be stated for what it is.'[68]

This moralizing framework continued to be a feature of the campaign, but the *Mirror* did deliver on its promise to challenge the 'prudery' that had previously constrained the public discussion of the problem. On 19 August the paper announced on the front page that it had commissioned a series of eight articles from a specialist 'in charge of important VD clinics', writing under the pseudonym of Dr Glenn, to provide an expert summary of information about the recognition and treatment of infections.[69] This weekly series, covering syphilis, gonorrhoea and soft sore, was undoubtedly the most detailed exposition yet published in the popular press on the subject. Glenn discussed the problem in plain and direct language. 'The vast majority of Venereal Disease infections in the adult result from sexual intercourse with an infected partner', he explained.[70] The earliest sign of gonorrhoeal infection 'is a purulent discharge from the genital organs', which may be accompanied 'by soreness or pain on passing urine'. Syphilis could be recognized by 'the appearance of a sore—or sores—on or near the genital organs', in the form of 'shallow, round ulcers often with a firm or hard edge'.[71] The progress of the infections if unchecked was described, as was the appropriate treatment that would be provided by a doctor. Avoiding the diseases, he argued, was best achieved by adhering to strict moral standards. 'Married men should remain faithful to their wives, and single men should remain chaste'; he dismissed the suggestion that continence was damaging to health.[72] Glenn was 'overwhelmed with correspondence' as a result of the series, a testament to the considerable public appetite for information on this matter. The *Mirror* provided extra columns in

67 *Daily Mirror*, 10 Aug. 1942, 3.
68 Ibid.
69 *Daily Mirror*, 19 Aug. 1942, 1.
70 *Daily Mirror*, 20 Aug. 1942, 7.
71 *Daily Mirror*, 27 Aug. 1942, 7; 10 Sept. 1942, 7.
72 *Daily Mirror*, 20 Aug. 1942, 7.

which Glenn could reply to misguided correspondents, and the articles were later collected in a pamphlet entitled *Ignorance Must End*, sold by the paper for 3*d*.[73]

By the time that Dr Glenn's articles concluded on 8 October, a substantial amount of information and advice had been offered to the millions of *Mirror* readers. It was becoming increasingly clear that there was widespread support for an official campaign of public education on venereal diseases. The popular liberal daily *News Chronicle* published in mid-September the results of a Gallup poll showing 79 per cent of the public in favour of a network of bureaux to disseminate advice on VD.[74] In October 1942 the Chief Medical Officer responded by addressing the problem in a broadcast on the BBC Home Service and a follow-up press conference. In similar language to the *Mirror* he spoke of his determination that society 'shall no longer tolerate this hush-hush attitude regarding venereal diseases'. He also side-stepped the moral issues by arguing that VD posed 'just the same sort of problem as any other infectious disease such as smallpox, diphtheria measles or typhoid fever'.[75] The issuing of Regulation 33B on 10 November, providing for compulsory examination and treatment of anyone[76] suspected of having infected two or more people, generated further discussion in the press. Nevertheless, as the Labour MP Tom Driberg told the House of Commons, newspaper reports 'have mostly consisted merely of quoting some distinguished personage as saying that we must "lift the veil of secrecy". Very few have contained any practical advice, information, or instruction to the citizen.'[77] The *Mirror* continued to stand alone in the depth of the coverage it gave the problem.

The *Mirror*'s approach was vindicated by a detailed survey of public attitudes conducted by Mass-Observation in London in early December 1942. This survey revealed a 'great willingness and often active desire to know more about VD, and to have the whole problem brought out into the open'. The press coverage had clearly made a substantial impact: three-quarters of the sample had read something about venereal diseases in a newspaper, with 67 per cent of men, and 94 per cent of women, approving of this publicity.[78] Closer investigation revealed that it was indeed the *Mirror* that was responsible for this impressive recognition rate:

Though no specific question was asked as to where people had read articles about VD, it transpired that most of them had either read the whole series in the *Daily Mirror*, or been

[73] *Daily Mirror*, 12 Sept. 1942, 6; see also *Daily Mirror* 31 Aug. 1942, 6; 5 Sept. 1942, 6; pamphlet advertised 1 Mar. 1943, 7.

[74] *News Chronicle*, 16 Sept. 1942, 1; 18 Sept. 1942, 2.

[75] Goodman, *Wilson Jameson*, 190–4.

[76] Unlike the nineteenth-century Contagious Diseases Acts and Regulation 40D in 1918, this legislation was gender neutral.

[77] 385 H. C. Debs, 5s., Venereal Disease (Compulsory Treatment), 15 Dec. 1942, col. 1862.

[78] Mass-Observation file report 1573, Jan. 1943, 1–2.

shown one or two articles on VD in that paper. Only a few had seen something on VD in any other paper, usually in connection with [Regulation] 33B.[79]

Some women told Mass-Observation that they had never heard of venereal diseases until they read about them in the press; more generally the organization found a 'welter of half-knowledge and superstition'.[80] The *Mirror* series had clearly been well pitched, particularly for the female readership. One working-class woman, for example, told the investigators that the articles 'gave you a lot of knowledge and they weren't abusive and make you feel uncomfortable'.[81] The significantly higher approval rates of the press coverage among women than men was perhaps a reflection of the fact that women often had fewer sources of information about sex and sexual health, and appreciated readily available newspapers addressing these issues. A number of men, on the other hand, felt threatened that this information was being put into the hands of women and children. One protested that he did not 'like the idea in a family newspaper' while another argued it was 'disgraceful that any national newspaper should discourse on this subject'.[82]

That many people in Fleet Street agreed with the latter respondents became clear when the Ministry of Health and the CCHE decided to launch a public information campaign to be carried in all major national and regional newspapers. When the draft copy of this advertisement was sent to the Newspaper Proprietors' Association several representatives argued that it was 'too outspoken' and that 'one or two words should be deleted'.[83] The Ministry reluctantly accepted three amendments to the text to ensure that the campaign was not derailed, even though these changes significantly weakened the impact of the advertisement. The first alteration was to remove from the section identifying the main venereal diseases as syphilis and gonorrhoea the sub-clause 'vulgarly known as pox and clap'. The use of the correct medical terms was an advance on the traditional euphemisms, but by refusing to include the vernacular names as well the press substantially increased the likelihood of confusion among the working-class audience. The second amendment was the removal of the sentences 'Venereal disease contracted through irregular sex alliance is spread to innocent partners. An infected man may give the disease to his wife, who, in turn, may infect her unborn baby.' As similar warnings had been provided elsewhere, this cut did not so much alter the meaning as remove an emphasis that was clearly felt to threaten the sensibilities of some readers. The third, and most damaging, piece of editing came in a section describing the symptoms of infection. Whereas the original had made clear that 'The first sign of syphilis is a small ulcer on or near the sex organs', the revised version removed the reference to the 'sex organs' to leave the bald assertion that 'The first sign of syphilis is a small ulcer.' By suggesting that any

79 Ibid., further notes, 3.
80 M-O file report 1599, Feb. 1943, 2–3.
81 M-O file report 1573, notes, 1.
82 Ibid, 2.
83 *Newspaper World*, 27 Feb. 1943, 17, 19.

ulcer could be regarded as a sign of syphilis, the advertisement in its final form risked provoking the sort of alarm and fear that officials were keen to avoid.[84] In Scotland, the final sections describing symptoms were omitted altogether: this cut was made at the recommendation of the Department of Health for Scotland, before any intervention by the Scottish press. Those papers sending editions over to Ireland were forced to remove the announcement altogether, and replace it with other advertising.[85]

The guidance provided by the expurgated advertisement was therefore significantly less explicit than that offered in the *Mirror*'s own series on the subject. The *Mirror* made clear its disappointment with the timidity of its competitors. When the first advertisements were published on 19 February 1943 it 'startled Fleet Street'[86] by making public the process by which 'the announcement was toned down, and the stark red warning of danger changed to an inoffensive pink'. Showing that it would not be bound by the decisions of the NPA, it printed the original versions of the edited sections of the advert. Under a cartoon portraying a burly workman chopping through the dark undergrowth of 'Sex Ignorance and Diseases', the paper pledged to continue to speak boldly in advance of conventional ideas'.[87] (**Illustrations 2.1 and 2.2**).

In contrast, the *Daily Express*, the *Mirror*'s main rival, remained silent. Along with the *Sunday Express*, the *Observer*, the *Yorkshire Evening Press*, and a number of Scottish papers including the *Glasgow Citizen,* it simply refused to print the announcement even in its edited form.[88] Maintaining its reputation as a respectable 'family newspaper', suitable for all, was as important to the *Express* editorial team as cultivating a crusading image was to that of the *Mirror*, and this advertisement seemed to conflict with their policy on 'cleanliness'. As E. J. Robertson, the chairman of Express Newspapers, explained to the Royal Commission on the Press in 1948, 'Our test is that our papers should be such that we should never be ashamed of our daughters reading them, and I defy anybody to find anything that we have done contrary to that rule.'[89] The paper suggested to the NPA that newspapers were not the best means of conveying information on venereal diseases: 'legislation and health talks to the Forces' were put forward as 'alternative and superior methods of combating the evil'. It is revealing that one of the few mentions of venereal diseases in the *Express* in this period was to report the Archbishop of Canterbury's speech that the moral aspect of the venereal disease problem was more important than the medical one.[90] The editorial team shared this view, and regarded an untargeted information campaign with little moral guidance as potentially counter-productive. The *Express* was representing those people who told Mass-Observation of their concern that 'by removing the

[84] *Daily Mirror*, 19 Feb. 1943, 3.
[85] *Newspaper World*, 27 Feb. 1943, 17.
[86] *World's Press News*, 25 Feb. 1943, 12.
[87] *Daily Mirror*, 19 Feb. 1943, 3.
[88] *Newspaper World*, 27 Feb. 1943, 17.
[89] Royal Commission on the Press, *Minutes*, Day 16, Cmd. 7364, 29.
[90] *Daily Express*, 27 Feb. 1943, 3.

Page 2 THE DAILY MIRROR Friday, February 19, 1943

Wealthy widow wins in 'blackmail case'

"I'VE been a very foolish woman, and I've regretted the whole thing," Mrs. Ethel B. Drew, wealthy widow, told the *Daily Mirror* yesterday after she had won what the Judge described as a "blackmailing action" brought against her by a Cypriot to whom she was once engaged.

"My friends asked me not to bring the case to court, but I thought it better to have it decided finally. It was dreadful having it all dragged up, but it is a relief to have it all over," she added.

Mrs. Drew, who is 56, of Cauldwell House, Bedford, was sued by Mr. Klear Demet, 37, of Sloane-avenue, S.W., for salary due under an alleged agreement to employ him as her secretary.

She counter-claimed for an account of money she said he had had from her.

Mr. Demet also claimed £28, cost of an engagement ring which he said he gave her at her request after they had discussed being married.

Lord Justice Goddard ruled that Mr. Demet had had a sum in excess of his salary, and Mrs. Drew was entitled to judgment on the claim and counter-claim for £26 11s. 8d. and costs.

She Had Courage

It was the not uncommon case of an elderly woman who had fallen under the fascination of a man very much younger than she was and behaving in a somewhat foolish fashion, said the Judge.

Although he did not intend to censure, in any way, the plaintiff's legal advisers, the action was a blackmailing action.

"Every blackmailer has his stock-in-trade, and in this case it was the foolish conduct of this woman.

"It is to her credit that she had the courage to come to Court and face the unpleasant publicity.

Un-English Ideas

"He is a most unsatisfactory person. He has consciously lied to me on several matters."

Mr. Demet, from the first, did not disguise his feeling that it was purely a commercial undertaking.

Bearing in mind that Mr. Demet came from the Levant and probably had not the same ideas as Englishmen, it was not surprising that he made up his mind to "make hay while the sun shone."

He was satisfied that the engagement ring was bought out of the woman's money.

BOMB "INTEREST"

Post Office Savings Bank depositors last year surrendered over £60,000 interest on their deposits. About 32,000 depositors are forgoing interest while the war lasts. Interest surrendered since the war would purchase nearly 250,000 incendiary bombs.

£700 FLOWERS SEIZED, GIVEN TO HOSPITALS

RAILWAY vans handed out to London hospitals on their rounds £700 worth of cut flowers impounded yesterday in the first case under the new Order prohibiting the carriage of cut flowers by rail.

Six men who brought the flowers from Penzance to London by train were fined at Marylebone—one £5 and the others £30 each.

It was stated that the flowers were carried in suitcases, a carton, a bag and a tin trunk.

For the Great Western Railway it was stated that before the Order under which the men were charged came into force on February 15, a previous Order had been brought in on November 1 providing that flowers or plants should not be accepted for conveyance by rail.

That had been got over by what these men were doing.

It was in consequence of this new racket that action was taken.

FIX PAY FOR ENGINEERS

A settlement of the wage claim for about 1,250,000 men in the engineering industry is expected today as a result of negotiations between the engineering unions and the employers.

The unions claimed an increase in basic rates of 11s. a week, an addition of thirty-three and one-third per cent. on the basic rate to all plain time workers, and the restoration of the 1939 working conditions.

Better lights for cycles

The Lighting Order is being amended to permit an alternative method of screening bicycle lamps, the Home Secretary announced yesterday.

The top half of the front glass will be blacked out, as at present, but the inside of the top half of the glass and the whole of the reflector will be white. This can be done with either paint or white paper.

"I am advised that the driving light thus produced is a considerable improvement on that obtained by the existing method and is welcomed by representatives of the cyclists' association," said the Minister.

Found husband dead in balloon fabric bag

HENRY ASTBURY, 35, of Dawson-road, Altrincham, Cheshire, was found by his wife dead inside a balloon-fabric bag in a bedroom at his home.

Death was apparently due to suffocation, and police are investigating the theory that the bag had been tied from the inside. The body was unclothed.

The bag was hand-made, gummed at the bottom and sides, and the string at the top was tied.

It is understood that when Mrs. Astbury found the house door locked she sought help from a passer-by.

The door was forced and Astbury was found inside the bag which was lying on the bed.

He was a big man, and was employed as a lorry driver by a firm of coal merchants, and was also a part-time member of the NFS.

Warns of "reactionary hospitals"

THE Minister of Health was told yesterday by Dr. Edith Summerskill (Soc., Fulham, W.) that unless he made the Rushcliffe Committee recommendations on the nursing services compulsory certain "reactionary hospitals" will never adopt them.

Dr. Summerskill gave this warning in the Commons when she asked why the recommendations were not made obligatory on all hospital authorities.

Mr. Brown said he had no power to impose the obligation suggested, but he did not believe that such action would be necessary to secure adoption of the recommendations.

U.S. BOMBERS GET NEW SUPER-GUN

U.S. bombers are to have a new quick-firing cannon which can spit more rounds a minute than a machine-gun, and "blow a Messerschmitt to pieces with one shell."

The inventor, **Mr. Antoine Gazda**, who created the Oerlikon gun, claims that bombers equipped with his cannon will be able to bomb Germany in daylight without fighter escort.

Quiet Corner - - - By Patience Strong

Loss

When God calls dear ones to Himself we are rebellious—Forgetting that their souls belong to Him and not to us... Blindly and possessively we hold to things most dear—But they are only lent to us for our brief sojourn here.

God, the Father, giveth life. All power is in His hand. Death is subject unto Him and comes at His command... So when loved ones must depart—Let not your faith grow dim. Yield with grace, remembering that they belong to Him.

M.P. ALLEGES FIRE TANKS ARE FAULTY

The allegation that many emergency NFS water tanks in London boroughs are "faulty in design and construction" is made by Mr. S. S. Hammersley (Cons., E. Willesden) in a Commons question of which he has given notice.

He is asking the Home Secretary what steps are being taken to prevent waste of public money.

POLICE COMB-OUT

There is to be a new comb-out of whole-time police establishments for the Forces and for industry, the Home Secretary, Mr. Morrison, announced in the Commons yesterday.

PATHETIC...

By BILL GREIG

THE Parliamentary joke of yesterday was that Sir Kingsley Wood had been offered honorary membership of the Labour Party "for services rendered."

It was a sad joke, a pathetic and uneasy effort to laugh away the greatest front bench failure for many a day.

Yet there can be no doubt that Sir Kingsley Wood succeeded where many of the most sincere men of the Labour Party have failed.

His strangely inept revelation of the failure of the Government front bench to realise the change in the tone of the country bound together the Socialist back benchers in common cause—the cause of the people—as has not happened before.

That is the major issue. The minor issue is that Sir Kingsley Wood, by one speech, has written "finis" to his political career. Statesmen may survive failures, but ridicule and laughter are things from which they never recover.

The oratory of the Chancellor has in the past been noteworthy for its competence rather than its brilliance. There were few who believed that his standard was high enough to allow of a fall which would resemble a death dive. Yet it happened.

Even stranger is the complete failure of the front bench to realise the depth of feeling in the country which has made the Beveridge Report, in itself of no paramount importance, into a symbol of a new Britain.

The younger back benchers, anxious to save something from the wreckage of Toryism, have grasped this fact, and realising the danger of political doom, found the courage of momentary revolt although it failed them with the division Lobby in sight.

The blind eye tactics of the Government have dismayed them, and today we see the once proud and united Conservative Party split in twain while the once divided back bench Socialists stand in firm ranks.

If there is one other bright aspect to the picture it is that the Liberals, under the goad of Horabin, Wilfrid Roberts and Megan Lloyd George, seem to have discovered again that they possess a conscience. Or is it that they, too, have heard the voice of the people?

Ten plain facts about

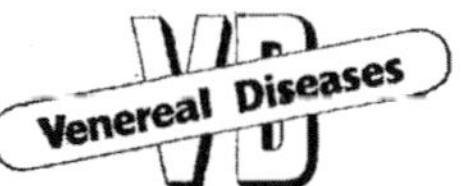

"It is very important under present conditions that the public should know of the existence of venereal diseases; their prevalence in war-time; how they are caused; the urgent necessity for early treatment; and where advice and treatment can be obtained."—THE MINISTER OF HEALTH.

1. Venereal Diseases have increased since the war and are still increasing; 70,000 new cases are now occurring yearly among civilians alone. Venereal diseases cause much misery. They bring tragedy into many homes, and considerably damage our war effort by causing reduced efficiency and wasted hours.

2. Ignorance and secrecy are highly dangerous. Only from a plain and frank statement of the facts can we all know what these diseases are, how they are spread, how they can be avoided and how and where they can be cured.

3. The two principal venereal diseases are syphilis and gonorrhœa. They are caused by quite different living organisms or germs.

4. Syphilis is a dangerous, a killing disease. If not treated early and thoroughly by a doctor it can cause serious mutilation, heart disease, paralysis, and insanity, any of which may be fatal. Syphilis can be passed on to an unborn child from its mother and (unless skilled treatment is given early in pregnancy) is one of the causes of blindness, deafness, and mental defects.

5. Gonorrhœa, though not so dangerous to life, is more serious than is generally believed, and is one of the causes of arthritis, sterility, and chronic ill-health.

6. Syphilis and gonorrhœa are almost always contracted through intercourse with an infected person. The germs of these diseases quickly die outside the human body. In practice, therefore, there is no need to fear their spread by accidental infection.

7. Professional prostitutes are not the only source of infection. Any free-and-easy sex behaviour must mean a risk of infection and cannot be made safe. Clean living is the only way to escape infection—abstinence is not harmful.

8. Venereal diseases can be cured if treated *early* by a specialist doctor. Advice and treatment are available at the clinics set up by County and County Borough Councils for the purpose. Treatment is free, confidential and *effective*. Any family doctor or Medical Officer of Health will give the address of the nearest clinic. Quack treatment or self-treatment is absolutely useless and may even be disastrous.

9. Disappearance of the early symptoms does not necessarily mean that the patient has been cured. It is essential to continue the treatment until the doctor says it may be stopped.

10. Anyone who has the slightest reason to suspect infection should seek medical treatment AT ONCE. A doctor or clinic should be consulted immediately about any suspicious sore or unusual discharge. It may not be venereal disease, but it is best to be sure.

These are the signs The first sign of syphilis is a small ulcer. It appears from 10 to 90 days after infection; usually about three weeks.

Gonorrhœa first shows itself as a discharge which usually appears from 2 to 10 days after infection.

Further information can be obtained IN CONFIDENCE from the local Health Department, or from the Medical Adviser, Central Council for Health Education, Tavistock House, Tavistock Square, London, W.C.1. (Phone: Euston 3341)

ISSUED BY THE MINISTRY OF HEALTH AND THE CENTRAL COUNCIL FOR HEALTH EDUCATION

(V.D.4-3)

Illustration 2.1. 'Ten plain facts about VD', Ministry of Health advertisement, *Daily Mirror*, 19 Feb. 1943, 2. This 1943 Ministry of Health advertisement, warning the public about the dangers of venereal diseases, was toned down after protests by some newspapers about its explicitness.

Friday, February 19, 1943 THE DAILY MIRROR Page 3

False modesty won't stop this disease

THE advertisement which we publish on the opposite page today is of great importance. It is the frankest official announcement ever made on a "delicate" subject, and we, of this newspaper, fully associate ourselves with it; recommend it to the close attention of all our readers, and congratulate the Government on at last having come right into the open in a matter which for some time past has been calling for the most candid type of publicity.

Our only criticism of this Ministry of Health appeal is that, while it is frank, it is not frank enough, and we have no hesitation in stating the reason why.

As originally presented the advertisement was clear and candid in its terms. It called a spade a spade. But Fleet-street, with a delicacy of feeling not hitherto considered its predominant characteristic, felt perturbed.

The newspapers as a whole thought that the Ministry's wording was too blunt. Consequently, to placate this unexpected sensitiveness of feeling, the announcement was toned down, and the stark red warning of danger changed to an *inoffensive* pink. For example

CLAUSE 3

In the original advertisement this read: "The two principal venereal diseases are syphilis and gonorrhœa (vulgarly known as pox and clap). Both are caused by tiny living organisms or germs, but the germ of syphilis is quite different from that of gonorrhœa."

That passage was modified thus: "The two principal venereal diseases are syphilis and gonorrhœa. They are caused by quite different living organisms or germs."

CLAUSE 7

The original clause was "Professional prostitutes are not the only source of infection. Any free and easy sex behaviour must mean a risk of infection and cannot be made safe. Venereal disease contracted through irregular sex alliance is spread to innocent partners. An infected man may give the disease to his wife, who, in turn, may infect her unborn baby. Clean living is the only way to escape infection—abstinence is not harmful."

The revised version merely says: "Professional prostitutes are not the only source of infection. Any free and easy sex behaviour must mean a risk of infection and cannot be made safe. Clean living is the only way to escape infection—abstinence is not harmful."

CLAUSE 10

As first issued this said: "Anyone who has the slightest reason to suspect infection should seek medical treatment at once. A doctor or clinic should be consulted immediately about any suspicious sore or unusual discharge. It may not be venereal disease, but it is best to be sure. These are the signs. The first sign of syphilis is a small ulcer on or near the sex organs. It appears from ten to ninety days after infection, usually about three weeks. Gonorrhœa first shows itself as a discharge from the sex organs and usually appears from two to ten days after infection."

This paragraph now reads: "Anyone who has the slightest reason to suspect infection should seek medical treatment at once. A doctor or clinic should be consulted immediately about any suspicious sore or unusual discharge. It may not be venereal disease, but it is best to be sure. These are the signs: The first sign of syphilis is a small ulcer. It appears from ten to ninety days after infection, usually about three weeks. Gonorrhœa first shows itself as a discharge which usually appears from two to ten days after infection."

Letting in some daylight!

THE *Daily Mirror* has, on certain occasions, shocked public opinion, and will not hesitate to do so again. The truth on ugly subjects is seldom popular. Those who tell that truth are often regarded as having done something scandalous. So it has been with this newspaper, when our only offence has been to speak boldly in advance of conventional ideas. As time goes on, however, people come to recognise that what has been said was necessary in the public interest.

NICE people are too easily offended

ON the subject of venereal disease we have played a pioneer role in warning young people of its dangers and in pressing on the authorities the urgent need for remedial measures of a drastic and comprehensive character. It has not been easy. *Nice* people are so easily offended. Officialdom too often hides its head in the sand and hopes for the best. But we are glad to say that in this instance we were soon able to secure the eager co-operation of the Ministry of Health who, though alive to the alarming spread of the disease in war-time, found themselves badly handicapped, first by public ignorance, and, secondly, by apathy on the part of local authorities.

Newspapers can do much to enlighten the public, and the *Daily Mirror* having introduced the subject anew in a leader headed "The Forbidden Topic" published a series of expert articles by a Harley-street specialist, and so paved the way for a campaign of education on an unsavoury but highly important subject.

Since then the matter has been discussed in Parliament and by various bodies, including the Church, whose leaders see the necessity of plain speaking and vigorous action.

Let us hope that today's official advertisement marks the beginning of the end of the humbug and hypocrisy with which the subject of venereal disease has been surrounded, and of, what is worse, that optimistic complacency which is based on the assumption that if only a thing can be kept hidden it will disappear.

The truth about V.D. has been hidden too long. Under war conditions the disease has increased rapidly. There was an increase, also, in the last war, but the conditions this time are different and more ominous for the future health of the country. As Lord Dawson of Penn, the physician, has pointed out, the women who are open to danger today come from more classes than before. There are girls who, while they regard prostitution with horror, affect to believe in "sexual freedom." It is this class which at the present time is running grave risks for the sake of momentary gratification.

Pious horror is no remedy

WHATEVER view may be taken of the moral aspect of V.D. there can be only one view on the practical side. A virulent infectious disease exists and is on the increase. The only thing to do is to face up to the facts and see that the disease is wiped out. It is no remedy to hold up one's hands and piously remark that the "sins of the fathers are visited upon the children, even unto the third and fourth generation."

Let us make up our minds that this shall not happen; that the innocent shall not be allowed to suffer for the guilty; and the fathers (and mothers too) must be taught the consequences of their "sin" in practical terms and be compelled to make themselves no danger to the community. We do not attempt in this article to define what is sin, and what is not sin, in regard to the relationship of the sexes, but we do most solemnly say that it is a sin against the nation and against humanity to acquire venereal disease and to pass its consequences on to others; it is a sin, when the disease has been acquired, to keep the fact secret and take no steps to effect a cure; it is a sin, on the part of good people to remain ignorant, indifferent, or complacent on this subject.

The war against V.D. is on. It is a war that can be won now.

It is everybody's duty to take a hand in the fight. Merely to study this page today; merely to acquire knowledge of the facts and to enlighten others; merely to help raise the veil of secrecy: these things are all steps in the campaign. Let the public co-operate seriously with the authorities, and a running sore in the social body of Britain can be controlled and eventually healed.

B.B.B.

Illustration 2.2. **'False modesty won't stop this disease'**, *Daily Mirror*, 19 Feb. 1943, 3. The *Daily Mirror* exposed the ways in which Fleet Street's reticence about VD was undermining the government's public health campaign.

taboo on sex and regarding venereal disease in the light of an ordinary ailment, they feared that illicit intercourse would now take place more frequently as shame and horror of the possible consequences were removed.'[91]

The controversy flared up again when the Ministry of Information decided that too many concessions had been made to the NPA. Little more than a week into the campaign, officials told newspapers that the sub-edited version of the advertisement was 'liable to cause misery and misunderstanding through not stating clearly the symptoms', and suggested that the phrase 'reproductive organs' could be substituted for the words 'sex organs' that had been expunged from the original. The NPA, realizing that consensus was now unlikely in Fleet Street, left individual editors to decide for themselves. Some papers, including the *Mirror* and *The Times*, now decided to print the original 'sex organs' in the new version of the advertisement, entitled 'VD—Plain Speaking'.[92] Others, including the *News Chronicle*, the *Herald*, the *News of the World*, and the *People*, accepted the Ministry's recommendation and chose the term 'reproductive organs', while the *Daily Mail* refused to accept either phrase and continued to print the original, misleading, copy.[93] The powerful anxieties caused by sexual terminology were highlighted once again. And as the campaign continued, there would be further complaints from the press about the style and content of particular advertisements.[94]

These obstructions from Fleet Street were deeply frustrating for health officials who wanted newspapers to play a far more active role in educating the public. The Ministry of Health's joint committee on venereal diseases, chaired by Sir Weldon Dalrymple-Champneys, observed in August 1943 that 'the press though prepared to accept the paid advertisements as a measure of national service are not enthusiastic in devoting more space to the subject.'[95] The committee agreed that this was a missed opportunity, especially in light of the evidence that the advertising campaign had made a powerful impact. An investigation conducted by Wartime Social Survey for the Ministry of Information found that 86 per cent of the public had seen the VD announcements in the press, and 92 per cent approved of the publicity. The survey also revealed that 'Those who had read the statement consistently showed more knowledge of the subject than those who had not'; indeed, 36 per cent of those who had read it admitted that 'either some or all of the information given in it was new to them'.[96] This data demonstrated that newspapers could play a substantial role in educating the public on sexual issues. Those individuals who did not find sufficient information for their needs were encouraged to seek help elsewhere. By October 1943, the

91 Mass-Observation file report 1633, 3.

92 *Newspaper World*, 6 Mar. 1943, 15; *Daily Mirror*, 5 Mar. 1943, 4; *The Times*, 2 Mar. 1943, 2.

93 *News of the World*, 7 Mar. 1943, 8; *Daily Mail*, 5 Mar. 1943, 4.

94 Bingham, 'The British Popular Press and Venereal Disease', 1072.

95 NA, MH/55/2325, Minutes of third meeting of JCVD, 10 Aug. 1943.

96 NA, RG/23/38 Wartime Social Survey Inquiry 18 Mar. to 17 Apr. 1943.

CCHE had received over 66,000 letters from the public in response to the adverts, and there were thousands of requests for the sex education pamphlets it produced.[97]

All of this activity reinforced the idea that being sexually informed—and by extension, sexually responsible—was an essential part of modern citizenship, for both men and women.[98] One government advertisement produced for Scotland actually stated, in an echo of the *Mirror*'s rhetoric, that 'Prudes and hypocrites may refuse to discuss venereal diseases frankly and openly. The good citizen understands that these diseases, like all diseases which lower public health, are the concern of everybody.'[99] It is significant that the wartime concern about venereal diseases prompted the establishment of an investigation by Her Majesty's Inspectorate into the provision of sex education, which resulted in the first guidance from central government on the subject for schools and youth organizations.[100]

The editorial team at the *Mirror* was perceptive enough to recognize the popular hunger for information about sex and to feed it as part of a high-minded campaign of education. 'It is a sin on the part of good people to remain ignorant, indifferent or complacent on this subject', one editorial argued, '. . . It is everybody's duty to take a hand in the fight.'[101] Of course the paper was not purely motivated by altruism—it used the issue to cultivate its growing reputation as a radical, outspoken paper of the people—but many of the staff did have an idealistic desire to challenge the prudery identified by Sir Wilson Jameson. The campaign was regarded as an 'immense success' by Cecil King and Harry Bartholomew, and soon acquired a central place in the growing mythology of the *Mirror*.[102] When Sylvester Bolam took over as editor of the *Mirror* in 1948, the wartime venereal diseases crusade was one of two examples used in a front-page statement championing the benefits of sensationalism.[103] Hugh Cudlipp devoted a short chapter to it in his half-centenary history of the paper in 1953.[104] This critical and commercial triumph provided a powerful impetus for both the *Mirror* and the *Sunday Pictorial* to extend their efforts to open up the discussion of sex in the years after the war.

97 NA, HO/45/25599 CCHE, VD publicity campaign, Medical Adviser's correspondence, Oct. 1943, Minutes of third meeting of JCVD, 10 Aug. 1943.

98 As Sonya Rose has argued, those who transgressed notions of sexual responsibility were criticized for failing to be 'good citizens': S. Rose, 'Sex, Citizenship, and the Nation in World War II Britain', *American Historical Review*, 103/4 (1998), 1147–1176.

99 NA, BN/10/220, Advertisement appearing in Scottish newspapers 22 Mar. 1943.

100 J. Hampshire and J. Lewis, '"The Ravages of Permissiveness": Sex Education and the Permissive Society', *Twentieth Century British History*, 15 (2004), 294.

101 *Daily Mirror*, 19 Feb. 1943, 3.

102 Cudlipp Papers, H.C. 2/1, Cecil King to Hugh Cudlipp, 25 Nov. 1942; King to Cudlipp, 25 Feb. 1943.

103 H. Cudlipp, *Publish and Be Damned! The Astonishing Story of the Daily Mirror* (London: Andrew Dakers, 1953), 251.

104 Ibid., ch. 31.

SEX EDUCATION AND ADVICE

In the two decades after the Second World War, the popular press gradually took up the challenge of educating the public about sexual questions. This was both a commercial response to the success of the *Mirror* and a reflection of wider social support for sex education. Rather than merely reacting to external controversies (such as those provoked in the inter-war period by Stopes and Dawson), newspapers increasingly took the initiative and investigated topics themselves. The resulting journalism remained moralistic and euphemistic, but medical and scientific language became more prominent and doctors, sexologists, psychologists, and counsellors were asked to offer their perspectives. Papers deliberately stirred up debate and invited responses from readers; agony aunts were given more space and greater licence to discuss sexual problems. Campaigning organizations found the press more receptive to their approaches and obtained greater coverage. In a period when the coverage of sex in other popular media (radio and television broadcasting, mass market magazines) remained restricted, newspapers had considerable power to shape public opinion. And while all national papers continued to support marriage and the family, they did not maintain an unthinking moral conservatism: many challenged readers and encouraged a reassessment of conventional positions. In relation to divorce and abortion, in particular, some popular papers contributed significantly to the climate of reform that produced the legislation of the 1960s.

One sign of the press's changing approach was the post-war interest in sex education. The *Mirror*'s sister paper, the *Sunday Pictorial*, edited by Hugh Cudlipp on his return from wartime military service, was particularly keen to counter the remaining resistance to sex education. This was part of the Mirror Group's wider attack on what it regarded as an outdated education system which failed to prepare young citizens for the realities of modern life. 'At present the great bulk of what people are taught isn't either true or interesting', complained the *Mirror* in 1943. 'Boys aren't taught how to be handy about the house, girls know far too little about running a home, both know next to nothing about sex-life and the managing of children. Isn't this more important than knowing who Habakkuk was?'[105]

The *Pictorial* provided space for those campaigning for the introduction of coherent programmes of sex education in schools and elsewhere. In January 1947, for example, a piece on this subject by Dr Norman Haire, the noted Australian doctor and a leading participant in the main sex reform groups, was significant enough to be advertised as 'Today's Important Article'.[106] Sex instruction, argued Haire, was a necessity in a 'civilised community' and provided

[105] *Daily Mirror*, 8 Feb. 1943, 4–5.

[106] *Sunday Pictorial*, 5 Jan. 1947, 5.

the only means to combat successfully 'such social evils as prostitution, venereal disease and promiscuity'. In Britain, however, most parents were 'not fully educated in either the biology or psychology of sex' and not in a position to provide the necessary teaching to their children. A comprehensive programme was required both to enlighten parents about the importance of such education and to establish appropriate courses in schools and universities. 'The frank, objective, and casual answering of all children's questions on sex matters' was 'essential' from nursery school stage.[107] The following month a feature article on marital problems highlighted the role of ignorance and anxiety about sex in destabilizing relationships. 'Efficient preparation for marriage by sex education' was the central recommendation for young couples; 'Parental frankness about sex matters' was identified as one of the key factors behind a happy marriage.[108] The readers of the *Pictorial* were presented with a series of powerful arguments that sex education provided a key means of addressing contemporary concerns about the break-up of families and juvenile delinquency.

Rather than just highlighting the problem, though, the *Pictorial* followed the example of the wartime *Mirror* and adopted the role of public educator. In December 1947 and January 1948 the *Pictorial* published a four-part serialization of a sex education pamphlet entitled *How a Baby is Born*. Designed specifically for children, the series discussed in simple language the basics of fertilization, pregnancy, and birth, often drawing analogies from nature. 'The male animal sends the sperms to the female through an opening in her body . . . The sperms of men, like those of the four-legged animals, live in a little bag. The father places the sperms in the body of the mother in very much the same way that the animals do'.[109] Cudlipp was sufficiently nervous to show the articles in advance to a panel of one hundred families he had assembled to advise the *Pictorial* on post-war issues; having obtained their approval he gave the series front-page publicity and presented it as 'a bold new educational experiment in newspaper production'.[110] Dr David Mace, the secretary of the Marriage Guidance Council, praised the initiative warmly, writing that 'thousands of parents will be grateful to the *Sunday Pictorial* for giving them such sound guidance in the fulfilment of one of their most important duties to their boys and girls.'[111] Some readers did indeed write to express their gratitude, and the series may well have been a useful tool for those who agreed with a correspondent who admitted 'I can't seem to bring myself to talk about sex with my children'.[112]

For some Fleet Street observers, such serializations were nothing other than cynical attempts to build circulation by exploiting the public's interest in sex.

107 *Sunday Pictorial*, 5 Jan. 1947, 5.

108 *Sunday Pictorial*, 9 Feb. 1947, 7.

109 *Sunday Pictorial*, 4 Jan. 1948, 8–9.

110 *Sunday Pictorial*, 4 Jan. 1948, 1; 11 Jan. 1948, 5.

111 H. Cudlipp, *Walking on Water* (London: Bodley Head, 1976), 182; *Sunday Pictorial*, 4 Jan. 1948, 1.

112 *Sunday Pictorial*, 8 Feb. 1948, 9.

John Gordon, the editor of the *Sunday Express*, told Beaverbrook that although the *How a Baby is Born* series must have seemed 'a certain winner', it wasn't 'hitting the bulls-eye': he believed that this was because the *Pictorial* had 'rather over-dosed its readers with sex.'[113] Because Gordon did not accept that sex was a suitable subject for discussion in a 'family newspaper', he refused to distinguish between different types of coverage. Educational material was lumped together with explicitly titillating content and dismissed as 'salacity'. Cudlipp, by contrast, was more sensitive to the changing social climate and recognized that there was a market for informative content presented in idealistic terms. But the *Pictorial* gave ammunition to its critics by occasionally giving credence to dubious science. A notorious example of this occurred in November 1955 with the *Pictorial*'s front-page headline 'Virgin Births—Doctors Now Say—It doesn't always need a man to make a baby'.[114] The paper claimed that doctors were exploring the 'sensational possibility' that there 'may be ten or more women in this country who have given birth to a baby without having association with a man.' Readers were invited to come forward if they believed they had experienced a virgin birth, and, predictably, the front page the following week declared 'Three Women Claim: "It Happened To Me"'.[115] 'It really is hard to imagine anything more obscene', a dismayed Arthur Christiansen told Beaverbrook after the first article, 'but it will certainly sell next week's paper'.[116] Such incidents were rare, but the cumulative impact of inaccuracies in reporting of all kinds undoubtedly damaged trust in the popular press, and inevitably weakened its effectiveness as an educator.

A more regular forum for the discussion of sexual welfare was provided by the 'agony aunt' and advice columns that became an increasingly prominent feature in many popular papers after the war. Columns addressing correspondents' problems have a very long history, dating back to periodicals of the late seventeenth century, although it has been argued that the first modern magazine 'agony aunt' was Annie Swan in *Women at Home* (1892–1920).[117] By the 1920s there were regular named advice columns in some popular newspapers, but most editors simply commissioned occasional features on various aspects of interpersonal relationships from their pools of contributors. In the second-half of the 1930s, however, as competition to provide human interest intensified, problem columnists began to be regarded as an important part of the editorial formula: Anne Temple at the *Daily Mail* and Dorothy Dix at the *Daily Mirror* were particularly successful. After the Second World War this form of journalism

113 Beaverbrook papers, H/128, John Gordon to Beaverbrook, 9 Jan. 1948.

114 *Sunday Pictorial*, 6 Nov. 1955, 1. 115 *Sunday Pictorial*, 13 Nov. 1955, 1.

116 Beaverbrook Papers, H/177, Christiansen to Beaverbrook, 10 Nov. 1955.

117 R. Kent, *Agony: Problem Pages Through The Ages* (London: Star, 1987), ch. 1; M. Beetham, 'The Agony Aunt, the Romancing Uncle and the Family of Empire: Defining the Sixpenny Reading Public in the 1890s', in L. Brake, B. Bell, and D. Finkelstein (eds.), *Nineteenth Century Media and the Construction of Identities* (Basingstoke: Palgrave, 2000).

flourished. Notable exponents of the genre included Mary Brown and Marjorie Proops (*Daily Mirror*), Mary Marshall (*Daily Herald*), Claire Rayner (*Sun*), Nora Downey and Unity Hall (*News of the World*). Other papers invited experienced counsellors or doctors to respond to readers: in the late 1940s and early 1950s, for example, the *Star* ran a regular column penned by Dr David Mace. Perhaps the most famous advice column of all was the *News of the World*'s John Hilton bureau, which responded to questions on issues of all kinds, whether emotional, financial, or professional.

The consistently high interest ratings these columns obtained in readership surveys, and the sheer volume of letters they attracted, provide the most persuasive evidence of the importance of popular newspapers as a source of advice and guidance on personal and sexual questions. In its investigation of the national press in 1948, Mass-Observation found that the *Mail*'s Ann Temple received 'warmer tributes than perhaps any other feature writer encountered in this analysis'.[118] Some four decades later, research carried out for the *Mirror* found Marje Proops was well ahead of the paper's other columnists in terms of reader interest.[119] In the 1970s, Proops received around 40,000 letters a year and Claire Rayner at the *Sun* around 13,000; the *News of the World*'s John Hilton bureau received more than 100,000.[120] These columnists represented convenient, approachable, and knowledgeable figures to whom readers could turn, at a time when many people felt it difficult to discuss sex in person. They sought to combine the authority of doctors and counsellors with the intimacy of a friend or family member. Behind the scenes they all had a support infrastructure to manage the task of replying to the letters: writing in 1976, Proops revealed that she had a staff of 'eight dedicated girls' helping her.[121]

Advice columnists in the middle decades of the century almost invariably provided a staunch defence of conventional morality. They repeatedly highlighted the virtues of sexual restraint outside marriage and defended the expectation that women (if not men) should be virgins when they wed. Many articles assumed a young female reader, and guided them how to act in a world of gender inequality and sexual double standards, which, it seemed, there was little prospect of reforming. 'We have a definite moral standard in this country, which states "chastity before marriage"' observed Thomas Bowen Partington in the *Mirror* in 1935, adding more pragmatically that 'Men despise in their hearts the girls

[118] M-O file report, 2557, Attitudes to Daily Newspapers, Jan. 1948, 27.

[119] A. Patmore, *Marge: The Guilt and the Gingerbread: The Authorized Biography* (London: Warner, 1993), 314.

[120] Press Council, *The Press and People*: Annual Report 1976 (London: Press Council, 1977), 100; M. Bromley, '"Watching the Watchdogs"? The Role of Readers' Letters in Calling the Press to Account', in H. Stephenson and M. Bromley (eds.), *Sex, Lies and Democracy: The Press and the Public* (London: Longman, 1998), 151; L. Lamb, *Sunrise: The Remarkable Rise of the Best-Selling Soaraway Sun* (London: Papermac, 1989), 183.

[121] M. Proops, *Dear Marje* . . . (London: Book Club Associates, 1976), 18.

who make themselves cheap.'[122] Writing in the same paper in 1953, Mary Brown admitted that the girl who 'dreams of the man she will marry and keeps herself exclusively for him' was now 'old-fashioned', but she used similar arguments to Partington to support this traditional wisdom. 'You will not believe me now,' Brown told her readers, 'but the day will come when you would give anything to look into the eye of one man and say: "There's never been anyone but you".' She was far more critical than Partington of the sexual double standard—it was 'crazy, illogical and grossly unfair' that 'nearly all men will take from any girl at every opportunity and still expect to marry a virgin'—but she advised young women to reconcile themselves to its existence. 'It is a fundamental element in masculine make-up and a girl who ignores the fact is laying up future trouble for herself.'[123]

This double standard was never more clearly exposed than on the rare, but notable, occasions when different advice was given to young men, or to their parents. A picture-story in the *Mirror* in 1939, for example, portrayed a father allowing his restless son to go about 'sowing his wild oats in his own way'. He ran 'wild about the town' and had a dalliance with a woman who 'didn't appear to be exactly an angel', but he soon got bored and settled down with an (implicitly virginal) 'sweet girl'. 'Encourage your son to have his fling early in life,' the fictional father concluded, 'Trust him. He won't let you down unless he's a born wrong 'un. And that's not likely.'[124] Such guidance, although infrequent, merely reinforced the notion that it was ultimately the duty of women to defend sexual morality. Columnists warned women about the potential consequences of premarital sex by describing in unsparing detail the miseries of unwanted pregnancy and abandonment. In 1948, David Mace displayed little sympathy for a Miss M, whose fiancé left her after she became pregnant: 'Miss M did something which involved the possibility of a new human life beginning its progress. . . . Knowing this, she deliberately gambled with this solemn responsibility for a stake which was no higher than the pursuit of a personal pleasure'. The absent father was denounced as a 'coward and a cad', but the bulk of the column focused on Miss M, because Mace wanted 'her to realise that the final responsibility for her plight rests solidly on her own shoulders'.[125]

Some columnists discouraged any form of physical intimacy among the unmarried, on the grounds that 'petting' might lead to further temptation. This reflected the assumption that anything short of intercourse was inherently frustrating. 'Do not put yourself under conditions whereby your natural desires tend to be unduly aroused', advised Partington, while Dorothy Dix declared firmly in 1938 that 'I don't believe in petting among boys and girls'.[126] Few columnists maintained such a strict line, however, as long as there was genuine

[122] *Daily Mirror*, 13 Nov. 1935, 12.
[123] *Daily Mirror*, 9 July 1953, 10.
[124] *Daily Mirror*, 17 Aug. 1939, 16.
[125] *The Star*, 20 Jan. 1948, 6.
[126] *Daily Mirror*, 16 July 1938, 20.

romantic attachment. Advice columnists were keen to maintain the romantic ideal of true love. Jean Fairfax in the *Sunday Pictorial* suggested in 1938 that the 'wise girl reserves her kisses for the man she really loves—even though sometimes she may be mistaken. At least, she has faith in her choice for the time being.'[127] Ten years later, a feature in the same paper suggested that petting might actually have some value 'as a step in normal sexual development and a preparation for marriage', because there were real dangers 'especially for women, in waiting too long for sexual awakening'. Such activity was only validated by 'love', however: 'physical experience is empty unless it is combined with real affection'.[128] The central message from the more liberal columnists was that young women should have the confidence to make their own judgements, and to reject unwanted male advances if necessary. Jane Peters suggested in 1952 that the 'smart girl' should 'make up her mind and stick to her decision . . . Once a girl can be firm without making him feel a clumsy fool, she has the secret of success with men'.[129]

Married readers, meanwhile, were warned about the disastrous repercussions of extra-marital affairs. Appeals to the romantic ideal could not be allowed to challenge the sacred bond of marriage. Once betrothed, the duty of maintaining the relationship was deemed to outweigh the temptations of love with another person. A couple who had found love and happiness in each others' arms, despite both being married to other partners, were told by Dorothy Dix in 1938 to stop their affair immediately. Her language was clearly informed by Christian teaching:

> You know that there is only one righteous solution to a problem like this . . . don't dally with temptation . . . you have no right to sacrifice your innocent families to your passion . . . . There is something more worthwhile having in life than love, and that is the integrity of your own soul, and the knowledge that you had the strength to do your duty.[130]

During the war advice columns were restricted due to shortages of space in the rationed papers, but they often continued in some form, partly because newspapers felt a strong responsibility to defend relationships put under strain by military service and extended absences from home. Cecil King told Hugh Cudlipp in 1943 that 'breaking and broken marriages' was the 'main theme' of the thousand or so letters that poured into the *Mirror*'s office every week.[131] Unsurprisingly, the editors of the Live Letters column reinforced the advice provided by Dorothy Dix. When a married man declared himself 'very much in love' with a 'single girl', the reply to his request for guidance was unequivocal: 'Forget each other, quickly.'[132] Anne Temple in the *Mail* was fiercely critical of

127 *Sunday Pictorial*, 6 Mar. 1938, 19.
128 *Sunday Pictorial*, 1 Feb. 1948, 19.
129 *Sunday Pictorial*, 11 May 1952, 9.
130 *Daily Mirror*, 7 Sept. 1938, 22.
131 Cudlipp Papers, Cecil King to Hugh Cudlipp, 12 Jan. 1943.
132 *Daily Mirror*, 10 Aug. 1943, 3.

the 'Girls who want Excitement from the War', tempting lonely soldiers into infidelity; other columnists warned women against consorting with American GIs.[133]

Similar advice continued to be offered long after the war. As women increasingly moved into the workplace and mixed more regularly with men, articles discussed how the correct boundaries were to be maintained. The unmarried were warned not to be seduced by the attentions of married bosses—such predators were, Anne Temple declared, men of 'contemptible irresponsibility'.[134] Married women were advised to be careful about their friendships with men, in case latent sexual urges emerged. 'Friendship between a man and a woman is a tricky business', observed Mary Brown in the *Mirror* in 1955. 'Quite suddenly it may flare up, above and beyond their innocent intentions, into a moment of blind passion'.[135] Columnists portrayed sexual desire as a mysterious force that was very difficult to control: those regarded as potentially 'impulsive' and 'emotional', namely teenagers and married women, had to be advised not to put themselves in situations where they might not be able to manage their feelings.

The key shift in this period was the increased emphasis placed on sex within marriage. The arguments developed by Marie Stopes and others in the inter-war period about the importance of a mutually enjoyable physical relationship for a healthy marriage were in the 1950s championed by newspaper columnists. Female readers, in particular, were encouraged to lose their inhibitions and explore the possibilities of sexual pleasure; both men and women were encouraged to learn more about sex to ensure mutual satisfaction. In 1952, for example, Ann Douglas identified 'Ignorance of Sex' as the second most significant cause of 'marriage wrecks'. Men were prone to 'confuse sex experience with knowledge' and generally refused to consult those who could usefully instruct them; women, meanwhile, 'still feel guilty about sex, regarding it as something shameful but necessary'. The result was unsatisfying sex which caused tensions.[136] When the *News of the World* invited Lady (Elizabeth) Pakenham (introduced as a 'mother of eight') to review the Marriage Guidance Council's 'ten commandments' for a happy marriage in 1955, she emphasized the importance of sexual compatibility. Indeed, she believed the Council's commandment to be 'patient, unselfish, and seek to understand in sex relationships' was insufficiently strong:

> Personally, I should have started off with a good, thumping, positive resolve—'I will be generous in sex relationships.' Too many married people, especially women, think their duty is done if they refrain from casting their eyes beyond their marriage partner; or if they concede marital rights with patience. I would like to see a little more generosity and joy injected into the council's seventh commandment.[137]

[133] *Daily Mail*, 15 Feb. 1943, 2; Rose, 'Sex, Citizenship, and the Nation'.
[134] *Daily Mail*, 22 Mar. 1954, 4.
[135] *Daily Mirror*, 17 Oct. 1955, 12.
[136] *Sunday Pictorial*, 4 May 1952, 12.
[137] *News of the World*, 27 Nov. 1955, 6.

Dr Robert Fagan, an American counsellor writing in the *News of the World* in 1960, agreed that a woman should 'make love to her husband' and act in a 'feminine aggressive way', rather than merely being the 'recipient of love-making'.[138] The language of gender difference had not disappeared—it was still widely assumed that men and women had slightly different roles to play in the physical side of marriages, as in other aspects—but levels of enjoyment were increasingly expected to be equal.

By the 1960s it was commonplace not just for columnists to encourage women to enjoy sex, but to ensure that they were self-reflective about sexual pleasure. In 1963 Marje Proops told the 'recent bride' to 'make sure' that she shed her inhibitions—or she would 'be sorry'. She encouraged these women—revealingly, she assumed that they had already had some sexual experience—to take the initiative in communicating their sexual desires. 'Tell him what you need and ask him about his needs.' Sex was a skill to be mastered gradually, with the appropriate assistance if necessary: 'You'll discover the art of sex by experiment, learning as you go. And if you find you are a bit slow on the uptake—or he is—buy a book.'[139] Advice columnists contributed significantly to the re-evaluation of the sexual from being a dangerous instinct that needed to be restrained, to a positive and pleasurable force that needed to be expressed for personal and psychological well-being. In July 1963, for example, Proops challenged the myth that 'sex isn't everything', and although written with light-hearted exaggeration, the sentiments matched much of the rest of her writing:

> those who assert that it isn't, can't possibly have heard of Freud, who maintained it was the impulse behind everything we do, say, think, feel, dream. Without it (or without the best of it) life is arid, boring, wearying, unenticing, uneventful, uninspiring. With it (or the best of it) life is rewarding, exciting, moving, amusing, exhilarating and splendid. Those who maintain the myth that sex isn't everything have my profound pity.[140]

The reference to Freud indicated the growing acceptance of psychological and psychoanalytical explanations of human behaviour by press commentators in the 1950s and 1960s. Freud's work had come to the attention of popular newspapers in the early 1920s, but during the inter-war years it was commonly dismissed as a passing craze lacking intellectual credibility, and there was little substantial engagement with it. 'The most popular member of a social gathering nowadays is the one whose smattering of knowledge of psychoanalysis enables her to chatter glibly about "complexes" and the workings of the subconscious mind' sneered a commentator in the *Weekly Dispatch* in 1921.[141] 'More nonsense is talked under the long name of "psycho-analysis" in these days than any other of the recent fads of pseudo-science' observed a *Mirror* editorial two years later.[142]

[138] *News of the World*, 3 Apr. 1960, 3–4.
[139] *Daily Mirror*, 14 Apr. 1963, 13.
[140] *Daily Mirror*, 7 July 1963, 13.
[141] *Weekly Dispatch*, 9 Jan. 1921, 8.
[142] *Daily Mirror*, 15 Mar. 1923, 7.

By the 1930s psychoanalysts occasionally appeared on problem pages,[143] but they were rarely able to discuss sexuality in any detail, and there was still a widely shared belief that, as the *Sketch* suggested in 1938, they were charlatans who 'revel in the sordid and unusual'.[144] These perceptions did not entirely disappear, but after the Second World War there was a more consistent use by journalists of psychoanalytical language and perspectives. This served to encourage the idea that the denial of sexual impulses could be very damaging to the individual and to their relationship. Proops, for example, suggested the 'commonest reason' that husbands were unfaithful was a lack of sexual responsiveness among their wives. She warned the many women who were 'frigid in bed, thinking of sex as something not very nice' that they were storing up problems for themselves: 'Don't be smug. Don't think it couldn't happen to you. It could.'[145]

In comparison to earlier columnists who had refused to accept any excuses for adultery, writers in the 1960s were more sympathetic to those who cited the absence of a satisfying sex life to explain their behaviour. This sympathy was not confined to straying men. In 1966 Sara Robson in the *News of the World* was far more compassionate than Dorothy Dix would have been to a woman who had engaged in a brief one night affair after being frustrated by the sexual coldness of her husband. 'A normally passionate woman living with a husband she loves, but seldom makes love with, is dreadfully vulnerable to the temptation you fell for. The perfectly natural and proper sexual side of her nature can only be held down at great cost.'[146] Robson recommended visiting a doctor or a Family Planning clinic with the husband to try to discover the root of his sexual problem, because if the issue was not addressed, 'similar incidents will happen again'. Even a 'normally passionate' woman could not be expected to control her sex drive indefinitely. 'I'm not an over-sexed woman', one reader told the *Sun* in 1969, 'but I do feel that my husband and I should make love more than twice a month—which is how often he feels like it.' Advice in this instance was supplied by another reader, who had 'mended' her marriage by convincing her partner that she desired him 'for her pleasure, more than his'.[147] Experienced columnists were quite clear that women's sexual expectations were changing. Reviewing her career as an agony aunt in 1976, Proops observed that 'Twenty years ago women wrote about their sexually demanding men. Now, many men write about sexually demanding women.'[148] Newspaper advice columns both encouraged and reflected the move by which sexual pleasure became seen as being central to the identity and well-being of men and women.

[143] For example, *Daily Mirror*, 2 Nov. 1935, 12. [144] *Daily Sketch*, 7 July 1938, 17.

[145] *Daily Mirror*, 5 May 1963, 15. [146] *News of the World*, 20 July 1966, 24.

[147] *Sun*, 12 Dec. 1969, 7.

[148] Proops, *Dear Marje*, 24. David Mace observed a similar trend: M. Collins, *Modern Love: An Intimate History of Men and Women in Twentieth Century Britain* (London: Atlantic Books, 2003), 125.

It is important not to exaggerate the contribution of advice columns to the education of the public. The responses to problems were necessarily brief and frequently banal. Despite their claims to frankness, columnists in newspapers could not be as specific and detailed as doctors and counsellors. Letters about minority or 'unorthodox' sexual practices could receive short shrift, and, certainly before the 1970s, gay men and women were not always treated sensitively. One reader, born in 1948, recalled her disappointment when as a teenager she had written to Marje Proops about her belief that she was a lesbian, and eventually received the reply 'Don't worry, dear, you'll grow out of it.'[149] On the other hand, many correspondents testified to the value of the advice they were given, and the columns remained very popular throughout the period. Their significance lies not so much in the specific advice given as in the general encouragement they gave readers, and especially women, to reflect on their personal relationships and to be confident in claiming sexual pleasure, at least in marriage. They suggested that readers talk about their problems with partners and provided them with some of the vocabulary to do so; they also advised them to seek help from doctors, counsellors, or relevant support organizations where necessary. In so doing, advice columns contributed to the climate of reform of the 1950s and 1960s.

THE PRESS AND THE CLIMATE OF REFORM IN THE 1950S AND 1960S

Advice columns were one of the avenues through which campaigning organizations such as the Family Planning Association and the Abortion Law Reform Association gained greater publicity in this period. After finding it difficult to make a significant impact on public consciousness through the press in the inter-war decades, in the 1950s the FPA and ALRA discovered that popular newspapers were becoming more interested in their work. These organizations improved their media operations considerably, briefing journalists, supplying ideas for articles and commissioning opinion polls with significant news value. In the late 1950s the development of the contraceptive pill received huge publicity and opened up the discussion of family planning. At the same time the dangers of back streets abortions started to move up the press agenda. Several popular newspapers also gave space to those dissatisfied with the operation of the divorce laws. In all of these ways, the press contributed to a climate of reform which produced the important legislation of 1967–9.

One major factor inhibiting official support for the provision of contraception in the first half of the twentieth century was concern about what a declining birth

[149] A. Oram and A. Turnbull (eds.), *The Lesbian History Sourcebook* (London: Routledge, 2001), 265.

rate might mean for Britain's economic and international position. This concern prompted the appointment of a Royal Commission on Population in 1944, although by the time it reported in May 1949, the birth-rate had risen slightly. The final report did not view the prospect of population decline with equanimity, but the commission believed that the trend towards using contraception was a reflection of the rise in status of women, which it was neither possible nor desirable to reverse.[150] The commission placed the issue of birth control firmly on the public agenda and provided an excellent opportunity for the FPA, in particular, to publicize its work. That the FPA was unable to capitalize on this opening was partly due to the lack of sophistication in its press operation. The General Secretary felt the need to write to an *Observer* journalist, Alison Settle, for advice on whom to invite to an FPA press conference designed to coordinate with the publication of the Royal Commission's report. 'We are children in these matters,' she admitted, 'and would very much appreciate your guidance'.[151] Settle's recommendations were enough to ensure that the FPA conference did receive some newspaper attention, including in the *Mirror* and the *News Chronicle*, but this was by no means the breakthrough with the press that it could have been.[152]

FPA-sponsored articles continued to be sufficiently rare that they generated huge interest when they appeared. A small piece in a (unspecified) popular daily newspaper in 1950, for example, led to the association receiving over 5,000 letters.[153] Determined that the FPA achieve greater visibility in its silver jubilee year of 1955, Margaret Pyke, the Honorary Secretary, organized meetings with key figures in Fleet Street to discover why the association continued to struggle with the press. A particularly revealing conversation was held with Michael Curtis, the editor of the *News Chronicle*. Curtis told Pyke that the press's reluctance to address the issue of birth control was not (as Stopes and others believed) due to the sensitivities of the Irish: 'few [papers] have much Irish circulation and if they do they could easily leave out any particular article from one edition'. The 'real difficulty' was that popular newspapers 'set out to be a "family paper" suitable for children if they get hold of it'. After Pyke pressed him, Curtis was forced to admit that 'perhaps Fleet Street overdid this fear (of arousing "family indignation") and that many things were quite as unsuitable or more so but inevitably had to appear'—such as the details of the Montagu homosexuality case.[154] Entrenched definitions of what sort of material was appropriate for a 'family newspaper' were

150 P. Thane, 'Population Politics in Post-War British Culture', in B. Conekin, F. Mort, and C. Waters (eds.), *Moments of Modernity: Reconstructing Britain 1945–64* (London: Rivers Oram Press, 1999).

151 Wellcome Library, London, FPA Papers, A17, Publicity, S. Robinson to A. Settle, 9 May 1949.

152 FPA Papers, A17, Executive Minutes, 27 July 1949.

153 FPA Papers, A17, BBC Woman's Hour transcript, 1 Dec. 1955.

154 FPA Papers, A17, Mrs Pyke, Report of Lunch with Michael Curtis, 24 Oct. 1955.

continuing to hinder the discussion of contraception decades after Stopes and Lord Dawson had propelled the subject into the deadlines.

Editorial attitudes were undoubtedly shifting, however, and in the closing months of 1955 the FPA finally achieved its publicity breakthrough. The visit of Iain Macleod, the Minister of Health, to the FPA headquarters in November received considerable attention and conferred respectability on the association. In June 1956 a memo looking back over the previous year celebrated 'a triumphant progress to recognition of the birth control position generally and the propriety of the FPA providing the service particularly'. It highlighted the 'strengthening resolution of the Press' in discussing the issue and breaking what it regarded as a 'conspiracy of silence'.[155] Birth control remained in the spotlight over the coming years, partly because of the considerable interest in the development of the contraceptive pill, and partly because of the concern about world population levels.

Report of 'X-Pills' appearing in British pharmacists—as remedies for menstrual pain, but with the potential to prevent pregnancy—emerged in the *Sunday Pictorial* in October 1958. The paper declared that it was 'appalling that such an important scientific achievement—with its possible dangers through inexpert use—should be allowed to sneak into the country' without proper medical oversight.[156] Within a fortnight this had been transformed into a more positive front-page story about the official experiments on the pill conducted by the Council for the Investigation of Fertility Control. The Council was seeking more recruits for the experiments, and the article in the *Pictorial* drew a 'staggering response', with over five hundred women volunteering in the first week.[157] By 1960 popular newspapers were competing to provide readers with the latest information about this invention. In February the *News of the World* offered the 'truth about the new birth-control pills', while in August the *Sunday Pictorial* produced a substantial three-part report on 'the Life Pill', which it described as 'the most important project of our time'.[158] The pill was much easier for newspapers to discuss than other forms of contraception because genitals did not need to be mentioned: this was an advanced, user-friendly invention for the scientific age.[159]

The three angles that dominated the early coverage of the pill were all to be found in this 1960 *Pictorial* series. First, and most prominent, was the potential value of the pill to women in removing the anxieties surrounding the risk of pregnancy and enabling fertility to be managed safely, effectively, and discreetly. The *Pictorial* raised the prospect that this was the 'ideal method of birth control' and highlighted the claim of Dr Pincus and his team that 'the pills

155 FPA Papers, A17, Memo 6 June 1956.

156 *Sunday Pictorial*, 19 Oct. 1958, 32.

157 *Sunday Pictorial*, 2 Nov. 1958, 1, 32; 9 Nov. 1958, 15.

158 *News of the World*, 14 Feb. 1960, 3; *Sunday Pictorial*, 7–21 Aug. 1960.

159 Cook, *The Long Sexual Revolution*, ch. 13.

make love-making more satisfying because of the complete freedom from fear and because the natural flow of affection need not be interrupted'.[160] Associated with this, of course, were concerns about the sexual freedom the pill might grant women.

Second, the role of the pill in countering the threat of world over-population was widely discussed. The 'population time-bomb' began to hit press headlines with regularity from the late 1950s, and in the 1960s was commonly regarded as one of the central political challenges of the age. Scientists 'believe the world's present birth rate is a greater menace than the H-bomb,' warned the *Pictorial*; if the birth-rate is not slowed down, 'the world will ultimately become a huge starving Belsen'.[161] The argument that the pill was a necessary part of world health policy became an effective way of outmanoeuvring moralist critics of the easier access to contraception.

The third area of debate was the health risks associated with the pill. Various scholars have explored the periodic health scares surrounding the pill after it had become widely used; the first major scare was in 1969.[162] Yet the reception of the pill cannot be properly appreciated unless it is recognized that concerns about potential ill effects were prominent from the start. In 1960 the *Pictorial* noted that in the trials 'So many suffered from side-effects that one in four dropped out'; it concluded that while the pill was generally considered safe, its long-term problems could not be assessed.[163] Warnings in the early 1960s about a potential connection with thrombosis, and about unknown long-term dangers, received considerable publicity.[164] In 1964 a *Daily Mail* editorial reminded readers of the delay in discovering the risks associated with thalidomide, and the paper's health correspondent found that none of the eleven doctors he stopped at a BMA conference would be happy for their wives to take the pill.[165] Other articles were more reassuring, but no newspaper was able to rule out the possibility of long-term effects. Whatever the particular concerns about the pill, however, the need for effective forms of contraception was becoming increasingly widely accepted. The continuing controversy over all three of these news angles ensured that the pill remained in the headlines and achieved far more newspaper publicity than any previous form of contraception. This subject was finally achieving the sort of detailed coverage that Stopes had sought.

In the inter-war period a sharp distinction was frequently drawn between birth control and abortion. Many campaigners (including Stopes) argued that by spreading knowledge about contraception women would not have to resort

160 *Sunday Pictorial*, 7 Aug. 1960, 6–7. 161 Ibid.

162 Cook, *Long Sexual Revolution*, 292; K. Wellings, 'Help or Hype: An Analysis of Media Coverage of the 1983 "Pill Scare"', *British Journal of Family Planning*, 12 (1986), 92–8.

163 *Sunday Pictorial*, 14 Aug. 1960, 6–7.

164 *Daily Mirror*, 29 Nov. 1962, 4; *Daily Mail*, 21 July 1964, 1.

165 *Daily Mail*, 22 July 1964, 1, 6.

to the illegal, and frequently dangerous, practice of abortion. Understood by some as nothing less than a form of murder, abortion inflamed passions and editors handled the subject very cautiously. Abortion cases were recorded in the court columns of Sunday papers but the campaign to reform the laws remained marginalized. Only slowly in the post-war period did this campaign come to be seen as a respectable one. The angle that forced the issue up the press agenda in the late 1940s and 1950s was the pragmatic concern about the dangers of back-street operations. Sunday papers, often with considerable input from the ALRA, produced articles drawing attention to the 'scandals of back-street surgery', the 'Big Money Operations [That] Kill 500 Every Year' or the '60,000 Unwanted Babies A Year'.[166]

Focusing on the traumatic experiences of women prepared to resort to almost any means to end their pregnancies provided a human interest element with which to capture the interest, and perhaps evoke the sympathy, of readers. They certainly generated a response. When the ALRA address was included in such articles, the association received a 'heavy correspondence', often from women desperate for reliable information; newspapers also noted the 'great number of letters' reaching the office when they raised the subject.[167] But if they were prepared to publicize the issue, few papers in the 1950s were prepared to commit themselves to supporting reform directly. The left-wing *Reynolds News* was an exception, demanding in 1952 that 'If the misery and suffering that is a consequence of back-street surgery is to be driven out of our social life, the law of the country must be changed. More important! The conspiracy of silence surrounding this problem of abortion must be ended.'[168] Other papers maintained some distance from the controversy. The *News of the World*, for example, was careful to remind readers that the author of one article on abortion was expressing 'his own personal views'.[169]

By the early 1960s, however, voices explicitly calling for legislative reform became more common. The issue of back-street operations remained prominent, but further momentum was generated when a connection was made between the drug thalidomide (contained in 'Distaval', a sedative marketed by the Distillers' Company) and foetal abnormalities.[170] The press featured heart-wrenching stories of parents looking after babies without limbs, which raised the issue of whether women should have greater access to abortion facilities in such cases. A *Daily Mail* survey, run by National Opinion Polls, found in 1962 that no less than 72.9 per cent of the public would be 'in favour of a change in the law

[166] ALRA Press Cuttings, SA/ALRA/E4, *Sunday Pictorial*, 23 Nov. 1947; SA/ALRA/E7, *Reynolds News*, 5 Dec. 1952; SA/ALRA/E6, *News of the World*, 3 Feb. 1952.

[167] ALRA Press Cuttings, SA/ALRA/E6, note from Alice Jenkins on *News of the World* clipping; SA/ALRA/E7, *Reynolds News*, 12 Dec. 1952.

[168] ALRA Press Cuttings, SA/ALRA/E7, *Reynolds News*, 12 Dec. 1952.

[169] *News of the World*, 3 Feb. 1952.

[170] Brookes, *Abortion in England*, 150–2.

allowing doctors to terminate pregnancy where there is good reason to believe that the baby would be badly deformed'.[171]

The changing coverage of abortion was also due to the efforts of an increasingly prominent and outspoken group of female columnists. Marje Proops (*Daily Mirror*), Anne Allen (*Sunday Mirror*), Dee Wells (*Daily Herald*), Monica Furlong (*Daily Mail*), Anne Batt (*Daily Express*), Lena Jeger (*Guardian*), and Katherine Whitehorn (*Observer*) all produced powerful articles in favour of reform.[172] Many of these writers continued to focus on the horrors of illegal operations, and particularly on the unfairness of a situation in which wealthy women could avoid the dangers of the back-streets by paying at a clinic. 'The present abortion laws are laws which favour the well-heeled' complained Proops.[173] 'As having an abortion has become so much a matter of having £200 and the right address, it seems grossly unfair that it should be denied to the have-nots', agreed Anne Batt in the *Daily Express*.[174] But arguments based around women's rights also became significantly more common. Anne Allen contended that 'every woman should have the right to decide what should happen to her own body' and asked 'What right has anyone to tell another human being that they must, or must not, bear a child?'[175] Marje Proops posed the same question: 'why should the majority of women who become pregnant and, for some very good reason, want or need to terminate their pregnancy, be denied the right to decide for themselves whether or not they should go on with the pregnancy?'[176] Surveying the response to her articles, Proops believed that this line of argument was striking a chord with the public: she told the ALRA that 'On the whole, there is clearly powerful support for the reform of the abortion laws and most readers—including many men—felt that women should be the ones to make the final decision'.[177]

The ALRA believed that the media played a very important role in creating a climate in favour of reform. Madeleine Simms, one of the leading campaigners, writing in 1964, was struck by the way that the popular press as well as the 'serious Press' had recently taken up the issue: she noted, moreover, that 'nearly all the comment has been both informed and sympathetic'.[178] 'With each article and programme it becomes much more difficult to utter the same old catch-phrases quite so unthinkingly', declared the ALRA newsletter in spring 1966.[179]

[171] ALRA Press Cuttings, SA/ALR/E14, *Daily Mail*, 25 July 1962.
[172] ALRA Papers, A11/2, *The Humanist*, 1964, 337–9.
[173] ALRA Press Cuttings, SA/ALRA/E15, *Daily Mirror*, 26 Nov. 1964.
[174] *Daily Express*, 22 Nov. 1965, 13.
[175] ALRA Press Cuttings, SA/ALRA/E14 *Sunday Mirror*, 14 July 1964.
[176] ALRA Press Cuttings, SA/ALRA/E15, *Daily Mirror*, 26 Nov. 1964.
[177] ALRA Papers, A11/1, Marje Proops to Dr D. Simms, 28 Sept. 1966.
[178] ALRA Papers, A11/2 *The Humanist*, 1964, 337–9.
[179] ALRA Papers, A11/3, *ALRA Newsletter*, spring 1966, No. 14, 4.

Looking back at the end of 1967, after David Steel's bill had successfully secured its passage through Parliament, the ALRA suggested that the 'support of certain newspapers and journals was invaluable'. Among the popular papers it singled out the *Daily Mail*, the *Sun* (previously the *Daily Herald*), the *Morning Star*, and the *Sunday Mirror*. (The *Daily Mirror* is a surprising omission from this list.) The main press opposition it identified as coming from the *Daily Telegraph* and *The Times* rather than popular papers.[180] The *Express*, the most likely source of popular opposition, had in fact generally supported reform.[181] The coverage of abortion provides one of the clearest examples of how the popular press could play a role in encouraging the public to rethink issues of sexual morality by exposing the failings of existing practice, and by giving space to passionate and persuasive journalists demanding change.

SEXUAL PLEASURE

Much of the popular press's writing about sex in the post-Second World War period was based on the notion of widespread sexual ignorance among the public. The favourite motifs of papers such as the *Mirror* were those of breaking the 'conspiracy of silence' and challenging the 'prudes'; journalists could present themselves as modern and progressive, conducting a service on behalf of a confused and unenlightened readers, raising 'controversial' issues and calling for reform. Although such rhetoric could be overblown, it was close enough to reality to appear convincing. By the late 1960s, however, it became increasingly implausible for popular journalists to cast themselves as crusaders uncovering secrets about sex. The liberalization of the censorship regime in the 1960s gave television, films, theatre, and novels greater freedom in discussing and portraying sex, and they now often did so more explicitly than 'family newspapers' could. The idea that there had been a 'permissive revolution' gained ground, and with it the assumption that ordinary people were sexually informed at ever younger ages.

Popular journalists sought new ways of writing about sex, and the paper that adapted most successfully was Rupert Murdoch's relaunched *Sun*. It developed a hedonistic and consumerist language of (heterosexual) sex, focusing on sexual pleasure and the creation of a liberated lifestyle—of which the 'page three girl' became the central visual image.[182] The paper tended to assume a certain level of sexual knowledge and experience of its readers, but offered advice on how to improve sexual technique and develop an understanding of the opposite sex. Some more basic educational material remained, as did moralizing condemnations of

[180] ALRA Papers, A11, *ALRA Newsletter*, winter 1967, No. 20, 9.

[181] For example, *Daily Express*, 22 Nov. 1965, 13; *Daily Express*, 23 July 1966, 6.

[182] P. Holland, 'The Page Three Girl Speaks to Women, Too: A Sun-Sational Survey', *Screen*, 24/3 (1983), 84–102.

those who deviated from the paper's sexual norms, but there was a clear shift in emphasis towards fun and fantasy.

The paper's pleasure agenda was evident in the first week of the relaunch in November 1969. 'We Enjoy Life and We Want You to Enjoy it with Us' declared the first Pacesetters section for women.[183] The sexual dimension of this enjoyment was clear in the feature 'Undies for Undressing', illustrated with a photo of a model in satin bra and knickers set.[184] Readers were also enticed with the first instalment of a week-long serialization of 'The Book Every Woman Wants to Read'—Jacqueline Susann's erotic bestseller *The Love Machine*.[185] The second issue included the first topless pin-up, and two days later the paper led the front-page with the headline 'Men are better lovers in the morning—Official'.[186] The paper was unapologetically providing entertainment, information, and guidance for a young, sexually informed target audience. 'The *Sun* is on the side of youth' declared an editorial at the end of the first week. 'It will never think that what is prim must be proper. . . . It believes that the only real crime is to hurt people.'[187]

Characteristic of the *Sun*'s approach was the serialization in October 1970 of Joan Garrity's sex manual *The Sensuous Woman*. The paper tantalized its readers with the fact that the book was so explicit that its own copies of the book had at first been impounded by British customs officials. 'It is the most outspoken sex manual ever written', the paper claimed, although it added that it would omit sections 'not suitable for publication in a family newspaper'.[188] Garrity claimed to be able to show all women how to be 'sexually irresistible' and 'experience a full, fulfilling and joyous sex life' by improving their self-awareness and honing their sensuality through a series of 'sexercises'.[189] The *Sun* printed several of these 'sexercises', through which women would 'train like an athlete for the act of love': most involved developing the sense of touch by caressing and massaging the body or using the tongue. Readers were also advised to practise moving their 'pelvis and bottom as if they were loaded with ball-bearings'.[190] As well as working on physical technique, women were encouraged to lose their inhibitions and become more adventurous. Garrity suggested experimenting with the 'enticing possibilities of body paint and harem costumes', moving out of the bedroom—'Unusual surroundings excite most men'—and discovering 'secret sexual longings': 'If you can act the fantasy out for him, what a thrill you'll give him. Go on—try!'[191] The series encouraged women to enjoy and indulge their sexuality, but conventional gender stereotypes were still evident—much of the advice was framed around the traditional goal of pleasing a man.

[183] *The Sun*, 17 Nov. 1969, 14. [184] Ibid., 33. [185] Ibid., 23–6.

[186] *The Sun*, 18 Nov. 1969, 2; *The Sun*, 20 Nov. 1969, 1. [187] *The Sun*, 22 Nov. 1969, 2.

[188] *The Sun*, 6 Oct. 1970, 1. [189] *The Sun*, 6 Oct.1970, 6; 7 Oct. 1970, 6–7.

[190] *The Sun*, 7 Oct. 1970, 6–7; 8 Oct. 1970, 8–9.

[191] *The Sun*, 10 Oct., 1970, 11; 13 Oct. 1970, 9; 9 Oct. 1970, 10–11.

Underlying this advice was a post-Christian, consumerist vision of relationships, in which loyalty could not be expected and unsatisfied partners would seek a better experience elsewhere. 'If you are going to stop him from straying, you must give him the variety and adventure of love at home that he might find, and easily, elsewhere. . . . Married or not, loving you as he does, he will not stop looking and maybe sampling another woman.'[192] But women were told to be equally demanding. Garrity advised women who had found partners who were ideal 'in every way' but lacked sexual chemistry to pass them on to sisters or friends.[193] The expression of sexuality was defined as the chief function of a good relationship: without sexual fulfilment, it seemed, a relationship could not survive.

At the end of the serialization, the *Sun* gave its columnist Elizabeth Prosser space in which to express her dismay at the lack of attention to love and romance in Garrity's advice.[194] But editorial staff were delighted with the impact it had with readers. It became known in the *Sun*'s office as 'the "definitive corker", the standard against which all other serialisations were measured'.[195] With its emphasis on pleasure, physical technique, and the realization of fantasy, *The Sensual Woman* was an accurate guide to the way in which the press coverage of sex was moving. Such features became common: a sequel, *The Sensuous Couple*, was serialized, and in subsequent years the *Sun* also offered its readers a 'Guide To Sensual Massage' and 'The Lovers' Virility Guide' (with six 'Sexercises For The Passionate Twosome').[196] These were supported by fashion pages which showed women how to 'Be his dream girl in clothes that tempt'.[197] Sex had become the central feature of the private self and great sex a required part of modern lifestyle. Proops noted in 1976 that 'Aggrieved women ask why they don't get an adequate number of orgasms'; indeed 'questions about orgasms are as commonplace as complaints about mothers-in-law'. Yet had she received such a letter when at the *Herald* in the early 1950s, she would 'have fainted dead away on the office floor'.[198]

The success of the *Sun* encouraged rivals to produce similar features, and this style of writing about sex gradually spread throughout the popular press. Some journalists, such as Proops, remained committed to older, more 'educational' approaches. In order to compete, however, this material had to become ever more direct and detailed. The best example of this approach was the *Daily Mirror*'s 'Guide to Sexual Knowledge' in August 1975, overseen by Proops. This was probably the most explicit series on sex ever printed in the national press, and in many ways the apogee of this form of educational popular journalism.

[192] *The Sun*, 10 Oct. 1970, 11.
[193] *The Sun*, 12 Oct. 1970, 12.
[194] *The Sun*, 14 Oct.1970, 9.
[195] P. Chippindale, and C. Horrie, *Stick it up your Punter! The Uncut Story of the Sun Newspaper* (London: Simon and Schuster, 1999), 33.
[196] Ibid; *The Sun*, 15 Jan. 1973, 14–15; *The Sun*, 23 Jan. 1973, 16–17.
[197] *The Sun*, 9 Feb. 1976, 14–15.
[198] Proops, *Dear Marje*, 24–5.

Parents were warned to 'allow your children to read it at your discretion'.[199] Covering several pages over two days, it was in many respects an uncomfortable mix of traditional and more modern styles of writing about sex. The series was justified squarely in terms of public ignorance. 'It is shocking that even mature men and women know so little about the facts of life that they are unable to teach their children how they came into the world', the paper declared. 'Only knowledge and understanding' could reduce the 'appalling statistics' of unwanted pregnancies and abortions.[200] There was a clear moral dimension, with the writers trying to maintain an essential connection between sex and love: 'When it is nothing more than physical gratification, sexual intercourse holds little significance. When it is part of a loving relationship, it can be the perfect culmination of love.'[201]

At the same time, the series demonstrated that popular journalism by the 1970s was able to shed the euphemisms that had been so typical in earlier decades. The sheath, for example, was described as 'a soft thin rubber covering for the penis which prevents ejaculatory fluid coming into contact with the vagina'.[202] The advantages and disadvantages of different methods of contraception were discussed in considerable detail, and illustrated with diagrams which would not have been out of place in a biology textbook (**Illustration 2.3**). The sexuality of babies and young children was addressed, as were the sexual needs of older men and women.[203] And in a nod to more recent trends, explicit advice was given about sexual technique, aimed in particular at men who were failing to satisfy their partners:

> the technique of bringing a woman to climax is simple. Arousing the woman before the sexual act is both necessary and important. It is best achieved by gentle stroking of her sexual zones: the breasts and nipples, inner thighs and arms, lower back and the clitoris—the small sensitive organ, a kind of miniature penis, lying between the folds of skin above the entrance to the vagina. But there are endless variations which lovers can employ to excite each other. Kissing is part of arousal and the exploration by the tongue of the sexual zones can bring quick response. Kissing of the genitals, known as oral sex, while highly gratifying to many, is repugnant to some. No practice which offends either partner ought to be persisted in, though at the same time, unless lovers are experimental they will never discover new pleasures.[204]

This passage provides a vivid demonstration of the extent of the shift since 1918.

For some readers, the *Mirror* had exceeded the bounds of what was possible in a 'family newspaper'. A Mrs de Luca from Edinburgh complained to the Press Council that the level of detail was 'out of place in a national newspaper within easy reach of children' and the series could in fact be seen as being 'pornography

[199] *Daily Mirror*, 12 Aug 1975, 1.
[200] Ibid.
[201] *Daily Mirror*, 12 Aug. 1975, 5.
[202] *Daily Mirror*, 12 Aug. 1975, 13.
[203] *Daily Mirror*, 12 Aug. 1975, 5, 12–13; 13 Aug. 1975, 5.
[204] *Daily Mirror*, 12 Aug. 1975, 5.

EUROPE'S BIGGEST DAILY SALE

5p Tuesday, August 12, 1975 * * * No. 22,252

IGNORANCE, irresponsibility, apathy: these are the main reasons why more than a third of the 600,000 babies which will be conceived this year will be unplanned and unwanted.

- IT IS SHOCKING that between three and four million couples take no contraceptive precautions when they make love.
- IT IS SHOCKING that adolescents as young as 12 and 13, engage in sex without knowledge of the act of love, or its consequences; that some teenagers regard the use of a contraceptive as "chicken."
- IT IS SHOCKING that even mature men and women know so little about the facts of life that they are unable to teach their children how they came into the world.

Irresponsibility and ignorance resulted, last year alone, in 220,000 unwanted pregnancies. Out of this number, there were 110,000 abortions and 64,617 illegitimate births.

THESE FIGURES ADD UP TO A DEVASTATING TOTAL OF HUMAN MISERY.

Today and tomorrow we publish a no-nonsense guide to sex. Only knowledge and understanding can reduce the appalling statistics.

PARENTS PLEASE NOTE:
This issue of the Daily Mirror contains a guide to sexual knowledge: allow your children to read it at your discretion

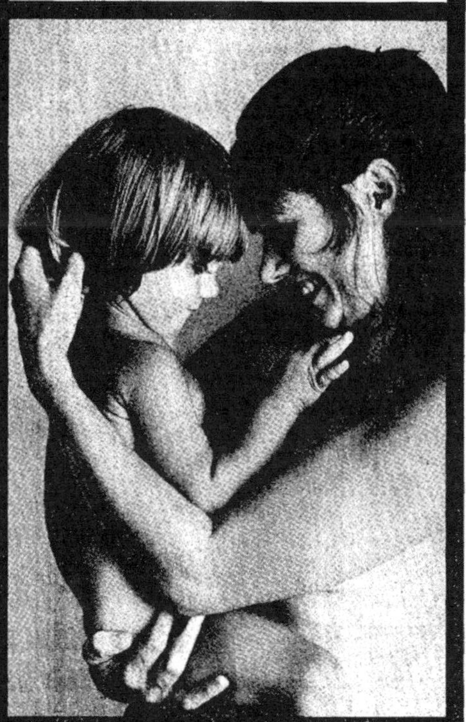

THE MIRROR GUIDE TO SEXUAL KNOWLEDGE

EDITED by MARJORIE PROOPS

PLEASE TURN TO PAGE 5

Illustration 2.3. **'The *Mirror* Guide to Sexual Knowledge'**, *Daily Mirror*, 12 Aug. 1975, 1, 13. This 1975 *Daily Mirror* series illustrates how explicit sex education features had become by the end of the period.

THE MIRROR GUIDE TO SEXUAL KNOWLEDGE

BIRTH CONTROL

What must be remembered is that a method which suits one couple may not be enjoyed by another

IN the past people thought man had nothing to do with procreation.

Those nine months between the sex act and child-birth puzzled our ancestors and they assumed a woman must have eaten something or fallen under a spell to produce a baby.

Even when the link between a woman's menstrual cycle and producing a baby became apparent, men stood aside from what was thought to be entirely women's work.

Fortunately today, science replaces superstition; the Pill replaces prayer.

Since women are less embarrassed about asking to "go on the Pill" than they were about making hesitant inquiries about Dutch caps, more than two million British women use this method—easily the most widely-prescribed system of birth control.

While all contraceptive methods have their good and bad points it must be remembered that a method which suits one couple may not necessarily suit another.

But it's safe to say, as far as reliability is concerned, that the contraceptive Pill, intra-uterine devices, Dutch caps and sheaths are the most efficient.

Only where they prove impractical or unacceptable should sterilisation be considered.

The Pill

WHEN a woman is pregnant she cannot produce another egg for fertilisation—her sex glands secrete hormones which prevent it.

Oral contraception, [illegible] pill made from two manufactured chemicals called progrestogen and oestrogen, produces the same effect.

Oral contraceptives neither affect a woman's ability to have a baby nor make it likely that her fertile span will be prolonged.

The Pill can be obtained only on a doctor's prescription and is available free on the National Health Service for any woman, regardless of age or whether you are married or single.

ADVANTAGES: Simple to use, it gives the woman final say in the size of her family. And provides virtually 100 per cent protection against pregnancy.

Free from fear of an unwanted pregnancy women appear to enjoy a more satisfying sexual relationship with their husbands.

The Pill also provides special benefit for women with heavy, painful or irregular periods.

DISADVANTAGES: Because of its action on the rest of the body, the Pill could speed up blood-clotting. For women with a history of high blood pressure, obesity, diabetes, phlebitis or severe varicose veins there can be a danger of thrombosis.

There can be side-effects like depression, lack of sexual feeling, headaches, gaining weight, rashes and vaginal discharge.

Often though, a change of pill eliminates side effects.

The Sheath

THIS is a soft, thin rubber covering for the penis which prevents ejaculatory fluid coming into contact with the vagina. [illegible] years of use, the sheath has proved itself efficient and any failure is likely to come from faulty use.

ADVANTAGES: Cheap and easy to buy. A sheath is easily put on by unrolling it over an erect penis before intercourse.

DISADVANTAGES: The chief one is the interruption in the rhythm of intercourse. All sexual contact between penis and vagina must be limited to when the sheath is on. Otherwise, there is a danger of pregnancy when slight escape of seminal fluid precedes ejaculation. They have been known to tear.

Rhythm method

DEVOUT Roman Catholics who regard all artificial methods of contraception as sinful, practise the natural rhythm method, also known as "the safe period."

This is based on having no intercourse at all during the fertile days in a woman's menstrual cycle.

Her fertile days—when ovulation takes place—are fourteen to sixteen days before a period starts, so a woman who practises this method must keep an accurate record of her cycle.

Since so many women have irregular periods, even the most conscientious record-keeper is liable to blunder.

ADVANTAGES: More spiritual than practical.

DISADVANTAGES: A totally unreliable method.

Chemical contraceptives

IN the form of creams, jellies, pastes, vaginal pessaries and aerosol foams, these contraceptives form a barrier and are lethal to sperms but harmless to the body tissues.

The most efficient is an aerosol foam, which, like all the chemical contraceptives, is used only by women and does not need a doctor's prescription.

A measured dose of foam is released into a plastic applicator which the woman presses into her vagina and the foam is pushed out into the neck of the womb.

ADVANTAGES: Cheap and easily bought at chemists.

DISADVANTAGES: Used by themselves, chemical contraceptives are highly unreliable.

Aerosols apart, the creams, pastes and jellies do not penetrate the deepest parts of the vagina to destroy the millions of sperms in each ejaculation.

TOMORROW: What to tell your children

INTRA-UTERINE DEVICES

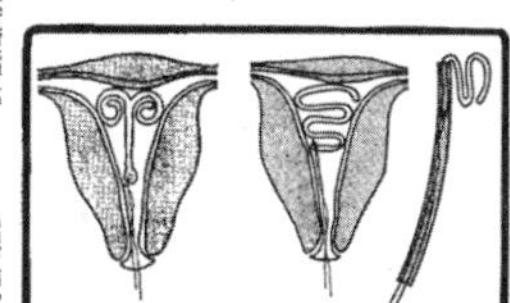

NO one quite knows how the Loop, Bow and Spiral work—but they do.

They are made of light plastic and insertion into the womb by a doctor is speedy—five to fifteen minutes—and relatively pain-free for a woman who already has children.

ADVANTAGES: Once it is in position, the device can stay there indefinitely and it needs no help from the woman.

DISADVANTAGES: A doctor will rarely fit a device into a woman who has had no children because her narrow womb entrance makes insertion more complicated.

Heavy painful periods can be made worse.

A woman who has persistent abdominal pains might find it unsuitable and it can be expelled involuntarily and unnoticed.

STERILISATION

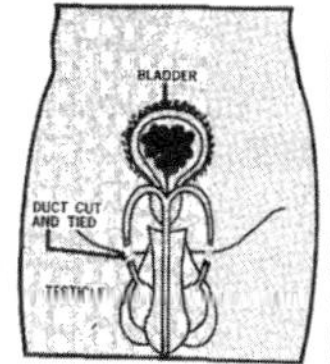

BECOMING more and more popular. Sterilisation is claimed to be a permanent method suitable for a couple who already have a large enough family. Either adult can be sterilised but whoever has the operation must have their spouse's written permission.

For a man, sterilisation is a simple operation. For a woman, the Fallopian tubes are cut and tied which involves a seven to ten day stay in hospital.

ADVANTAGES: Unplanned pregnancies cannot happen. For men, virility and sexual performance remain unchanged.

For women, sexual feelings and performance are unimpaired.

DISADVANTAGES: For men, the operation is irreversible. For women with heavy family responsibilities, the main disadvantage is a stay in hospital.

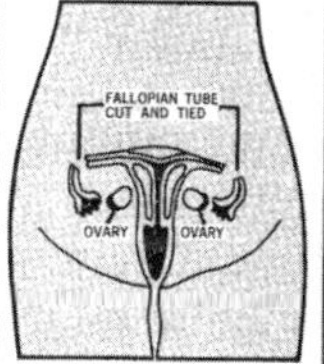

DUTCH CAPS

THE cap, which looks like a small saucer, comes in sizes to suit individual pelvic measurements. After the first fitting and instruction by doctor or nurse, a woman can handle a cap herself.

Some time before intercourse she must squeeze special sperm-killing jelly or cream over the cap. Then she inserts it in much the same way that she inserts an internal sanitary tampon.

The cap must not be removed until at least six hours after the sexual act.

ADVANTAGES: Highly efficient, it has no physical side-effects. It does not interfere with intercourse.

DISADVANTAGES: There is a risk of pregnancy for the woman who had had faulty instruction in fitting the cap or who inserts it wrongly.

NECK OF WOMB (CERVIX)
WOMB
CAP
VAGINA
BLADDER

GRAPHICS by LEE and TERRY DICKIE

Illustration 2.3. continued

used solely for boosting sales'. The editor of the *Mirror*, Michael Christiansen, defended the paper by employing the idealistic language developed since the Second World War, arguing that the series had been placed with the 'sole object of helping to prevent so much human unhappiness'. The Press Council rejected the complaint, recognizing that the series 'could have given offence to some people' but concluding that it could not 'reasonably be interpreted as pornographic'.[205] In many respects, however, this controversy had a rather dated feel. This sort of material would become less common, as the emphasis on sexual pleasure and titillation increased. Advising and informing came to seem rather old-fashioned: entertainment was now pushed to the forefront. In the years ahead, the resources devoted to reader advice services would be cut back severely. Soon after taking over the *News of the World*, Rupert Murdoch closed the John Hilton bureau to cut costs—indeed advice columns would soon be expected to make money by advertising expensive pay phone lines.[206] In this new era, problem columns would need to fulfil different needs. Kelvin MacKenzie, editor of the *Sun* between 1981 and 1994, asked for the printed letters to be more 'dirty', and remodelled the advice pages to included titillating photo strips.[207]

Amongst all the sensational and titillating material in popular newspapers it is easy to overlook the more serious and informative articles about sex. There is a long tradition of sneering at the advice column;[208] historians have, furthermore, tended to highlight those moments when the popular press made conservative or obstructive interventions in debates about sexual welfare.[209] And it is true that newspaper articles on sex frequently came laced with heavy doses of morality and prejudice. Yet for many ordinary readers, with many fundamental gaps in their knowledge about sex, newspapers could offer useful guidance and instruction. Thousands and thousands wrote to advice columnists; millions read with interest educational features. The surveys following the *Mirror*'s 1942 VD campaign demonstrated that newspapers could have a major impact on the public understanding of sexual welfare issues. For women, in particular, advice columns and feature articles by prominent female columnists provided a space in

205 Press Council, *Annual Report 1976*, 99–100.

206 C. Bainbridge, and R. Stockdill, *The News of the World Story: 150 Years of the World's Bestselling Newspaper* (London: HarperCollins, 1993), 234.

207 Chippindale and Horrie, *Stick it up your Punter*, 109.

208 Kent, *Agony*, Introduction.

209 For example, the *Express*'s 'Lord Dawson Must Go' piece (Soloway, *Birth Control*, 187), and its resistance to the wartime VD campaign (J. Weeks, *Sex, Politics and Society: The Regulation of Sexuality since 1800* (London: Longman, 1981), 216; Davenport-Hines, *Sex, Death and Punishment*, 266–7; R. Porter and L. Hall, *The Facts of Life: The Creation of Sexual Knowledge in Britain, 1650–1950* (New Haven: Yale University Press, 1995), 241–2; Hall, *Sex, Gender and Social Change*, 134–5); the resistance to sex education programmes in schools (Hampshire and Lewis, 'The Ravages of Permissiveness', 302–4; the reaction to the AIDS crisis (Davenport-Hines, *Sex, Death and Punishment*, 6–7).

which female sexuality and issues of concern such as contraception and abortion could be discussed sympathetically and sensitively. By coming to define sexual health as a matter of public, rather than merely private, concern, the popular press made a significant contribution to the process in which Britons became more knowledgeable and self-conscious about sex.

3

Surveying Sexual Attitudes and Behaviour

Popular newspapers have an insatiable demand for information about the habits and opinions of the public. Such information has always had a considerable news value, because most people are curious to find out more about the lives of others; it is also of great professional interest to journalists who want to understand their audience. Popular papers rhetorically claim an allegiance with their readers, and work hard to convey the impression that they are 'in touch' with them and take their views seriously.[1] The traditional conduit for this information was the reader's letter, and in many papers the letters page had a genuine editorial and symbolic significance. Readers were invited to express their views on the issues of the day, and it was believed in Fleet Street that the stream of letters into newspaper offices could be used to track shifts in the state of public opinion. The *Daily Mirror* could feel the 'people's pulse-beat' during the Second World War, Hugh Cudlipp argued, because 'All the clues were in the *Mirror*'s postbag from its readers'.[2]

The development of modern, statistically weighted techniques of market research and opinion polling in the late 1920s and early 1930s raised the prospect that large populations could be studied much more 'scientifically'. The British Institute of Public Opinion (BIPO) introduced George Gallup's random sample methodology into Britain in 1937; in the same year Tom Harrisson, Charles Madge, and Humphrey Jennings established Mass-Observation to conduct an 'anthropology of ourselves'.[3] Popular newspapers were soon using the findings of these and other organizations. The *News Chronicle* took the lead, regularly publishing the results of BIPO surveys from October 1938: these would, the paper claimed, reveal 'with accuracy and without bias, what Britain thinks'.[4] In 1942 Beaverbrook suggested that the *Express* develop its own system for carrying out surveys, and an *Express* Centre of Public Opinion was accordingly

[1] On the rhetoric of allegiance, M. Conboy, *The Press and Popular Culture* (London: Sage, 2002).

[2] H. Cudlipp, *Publish and Be Damned! The Astonishing Story of the Daily Mirror* (London: Andrew Dakers, 1953), 136.

[3] L. Beers, 'Whose Opinion? Changing Attitudes Towards Opinion Polling in British Politics 1937–64', *Twentieth Century British History*, 17/2 (2006), 177–205; N. Hubble, *Mass Observation and Everyday Life: Culture, History and Theory* (Basingstoke: Palgrave Macmillan, 2006).

[4] Beers, 'Whose Opinion?', 183.

established.[5] Polls and surveys of all kinds, covering everything from voting intentions to shopping preferences, became a staple of the newspaper formula in the post-war years. In the process, the press consolidated certain ideas about the state of contemporary society, about trends in opinion, about 'normal' behaviour; readers were able to compare themselves to others more directly than ever before.

The introduction of surveys had a particularly significant impact on the understanding of 'normal' sexual attitudes and behaviour. Before the Second World War, reliable evidence about sexual activity was very scarce, and journalists and commentators were free to offer their own opinions with little fear of being proven wrong. Most shared the belief that Britons, and British women in particular, generally exercised a high degree of sexual restraint and adhered to strict moral standards. This was part of an imperial world view which portrayed the British as a 'civilized' race able to control their physical and sexual urges, unlike the more animalistic and expressive peoples of Africa and Asia. Many agreed that habits had changed since the Victorian period, and there were anxieties that sexual restraint had been dangerously undermined by the upheavals of the Great War. Despite this, faith in the underlying decency and morality of the British people remained very strong.

After the Second World War, these assumptions were placed under increasing scrutiny by the new methods of social investigation, often with unsettling results. Sexologists, doctors, psychologists, and social scientists displayed a new determination to collect data that would enable more rigorous and ambitious research into sexual behaviour. Inspiration was provided by the pioneering work of the American scientist Dr Alfred Kinsey, whose *Sexual Behavior in the Human Male* (1947) and *Sexual Behavior in the Human Female* (1953) were based on thousands of interviews conducted across the United States. The British press not only gave considerable publicity to Kinsey's work, it also encouraged related research in Britain. The *Sunday Pictorial* provided the funds for Mass-Observation to conduct its 'Little Kinsey' survey in 1949, and the following year *The People* commissioned Geoffrey Gorer to investigate marriage and sex as part of his exploration of English character. These early British surveys focused on attitudes to sex rather than on sexual behaviour itself, but they helped to undermine the notion that the British public would not respond favourably to direct questioning on sexual issues, and hence paved the way for further studies. Popular newspapers developed an ongoing interest in sex surveys of every type, enthusiastically speculating about the meaning of the latest findings. Many of these findings challenged older assumptions about patterns of sexual behaviour—for example, about the extent of extra-marital sex, or the prevalence of homosexual activity—and press reports helped to establish new ideas and

[5] House of Lords Record Office, Beaverbrook Papers, H/112, Beaverbrook to Robertson, 7 May 1942.

expectations of 'normal' sexuality. More broadly, the discussion of the 'sex lives' of ordinary men and women reinforced the notion that the old reticence surrounding sex was unnecessary, and that it was natural, and indeed productive, to talk about and reflect on one's sexual experiences.

By the end of the 1960s, press reports about the sexual behaviour and attitudes of the young generation had considerably eroded older assumptions about a chaste Britain. There was much discussion of contemporary 'permissiveness', and Britannia was now often portrayed as a flirtatious youth rather than a demure maiden. The diversity of British society was ever more apparent, and it became harder and harder for the popular press to identify and champion shared attitudes and standards of behaviour. In particular, it was more difficult for newspapers to keep 'in touch' with younger readers while defending the family values that were such a central part of their identity, and divisions opened up between those papers prepared to welcome the new sexual freedoms and those nostalgic for a Britain that had disappeared.

THE GREAT WAR AND CHANGING SEXUAL MORES

In July 1922, at the conclusion of a sensational three-week divorce trial in which Lord John Russell, the heir of the Ampthill peerage, accused his wife of adultery and promiscuity (see Chapter 4), the *Daily Express* reassured its readers that the proceedings in the courtroom did not reflect the reality of married life in post-war England. 'The manners and morals laid bare during this case were so freakish,' the paper protested, 'that it is absurd for moralists to use the "revelations" as whips with which to chastise modern society'.[6] A retrial was conducted the following March, and the *Express*'s response was identical:

> The mass of Englishmen and Englishwomen, whatever their birth, means, and education, continue to lead orderly and decent lives—to sleep, eat, work, and love—undisturbed and, we believe, uninfluenced by these revelations of a state of affairs that by the very token of its notoriety is proved the exception to the rule . . . life and love, loyalty and goodness remain among us. The ideals are not dethroned by the folly of fools.[7]

This insistence that most ordinary people led 'orderly and decent lives', and remained 'uninfluenced' by 'the folly of fools', was typical of the popular press. During the second half of the nineteenth century Victorian moralism fused with ideas of racial superiority to consolidate the belief that sexual respectability was a defining characteristic of the British (or, in this case, the English) people.[8] Sexual restraint became a central element of the versions of British identity championed in commercial forms of popular culture, from fiction to film.

[6] *Daily Express*, 24 July 1922, 6. [7] *Daily Express*, 17 Mar. 1923, 6.

[8] M. Mason, *The Making of Victorian Sexuality* (Oxford: Oxford University Press, 1994).

Journalists celebrated family values not only because they regarded it to be their social duty, but also because they thought these values were shared across classes and regions. 'No woman doubts marriage', declared another *Express* editorial during the first Russell trial, 'She knows that it is the most nearly perfect institution in this imperfect world'.[9]

It was widely recognized, nevertheless, that patterns of sexual behaviour were not static and during the inter-war period many commentators concluded that the younger generation no longer adhered to the strict moral standards laid down by their Victorian predecessors. Most identified the Great War as responsible for this shift. During the conflict many people were presented with new sexual opportunities as families were temporarily broken up and traditional forms of supervision curtailed. Rising rates of venereal disease and illegitimacy lent credence to stories of servicemen consorting with prostitutes or being seduced by 'khaki girls'.[10] Far from being a temporary suspension of normal standards, however, a consensus emerged in the early 1920s that the wartime experience had had a long-term impact on a whole generation. The war, it seemed, had irreversibly loosened some of the restraints imposed by society—as Viscountess Helmsley wrote in the *Weekly Dispatch*, it had 'stirred the primitive in men and women'.[11]

Although both sexes had been affected, most commentators were preoccupied with the change in young women. The 'girl of today' had lost her innocence, lamented 'W.A.S.' in the *Daily Express* in 1920: 'The great war has stamped its memory ineffaceably upon her mind with associations of a general collapse of morality'.[12] Explaining in the *Weekly Dispatch* 'Why Women's Manners Are Lax', the feminist writer Cicely Hamilton suggested that female manners and fashions could be explained by the fact that 'Prolonged warfare induces the spirit of savagery, which strives to get back to that lack of ceremony and scanty costume of the savage'.[13] For the novelist Elizabeth Marc, writing in the *Daily Mail* in 1921, the 'girl of today' was 'as much a war product as a high income tax and poison gas', and the 'extravagant manners of both sexes' were simply 'the result of extraordinary conditions'. She suggested sympathetically that the craving for excitement was an instinctive response to the pain of the war and that the laughter of the 'unmannerly girl' might 'hide tears'.[14] This interpretation of the impact of the war long retained its plausibility. Anthony Gibbs, son of the noted war correspondent Sir Philip Gibbs, argued in the *Daily Herald* in 1930 that during the war 'All standards were abolished, especially the standards of Christianity,

[9] *Daily Express*, 15 July 1922, 6.

[10] A. Woollacott, 'Khaki Fever and its Control: Gender, Class, Age and Sexual Morality on the British Homefront in World War 1', *Journal of Contemporary History*, 29/2 (1994); P. Levine, ' "Walking the streets in a way no decent woman should": Women Police in World War 1', *Journal of Modern History*, 66/1 (1994).

[11] *Weekly Dispatch*, 20 Mar. 1921, 8.

[12] *Daily Express*, 12 Nov. 1920, 6.

[13] *Weekly Dispatch*, 27 Feb. 1921, 8

[14] *Daily Mail*, 11 Aug. 1921, 4.

and the youth of the world discovered that, far from being nasty, sex was rather nice', with the result that Britain 'entered on a period of libertinism'.[15] Indeed, one of the most pressing fears on the outbreak of the Second World War was that sexual morality would degenerate once again.[16]

The actual evidence for a 'period of libertinism' is sketchy, and these contemporary judgements strike most historians as exaggerated.[17] Many commentators seem to have made unwarranted inferences about sexual behaviour after observing very real shifts in the social interaction of the sexes after the war. Mixed-sex environments were gradually becoming more common as women obtained new employment opportunities, gained political rights, and participated in new forms of leisure, such as the cinema. The spread of the practice of 'mixed bathing' on Britain's beaches was one of the prime symbols of this easier social interaction, and developed into a long-running talking point in the columns of the *Daily Mail* in the 1920s.[18] The expectation that unmarried women would be accompanied by chaperones was decreasing, and many observers were surprised by the confidence with which 'the girl of today' conversed with men. In February 1921, for example, the *Weekly Dispatch* highlighted some 'startling illustrations' of the 'freedom with which young men and women strike up acquaintance in public places'. The 'stories of haphazard friendships begun without prudence or modesty by young unmarried girls living in respectable homes' seemed 'incredible' to the leader-writer, only to be believed because of the reliability of the witnesses.[19]

For some commentators this social mixing was a healthy relief from the unnatural repressions of Victorian society. 'The girl of today has to thank the war for her emancipation from the restrictions which bad, sad old Mrs Grundy sought for her so long to place upon her masculine friendships', declared Mrs Gordon Stables in the *Express*. Greater freedom would enable her to develop a 'far profounder understanding of her fellow man'.[20] In 1925 a contributor to the *Mail* could celebrate the fact that 'the relations between the sexes have changed to such an extent that it is at last possible for two persons of opposite sexes to meet regularly without regarding each other as a potential husband or wife'.[21]

Others warned that such easy mixing of the sexes might threaten the ideal of (female) chastity before marriage. Mary Boazman in the *Mail* argued that

[15] *Daily Herald*, 23 May 1930, 8.

[16] S. Rose, 'Sex, Citizenship, and the Nation in World War II Britain', *American Historical Review*, 103/4 (1998), 1147–76.

[17] J. Weeks, *Sex, Politics and Society: The Regulation of Sexuality since 1800* (London: Longman, 1981), ch. 11; L. Hall, *Sex, Gender and Social Change in Britain since 1880* (Basingstoke: Macmillan, 2000), ch. 6.

[18] A. Bingham, *Gender, Modernity and the Popular Press in Inter-War Britain* (Oxford: Oxford University Press, 2004), 167–8, 171; C. Horwood, '"Girls Who Arouse Dangerous Passions": Women and Bathing 1900–39', *Women's History Review*, 9/4 (2000), 653–73.

[19] *Weekly Dispatch*, 27 Feb. 1921, 8.

[20] *Daily Express*, 7 May 1919, 3.

[21] *Daily Mail*, 23 Feb. 1925, 8.

the war had taught society that 'A girl cannot sow her wild oats as a man has been accustomed to do' and she advised the 'prudent mother' to accompany her daughter to 'all subscription dances, at least until she is over twenty'. The consequences for Britain of too great a freedom were dire: 'Its young girls are the nation's very precious jewels. Upon their purity and sense of right depends the future well-being of the nation, and the pity is great if either is injured by careless guardianship.'[22] The *Weekly Dispatch* was likewise adamant that Britain could not maintain its greatness if sexual morality was undermined: 'No community can exist indefinitely under such conditions. The standards of conduct will have to be altered, to revert to something of the regularity of Victorian days, if the race is to live up to its responsibilities in a very envious world.'[23]

If the freer mixing of the sexes prompted anxieties about declining sexual standards, so too did a perceived increase in the mixing of ethnic groups. The African and Asian communities in Britain increased in size in this period, and there were a number of incidents, including the race riots of 1919 in London, Liverpool, and a number of other major ports, and the post-war 'dope scare', that drew press attention to them.[24] The influence of national and racial stereotypes on assumptions about sexual behaviour was particularly conspicuous in the coverage of ethnic minorities. Reports repeatedly emphasized the physicality, sexual aggressiveness, and lack of restraint of non-white individuals. Newspapers were quick to identify sexual tensions as a contributing factor to the 1919 race riots. As the historian Lucy Bland has observed, 'over and over again the press and the authorities cited white men's fury at interracial relationships' as one of the main causes of the disturbances.[25]

Most commentators suggested that such relationships were inherently unstable and provocative due to racial incompatibility. 'It is naturally offensive to us that coloured men should consort with even the lowest of white women', argued the *Sunday Express*. 'Racial antipathy is always present, the sex jealousy inflames it to a violent, unreasoning wave of emotion.'[26] For the *Liverpool Courier*, the problem was simply that 'The average Negro is nearer the animal than is the average white man'.[27] Such notions were rarely challenged. Many left-wing commentators, despite professing to believe in racial equality, shared many of these assumptions about excessive black sexuality. It was, after all, the *Daily Herald* that gave greatest prominence to the campaign (led by the socialist journalist Edmund

[22] *Daily Mail*, 13 July 1920, 6. [23] *Weekly Dispatch*, 27 Feb. 1921, 8.

[24] P. Fryer, *Staying Power: Black People in Britain since 1504* (London: Pluto, 1984), ch. 10; C. Holmes, *John Bull's Island: Immigration and British Society 1881–1981* (Basingstoke: Macmillan, 1988); M. Kohn, *Dope Girls: The Birth of the British Drugs Underground* (London: Lawrence & Wishart, 1992).

[25] L. Bland, 'White Women and Men of Colour: Miscegenation Fears in Britain after the Great War', *Gender and History*, 17/1 (2005), 34.

[26] *Sunday Express*, 15 June 1919, cited in Bland, 'White Women', 36.

[27] *Liverpool Courier*, 11 June 1919, cited in Bland, 'White Women', 36.

Morel) against the 'Black Horror on the Rhine', namely the use by France of colonial African troops to police the German Rhineland. As headlines made clear, this was a specifically 'Sexual Horror', driven by allegations that the 'barely restrainable bestiality of the black troops' resulted in the rape of numerous white women.[28]

If African men were portrayed as potentially violent sexual predators, Asian men tended to be described, using well-entrenched stereotypes of the 'Oriental', as mysterious and devious individuals who seduced white women by trickery or the offer of drugs. The *Sunday Chronicle*'s 'special correspondent', travelling through Limehouse, 'London's Chinatown', in 1919, was 'impressed by the number of white women who lounge in the doorways, nurse their children on the steps, or wait in the small general shops which abound'. These women had been corrupted by some 'deep, irresistible influence' of their 'Asiatic' husbands: they were 'insensible to the degradation into which they sink, and unquestionably fulfil the behest of their masters', acting as 'decoys, or mediums, for the disposal of opium'.[29] Readers were advised that the 'half-caste' children would inherit 'the worst characteristics of both parents': 'any student of eugenics will tell you that the boy in whose blood surges the twin tides of Orientalism and Occidentalism has impulses only the slow process of western civilisation has kept in leash.'[30] In 1920 a magistrate warned of 'moral and physical suicide of unhappy girls fascinated by the yellow man', and a number of prominent court cases in the early 1920s consolidated the stereotype of British women being bewitched into the drug trade by inscrutable Chinese men.[31]

Such cases merely stiffened the resolve of newspaper contributors to advise against interracial relationships. In the *Daily News*, Helen Hope, one of the first regular press problem columnists, declared in 1922 that she was 'now perfectly convinced that racially-mixed marriages are a mistake and should be discouraged from every point of view'.[32] An article in the *People* drew attention to cases where Indian men had shocked their British wives by committing suicide when their marriages had run into difficulties, because their Oriental background encouraged them to consider death as a 'panacea' for all ills.[33] The weight of the evidence presented to readers of popular newspapers was that different ethnic groups were socially and sexually incompatible.

In the absence of any representative studies of sexual behaviour, press discussion of contemporary trends inevitably remained anecdotal and strongly swayed by existing assumptions about gender, race, and class. Journalists offered sweeping generalizations based on personal observation, hearsay, or the evidence of

[28] *Daily Herald*, 10 April 1920, 1; R. Reinders, 'Racialism on the Left: E. D. Morel and the "Black Horror on the Rhine"', *International Review of Social History*, 13 (1968), 1–28; P. Levine, *Prostitution, Race and Politics: Policing Venereal Disease in the British Empire* (New York: Routledge, 2003), 170–1.

[29] *Sunday Chronicle*, 23 Mar. 1919, 3.

[30] Ibid.

[31] Bland, 'White Women', 44.

[32] *Daily News*, 11 Nov. 1922, 6.

[33] *The People*, 28 Sept. 1928, 5.

the latest court case. The *Daily Mirror* came closest to conducting its own research when in 1937 the columnist Cassandra asked readers to tell him about their romantic experiences—although his questions were restricted to the relatively safe topics of the age of first date, first kiss, and marriage, and the number of marriage proposals received. From an impressive total of 50,432 replies, the paper calculated that the average age at the first kiss was fifteen years and three months, five months after the first date; here, once again, was evidence of the restraint of the British.[34] British women also seemed to be discerning in matters of the heart—Cassandra was 'amazed' to find that the average female respondent received three offers of marriage, before marrying at twenty-four.[35] But such features, entertaining as they were, revealed little about sexual activity. The popular press generally reinforced the idea that sexual mores were changing, and in particular that young women were becoming more assertive, but specific details were scarce. And for all the discussion of a swing away from 'Victorian' standards, it was clear whenever comparisons were made with other races and nations that the underlying faith in the decency and restraint of the British people remained more or less intact.

THE EMERGENCE OF THE SEX SURVEY

Cassandra's light-hearted poll of 1937 was a reflection of the growing press interest in public opinion surveys. By the late 1930s a wide range of social investigators and research organizations were developing what they presented as 'objective' and 'scientific' methods to measure trends of opinion and patterns of behaviour, and thereby offer the prospect of a constant flow of accurate and reliable information about society. Surveys were carried out on many topics, but it took an unusually determined American scholar, Professor Alfred Kinsey of Indiana University, to apply the methods to the large-scale study of sexual behaviour.[36] His pioneering *Sexual Behavior in the Human Male* (1948), based on 12,000 oral interviews, claimed to reveal, for the first time, the facts about intimate sexual activities in America, and it ushered in a new era of sex research. The press took up the task of completing the circle of communication, telling the public what had been discovered. In Britain, some newspapers went a step further by financing surveys and exclusively publishing the findings.

Despite the furore caused on its publication in America, Kinsey's *Human Male* initially received little attention in the British press. Much of the early

[34] *Daily Mirror*, 30 June 1037, 10; H. Cudlipp, *Walking on Water* (London: Bodley Head, 1976), 58.

[35] Ibid.

[36] J. Gathorne-Hardy, *Alfred C. Kinsey. Sex: The Measure of All Things—A Biography* (London: Pimlico, 1999).

coverage was due to the efforts of David Mace, the well-connected secretary of the Marriage Guidance Council. Mace praised Kinsey's 'most important research' in his regular column in *The Star* in January 1948, before producing a longer feature article for the *Sunday Pictorial* the following month.[37] Mace emphasized both Kinsey's impartiality—'He had no axe to grind, no theory to bolster up, no commodity to sell'—and his rigour. His 'skill as an interviewer' was 'superb', and he was able to extract the 'truth' from respondents. The result was nothing less than a record of 'what people are doing with sex, at the present time', in the United States, backed with irrefutable scientific evidence. He recognized that the work would provoke intense debate, but his faith in the power of education led him to declare that 'nothing but good can come . . . . Knowledge of the truth will set us free from false values.'[38]

Mace's analysis of the report's findings developed themes that would dominate the British press's discussion of Kinsey's work. First, he highlighted the extent and range of sexual activity uncovered by the survey—that 'masturbation among men is practically universal', that 'homosexual practices are far more common than is generally known' and that 'sexual power develops surprisingly early in some boys and continues till very late in life'. Indeed—and this was what Kinsey himself sought to emphasize—'variations in individual sexual patterns are so great that it is almost impossible to define what "normal" sex is'. Mace predicted that the findings would cause a 'sensation' among the public, and suggested in particular that 'Many who have suffered agonies because they thought themselves exceptional and abnormal will have a great burden lifted from their minds'.[39] It is indeed likely that the preconceptions and anxieties of many of the *Pictorial*'s 15 million readers were challenged by this summary of the work of the 'unshockable' American professor. Other articles reinforced the message of sexual variation. Jenny Nicholson, after admitting that she could only address a few aspects of the report in the 'non-scientific, medical-columnless' *Sunday Dispatch*, revealed that 'So-called perversions occur in "from 40 to nearly 75% of large segments of normal, socially well-adjusted populations" '. She also highlighted the extent of marital infidelity, noting that 'about one-third to one-half of all married men are unfaithful to their wives at one time or another.'[40] Like Mace, she pointed out that the results were not in line with conventional beliefs: American women were 'discovering all sorts of things about the American man they hadn't even guessed at'.[41]

At the same time, Mace's assumptions about British standards of behaviour led him to doubt that the results would have been quite so high had the research been conducted in Britain rather than the United States. The 'general impression in this country is that the code of sexual behaviour is more lax in America than in Britain', he observed, and suggested that 'on the whole it does look

[37] *The Star*, 6 Jan. 1948, 6; *Sunday Pictorial*, 1 Feb. 1948, 7.
[38] *Sunday Pictorial*, 1 Feb. 1948, 7.
[39] Ibid. [40] *Sunday Dispatch*, 29 Feb. 1948, 4. [41] Ibid.

as if this impression is justified'. Kinsey had found, for example, that some three-quarters of American men had engaged in premarital sex before the age of 20, but Mace declared he 'would be surprised if the figure proved as high' in Britain. He also believed that the average American child was 'allowed a great deal more freedom and is less severely disciplined than here'.[42] Similar comments were made when the study was published in Britain at the beginning of 1949. 'Kinsey's findings on pre-marital intercourse will certainly not be taken as applying to this country' declared a contributor to the *Pictorial.* British wives would be 'shocked' at rates of marital infidelity in America, 'but they will not accept the premise that the same thing happens here'.[43] The notion of America as a brash and emotionally unrestrained society was a powerful one in British culture, and had been reinforced by wartime tales of the behaviour of American GIs stationed in Britain.[44] Such ideas encouraged some to dismiss the relevance of Kinsey's figures to Britain's more moral society.

If the Kinsey Report could not provide a guide to British attitudes and behaviour, it stimulated curiosity about what research in Britain would uncover. The *Sunday Pictorial*, the paper that had given the most attention to the *Human Male*, believed such research worthy of investment as a continuation of its crusade to open up the public discussion of sex. It found a willing partner in the form of Mass-Observation. The organization had been interested in investigating sexual attitudes for some time, but had struggled to find the necessary finances to set up the project; Tom Harrisson was therefore 'deeply grateful' when the *Pictorial* offered to buy newspaper rights for the findings of its projected sex survey.[45] Mass-Observation's research was not on the same scale as Kinsey's, and the focus was on attitudes rather than behaviour. Interviews were conducted with 2,052 members of the public, and information about sexual experiences was obtained from 450 people from Mass-Observation's voluntary panel. For all its limitations, the research was, as the sociologist Liz Stanley has noted, of great importance as the 'first national random sample survey of sex to be carried out' in Britain.[46]

By financing and publishing what was dubbed the 'Little Kinsey' survey, the *Pictorial* made a very significant contribution to the cause of sex research in Britain. This survey has misleadingly been described as 'hidden', 'lost', and 'unpublished', because Mass-Observation did not produce the pamphlet it had originally intended, and because the *Pictorial*'s role has been downplayed.[47] In

[42] *Star*, 6 Jan. 1948. [43] *Sunday Pictorial*, 2 Jan. 1949, 5.

[44] Rose, 'Sex, Citizenship and the Nation'; D. Reynolds, *Rich Relations: The American Occupation of Britain, 1942–45* (London: HarperCollins, 1996).

[45] T. Harrisson, 'Preface' to Mass-Observation's Sex Survey of 1949, reprinted in L. Stanley, *Sex Surveyed* (London: Taylor & Francis, 1995), 68.

[46] Stanley, *Sex Surveyed*, 3–4.

[47] The press release for a BBC4 programme on Little Kinsey (first broadcast 5 October 2004) claimed that 'The findings of Little Kinsey were considered so outrageous and shocking that

fact the *Pictorial* gave the survey far greater publicity than Mass-Observation could have managed on its own. Harrisson and Mass-Observation director Len England were, moreover, impressed by the paper's hands-off approach to the project. Harrisson made clear that the *Pictorial* 'left us entirely free to do the survey in any way we liked' and provided 'an object lesson of editorial good manners' by not attempting to distort or exaggerate the results.[48] Mass-Observation sent full reports to the *Pictorial* 'for their own staff to condense into a form suitable for its own readership', and the final versions of the articles—including pictures and headlines—were returned to the organization and its assesors for comment before publication. England confirmed that 'in every case all suggestions made by MO and the assessors were incorporated without question in the articles'.[49]

The results of the research were published in five substantial articles under the title 'The Private Life of John Bull' in July 1949.[50] The articles were advertised heavily in the preceding weeks—including on the front page—as 'the most important human document of our times'.[51] Great emphasis was placed on the fact that the research had been conducted impartially by an 'independent scientific social research group' and was being presented neutrally with no attempt 'to draw any conclusions'.[52] The *Pictorial*, once again, deployed an idealistic rhetoric and displayed its faith that presenting the 'facts' to readers would change Britain's sexual culture. It argued that the series 'tears away the veil of false modesty which, for so long, has hampered frank discussion and recognition of certain facets of our way of life'.[53] Not only would the articles encourage this 'overdue' discussion, they would 'undoubtedly influence our standards of behaviour'.[54] And indeed the *Pictorial* could find support for its crusade to spread sexual knowledge in the results of the survey, with four-fifths of respondents admitting they had received no formal sex education, and the same proportion advocating that such education be given.[55]

The central theme of the report was the existence of 'considerable individual confusion in a world of rapidly changing moral values'. Traditional Christian morality remained important—and 'clear divisions of opinion' were found between churchgoers and non churchgoers—but Mass-Observation discerned 'a move away from the Church's teachings towards greater sexual freedom'.[56] The researchers were 'certain' that there was 'more tolerance or passive acceptance of

they have been buried in an archive in the University of Sussex', and this claim was repeated in many newspaper articles on the programme: http://www.bbc.co.uk/pressoffice/pressreleases/stories/2005/09_ september/06/4autumn_decade.shtml, accessed 19 Oct. 2007. See also Stanley, *Sex Surveyed*, ch. 2.

48 Ibid.

49 Mass-Observation File Report 3110A, Len England, 'Little Kinsey', 18.

50 *Sunday Pictorial*, 3, 10, 17, 24, 31 July 1949.

51 *Sunday Pictorial*, 19 June 1949, 9; 26 June 1949, 1.

52 *Sunday Pictorial*, 19 June 1949, 9.

53 *Sunday Pictorial*, 3 July 1949, 6–7.

54 *Sunday Pictorial*, 26 June 1949, 1.

55 *Sunday Pictorial*, 3 July 1949, 6–7.

56 Ibid.

practices which were vehemently denounced by our grandfathers'. For example, a third of respondents were prepared to 'give approval to some form of sexual relationship outside marriage', particularly those in which the partners were engaged or living together; the researchers suggested that a similar proportion, 'and probably more', had actually engaged in such extra-marital intercourse.[57] There was a 'general feeling' that divorce was 'often a regretful necessity' and should be available on grounds of incompatibility rather than just infidelity, cruelty, or desertion.[58] About two-thirds of respondents were also in favour of birth control.[59] Ignorance remained significant, and a majority believed that sex could in certain circumstances be 'unpleasant' and 'harmful', but the conviction that the sex instinct was 'natural' was widespread and a third felt that happiness was not possible without sex.[60]

The trend to 'greater sexual freedom' appeared to be confirmed by the article discussing the sexual behaviour of Mass-Observation's panel of 450 volunteers. This piece was advertised on the front page as 'the most intimate report ever published in a British newspaper', and given the detail it provided, the claim was not without foundation.[61] The results revealed that despite social disapproval a significant amount of extra-marital sex was occurring. A quarter of husbands and a fifth of wives admitted to being unfaithful, and 49 per cent of unmarried men and 38 per cent of unmarried women claimed to have had intercourse. One man in seven had slept with more than four women, and a quarter had slept with prostitutes. Within marriage sexual satisfaction was high at 75 per cent, although the report identified a 'very marked' gender divide with women less happy—a finding that would be replicated in many future surveys. Many husbands felt that 'more cooperation' from their wives would improve love-making, and their spouses often admitted the same, but women all too often found their sexual experiences 'unsatisfying emotionally'.[62]

The *Pictorial*'s boldest editorial decision, however, was to include figures concerning homosexuality, masturbation, and sexual fantasy. In a section entitled 'perversions', the paper recorded that 12 per cent of respondents had experienced 'homosexual relations' at some point in their life, and a further 8 per cent 'had known milder homosexual relations'. It also revealed that only 5 per cent of men, and a third of women, never masturbated, while half admitted to having day-dreams about 'love-making or other sexually-exciting situations'. Two per cent believed themselves to have abnormal 'sadistic and masochistic inclinations or fetishes'.[63] Such material was highly unusual in a British newspaper, and although the implications of the figures were not explored, many readers must have been surprised by the near universality of masturbation, and

[57] *Sunday Pictorial*, 10 July 1949, 6–7.
[58] Ibid.
[59] *Sunday Pictorial*, 24 July 1949, 5.
[60] *Sunday Pictorial*, 3 July 1949, 6–7.
[61] *Sunday Pictorial*, 17 July 1949, 1.
[62] *Sunday Pictorial*, 17 July 1949, 6–7.
[63] Ibid.

the commonness of homosexual experience, given the moral disapproval both provoked. Mass-Observation underlined that it was not possible to know how the habits of the sample compared with the rest of the population, but the findings seemed to confirm other evidence that everyday behaviour did not conform to traditional morality.

Len England monitored the reaction to the survey closely and found that the *Pictorial* articles elicited a broad range of responses. Some individuals simply dismissed the project as 'pornographic'.[64] The Labour backbencher Stanley Evans was among this number, lambasting the articles in the House of Commons as 'real "stinkers"' and declaring that 'who went to bed with whom and how many times is no sort of Sunday morning breakfast reading for young girls and boys'.[65] But England was pleased that such comments were 'rare' and that there had 'certainly been no public outcry of any description'. This was 'perhaps remarkable in view of the very popular circumstances of its first appearance and of its lack of the academic background of the Kinsey Report'.[66] Some complained that the survey was rather 'sketchy', which he was prepared to accept given the limitations imposed on the research, or that it was 'obvious', a harsh criticism given the pioneering nature of the project. Yet others reacted very positively. One man asked for his views on current affairs, and 'quite unaware that the investigator to whom he was talking was a Mass-Observer', ignored 'atom bombs, economic crises, strikes, and droughts', and said 'that the most important thing in the news was a series of articles in a Sunday newspaper telling him enlightening facts about the sex question!'[67] More prominent support was obtained from the Labour MP Marcus Lipton (then campaigning to reform the divorce laws) who argued that the survey 'shows what people are thinking on matters of vital importance to the nation' and suggested that copies of the series should be sent to all Members of the House of Commons.[68] More generally, the continuing circulation growth of the *Pictorial* seemed to show that readers were attracted to the paper's bold approach to sexual issues.

The impact the series made in Fleet Street is perhaps best indicated by the decision of *The People*, the *Pictorial*'s main competitor for 'second place' in the Sunday market behind the *News of the World*, to commission a survey of its own. In 1950 the *People* approached the social scientist Geoffrey Gorer to lead a wide-ranging investigation of English character, to be conducted by a large survey of the paper's readers. The focus of this exercise was by no means exclusively on sex, but attitudes to love, sex, and marriage did form a major part. Gorer admitted to having reservations about collaborating with a publication which, he noted wryly, 'did not automatically command the respect

[64] M-O File Report 3110A, 21.

[65] 467 H.C. Debs, 5s, Royal Commission on the Press (Report), 28 July 1949, col. 2786.

[66] M-O File Report 3110A, 21. [67] Ibid. [68] *Sunday Pictorial*, 17 July 1949, 1.

of my colleagues', but he was won over by the opportunity of using a substantial research department to process the results and by the paper's commitment to conducting parallel surveys to test the representativeness of the sample.[69] The *People* was just as willing as the *Pictorial* to invest in serious research that would appear credible to readers. The *People* was, however, rather more cautious than its rival about the sorts of questions that could be asked about personal matters. Its editorial team told Gorer that his question designed to uncover views about women's sexual nature might cause 'offence': to Gorer's regret, a specific enquiry about women's 'sexual climax' became a more general one about women's enjoyment of 'the physical side of sex'.[70] Once all such issues had been resolved, an invitation for volunteers appeared on 31 December 1950, and by the end of January 1950 over 10,500 completed questionnaires had been received.[71] The responses were analysed and Gorer produced a series of eight articles which were published in the *People* in August and September 1950.[72] A fuller discussion of the findings was published in book form in 1955 as *Exploring English Character*.

The *People* sought to capture public attention by leading with the material on sex and marriage. The first instalment was publicized with advertisements asking 'Are We An Immoral Nation?' and for the first three weeks the findings on personal relationships were examined. Rivals certainly identified the sexual content as the central element—the *Express* Director E. J. Robertson told Beaverbrook that the series was an 'English version of the Kinsey Report'—even if the discussion was not particularly explicit. (Robertson thought that the first article would 'disappoint people who bought *The People* in the hope of getting some salacious reading').[73] In contrast to the earlier surveys, however, Gorer emphasized the sexual conservatism of his respondents. 'The young people of England are terribly shy—particularly in relation to the opposite sex,' he observed, adding that he had 'impressive evidence that young English men and women have a very high standard of morality'.[74] ('I very much doubt whether the study of any other urban population would produce comparable figures of chastity and fidelity', he concluded in *Exploring English Character*.)[75] He found, for example, widespread disapproval of sex before marriage among young people, even for those who were engaged. Two-thirds of men married the first woman in which they were seriously interested.[76] Gorer argued that 'this strict code of sexual conduct is maintained in adult life', even though some two-fifths of husbands admitted to 'straying' after marriage (many of these were put down to prolonged separation, such as during the war). He believed it significant that very

[69] G. Gorer, *Exploring English Character* (London: Cresset Press, 1955), 4–6.
[70] Ibid, 26, 33. [71] Ibid., 8–9.
[72] *The People*, 12, 19, 26 Aug., 2, 9, 16, 23, 30 Sept. 1950.
[73] Beaverbrook Papers, H/151 Robertson to Beaverbrook 13 Aug. 1951.
[74] *The People*, 12 Aug. 1951, 4. [75] Gorer, *Exploring English Character*, 87.
[76] Ibid.

few men or women placed 'glamour' or 'sex appeal' high in their list of desirable attributes for partners.[77]

Gorer's results also indicated that the double standard of morality remained powerful, and that it was often upheld more strongly by women than men. A quarter of women wanted their 'future husband to know something about sex', but only one in eight expected the same privilege for themselves: many insisted that they would 'lose their self-respect' and 'would feel cheap and tawdry' if they engaged in premarital sex.[78] Women were less likely than men to cite sexual compatibility as the reason for a happy marriage, and whereas 60 per cent of men believed that women enjoyed sex as much as or more than men, only just over a third of women agreed.[79] Indeed, Gorer himself showed signs of the double standard he observed in others, implicitly accepting that it was part of the husband's role to take the lead in the bedroom.[80]

Gorer and Mass-Observation painted rather different pictures of British sexual culture. They wholeheartedly agreed, however, that a lack of sexual knowledge made it very difficult for many people to develop fulfilling physical relationships. 'Many marriages,' Gorer argued, were 'wrecked from the start simply because the bridegroom is woefully ignorant on sex matters'.[81] They also identified the problems caused by men and women having different expectations about sex and finding it hard to communicate their desires. Perhaps most important of all, they demonstrated that the supposedly reserved British people were prepared to talk about these private issues. In so doing they provided a justification for further research and inspired extensive public debate about everyday sexual activity.

THE KINSEY FURORE OF 1953

By the time Kinsey's research on *Sexual Behavior in the Human Female* was published in 1953, the British press was much more accustomed to discussing the sex lives of ordinary people than they had been in 1948. The contrast between the amount of space devoted to the two reports was remarkable. In 1949 David Mace declared himself surprised at how 'little attention' the *Male* volume had received; in 1953, one commentator lamented that the press had 'for weeks' in advance of the official publication date of 20 August been beating 'the publicity drum declaring that the day of glorious revelation was at hand'.[82] The *Daily Sketch*, the *Daily Mirror*, the *Sunday Pictorial*, and the *Sunday Dispatch* produced substantial articles on the research before the findings were released, but they were all outdone by the *People*, which provided an accurate preview of many of the key

[77] *The People*, 26 Aug. 1951, 4; 19 Aug. 1951, 4.
[78] *The People*, 19 Aug. 1951, 4.
[79] *The People*, 19 Aug. 1951, 4; 26 Aug. 1951, 4.
[80] *The People*, 12 Aug. 1951, 4.
[81] Ibid.
[82] *Sunday Pictorial*, 2 Jan. 1949, 5; *Sunday Express*, 23 Aug. 1953, 4.

statistics in the report.[83] On publication day the 'Kinsey Report' was front page news in many popular papers (**Illustration 3.1**). The following Sunday, no fewer than eight of the main eleven national papers featured Kinsey—the exceptions were the *News of the World*, the *Sunday Times* and the *Observer*—and all printed extra copies to meet the expected demand.[84]

The British public was therefore bombarded with articles discussing the sex lives of women across the Atlantic. As in 1948, the general tone was one of surprise at the extent of sexual activity that Kinsey had uncovered; indeed, the expectation that women had stricter standards of sexual behaviour than men made the statistics shocking to many. The most widely reproduced findings were that nearly half of respondents had engaged in premarital sex, and that more than a quarter of wives had had affairs while married (many of the latter with encouragement from their husbands). There was also considerable interest in the finding that masturbation and sex with other women were both common, albeit not at the levels found in the male population. '62% had engaged in self-stimulation, 58% to the point of climax', while a fifth 'had had sexual contacts with other females' noted the *Herald*.[85] The *People* provided information about the frequency of sexual activity. Younger married women, the paper reported, 'have sex relations on an average three times a week. By the time the woman is 30 this drops to just over twice a week'. It added that the 'average unmarried girl between the ages of 15 and 35 goes on two "petting expeditions" a month'.[86]

As well as evidence of women's sexual appetite, however, the report confirmed the significant levels of sexual incompatibility and ignorance found in other surveys. The *Mirror* highlighted Kinsey's argument that women were as sexually responsive as men, but were often turned off by their partner's poor technique: 'Female "frigidity" is a man-made situation . . . . They [men] go far too quickly and offer a variety of love-making that may mean little to a woman'.[87] All of this coverage seems to have been lapped up by curious readers. A circulation report for the *Sunday Express* found 'considerable public interest' in the articles but because 'the subject was so well catered for' no particular paper gained an advantage.[88]

The report provoked far more controversy in the British press than any earlier sex survey. Some sceptics questioned the whole basis of Kinsey's research. Peter Marshall in the *Sketch* suggested that Kinsey was 'selling sex' in a bid for personal fame; for Cassandra in the *Mirror* Kinsey was a 'ghastly post-mortemist

[83] *Daily Sketch*, 12, 14, 15 Aug. 1953; *Daily Mirror*, 12, 14 Aug. 1953; *The People* 16 Aug. 1953, 1, 7; Beaverbrook Papers, H/164 Robertson to Beaverbrook, 17 Aug. 1953.

[84] Beaverbrook Papers, H/164, E. J. Robertson to Beaverbrook, 26 Aug. 1953.

[85] *Daily Herald*, 20 Aug. 1953, 4.

[86] *The People*, 16 Aug. 1953, 1.

[87] *Daily Mirror*, 20 Aug. 1953, 8–9.

[88] Beaverbrook Papers, H/164, E. J. Robertson to Beaverbrook, 26 Aug. 1953.

Daily Mirror

THURS AUG. 20 1953

1½d FORWARD WITH THE PEOPLE No. 15,479

WOMEN

THE SHOCKS IN THE KINSEY REPORT

DR. ALFRED C. KINSEY, THE WORLD'S No. 1 SEXO-ANALYST, BLOWS THE GAFF TODAY ON ALL ABOUT EVE. HIS AMAZING REVELATIONS ABOUT AMERICAN WOMEN WILL SET THE WORLD TALKING, BLUSHING OR SCOFFING.

These are some of the shocks:

NEARLY HALF the married women questioned had not been virgins when they walked to the altar.

MORE THAN A QUARTER had been unfaithful to their husbands.

FOUR OUT OF FIVE WOMEN had indulged in petting or necking by the time they were eighteen.

[Startlingly, too, petting gets a good mark from Kinsey. The girl who pets, he says, is more likely to wed than the girl who doesn't.

Parents, he finds, indulge in widespread petting as well—with other men or women—because it is socially more acceptable than adultery.]

ABOUT TWO-THIRDS of marriages run into trouble over sex.

MEN, despite their many affairs, still like to marry virgins. But few **WOMEN** think their husbands-to-be should be "innocent."

MOST MEN don't know how to make love. They approach it wrongly, think women are stimulated by the things that arouse men.

WOMEN stay young longer than men in the business of love making. Women reach their peak around thirty, and keep it well through their fifties.

MEN are at their peak between 15-20—decline in the middle twenties and go on declining.

MODERN WOMEN are less inhibited than their mothers and grandmothers were. This change has been going on since the "new freedom" that women found after World War I. And it is the reason why parents don't worry about youth today as much as their own parents did.

WOMEN are not different from men when it comes to love. They can respond as quickly as men. They don't, though, mainly for psychological reasons—which the men have much to do with.

FEMALE FRIGIDITY is a man-made situation.

Kinsey makes it plain that his sensational findings do not represent the love life of women all over the world.

The investigation took him and his associates fifteen years to prepare. Nearly 6,000 females, from children to grandmas, revealed their secrets.

The result is a mighty volume called "Sexual Behaviour in the Human Female." It will be published next month.

KINSEY'S BIGGEST BOMBSHELL—SEE CENTRE PAGES

300 killed as army throws out Mossadeq

AFTER nine hours of bloody street fighting, Persia's Premier Mossadeq and his Government were thrown out last night by troops loyal to the Shah.

And the Army—on the side of the Shah—now rules Persia.

More than 300 people died in the savage battles that raged in Teheran, the capital. Hundreds more were injured.

Mossadeq escaped the mob that for hours fought in pitched battle outside his house with his personal bodyguard.

But his right-hand man, Hussein Fatemi, his Foreign Minister, was caught by the mob and hacked to pieces in the street.

Fatemi.

Mossadeq is reported to be under arrest. His rescue from the mob was carried out by the new Premier, Major-General Zahedi, who sent an armed guard to [illegible] (American).

They got him out just as the big iron gates were battered down. The mob found the house fortified with steel and concrete like a Hitler bunker. They tore through it smashing windows, breaking doors and wrecking furniture.

Most of the day's casualties were in the battle outside Mossadeq's house. His guard fought on until their ammunition was finished. Teheran officials said their last stand cost 200 lives.

'Bomb Him Out' Order

General Zahedi, as a last resort, had ordered the loyalist air force to bomb the house. But a message thrown from it announced Mossadeq's resignation and pleaded with the mob not to attack him.

Reports from all over Persia said that the pro-Shah forces were in control of the situation everywhere.

Late last night the victorious loyalists were clearing out the last remnants of pro-Mossadeq resistance. They had used Sherman tanks, guns and bazookas to bombard strongholds.

General Zahedi, the man named as Premier by the Shah before he left Persia at the week-end, last night ordered martial law, a curfew, and the closing of all shops except those of butchers, grocers and bakers.

The gaol doors in Teheran were opened and all Mossadeq's political prisoners were freed.

Before the curfew came into operation crowds roamed the streets of Teheran shouting "Long live the Shah" and "Down with his enemies," and re-erecting statues of the Shah which had been taken down by Mossadeq's supporters.

Mob Fires Buildings

General Zahedi's coup started at 9 a.m. Mobs armed with sticks and stones massed in the southern part of the capital and they were joined by soldiers and uniformed police.

By noon the mobs closed in on the centre of Teheran. Eight buildings were fired as the marching crowds, flanked by five tanks and twenty lorries, moved on.

By 4 p.m. the loyalists had control of most Government offices—and the radio station.

Then in short dramatic sentences, the story of the victory was broadcast to the world.

Finally, the radio announced that the Shah, now in Rome with his Queen Soraya, had been recalled.

The "Daily Mirror" Correspondent in Rome reported last night:

The Shah, overcome with emotion at the news of General Zahedi's victory said that he would return to his country as soon as calm had been restored.

But he said that Queen Soraya would not go back with him yet. She would stay in Europe for a time on holiday.

How's that!

WELL, here it is—the victory wave all Britain had been hoping for. And this is England skipper Len Hutton giving it soon after his Test team's smashing win over the Australians at the Oval yesterday.

Later, the England team held a party in the Oval pavilion. It broke up soon after six o'clock when several players, smoking cigars, left carrying bottles of champagne.

And last night the little town of Pudsey, in Yorkshire, Hutton's birthplace, was preparing a "proper do" for England's captain, with a public reception in the market square.

"We saw a mighty victory," says Peter Wilson.—Page 15.

Illustration 3.1. 'Women—The Shocks in the Kinsey Report', *Daily Mirror*, 20 Aug. 1953, 1. This *Daily Mirror* front page demonstrates the press's intense interest in Professor Alfred Kinsey's research into the sex lives of American women.

tearing out the entrails of incipient love', unnecessarily scavenging in the 'colossal compost heap of rotting human behaviour'.[89] Several right-wing or traditionalist commentators were disturbed at what they saw as the absence of any moral dimension, and accused Kinsey of encouraging promiscuity, particularly with his suggestion that petting often aided later sexual adjustment. 'This is propaganda for what is sometimes called Free Love' declared 'Candidus' in the *Sketch*: Kinsey is recommending laws to suit the sex urge . . . legislation which would sweep away the present structure which is commonly called the moral code.'[90] In a more measured article in the *Mirror*, headlined 'Stop Praising Petting', advice columnist Mary Brown challenged Kinsey's 'tacit' support for petting, warning that 'petting to the limit' could cause 'psychological and spiritual harm'.[91]

In the left of centre papers, by contrast, there were some notable defences of both sexological research and the public discussion of sex. The Methodist leader Leslie Weatherhead, writing in the *News Chronicle*, argued that by improving public understanding of sex, the report would improve marital happiness and lessen delinquency. 'The place where evil most flourishes', he contended, 'is in the shadows of ignorance, half-knowledge, false values and distortion'.[92] The *Daily Herald* used similar rhetoric to assert that 'Lack of information about sex has caused immense mischief and misery' and concluded that 'Dr Kinsey's work brings into the open facts which ought to be known and frankly discussed'.[93] And although it gave space to critical voices, a *Mirror* editorial outlined the paper's conviction that Kinsey had produced a 'serious and important book' and that the public was 'entitled to know what he says and discuss what they think about it': 'We do not treat the public as babies. We do not want to censor their information.'[94] These papers remained wedded to the arguments of the educationalists that spreading knowledge would help to eradicate the incompatibility and unhappiness that Kinsey and others had graphically documented.

There were similar divisions over whether Kinsey's findings reflected behaviour in Britain. Many conservative critics held fast to the conviction that Britain remained a moral and restrained nation, as Gorer had found. 'Is one of every four wives in the City of Birmingham unfaithful to her husband?' asked 'Candidus' in the *Sketch*. 'The thought is just too fantastic for any reasonable man and woman to believe.'[95] The findings were based on 'confessions of exhibitionists'.[96] Mary Brown posed the same question and suggested that in Britain one unfaithful wife in fifty might still be too high, based on the 'thousands of letters' she had

[89] *Daily Sketch*, 12 Aug. 1953, 4; *Daily Mirror*, 14. Aug. 1953, 4.
[90] *Daily Sketch*, 21 Aug. 1953, 4.
[91] *Daily Mirror*, 22 Aug. 1953, 5.
[92] Cited in *Daily Herald*, 21 Aug. 1953, 4.
[93] *Daily Herald*, 21 Aug 1953, 4.
[94] *Daily Mirror*, 22 Aug 1953, 2.
[95] *Daily Sketch*, 20 Aug. 1953, 4.
[96] *Daily Sketch*, 14 Aug. 1953, 4.

read as an agony aunt.[97] The '*Herald* Doctor', on the other hand, accepted that Kinsey's results probably applied 'to many other women in many other countries'. He certainly agreed that the overall trend was that 'Younger women have a more complete, more enjoyable, less inhibited sexual life today than their mothers ever knew'.[98] The *Mirror*'s leader-writer was uncertain, but argued that it was disingenuous of critics to claim that all of Kinsey's respondents were exhibitionists: 'the whole lot can't have been freaks'.[99]

Enterprising journalists sought to uncover some relevant evidence in Britain. Eric Wainwright surveyed ten youth clubs for the *Mirror* and found that 'a lot of necking went on'; leaders in every district complained, moreover, that 'parents allow girls of fourteen and fifteen to stay out until midnight and later'. This 'parental fecklessness' shocked Wainwright 'more than anything Kinsey has unearthed'.[100] More ambitiously, the *People* conducted a nationally representative survey of 1000 randomly selected women on many of the issues raised by Kinsey. Although the methodological differences between the surveys made direct comparisons problematic, the *People* confidently asserted that its results indicated that British women were 'much more moral, more conventional and more faithful to the marriage bond than the American women of the Kinsey Report'. Whereas more than a quarter of Kinsey's respondents admitted infidelity, for example, only one in nine of the *People*'s sample did so.[101] At the same time, the *People*'s survey did find evidence that 'the sexual urge of women is greater than is commonly supposed, that it is strongest among mature women and is not entirely satisfied inside the marriage convention'. Many women expressed discontent with their sexual relationships, with the average respondent satisfied by intercourse less than half the time.[102] Once again, the obstacles that women faced in achieving sexual pleasure were placed under the spotlight.

The intense debate surrounding the Kinsey Report in August 1953 was the first time that ordinary sexual behaviour had been discussed in detail across the spectrum of the press. Previous surveys had either been exclusive serializations or had stirred only limited attention; this time very few popular papers—the *Daily Express* was the notable example—chose to ignore the report. This sense of a turning point in the press coverage of sex was reflected in the numerous protests and complaints that this journalism provoked. One of the most prominent of these was made by the *Sunday Express*'s veteran columnist (and former editor) John Gordon at the height of the Kinsey frenzy. Under the headline 'Our Sex-Sodden Newspapers—It is Time to Speak Out Against this Degradation', Gordon lamented that the Kinsey report had provided British papers with the opportunity to engage in 'a sexual orgy beyond all their previous exhibitions'. As a relatively expensive book, he argued, the report carried little moral danger,

[97] *Daily Mirror*, 22 Aug. 1953, 5
[98] *Daily Herald*, 21 Aug. 1953, 4; 22 Aug. 1953, 3.
[99] *Daily Mirror*, 22 Aug. 1953, 3.
[100] *Daily Mirror*, 22 Aug. 1953, 5.
[101] *The People*, 23 Aug. 1953, 6.
[102] Ibid.

but 'spread across the pages of newspapers with its salacities highlighted, it is deliberate, calculated pornography'. By the 'skilful handling of type, headlines and layout', furthermore, the press gave 'salacity an emphasis and a glamour which may well convince young and impressionable minds that morality is old fashioned and immorality the right thing in this new age'. He concluded that 'a considerable section of our Sunday Press, and a smaller section of our daily Press, has become a menace of some considerable gravity to the moral standards of the nation', and called on all responsible citizens to take a stand against 'brothel journalism'.[103] Gordon's article, *Express* director Robertson told Beaverbrook, 'produced the biggest response from readers for many years', with the paper receiving a total of 575 letters commenting on the column (Gordon claimed that only two of these letters were not supportive of his position).[104]

Another well-publicized attack came from Reverend Joseph Christie in a sermon delivered in Westminster Cathedral, in which he complained that the press had transformed a scientific inquiry into 'cheap pornography'.'In order to indulge the profit motive the proprietors of some of our newspapers are prepared to invade the sanctuary of young souls and encourage them to viciousness.' 'Their work', he cautioned, 'can warp young lives'.[105] A number of religious bodies and citizens' organizations, including the British Council of Churches, the National Women Citizens Association, and the Public Morality Council, sent complaints to the newly established Press Council. Discussing the matter in its second ever meeting, the Council concluded that it was necessary to respond to the public unease and issue a warning to Fleet Street. While 'defending the right of the Press in the contemporary world to deal in an adult manner with matters of sex', the Council declared that it was 'deeply concerned by the unwholesome exploitation of sex by certain newspapers and periodicals'. It recorded its view that 'such treatment is calculated to injure public morals especially because newspapers and periodicals are seen and read by young persons'.[106]

This resolution appeased some of the press's critics, but because the Council had no disciplinary powers, Fleet Street could safely ignore it. In reality, the ruling was imprecise and confused, and offered little genuine guidance for the future. It made no attempt to identify when and in what ways the discussion of a serious piece of sex research had drifted into 'exploitation'. The Council simply highlighted the eternal ambiguity of the popular press's position by imploring it to write in an 'adult manner' while remaining conscious of its younger audience. Editors and journalists continued to outmanoeuvre critics by switching between these two positions as necessary. The *Mirror* defended its coverage by arguing 'We

[103] *Sunday Express*, 23 Aug. 1953, 4.

[104] Beaverbrook Papers, H/161, Robertson to Beaverbrook, 26 Aug. 1953; Atkins to Robertson, 8 Sept. 1953; *World's Press News*, 11 Sept. 1953, 11.

[105] As reported in *The Times*, 31 Aug. 1953, 2; *Sunday Express*, 30 Aug. 1953, 4.

[106] Press Council, *The Press and the People: First Annual Report* (London: Press Council, 1954), 21.

do not treat the public as babies. We do not want to censor their information'.[107] But, of course, it continued to use the 'family newspaper' tag when it suited. Unwilling and unable to address this confusion, it was evident that the Press Council would find it impossible to restrain newspapers from exploring sexual issues.

Despite the warning of 1953, therefore, the sexual habits of the public remained an important topic for the popular press. The *Sunday Pictorial*, for example, devoted seven weeks in 1956 to a serialization of Dr Eustace Chesser's survey of *The Sexual, Marital and Family Relationships of the Englishwoman*.[108] Journalists pored over the results of investigations conducted in other nations to see what lessons could be learned for Britain.[109] Each survey provided different results with slightly different implications, but it is reasonable to conclude that the overall impact was to encourage a greater self-reflexivity about sex.[110] Individuals were invited as never before to compare themselves to others, to think about the quality of their sexual experience. Everyone was now regarded as having a 'sex life' which could be scrutinized, measured, and improved.

PERMISSIVE BRITAIN?

During the 1960s and 1970s many of the assumptions underpinning earlier discussions of sexual behaviour were challenged. As British society became conspicuously more pluralistic it became increasingly difficult to invoke shared standards of sexual morality. Church attendances were in steady decline and the Christian teachings on marriage and the family lost much of their influence; higher levels of immigration into Britain brought different ideas about sexuality and relationships; a consumerist youth culture and hedonistic counter-culture placed greater emphasis on pleasure and instant gratification.[111] As Britain's international position declined, moreover, it became harder to defend notions of British superiority. The idea that British people were uniquely pure and sexually restrained became the object of satire. For Bernard Levin, writing in the *Daily Mail* in 1962, the stereotype that 'English girls are more chaste than Continental girls' was nothing more than a dangerous 'national lie'—on a par with such myths as 'This is a Christian country' and 'Our police are the

[107] *Daily Mirror*, 22 Aug. 1953, 2; see also 12–14 Nov. 1953

[108] *Sunday Pictorial*, 22 Jan.–4 Mar. 1956.

[109] For example, the *Daily Mirror*'s investigation of Sweden's 'new morality': 29 Nov–1 Dec. 1955.

[110] A. Giddens, *The Transformation of Intimacy: Sexuality, Love and Eroticism in Modern Societies* (Cambridge: Polity Press, 1992).

[111] C. Brown, *The Death of Christian Britain: Understanding Secularisation 1800–2000* (London: Routledge, 2001), ch. 8; T. Newburn, *Permission and Regulation: Laws and Morals in Post-War Britain* (London: Routledge, 1992).

best in the world'—that blinded people to the realities of modern Britain.[112] The notion that Britain was becoming a 'permissive society' gradually gained momentum in Fleet Street as journalists pounced on every sign that British sexual mores were changing. This tendency was reinforced by the metropolitan bias of British popular journalism. It was far easier to believe in the 'permissive society' when pounding the colourful streets of London than when stuck in suburbia or sleepy provincial towns.

The resilience of the idea that Afro-Caribbean and Asian people were in various ways sexually different to white Britons ensured that the historically high levels of immigration from the new Commonwealth in the post-war period were seen as posing a challenge to Britain's sexual regime. The historian Bill Schwarz has suggested that miscegenation was the 'central issue in terms of white perceptions of race' in the 1940s and 1950s, and anxieties about cross-race relationships continued to feature prominently in the popular press in these years.[113] In 1953, for example, Pat Roller argued in the *Daily Record* that Cable Street in Stepney had become an even worse place to live than Glasgow's deprived Gorbals because of the problem of racial mixing: 'The association of black and white all along these streets has changed this part of Stepney into a shameless Harlem'.[114] Black men were presented as possessing an irresistible sexual magnetism which lured impressionable women from all over Britain, and which welfare workers tried valiantly to counteract. One told Roller that her organization 'had rescued "quite a lot" of girls from black Stepney and brought them back into the family fold', but that it was 'not easy' to do so.[115] Popular newspapers created a talking point out of these fears: 'Would You let your Daughter Marry a Black Man?' asked the *Daily Express* in 1956, copying a similar feature in *Picture Post*.[116] Sexual jealousies seemed to have been one of the causes of the outbreak of rioting in Nottingham and Notting Hill in 1958, and these incidents reinforced the notion that cross-race relationships produced social disruption.[117]

As the issue of racial integration rose up the political agenda in the wake of the riots, white journalists were increasingly sent out to investigate the patterns of behaviour in Afro-Caribbean and Asian communities in Britain—just as their predecessors in earlier decades had reported on exotic customs of Empire. The resulting articles repeatedly emphasized the ways in which immigrants' habits varied from the norms of white Britain. Anne Sharpley's series on West Indian migrants in the *Evening Standard* in 1961 was typical of this genre.

112 *Daily Mail*, 26 Oct. 1962, 2.

113 B. Schwarz, 'Black Metropolis, White England' in M. Nava and A. O'Shea (eds.), *Modern Times: Reflections on a Century of English Modernity* (London: Routledge, 1996), 197.

114 *Daily Record*, 13 Aug. 1953, 4.

115 Ibid.

116 *Daily Express*, 18 July 1956; *Picture Post*, 30 Oct. 1954, both cited in W. Webster, *Englishness and Empire 1939–1965* (Oxford: Oxford University Press, 2005), 157.

117 See, for example, *Daily Mirror*, 2 Sept. 1958; Webster, *Englishness and Empire*, ch. 6; M. Phillips and T. Phillips, *Windrush: The Irresistible Rise of Multi-Racial Britain* (London: HarperCollins, 1998), ch. 12.

After interviewing several men and women from Kingston, Jamaica, Sharpley explained that West Indians had a 'very different attitude towards marriage'. She admitted that she thought their 'manner' of having children was 'to say the least, random', and noted that some 45 per cent of Jamaican children were born out of wedlock. This was, she found, because marriage was considered by West Indians to be 'a status to be achieved in maturity—and is not merely an institution for the procreation and protection of children'. 'Girlie', a 21-year-old unmarried mother who was expecting her second child, told Sharpley that her pregnancies proved that she was a desirable partner rather than an infertile 'mule'. 'Girlie' insisted that she had no plans to marry until the age of 30, although she was considering aborting her current pregnancy.[118]

Other newspapers attempted to provide greater detail and sophistication by publishing extracts from academic reports and inquiries. In 1963, for example, *The People* serialized Sheila Patterson's influential sociological study, *Dark Strangers*, which explored the 'different social customs' of immigrants into Brixton.[119] Patterson reinforced perceptions of black promiscuity, concluding that 'West Indian men look upon the fathering of children as evidence for all to see of their manhood and virility'; wealthier West Indian women, meanwhile, were prone to avoid 'all permanent liaisons, taking and discarding male consorts in a "queen bee" fashion.'[120] She also provided further evidence that anxieties about miscegenation produced community tensions. 'It was rare to find any Brixtonians who accepted intermarriage and sexual intercourse between white women and coloured men as normal', she revealed, and confirmed that 'if a white woman is seen in the streets with a black man it will often cause unpleasant remarks to be made by other white people'.[121] Sharpley and Patterson were actually relatively sympathetic observers, emphasizing the love that West Indian men and women displayed to their children, but the impression for many British readers must have been one of fecklessness and irresponsibility.

Journalists suggested that these different standards of behaviour could generate serious social problems in Britain. Some highlighted the strain placed on local housing and welfare systems. In 1961 the *News of the World*'s David Roxan investigated the case of Birmingham, where a sudden 'uprush of violence and sin' had overburdened the city's services. He asserted that 'The coloured population is without doubt one of the biggest headaches', having found that '20,000 West Indians fathered more children than 250,000 whites', and that rates of illegitimacy were far higher for the former. Of the 129 men who contracted VD twice in one year, Roxan added, 108 were West Indians, while only six

[118] *Evening Standard*, 25 Oct. 1961, 8.

[119] S. Patterson, *Dark Strangers: A Study of West Indians in London* (London: Tavistock Publications, 1963); on Patterson see C. Waters, '"Dark Strangers" in our Midst: Discourse of Race and Nation in Britain, 1947–63', *Journal of British Studies*, 36 (1997), 207–38.

[120] *The People*, 6 Jan. 1963, 2–3.

[121] *The People*, 13 Jan. 1963, 2–4.

were English.[122] The sheer presence of such men seemed to incite immorality in the local population. 'White girls with low morals', were 'pursuing coloured men' Roxan claimed, with 'heavily painted 15-year-olds' luring them at railway stations. The result was that adoption agencies were faced with the 'increasing problem' of finding homes for 'half-caste' children.[123]

Most of these investigations found consolation in the prediction that immigrants would gradually alter their behaviour to suit British norms. The responsibility for change was routinely placed on the newcomers. 'Many immigrants are realising they will not be accepted until they conform to existing social standards', observed Roxan, while Patterson believed that the newcomers would 'learn local ways'.[124] But by reinforcing negative sexual stereotypes and consistently highlighting the differences between communities, this journalism did little to ease tensions.

But it was not just incomers who were perceived to be rejecting traditional British standards of sexual behaviour. Even more alarming to many observers was the growing evidence that British teenagers were, on a far greater scale than ever before, ignoring Christian moral teaching. Professor George Carstairs, an esteemed expert in psychological medicine, highlighted this tendency in a Reith Lecture broadcast on the BBC Home Service in November 1962, and widely reported by the press. When Carstairs suggested that 'our young people are rapidly turning our own society into one in which sexual experience, with precautions against conception, is becoming accepted as a sensible preliminary to marriage', he was amazed to find his words 'taken up by national and local newspapers all over Britain, and echoed in the Press of Europe and North America'.[125] But he had, as he quickly realized, touched on 'a very live issue'. Newspapers used the occasion to explore the habits of this younger generation and many claimed that mores were changing rapidly. Interviewing a number of 'Young Ones', for example, the *Sunday Pictorial* found a sole individual who disapproved of premarital sex. 'If you like a boy enough and he likes you enough then what is wrong?' remarked one 'typical' 17-year-old girl.[126] The *Pictorial* asked its readers whether 'chastity is out of date', and found that a 'small majority' of respondents believed that it was not—but this was hardly a ringing endorsement from a group of letter-writers of all ages.[127] A survey of students at London University taken a few months later seemed to reinforce the idea of a liberal young generation. Discussing the results in the *Sunday Mirror*, advice columnist Anne Allen noted that a third of student couples 'were living together as man and wife' and 'almost all had sexual experience before marriage'. The respondents identified sexual pleasure as a priority. One 17-year-old boy

122 *News of the World*, 10 Dec. 1961, 11.

123 Ibid.

124 Ibid.; *The People*, 20 Jan. 1963, 14–15.

125 G. Carstairs, *This Island Now: The BBC Reith Lectures 1962* (Harmondsworth: Penguin, 1964), 49, 105.

126 *Sunday Pictorial*, 2 Dec. 1962, 18–19.

127 *Sunday Pictorial*, 9 Dec. 1963, 6.

remarked, to Allen's consternation, that 'The best human happiness is sex. . . . I take it when I can find it.'[128] 'When I was in my teens,' Allen told her readers, 'I swore that when my turn came to be grown-up I'd never say, "When I was young things were different . . ." But things HAVE changed.'[129]

By the mid-1960s a flood of similar articles had rendered it platitudinous to observe that sexual habits had shifted. Television, cinema, literature, and popular music were all increasingly sexually explicit: sex seemed to be everywhere. It was widely accepted that by easing the fear of pregnancy, the pill had allowed the casting off of inhibitions. And far from being a beacon of restraint, Britain seemed to be at the heart of the sexual revolution. *Time* magazine's 'Swinging London' feature of April 1966 identified London as the global centre of the new lifestyle.[130] Newspapers competed to reveal the latest evidence of looser morals. In March 1966, for example, the *People* claimed that 'decadent moral behaviour' was 'touching every corner of this once so-respectable land'. This 'decadence' amongst 'ordinary' citizens included ' "orgy" parties, home-made "blue-films", a mania for pornography, indulgence in pep-up sex drugs'; most shocking of all, though, was the practice of 'wife-swapping' on a 'scale that will startle and revolt all decent-minded people'.[131] The paper quoted figures from the Institute of Sex Research in Indiana estimating that 5 million married couples in America had exchanged partners at least once, and suggested that similar proportions could be expected in Britain.[132] The following month the author Betty James talked to that 'incredible new breed, the girls of 1966' for the *News of the World*, and concluded that they were 'very, very "advanced" indeed', with the result that illegitimacy rates were 'rising sharply year by year'.[133] By 1968 the *People* had decided that Britain had gone 'Strip Crazy', with 'housewives, mothers, typists and shop assistants' rushing to join the striptease 'bandwagon' and perform in front of audiences without 'social or class barriers'.[134] Generalizing wildly from small samples, journalists suggested that a generation of men and women were indulging their sexuality with a casual indifference to traditional restraints.

The phrase 'permissive society', which was coined in 1968, soon became a journalistic cliché, as it seemed to encapsulate perfectly the nature of the perceived new era.[135] 'We cannot halt the ever-growing Permissive Society', argued Rosalie Shann in the *News of the World* in September 1969.[136] The 'climate of Britain' agreed David Farr in the *People* on the same day, was 'free, swinging and totally permissive'.[137] 'The permissive society is not an opinion. It is a fact,' argued the

[128] *Sunday Mirror*, 7 April 1963, 18–19. [129] Ibid.

[130] *Time*, 15 April 1966. On the contemporary sense of sexual change, see J. Green, *All Dressed Up: The Sixties and the Counterculture* (London: Pimlico, 1999).

[131] *The People*, 6 Mar. 1966, 2–3. [132] *The People*, 13 Mar. 1966, 2–3.

[133] *News of the World*, 26 June 1966, 2.

[134] *The People*, 14 April 1968, 1; 7 April 1968, 2–3.

[135] J. Ayto, *Twentieth-Century Words* (Oxford: Oxford University Press, 1999), 429.

[136] *News of the World*, 28 Sept. 1963, 14. [137] *The People*, 28 Sept. 1969, 14–15.

Sun in an editorial shortly after its relaunch in November 1969. 'People who pretend that yesterday's standards are today's, let alone tomorrow's, are living a lie.'[138] This press fascination with the 'permissive society' was more than just the latest episode in the long history of journalistic moral panics about the loose morals of the younger generation. In the second half of the 1960s the press consolidated the idea that British society had fundamentally changed, that the moral codes that had governed the nation for generations were being abandoned by huge swathes of the community. The reforming legislation of 1967–9 was portrayed as contributing to this shift, as was abolition of the Lord Chamberlain's role in theatre censorship. Britain appeared to have entered an entirely new era.

Some did raise doubts about the reality of the 'sexual revolution'. Looking back over the decade at the end of 1969, several commentators drew attention to the social continuities. 'Despite the vivid memories and meagre mini-skirts of the Swinging Sixties under the surface much was constant', argued Nicholas Lloyd in the *Sun*.[139] Discussing an opinion poll suggesting a high level of public scepticism about recent reforms, Paul Barker in *New Society* asked whether the decade would not be more appropriately labelled the 'Cautious Sixties' than the 'Swinging Sixties'.[140] And when Geoffrey Gorer conducted another survey of the nation—this time for the *Sunday Times*, in a revealing sign of the greater respectability of such investigations—he argued that 'England still appears to be a very chaste society'.[141] But these voices tended to be drowned out by the more persistent focus on signs of 'permissiveness', on challenges to authority, on daring fashions, and explicit books and films. 'The moral structure of two thousand years of civilisation is collapsing' declared the *Daily Mail* in 1971, opening up yet another 'Great Debate' on the 'subject of our times'.[142] The 'permissive society' had become the frame through which journalists observed the nation, and they ceaselessly looked for new angles on this defining story of the age. Every rise in the figures for divorce, abortion, and venereal diseases appeared to confirm this belief. 'Britain is in the grip of a permissive epidemic which is still growing' declared a front-page article in the *Sun* in January 1973. 'The cost of careless love will mean a record number of venereal disease cases and a staggering rise in abortions'.[143]

These perceived changes in sexual behaviour opened up significant divisions between different popular papers. All of them shared a commitment to family values, a commitment that was far too deeply engrained for them not to attack the worst excesses of 'permissiveness'. At the same time the *Sun* and the *Mirror*, in particular, relied heavily on young readers and were wary of appearing 'out-dated'

138 *The Sun*, 22 Nov. 1969, 2.

139 *The Sun*, 31 Dec. 1969, 13.

140 *New Society*, 27 Nov. 1969, 847–50.

141 G. Gorer, *Sex and Marriage in England Today: A Study of the Views and Experience of the Under-45s* (London: Thomas Nelson, 1971), 30. The *Sunday Times* articles were printed on 15, 22, 29 March 1970.

142 *Daily Mail*, 6 May 1971, 18–19.

143 *The Sun*, 29 Jan. 1973, 2.

by identifying too closely with stuffy moralists; they were, moreover, themselves taking advantage of more liberal attitudes by including more sexually explicit images and features. The result was that these papers generally displayed a cautious approval of the new sexual freedoms. The *Sun* lamented the rising numbers of schoolgirls seeking abortions, but denied that this was a reason to restrict their availability: 'We mustn't stop them getting abortions. We must stop them getting pregnant.'[144] When the Commons re-examined the abortion laws in 1976, the paper made clear its view that it 'did not want to see us back in the bad old days of backstreet abortions'.[145] In any case, the *Sun*'s celebration of sexual pleasure hardly left it in a position to recommend abstention: it remained comfortable in recommending the pill for 'single girls'.[146] Only in the 1980s, under the editorship of Kelvin MacKenzie, did the paper begin to develop a more aggressively right-wing rhetoric on such issues.[147] The *Mirror*, for its part, remained faithful to its educational agenda, arguing that the pressing problem was not immorality but a lack of sexual knowledge. 'The alarming statistics of unwanted pregnancies, illegitimate births and the massive number of abortions highlight an appalling ignorance about contraception', argued Marje Proops in 1975. 'Too few schools offer pupils worthwhile sex and contraceptive advice. Too few mothers teach their children.'[148] The *Sun* and the *Mirror* tended to target their moralizing rhetoric on counter-cultural or feminist figures whom they believed were too radical for mainstream opinion.[149]

The conservative mid-market newspapers, notably the *Express* and the *Mail*, were far more openly nostalgic for the Britain that had disappeared, and offered thoroughgoing critiques of permissiveness. These papers were more comfortable using a language of responsibility, restraint, law and order. Columnists such as Jean Rook (who left the *Mail* for the *Express* in 1972) and Lynda Lee-Potter (who replaced Rook at the *Mail*) offered scathing commentaries on what they saw as the decline of decent standards of behaviour. 'I see no great gain in the loss of inhibitions, discipline, the three Rs, white £5 notes and self-respect' lamented Rook in 1976.[150] The solution they and their colleagues prescribed for the problems of modern society was essentially individual moral improvement. 'Those who are concerned at the coarsening and increasing violence in our life have to argue for voluntary restraint in a quiet, rational way', insisted the *Express* in 1976. 'There is little that legislation can do—except possibly reduce the flaunting of the brutalisation of sex. But there is an increasing responsibility placed on individuals of all age groups to promote reticence.'[151] Such journalism prepared sections of middle-class Britain for Margaret Thatcher and the new

[144] *The Sun*, 1 Oct. 1970, 2. [145] *The Sun*, 18 Feb. 1976, 2.

[146] *The Sun*, 10 May 1978, 9.

[147] P. Chippindale and C. Horrie, *Stick it up your Punter: The Uncut Story of the Sun Newspaper* (London: Simon and Schuster, 1999).

[148] *Daily Mirror*, 8 Aug. 1975, 3. [149] e.g. *The Sun* 9 Nov. 1970, 2.

[150] *Daily Express*, 21 Jan. 1976, 5. [151] *Daily Express*, 30 Jan. 1976, 6.

right. (Indeed, Jean Rook boasted in 1979 that she 'was the first in Fleet Street to take Margaret Thatcher seriously as a possible Prime Minister. Or even to take her seriously.')[152] Having given so much publicity to the changes in sexual behaviour, the popular press helped to make moral standards a political battleground.

In 1976, Hugh Cudlipp, the man who had done so much to encourage the popular press to report on everyday sexual behaviour, looked back with amusement at the *Mirror*'s first effort to survey its readers in 1937. The finding that the average first kiss occurred at the age of 15 and a quarter reflected a far more innocent age. 'A similar investigation today would yield different results,' he noted wryly; 'for kiss read coitus'. Yet the rationale behind the exercise had been a serious one. 'The point of it all was that the *Daily Mirror* was now dealing with life as it was and is lived by ordinary people.'[153] This early sex survey journalism had the progressive aim of trying to explore sex as it was actually practised, thereby opening up debates about sensitive issues such as extra-marital sex, masturbation, and homosexuality. Many people consumed with guilt about their 'immoral' habits must have been reassured that they were not as unusual as they had imagined. The surveys also highlighted the different attitudes and expectations held by men and women, and stimulated efforts to overcome problems of communication. It was not recognized at that time how a flood of similar surveys could create an alternative set of anxieties about whether or not one was meeting rising standards of pleasure and performance. In the more sexualized post-1960s society, surveys lost their radical edge and came to be used either as entertainment or as moral warnings—to measure the fun being had by a liberated younger generation, or to demonstrate the depravity of a population that had lost its moral anchor. Above all, they were used to show how far the British had travelled from an earlier age of assumed sexual fidelity and restraint.

[152] J. Rook, *Rook Eye's View* (London: Express Books, 1979), 67.
[153] Cudlipp, *Walking on Water*, 58.

4

Court Reporting

In the news values of the popular press, criminal and morally transgressive activities have traditionally received greater attention than the mundane realities of everyday behaviour. Stories of crime and punishment have been a staple of popular culture in the form of ballads and broadsheets for hundreds of years, and in the mid-nineteenth century court reports became the main selling point of the new mass-circulation Sunday newspapers such as *Lloyd's Weekly News* and the *News of the World.*[1] So while information and advice about ordinary, consensual adult sexual relationships only gradually came to be regarded as suitable content for popular newspapers in the mid-twentieth century, there was already by then a long history of reporting on illicit expressions of sexuality. The authority of the judicial process gave legitimacy to the coverage of subjects that would have been considered inappropriate for discussion in other contexts, although journalists had to use a euphemistic style that drew a veil around the most explicit details. Week after week, readers of the Sunday papers were presented with courtroom dramas featuring everything from adultery and bigamy to sexual violence and indecent assaults. The popular daily papers that emerged after 1896 sought to be more respectable than their Sunday rivals, and did not provide quite such an extensive and detailed coverage of crime; they did, nevertheless, devote considerable amounts of space to the most high profile or titillating trials. For all the changes in newspaper content across the twentieth century, court reporting remained central to popular journalism, a cheap, convenient and reliable means of providing the human interest stories that fascinated, entertained, and shocked readers.

Court reporting could never be viewed purely in commercial terms, however. It was a peculiarly sensitive form of journalism which had consequences for the administration of justice, and, many argued, the moral balance of society. The British tradition of open courts was meant to ensure that the workings of the judicial system were transparent and that criminals were punished in sight of the community. Publicity was a vital element of this punishment, designed to act as a deterrent to those contemplating similar offences; conversely those who

[1] M. Conboy, *The Press and Popular Culture* (London: Sage, 2002); V. Berridge, 'Popular Sunday Papers and Mid-Victorian Society', in G. Boyce, J. Curran, and P. Wingate (eds.), *Newspaper History from the Seventeenth Century to the Present Day* (London: Constable, 1978).

were acquitted deserved to have their innocence declared so that their reputation was restored. The press had an important role in accurately recording the proceedings of the courts and preventing the circulation of unfounded rumours. The seriousness of this task was underlined by the contempt of court laws which could lead to severe punishments for editors and journalists producing inaccurate, prejudiced, or critical reporting. More broadly, it was recognized that the press coverage of the judicial system had a significant influence on public perceptions of crime, and, by extension, of the 'state of society'. Governments feared that 'disproportionate' crime journalism would cause anxiety among voters or damage the nation's reputation abroad. Others were more worried about the impact of reporting on criminals themselves, arguing that the public demonization of offenders could create obstacles to rehabilitation or treatment.[2]

Throughout the twentieth century, the popular press was accused of placing its commercial interest in sensational stories ahead of its wider social responsibilities when reporting crime. In the first half of the century, particularly, critics claimed that court reporting posed a serious threat to public morality. The press gave far too much prominence to criminal and immoral activities, they argued, describing them in unnecessary detail, and all too frequently glamorizing the protagonists of major trials. Rather than acting as a deterrent, newspaper reports might actually encourage imitation and experimentation; at the very least, it was suggested, exposure to endless stories of illicit behaviour dulled the horror of such activity and weakened the moral sense of readers. Such anxieties were particularly acute, of course, because newspapers now circulated throughout society and reached those deemed to be the most impressionable. The main preoccupation was about the corruption of young readers, but there was also some concern about women being exposed to reports of sexual offences. Before the First World War women had often been asked to leave the public galleries of courtrooms when graphic sexual evidence was being considered, and when women became jurors after 1919 there were numerous examples of judges excusing them because of the nature of the evidence.[3] Newspapers did not, of course, report all of the evidence placed before the court, and certainly did not give precise physical descriptions of sexual offences, but many critics argued that their coverage was still sufficiently salacious and suggestive to cause grave moral damage. Moral concern about court journalism peaked in the 1920s, when there was a high profile campaign against the excesses of divorce reporting, and in the

[2] There is now an extensive literature on crime journalism: see, for example, S. Cohen, *Folk Devils and Moral Panics: The Creation of the Mods and Rockers* (London: MacGibbon & Kee, 1972); S. Hall et al., *Policing the Crisis: Mugging, the State, and Law and Order* (London: Macmillan, 1978); S. Chibnall, *Law-and-Order News: An Analysis of Crime Reporting in the British Press* (London: Tavistock Publications, 1977); C. Critcher, *Moral Panics and the Media* (Buckingham: Open University Press, 2003).

[3] On women in the courtroom, see H. Fenn, *Thirty-Five Years in the Divorce Courts* (London: T. Werner Laurie, 1910), ch. XI.

1950s, when many complaints about explicit crime coverage were sent to the Press Council.

Fleet Street defended itself by arguing that the press was merely satisfying natural curiosity about those who broke the law, and by contending that many of its accusers were guilty of hypocrisy. Northcliffe observed that crime reports 'are the sort of dramatic news that the public always affect to criticise but is always in the greatest hurry to read'.[4] Editors denied that their court coverage was morally harmful, insisting that it was carefully edited and always unambiguously supportive of the forces of law and order. They also rejected claims that the press obstructed the administration of justice, pointing out how frequently the press assisted the police in prompting the public to volunteer information about crimes. MPs were not always convinced by such protestations, however, and they served notice that they were prepared to encroach on the hallowed 'freedom of the press' in order to protect public morality. In 1926, the Regulation of Reports Act, which significantly curtailed the coverage of divorce suits, passed with a substantial majority, and further restrictions on court reporting followed.

From the 1960s, anxieties about the moral impact of court reporting gradually faded, to be replaced by an increasing concern about the manner in which the press's unscrupulous pursuit of scoops were creating various obstacles to the operation of the law. On several occasions the payment of witnesses in high profile trials threatened to pervert the course of justice. After the inappropriate deals made by the *News of the World* during the Moors Murders trial of 1966, the Press Council attempted to ban the practice, but it was unable to enforce its ruling. During the 1970s, moreover, feminists argued that aggressive and sexist styles of journalism were discouraging victims of rape and sexual violence from coming forward, and reinforcing assumptions which prevented such offences being treated with the seriousness they deserved. Ultimately, however, these various restrictions, punishments, and criticisms did little to diminish the press's appetite for sex crime stories.

THE *NEWS OF THE WORLD* AND THE STRATEGIES OF COURT REPORTING

The commercial potential of court reporting was most clearly demonstrated by the success of the *News of the World*, which became Britain's most popular newspaper through its command of this form of journalism. The paper expertly squeezed every last drop of human interest from legal proceedings around the country: its coverage was more professional, more extensive, and more explicit than any of its rivals. Particularly serious or sensational cases, or those involving prominent

[4] T. Clarke, *My Northcliffe Diary* (London: Victor Gollancz, 1931), 199.

figures, were described as fully as possible, but considerable amounts of space were also devoted to recording relatively mundane cases of assault, deception, or indecency. The editorial assumption was that readers were intrigued by all crime and moral transgression, whether major or minor; if there was a sexual dimension, this interest would be heightened. Steadily rising sales seemed to confirm these assumptions. One Fleet Street veteran aptly described the *News of the World* as the 'Hansard of the Sleazy'; Stafford Somerfield, the editor of the paper in the 1960s, preferred the suggestion that it was the judges' 'trade paper', and boasted that one judge was known to delay his summings-up until the *News of the World* reporter was in the press box.[5]

The price of commercial success obtained in this way was sustained moral criticism from political, religious, and cultural elites. The *News of the World* was the least respectable of the mainstream national papers, and was widely agreed to exist in a category of its own. The Conservative MP Major Birchall did not need to identify the publication to which he was referring when he complained to the House of Commons in 1926 that 'one Sunday newspaper' devoted half of its news space to 'matters of crime of every kind, very largely connected with sexual offences'. This was, he argued, material that 'degrades and pollutes the reader's mind'. One of his colleagues agreed that it was possible to single out 'one newspaper that has been wrong in this matter'.[6] There were similar exchanges before the Royal Commission on the Press in 1947–8. When the editor of the *Newcastle Journal and North Mail* was asked whether 'it was common to find salacious or pornographic matter in the daily newspapers', he replied, 'Not in the sense that one gets in the pornographic treatment of material in a certain paper'.[7] The *News of the World* was a special case, both in the circulations it achieved and the opprobrium it attracted.

The editors of the *News of the World* were well aware that the paper's sex and crime formula would never win over educated critics. Their task was rather to ensure that the paper contained enough to interest and titillate a mass working-class readership without becoming so unrespectable that too many potential buyers or advertisers were put off. It was essential for circulation and advertising success that the *News of the World* should be able to present itself as a 'family newspaper', suitable for all. A number of strategies were adopted to ensure that the paper remained within the bounds of decency. The most important was self-censorship. Court reports were written very carefully, with the most sensitive evidence either omitted completely or described euphemistically. As Henry Fenn, an experienced court journalist, observed, 'what is published

[5] R. Greenslade, *Press Gang: How Newspapers make Profits from Propaganda* (London: Macmillan, 2003), 30: S. Somerfield, *Banner Headlines* (Shoreham-by-Sea: Scan Books, 1977), 126.

[6] 200 H. C. Debs, 5s, Judicial Proceedings (Regulation of Reports) Bill, 10 Dec. 1926, cols. 2445, 2447.

[7] Royal Commission on the Press, *Minutes of Evidence*, Day 13, 17 Dec. 1947 (London: HMSO, 1948), Cmd. 7351, 9.

in the leading newspapers regarding unsavoury matter is the merest bagatelle compared with the details which are eliminated . . . . Every case is and has to be sub-edited at the fountain source before leaving the hands of skilled reporters.'[8] Accounts of sexual misdemeanours were particularly evasive and oblique, relying on traditional circumlocutions rather than modern sexual terminology. Until the 1950s, at least, words such as 'intercourse', 'rape', 'abortion', and 'pregnancy' were used very rarely. Instead, journalists referred coyly to 'intimacy', 'grave offences', 'illegal operations', and 'a certain condition'. Editors could therefore protest that the paper contained only what was 'fit to print' and that it excluded unnecessary information about criminal and indecent activities; critics were denied ammunition that could have proved very dangerous. The key to this form of popular journalism, of course, was suggestion: tantalizing headlines introduced stories which gave just enough detail to set readers' imaginations racing.

A report of a case from Lincolnshire Assizes in November 1931 serves to illustrate the *News of the World*'s style. Underneath the intriguing headline 'Incident In Bathroom—Girl's Allegations In Grave Charge—Three Accused Persons Acquitted', the opening paragraph told how the court had heard 'extraordinary allegations of improper relations between a tradesman and a young girl assistant, and of steps which the man, his wife, and a third person were stated to have taken to get the girl out of trouble'. The allegations were not, of course, particularly extraordinary, merely a routine story of an unplanned, extra-marital pregnancy and a desperate attempt at abortion, of the type heard in courts around the country. The reporter chose his words carefully, but described enough to allow the informed reader a fairly clear idea of what had happened:

> The Hydes were charged with using an instrument on Joyce Mumby, 18, and with causing her to take certain noxious things . . . . On a date about her 16th birthday, the girl alleged, Mr Hyde was familiar with her, and this conduct continued until June last, when she discovered that she was an expectant mother. She spoke to Mr Hyde on the matter, and later, she declared, both he and his wife did something to her and gave her pills and medicine . . . [later] Miss Mumby declared that [the third defendant] Walsham then did something to her . . . Walsham stated that the girl took him up to the bathroom and pressed him to do something to her as she was in trouble, but he refused.[9]

For those readers unfamiliar with these euphemisms, the 'something' that was done to Joyce Mumby would have been mystifying, and their innocence would have been preserved. As the historian Jonathan Rose has pointed out, the levels of sexual ignorance in this period were such that many readers simply would not have understood this evasive language.[10] For those who did realize what was going on, the refusal to use more direct terminology reinforced the idea that sex and all its repercussions were 'dirty', and not to be discussed openly. At the

[8] Fenn, *Divorce Courts*, 291. [9] *News of the World*, 8 Nov. 1931, 4.

[10] J. Rose, *The Intellectual Life of the British Working Classes* (New Haven: Yale University Press, 2001), 207–11.

end of the report, moreover, the judge's summing-up underlined the dangers of transgressing the rules of sexual morality. The defendants were acquitted largely because the judge believed that Joyce Mumby was a tainted and unreliable witness, who 'seemed to be a shameless hussy, having, as she alleged, consorted with her employer for two years'.[11]

Vocal support for the law, the police, and conventional morality was another vital element of the paper's strategy. There must be no suspicion at all that the *News of the World* condoned the behaviour it recorded. Reporters scrupulously described the mechanics of the judicial process, giving prominence to the comments of the judges and the sentence that was handed down. The paper's standard defence to accusations that it dwelt on the worst aspects of human behaviour was that it reported not crime but punishment, and thereby helped to teach readers what they should not do.[12] The paper's columnists and leader writers consistently called for vigorous enforcement of the law and demanded the imposition of tough penalties. 'We were more concerned with the victims than the criminals,' wrote Stafford Somerfield; 'we believed in capital punishment and the lash for those who raped, for those who smashed old and crippled people over the head.'[13] The *News of the World* also developed a tradition of offering rewards for information about high profile crimes. In 1928, £1,000 was offered for intelligence relating to the murder of police constable Reginald Gutteridge, and similar rewards became almost a matter of routine in later years.[14] The paper's crime reporters worked hard to forge a close relationship with the police and the judiciary, trading favourable publicity for tip-offs and sympathetic treatment. Leading detectives and members of the bench, were often able to secure lucrative deals for the serialization of their memoirs.[15] Journalists tended to share and reinforce the conservative perspectives that prevailed in these institutions, and demonstrated little sympathy with the arguments of liberal criminologists and reformers.

Editors were also careful to ensure that the *News of the World* maintained the appearance of a respectable newspaper. Well into the 1960s the front page was dominated by political and international reports which must have been poorly read compared to the court coverage inside, but conveyed the message that the paper was a serious national publication rather than one unsuitable for domestic consumption. Substantial sums were spent, for similar reasons, on obtaining articles from politicians, churchmen, and authors commenting on contemporary affairs. The layout and typography was also relatively austere

[11] *News of the World*, 8 Nov. 1931, 4.

[12] For example, Royal Commission on the Press 1947–49, *Minutes of Evidence*, Day 22 (London: HMSO, 1948), Cmd. 7398, 27.

[13] S. Somerfield, *Banner Headlines* (Shoreham-by-Sea: Scan Books, 1979), 150.

[14] C. Bainbridge and R. Stockdill, *The News of the World Story: 150 Years of the World's Bestselling Newspaper* (London: HarperCollins, 1993), 103.

[15] Ibid., 141–50.

until the 1960s. The paper was considerably slower than many of its rivals to introduce photographs, bold headlines, and the modern 'jig-saw' make-up. The *Daily Mirror* and the *Sunday Pictorial* were, for example, far more daring in their use of pin-up photographs (see Chapter 6). This eventually left the *News of the World* looking rather dated and out-of-touch; for a long time, however, this conservatism played an important role in reassuring readers that it was reputable and 'decent'.

These strategies proved to be very successful, as the spectacular circulation figures testified. The paper's popularity, in turn, meant that leading politicians often felt the need to conceal their disdain and maintain good relations with it. In May 1941, Winston Churchill and the Chancellor of the Exchequer, Kingsley Wood, both took time from their hectic wartime schedules to attend a party at the Dorchester Hotel to celebrate Sir Emsley Carr's fiftieth year as *News of the World* editor. The King and Lloyd George both sent congratulatory telegrams. Many must have shared the moral reservations of one attendee, the Conservative politician Sir Cuthbert Headlam, who recorded in his diary that the *News of the World* 'is a foul paper and I cannot understand why a reputable man is its editor'.[16]

No other popular paper placed quite such emphasis on court reporting as the *News of the World*, but it was a significant part of the editorial mix for them all. A study for the first Royal Commission on the Press found that 15 per cent of news space in the *Daily Mirror* in 1927 was devoted to the composite category of 'Law, police and accidents', most of which was court coverage. This figure rose to 20 per cent in 1937 and 23 per cent in 1947: more space was devoted to this category than to any other apart from sport. The proportion was rather less in the *Daily Mail*, at around 10 per cent, but this was still more space than for home political, social, and economic news, except in the unusually small papers of 1947.[17] The figures would have been considerably higher for the Sunday papers had they been included—indeed, the fact they were not was a reflection of the Commission's assumption that the Sundays concentrated so much on sensational human interest content that they made little serious contribution to contemporary public debate, and hence were not worth studying.

A similar survey in 1975 found that the four national popular dailies all devoted about 10 per cent of their space to general 'legal and police' news: in each case this was the largest single category except sport. By the mid-1970s, however, the Sundays had considerably reduced their reliance on court reports. Even the *News of the World* devoted only 11 per cent of its news space to 'legal and police' stories, while the figures for the *Sunday Mirror* and the

[16] C. King, *With Malice Toward None: A War Diary* (London: Sidgwick & Jackson, 1970), 123; S. Ball (ed.), *The Headlam Diaries 1935–1951* (Cambridge: Cambridge University Press, 1999), 249.

[17] Royal Commission on the Press 1947–49, *Report* (London: HMSO, 1949), Cmd. 7700 250.

People were 8 per cent and 7 per cent respectively. Faced with declining circulations, the Sundays had tried to update their formula by replacing much of their court coverage with revelatory articles about celebrities and sex-related investigations. Even at this reduced level, however, the 'legal and police' content outstripped the combined amount of home and foreign political, social, and economic news.[18]

Other popular papers also used broadly similar editorial strategies to the *News of the World* in their court reporting. They emphasized the human drama of the proceedings but became euphemistic and evasive about the precise details of the offences; they combined an obvious interest in the criminal and transgressive with a vocal support of the authorities enforcing the law and protecting conventional morality. The main differences were in the selection policies and the detail provided. Until the 1950s, few other popular papers reported cases involving homosexuality, indecent assault, rape, or incest, unless they had some particularly sensational elements, or featured a prominent person. While the *News of the World* reported 22 rapes cases in 1951, for example, the *Daily Mirror* and the *Sunday People* reported only one.[19] When the same cases were reported, moreover, the *News of the World* tended to be slightly less euphemistic than its rivals, daring to hint at details others omitted. Other papers might have been more brightly written, more varied in content, and more visually attractive, but readers knew that the *News of the World* was the best source for the titillation, excitement, and scandal provided by the law courts. As one woman told Mass-Observation in 1948, she had taken the paper 'for years' because she liked 'to read all the crimes and sensational things'.[20] That was why it became the most popular paper in the world, read by over half of Britain's adult population at mid-century.

It is reasonable to conclude that the popularity of the *News of the World*, and of salacious court reporting in general, was a reflection of a society characterized by a combination of fascination, guilt, and ignorance about sex. Writing in 1951 after conducting a detailed survey of the habits of the English people, Geoffrey Gorer was struck by the avid attention paid to this form of journalism in a society which was so disciplined and sexually conservative. 'Though most English men and women cannot "let themselves go", they love to think and read about people who do throw off inhibitions, either with sex or violence—provided they are punished. In no nation that I know about is there so much general interest in what is called "police court" news.'[21] Readers were clearly intrigued by transgressions of the strict rules and expectations

[18] Royal Commission on the Press 1974–77, *An Analysis of Newspaper Content: A Report by Professor Denis McQuail*, Research Series 4 (London: HMSO, July 1977), Cmd. 6810-4, 24–5, 34–5.

[19] K. Soothill and S. Walby, *Sex Crime in the News* (London: Routledge, 1991), 18.

[20] Mass-Observation, *The Press and its Readers* (London: Arts and Technics Ltd, 1949), 45.

[21] *The People*, 30 Sept. 1951, 4.

that governed sexuality: some perhaps even enjoyed the vicarious thrill of imagining themselves engaging in similar behaviour. At the same time, there was widespread support for conventional family values, and these stories provided reassurance by recording the reassertion of order and morality provided by the judgement of the court. Readers could repeat the hypocritical assertions of the editors and journalists that they were interested in the punishment rather than the crime. The reports played on the idea that sex was a dirty and potentially dangerous activity; it is likely that they reinforced the common belief that sexual experimentation and indulgence could have disastrous personal consequences, and conversely that self-control and restraint were essential for respectability. They may have been highly evasive and euphemistic, but, such was the paucity of imagery and information about sex in the culture available to the ordinary working-class individual, they were still suggestive enough to seem daring and thrilling. When sexual mores shifted in the second half of the century, though, newspapers had to alter their approach towards court reporting.

DIVORCE COURT REPORTING

Of all the different types of court reporting, the most controversial in the late nineteenth and early twentieth centuries was that dealing with divorce cases. There were particular features of divorce cases that made them especially attractive to the whole spectrum of the popular press and ensured that they were covered extensively. They were civil suits in which the central issue was almost invariably the adultery of one of the spouses, so journalists had an excuse to delve into the private lives and personal relationships of the protagonists. At the same time they could be given rather lighter treatment than serious criminal proceedings, and they did not generally involve more violent, 'unnatural', or indecent activities that most editors preferred to leave to the *News of the World*. Divorce suits were expensive in this period and were usually brought only by relatively wealthy upper- or middle-class plaintiffs, adding a touch of glamour to the tales of infidelity. These cases had considerable news value, were titillating without being too sordid, and were therefore suitable for daily and Sunday papers. Indeed, it was their popularity with the more 'responsible' daily newspapers that evoked much of the concern.

There were complaints about the press coverage of the divorce court from its foundation in 1857. In 1859, for example, Queen Victoria expressed her disquiet to Lord Chancellor Campbell, lamenting that divorce cases 'fill now almost daily a large proportion of the newspapers, and are of so scandalous a character that it makes it almost impossible for a paper to be trusted in the hands of a young lady or boy'. She argued that the effect of this 'must be most pernicious to the public morals of the country'.[22] A number of attempts were made in subsequent years to give the court the power to conduct its proceedings *in camera*, but these were defeated by those determined to maintain the tradition of legal openness and preserve the deterrent effect of newspaper publicity. In the first decades of the twentieth century, however, the campaign gathered momentum. The Royal Commission on Divorce, reporting in 1912, made clear its opposition to sensational press coverage and called on Fleet Street to remove such material; if such action was not forthcoming, the Commission recommended statutory restrictions. Fleet Street did not act, and the result was a parliamentary campaign against divorce reporting led by the Conservative MP Sir Evelyn Cecil and supported by a wide range of organizations, including the Mothers' Union, the National Council of Women, the National Union of Teachers, and church societies representing all the main Christian denominations. Cecil's Judicial Proceedings (Regulation of Reports) Bill was finally passed in December 1926. The act restricted newspapers to printing the names, addresses, and descriptions of the parties and main witnesses; a concise statement for the grounds of the case; submissions on points of law; the judge's summing up; and the findings of the jury. Newspapers were no longer able to recount the evidence of the witnesses, exchanges that had provided intimate details for so many stories.

The historians Gail Savage and Anne Humphries have both discussed the debates about divorce reporting, demonstrating how attitudes gradually shifted in favour of regulation as the newspapers carrying these reports circulated ever more widely, and as concerns grew about the damage that accounts of the sexual indiscretions of upper classes posed to the reputation not only of the institution of marriage, but also to the wider social hierarchy.[23] Nevertheless, many aspects of this issue have not been fully explored, in particular those relating to the actual content of the divorce coverage in popular newspapers, and the attitudes of editors and journalists themselves. Nor has the longer-term impact of the 1926 Act been addressed. All of these elements need to be examined if the nature of the campaign and the ultimate significance of the legislation are to be properly understood.

Most of those seeking to restrict divorce reporting accepted that the newspapers rarely contained details that were so sexually explicit that they contravened existing obscenity legislation. As Sir Evelyn Cecil admitted when he introduced his initial bill to the House of Commons in May 1923, it was impossible to identify individual sentences that could be brought to the attention of the Director of

[22] 194 H. C. Debs, 5s, Judicial Proceedings (Regulation of Reports) Bill, 16 April 1926; G. Savage, 'Erotic Stories and Public Decency: Newspaper Reporting of Divorce Proceedings in England', *The Historical Journal*, 41 (1998), 513–14.

[23] Savage, 'Erotic stories'; A. Humphries, 'Coming Apart: The British Newspaper Press and the Divorce Court', in L. Brake, B. Bell, and D. Finkelstein (eds.), *Nineteenth-Century Media and the Construction of Identities* (Basingstoke: Palgrave, 2000).

Public Prosecutions (DPP) as being obscene.[24] Journalists and sub-editors made sure that such material was not allowed to slip through. Graham Campbell, a Bow Street magistrate, told the select committee considering Cecil's Bill that reporters were 'extremely careful' to avoid obscenity, and Sir Ellis Hume-Williams QC agreed that he could not 'recall any case' in which he had been involved where he had 'read the case afterwards and found that indecent details had been included'; he insisted that journalists exercised a 'wonderful discretion' in dealing with such cases.[25]

Rather than obscenity, the cause of the complaints was actually the prominence, the extent, and the 'suggestiveness', of the divorce court reports. Instead of focusing on important political, international or economic news, the press devoted large amounts of space to record the infidelities and intimacies of those seeking divorce. Readers' attention was unnecessarily directed away from public events to private immorality. Sir Archibald Bodkin, the DPP, told Cecil's Select Committee in 1923 that although the details of matrimonial causes were 'pale and colourless' beside the things that he had to read every day, he considered it harmful that the public had conjugal infidelity 'rammed down their throat in every evening paper . . . [and] again the next morning, when newspaper space could be so much better occupied'. 'Familiarity with what ought to be avoided,' he warned, 'takes away half the horror of it'.[26] Sir Edward Clarke KC agreed that 'the real mischief was done when a great divorce case was on lasting, perhaps, a week, and the public mind was excited by flaming posters, recording the progress of the case'.[27] By losing all sense of perspective, he suggested, the press was in danger of distorting the priorities of its readers. Similarly the Archbishop of York, speaking to a public meeting in support of Cecil's bill in 1926, contended that this type of journalism generated a 'pressure of sexual suggestion' by 'an accumulation of details' that 'defiled the mind and the imagination of the people'.[28]

With the most sensational cases receiving such extensive publicity that they became daily melodramas, the protagonists obtained the sort of attention usually accorded to film and theatre stars. Critics argued that instead of acting as a deterrent, court reporting actually glamorized immoral lifestyles. Cecil suggested that 'there are people who seem to glory in being the central figure of a horrible serial story', and Bodkin agreed that some of the press coverage had the effect of

> almost honouring, or at any rate putting on a pedestal for a time, two or three people who have been making fools of themselves in their conjugal life, almost raising them to a dignified position, and making heroes to be snap-shotted, and their dresses described, and their hats described as they come into and go out of Court.[29]

[24] 164 H. C. Debs, 5s, Matrimonial Causes (Regulation of Reports) Bill, 15 May 1923, col. 251.
[25] Parliamentary Papers, 1923, VII, Select Committee on the Matrimonial Causes (Regulation of Reports) Bill [SCRR], *Minutes of Evidence*, 34, 62, 65.
[26] Ibid., 23–4. [27] *The Times*, 14 July 1923, 12. [28] *The Times*, 20 Jan. 1926, 14.
[29] 164 H. C. Debs, 5s, 15 May 1923, col. 250; P. P. 1923, VII, SCRR, 27.

Even defenders of the press's right to report court cases often conceded this point. Hume-Williams, for example, admitted that 'the descriptions of the appearance of the principal parties and so on were somewhat extravagant'.[30] *The Times*, also instinctively in favour of the 'freedom of the press', was ultimately very doubtful whether 'any desirable purpose' was served by the detailed reporting provided by the popular papers:

> The passion for notoriety may, in fact, be a far stronger influence in the case than any desire to escape attention. To be the principal character in a number of popular papers for several days on end, to be photographed at every stage of the trial, to have the prospect of being badgered or bribed for 'reminiscences' and 'impressions' at the end of it all—all this may be sufficiently nauseating to some of the principal actors, but it possesses obvious attractions for others.[31]

It seemed to these observers that a new era had arrived in which the media overrode the traditional dictates of morality, and dispensed publicity indiscriminately, regardless of desert; the corollary of this was that for some people the desire for fame, or even notoriety, surpassed any feelings of shame or embarrassment about the reason for their public prominence. But if there were indeed some who revelled in the attention, there were certainly others who found the press spotlight distressing and disruptive to the process of coming to terms with the divorce process. One petitioner, who 'had the misfortune to be picked out for report in the Press, complete with photographs', described the consequences to the readers of *The Times*. 'I then received by almost every post letters from young men of the middle and lower class offering me their sympathy, congratulations, and affection, and requesting the commencement of a correspondence "with a view to further developments".' Such letters merely added 'insult to injury'.[32] Whether press publicity was welcomed or not, then, it appeared to have undesirable consequences.

It is clear from these arguments that critics were responding to the new forms of popular journalism that were developing in the post-war period. It was not just, as Savage and Humphries have observed, that newspapers were circulating through society more widely than in the past: it was that the style of coverage had changed, especially with the use of photography. Sunday newspapers such as the *News of the World* may have shocked some with the length and detail of their court reports, but visually they remained relatively sober. Headlines were tantalizing, but fairly modest in size, and only slowly did the Sundays make use of sketches and photography to illustrate their stories. By contrast, the new daily picture papers such as the *Mirror* and the *Sketch* devoted huge amounts of space to news photography, developing a different type of popular journalism in which images were as important as the text. The introduction of more convenient, lightweight

30 *The Times*, 6 July 1923, 9.
31 *The Times*, 15 April 1926, 15.
32 *The Times*, 13 June 1924, 5.

cameras in the 1920s enabled photographers to provide more spontaneous and dramatic shots, and in the increasingly competitive environment of post-war Fleet Street, these became vital tools for editors. Photographs were used to heighten the 'human interest' in divorce trials, and in the most sensational cases all of the leading participants could expect to be captured on film. They were far more immediate and eye-catching than the sketches that had been used in the past. Before 1925, furthermore, there were no statutory restrictions on the use of cameras in the courtroom itself. Photographic illustration not only made divorce reports seem more prominent, it also made them appear more 'suggestive'; visual images could now be used to give life to the evidence in the readers' imagination. It is no coincidence that alongside the campaign to restrict divorce reporting, a campaign to ban photography in the courtroom developed. This succeeded when Section 41 of the 1925 Criminal Justice Act prohibited photography in and around courts; henceforth only the sketches of official courtroom artists could be published.[33]

The coverage of the two hearings of the Russell divorce case in 1922 and 1923 illustrates these developments in popular journalism very well. This case involved Lord John Hugo Russell, scion of one of Britain's most notable landed families, suing his wife, Christabel, for divorce on the grounds of adultery, with the main evidence being that she had given birth to a son when the marriage had not been consummated. The detailed examination of the exact nature of the Russells' physical relationship, and the accusations that Mrs Russell had taken a number of lovers, provided a great deal of titillating copy for the press. The first trial in July 1922 was featured four times on the front page of the *Daily Mirror*, each time illustrated with photographs of the protagonists.[34] The most sensational of these front-page photographs was one showing John Russell 'In Women's Guise', the court having heard about his fondness for cross-dressing.[35] The *Daily Express* overcame its usual reticence and placed the case no fewer than six times on its front page.[36]

This coverage shocked George V, just as his grandmother had been shocked in 1859. George's private secretary, Lord Stamfordham, informed the Lord Chancellor that the King had been disgusted at the 'gross, scandalous' details that had been recorded by the press, and doubted whether there had been 'any similar instance of so repulsive an exposure of those intimate relations between man and woman' that the 'unwritten code of decency' had previously insisted be kept 'sacred and out of range of public Eye or Ear'.[37] The King's anxiety, shared by so many others, was that the discretion that traditionally protected

[33] K. Baynes (ed.), *Scoop, Scandal and Strife: A Study of Photography in Newspapers* (London: Lund Humphries, 1971); L. Nead, 'Courtroom Drama', in 'Powers of the Press', *BBC History Magazine*, Low Exhibition supplement, 2002.

[34] *Daily Mirror*, 8, 12, 13, 14 July 1922, 1.

[35] *Daily Mirror*, 13 July 1922, 1.

[36] *Daily Express*, 8, 12, 14, 15, 19, 22 July 1922, 1.

[37] National Archives, LCO 2/775, Lord Stamfordham to Lord Chancellor, 15 July 1922.

private behaviour was being eroded in a highly damaging way. It was this case that prompted Sir Evelyn Cecil's interest in imposing statutory restrictions on the press and led to him raising the issue in the House of Commons with a question to the Attorney-General.[38]

But the criticism provoked by the inconclusive first trial did nothing to restrain the press. Indeed when the suit returned to the divorce court in March 1923 the *Daily Mirror*'s coverage, in particular, was even more extensive than before. Its front page was dominated by the case on each of the first three days of evidence, with no fewer than fourteen photographs portraying the protagonists.[39] The case returned to the front page of the *Mirror* three more times before it concluded on 17 March; there were reports on the first inside spread (pages two and three) ten times in this period, and sometimes further material elsewhere in the paper.[40] Headlines gave tantalizing glimpses of the lurid evidence to follow: 'Many Lovers of Mrs. Russell—Twenty or Thirty—Did Not Believe Any of Them—Pride in Child—Dramatic Replies to Queries by Famous KC'.[41] This was the undue prominence, the 'accumulation of details', of which the moralists complained; the dailies could transform court cases into melodramas far more effectively than the Sundays, simply by being in a position to record every twist and turn of the proceedings, rather than merely summarizing the week's events. The *Daily Express* featured the case on its front page three times; on the second occasion the paper placed a large picture of Mrs Russell's baby under the headline 'Who Is My Daddy?'[42] At the end of the trial an editorial in the *Express* admitted that the reporting of the case had been 'intimate and unsavoury' and looked forward to being able to address 'cleaner and more important matters'—as if the paper bore no responsibility for the selection of news.[43] As was so often the case in Fleet Street, editors claimed merely to be meeting public demand.

The coverage of the Russell case was regarded as damaging not only because of the danger of corrupting impressionable readers, but also because it harmed the image of Britain abroad. In an increasingly inter-connected world, British journalism made a global impression. Frederick Peaker, President of the Institute of Journalists (IoJ), told Cecil's Select Committee that the details of many divorce trials were reproduced in the vernacular press in India, and 'instinctively led Indians to assume that this was the normal life in England'. That 'did not do any good for the British Empire' and could, he implied, weaken the moral authority which underpinned British rule.[44] Similar arguments were used by the sponsors of the Regulation of Reports Bill in 1925 and 1926. Lord Darling told the House of Lords in 1925 that he had been moved to take up the matter after being spoken to by 'representatives of foreign countries' who told him of the

[38] 164 H. C. Debs, 5s, col 249.
[39] *Daily Mirror*, 1–3 Mar. 1923, 1.
[40] *Daily Mirror*, 1–17 Mar. 1923.
[41] *Daily Mirror*, 8 Mar. 1929, 19.
[42] *Daily Express*, 2 Mar. 1923, 1.
[43] *Daily Express*, 17 Mar. 1923, 6.
[44] *The Times*, 11 July 1923, 9.

'great evil which was done to England' by the publication of details of sensational divorce cases. In most countries, newspapers were prohibited from recording the proceedings of such trials, and so foreign readers were particularly struck by the reports in the English press. Darling's informants told him that by reading such material people in their countries came to conclusions about the English which were 'thoroughly unjustified'.[45] Major Kindersley, introducing what was to be the successful bill in the Commons the following year, likewise observed that:

> The circulation of some of the most offending of our journals is not confined to this country, and there can be no doubt that foreign nations and our Eastern Empire and the Dominions derive from the altogether disproportionate space given to cases of this kind an entirely wrong impression of the social and domestic life of this country. This does infinite harm to our national prestige, and lowers us in the eyes of those to whom English domestic life and civilisation have in the past been an example and an inspiration.[46]

These critics articulated a powerful argument that the liberties granted to the press were being exploited for commercial gain by those with no concern for British standing in the world; statutory restrictions were essential to protect the nation's reputation for decency and morality.

In the face of this widespread criticism, Fleet Street was divided. After 1926 the press was keen to propagate the idea that it had supported the ban on divorce reporting, and had been relieved no longer to have to cover such sordid matters. Ralph Blumenfeld, the editor of the *Daily Express* from 1902 to 1929, wrote in 1933 that 'practically all the reputable newspapers' welcomed the Regulation of Reports Act, and that there was 'no doubt' this interference with the freedom of the press was 'amply justified'.[47] Fifteen years later Frank Owen, the editor of the *Daily Mail*, told the Royal Commission on the Press that 'every journal in Fleet Street of any responsibility welcomed the Act'.[48] The reality was more complex. The IoJ and the National Union of Journalists (NUJ) certainly pledged their support, and initially the Newspaper Proprietors' Association (NPA) told Cecil that they saw no difficulty in enacting his bill as drafted. The NPA soon changed its opinion, however, and in 1924 the Newspaper Society announced its objections to the measure. When William Joynson-Hicks, the Home Secretary, produced a memorandum on the matter in March 1925 he concluded that, 'speaking generally', the bill was 'opposed by the press'.[49] In August he confronted the 'leaders of the newspaper world', and clearly found them reluctant to agree to any restrictions: he told the Lord Chancellor that he had used 'plain Anglo-Saxon' to impress on them that 'they

[45] 62 H. C. Debs, 5s, Judicial Proceedings (Regulation of Reports) Bill, 16 July 1925, col. 131.

[46] 194 H. C. Debs, 5s, Judicial Proceedings (Regulation of Reports) Bill, 16 April 1926, col. 744. See also the comments of Major Astor, cols. 783–4.

[47] R. Blumenfeld, *The Press in My Time* (London: Rich & Cowan, 1933), 134.

[48] Royal Commission on the Press 1947–49, *Minutes of Evidence*, Day 32, 18.

[49] NA, CP 163 (25) Judicial Proceedings (Regulation of Reports) Bill—Memo by Home Sec., William Joynson-Hicks, 17 Mar. 1925.

had got to consent to something'.[50] Even then, the NPA resisted until the end, circulating a document to all MPs in April 1926 describing the proposed bill as 'unworkable' and 'unfair'.[51]

This resistance was also evident in the pages of popular newspapers. Editors did not alter the style of court reporting after the uproar surrounding the Russell trials, and they continued to defend the press's right to produce such reports. In March 1925, a case came before the court that was every bit as sensational as that of the Russells. It was not actually a divorce suit but a financial claim arising out of the recent divorce of a society couple, the Dennistouns; nevertheless, the evidence dealt at length with the couple's turbulent marriage, and in particular with the fact that Mrs Dennistoun had, with the knowledge of her husband, slept with General Sir John Cowans to further the husband's army career.[52] Like the Russell case, the Dennistoun trial provided material for titillating reports for nearly three weeks. It dominated the front page of the *Mirror* for each of the first three days of evidence, and returned to the front page three more times; the case even reached the front page of the relatively sober *Daily Herald* four times.[53] Once again, the King was moved to complain about the press coverage, Lord Stamfordham informing the Lord Chancellor that 'The King deplores the disastrous and far-reaching effects throughout all classes and on all ranks of the Army of the wholesale Press advertisement of this disgraceful Story.'[54] And once again, Fleet Street affected disgust while exploiting the story to the full.

The controversy did at least force some papers to justify their coverage. The *Mirror*, for example, admitted that there were now 'many critics' of the court reports, but pointed to the possibility of a 'grave legal scandal' if they were suppressed, and suggested that details might simply emerge through other channels: 'rumour is often a much more dangerous agency than plain statement'. It also implied that there were few readers who were not intrigued by this sort of content: 'We ask the average man to clear his mind of cant and say: "Does he or does he not read these reports himself? Is there not in them a 'human interest' that he cannot resist?"' The paper accepted that critics could be mollified if the press agreed to select details to report more carefully, but it offered no practical proposal as to how this would be achieved; it also immediately apportioned the blame elsewhere by criticizing the latitude allowed to lawyers in their cross-examinations.[55] The Dennistoun case showed an unapologetic press unwilling to bow to parliamentary pressure, exploiting the courtroom as readily as ever.

In the absence of any evidence of a change in the style of reporting, the campaign to restrict reports pressed ahead to a successful conclusion with a speed that surprised many in Fleet Street. The second reading of the Regulation

[50] NA, LCO 2/775, Joynson-Hicks to Lord Chancellor, 5 Aug. 1925.
[51] *The Times*, 17 April 1926, 7.
[52] Savage, 'Erotic Stories'.
[53] *Daily Mirror*, 4–26 Mar. 1925; *Daily Herald*, 12, 19, 24, 25 Mar. 1925, 1.
[54] NA, LCO 2/775, Lord Stamfordham to Lord Chancellor, 6 Mar. 1925.
[55] *Daily Mirror*, 26 Mar. 1925, 6.

of Reports Bill in April 1926 demonstrated just how extensive parliamentary support was for it, with the bill passing by a crushing 222 votes to three, and it crossed the remaining hurdles with ease. Faced with the new legislation at the end of the year, the trade journal *Newspaper World* admitted that it had come 'far sooner than expected' and attributed the bill's momentum to a decisive change in popular opinion: 'The people demanded the measure. Things were being reported by some journals that made men and women shudder.'[56] The act was a symbol that Parliament was prepared to encroach on the 'freedom of the press' in order to protect public morality. It was a product of deep anxieties, both inside and outside parliament, about discussing and drawing attention to activities that were perceived to belong in the private sphere. Fleet Street had underestimated the determination of its critics and failed to recognize that the new illustrated popular daily journalism, with its bright photographs and brash headlines, would intensify long-held concerns.

Yet did the act have the effect its proposers intended? It certainly reminded popular newspaper editors of the need to exercise caution when discussing intimate personal relationships, and ensured that evasive and euphemistic styles of reporting remained in place. Some observers detected a moral improvement in the press. Robert Graves and Alan Hodge argued in 1940 that after the passage of the act 'the Press got cleaner and cleaner as the period advanced'.[57] Robert Ensor, questioning witnesses as a member of the Royal Commission on the Press in 1948, accepted that 'a considerable contribution has been made by the Act of Parliament which prohibited divorce reports . . . no harm was done to anybody, but there was a great benefit to the public.'[58] The 1926 act also laid down an important precedent. It emboldened Parliament to impose further restrictions to prevent the press exploiting other types of court case. In 1933 it regulated the reporting of cases involving juveniles, in 1935 it permitted evidence of sexual incapacity in nullity proceedings to be given *in camera*, and in 1937 it prevented the publication of the details of certain domestic, matrimonial, and guardianship cases.[59] This process of regulating media coverage of the legal system continued in the second half of the century amid growing concern that the media could hinder or even pervert the course of justice. In 1962 the reporting of committal proceedings in magistrates' courts was restricted, and in 1981 the Contempt of Court Act tightened the law relating to the coverage of suspects who had been charged by the police.

[56] *Newspaper World*, 11 Dec. 1926, 7.

[57] R. Graves and A. Hodge, *The Long Week-End: A Social History of Great Britain 1918–1939* (first pub. 1940; Harmondsworth: Penguin, 1971), 108.

[58] Royal Commission on the Press 1947–49, *Minutes of Evidence*, Day 32, 18.

[59] The relevant acts were the Children and Young Persons Act 1933; the Supreme Court of Judicature (Amendment) Act 1935; and the Summary Procedure (Domestic Proceedings) Act 1937: see Political and Economic Planning, *Report on the British Press* (London: PEP, 1938), 221.

From another perspective, however, the 1926 act demonstrated how difficult it was to control the press by legislation. While divorce trials could no longer be built up into serial melodramas over several days, the basic details of the case and the judge's summing up could still be used to provide entertaining articles—and, as one editor observed, 'some judges provide fairly meaty reading when they get a contested case to review'.[60] Divorce court reports, therefore, continued to appear in both popular dailies and Sundays, and they continued to provoke complaints. In January 1952, for example, Arthur Christiansen told Beaverbrook that the *Mirror* was using a 'particularly dirty divorce case' to titillate readers; the same year, Conservative MP and respected journalist William Deedes lamented to the House of Commons that the Sunday press were still serving up 'divorce and dirt' under a 'very thinly veiled hypocrisy'.[61] More than three decades later a TUC study noted that one of the main ways in which 'ordinary women' received prominence in the press was as a party 'in a salaciously treated divorce case'.[62]

More importantly, though, the legislation was narrowly drawn and left plenty of trials other than divorce suits that could be used to provide drama and details of sexual transgression. Discussing the Regulation of Reports Bill on the eve of its Second Reading in 1926, *The Times* doubted 'whether its enactment will have any serious effect at all on the admitted evil which it sets out to attack . . . the ingenuity which ransacks all the world for garbage is not likely to be cramped by the loss of this particular field'.[63] The Dennistoun trial that had provoked such protests in 1925 was, after all, a financial action rather than a divorce suit, and hence would not have been covered by the legislation had it been in force. After 1926—and even after the further legislation of the 1930s—it was simple enough for the press to find similarly titillating cases that were not subject to reporting restrictions. *The Times*'s prediction proved to be correct, and complaints about how easily 'garbage' could be 'ransacked' from court rooms continued to be expressed frequently. The first Royal Commission on the Press was concerned about the prevalence of salacious court reporting, as were many MPs in the 1950s.[64] The Regulation of Reports Act ultimately did little to inhibit the development of popular journalism based on human interest, sex, and melodrama.

What conclusions can be drawn about the effect of divorce reports on readers? Anne Humphries has argued that the most important impact of divorce reports was to help 'to naturalize the idea of divorce' by creating the impression that

60 C. Wintour, *Pressures on the Press* (London: Andre Deutsch, 1972), 139.

61 Beaverbrook Papers, H/155, Christiansen to Beaverbrook, 31 Jan. 1952; 508 H. C. Debs, 5s, 28 Nov. 1952, col. 994.

62 Trades Union Congress, *Images of Inequality: The Portrayal of Women in the Media and Advertising* (London: TUC, 1984), 7.

63 *The Times*, 15 April 1926, 15; see also 16 May 1923, 15; 1 Aug. 1923, 11.

64 Royal Commission on the Press, *Minutes of Evidence*, Day 13; 570 H. C. Debs, 5s, 17 May 1957, State of the Press.

it was common: the press, she concludes, 'was a strong factor in the gradual acceptance of divorce as a means of dealing with an unsatisfactory marriage'.[65] This is a plausible contention, although it must be remembered that the expense and difficulty of obtaining a divorce meant that it remained out of reach for the majority of the population until the second half of the century. As Humphries observes, moreover, the 'gradual acceptance' of divorce did not damage the popularity of marriage as such—merely the idea that marriages should be unbreakable. The popular press maintained a stout defence of marriage against its critics, while accepting that some marriages needed to be dissolved. During the hearing of the Russell suit a *Daily Express* editorial was severely critical of the 'literary opportunists' who asked 'Is marriage a failure?'; two years later the paper argued that 'in nearly every case it is only the little mind and the little soul that find marriage a mistake'.[66] It was, nevertheless, increasingly difficult to maintain some of the more romantic idealizations of marriage in the face of the stream of stories about adultery and betrayal. One commentator observed in November 1920 that young girls were unable to keep their 'dreams of knights in armour' for long in the modern world: 'The croaking, mocking laughter of the Divorce Court shrieks out at her and shatters them. She sees her ideals mocked and travestied daily within its grim and dusty walls.'[67]

Some working-class readers may have been particularly struck by the extent of adultery and immorality among the social elites, which is one reason why this type of reporting caused such anxiety in many political circles. Some left-wing papers explicitly encouraged readers to think in this way. The *Daily Herald*, in particular, maintained the long radical tradition of using examples of immoral personal behaviour as evidence of the wider corruption of the political and social system. An editorial after the Dennistoun case suggested that the revelations in court confirmed that the standards of the upper class were probably lower 'than at any previous period in our history; never before have aristocratic prostitutes, pimps and paramours dragged their doings into public gaze'. Such depravity, the paper argued, was an inevitable consequence of a capitalist society.[68] Most popular papers, however, were reluctant to draw such lessons. The *Mirror* dismissed the idea that the Dennistoun trial suggested 'that "our betters" are not what they should be . . . it is more charitable, and also much more accurate, to assume that nobody is anybody else's "better", as far as the division of the classes goes, high or low, rich or poor'.[69] Divorce reports probably encouraged cynicism about upper-class behaviour, rather than fomenting political radicalism. It has been suggested that the ruling elites only lost their 'moral authority' as a result of the Profumo scandal in 1963, but

[65] Humphries, 'Coming Apart', 228.
[66] *Daily Express*, 15 July 1922, 6; 21 Oct. 1924, 8.
[67] *Daily Express*, 12 Nov. 1920, 6.
[68] *Daily Herald*, 25 Mar. 1925, 4.
[69] *Daily Mirror*, 24 Mar. 1925, 7. The *Daily Express* made a similar point at the end of the Russell trial: 17 Mar. 1923, 6.

the long history of scandalous tales from the divorce courts clearly eroded their authority before then.

It is reasonable to conclude that divorce reports, like other court coverage of the period, offered readers a convenient opportunity to satisfy some of their curiosity about sexual indulgence and moral transgression while maintaining their attachment to conventional values. For all that they gloried in the titillating details of adulteries and affairs, court reporters and leader writers invariably included conspicuous condemnations of promiscuity and unfaithfulness. If the reports hinted at the pleasures of illicit sex, they also underlined that such pleasures often produced serious consequences: not only the breakdown of marriage, but also unwelcome publicity and considerable damage to one's reputation. In this light, the anxieties of the critics of the press coverage seem ridiculously overblown. Yet contemporaries believed that newspapers carried a tremendous moral power, and when there was so little discussion of sex in mainstream popular culture, the ambivalences and ambiguities of the divorce reports could seem profoundly threatening. As the cultural environment changed in the second half of the century, however, some of these fears started to fade.

NEW STYLES OF COURT REPORTING IN THE 1950S AND 1960S

In the 1950s the popular press's greater willingness to discuss sexual issues led to some significant shifts in court reporting. Daily newspapers started to report a broader range of sexual offences, rather than leave them to the *News of the World*. This was most noticeable with regard to homosexual offences (discussed fully in Chapter 5), but popular dailies also included reports of rape and indecent assault cases more regularly.[70] At the *Express*, Arthur Christiansen certainly spotted this tendency: in 1952, for example, he sent Beaverbrook a clipping showing how the *Daily Mail* had reported an actual bodily harm case with a sexual element, of the type 'which is normally reserved for the *News of the World*'.[71] At the same time crime journalism was gradually becoming less evasive and euphemistic. Descriptions became fuller and medical, scientific and psychoanalytic terminology became more common.

These developments were evident in the coverage of the trial in June 1953 of John Christie for a series of murders at his house, 10 Rillington Place in Notting Hill, London. There was an obvious sexual dimension to the murders. Christie strangled most of his seven victims while having intercourse with them, and he had intercourse with some after they had died; he also removed pubic hairs as trophies. Such gruesome events left journalists in a dilemma about what they

70 Soothill and Walby, *Sex Crime*, 18.

71 Beaverbrook Papers, H/155, Arthur Christiansen to Beaverbrook, 8 Aug. 1952.

could report, but whereas in previous decades most of the daily papers would have been very cautious and evasive, now they gave a fairly accurate description of the nature of the murders. Both the *Express* and the *Mirror* reported the post-strangulation intercourse and the evidence regarding Christie's previous sexual problems, and they made vague references to the collection of hair.[72] The *Daily Herald* went further, explaining the source of the hair and, after the verdict, providing a psychological profile of the murderer. The *Herald* doctor described Christie as a 'necrophiliac sado-masochist, a hair-fetishist and a psychopath'; he explained the meanings of sadism and masochism and suggested that Christie's personality was the product of a bad 'child–parent relationship'.[73]

This reporting was significantly more direct than had been usual before the Second World War. The *Express*, which was most conspicuously breaking with its tradition of coyness on sexual matters, printed an editorial justifying its decisions in this case. It admitted that the 'dreadful and sordid issues' being discussed gave the paper 'a problem of good taste and fair presentation in preparing its account'. Nevertheless, it argued that 'the proceedings of a trial of this magnitude, where the life of a man is at stake, must be made available to the public for the same reason that they are held in a public court. Publicity is the ultimate safeguard of justice.' By 'striving to combine decency with completeness', the editorial concluded, 'the *Daily Express* carries out an essential, if unpleasant, part of its duty to the public.'[74] It might have added that the public interest in the case was such that the *Express* did not want to risk its readers having to follow proceedings in a rival publication.

These shifts in crime coverage, and the reporting of the Christie case in particular, were highly controversial. Conservative MP Christopher Hollis protested that 'It is incredible that newspapers should be found ready to pander to a public taste for every detail' of murders with sexual motives. 'So long as the Press continue to grab at these stories with an hysterical enthusiasm,' he argued, 'they must take a considerable share of the responsibility if from time to time other sordid and horrible crimes of the same kind are committed'.[75] For editors like Hugh Cudlipp, on the other hand, this more explicit style of journalism was a necessary response to the new attitudes of a more sexually informed younger generation of readers. In November 1953, Cudlipp took the highly unusual step of devoting four pages over three days—including one front page—to a series entitled 'Sex, Crime, and The Press', which explained in detail the paper's policies on these issues.[76] It dismissed complaints that 'newspapers make too much of horrors like the Christie case' by observing that 'The world is as it is. The newspapers are bound to reflect it or give a false picture.' The *Mirror*'s direct style of reporting, it claimed, was motivated by a democratic impulse

[72] *Daily Express*, *Daily Mirror* 22–6 June 1953.

[73] *Daily Herald*, 24 June 1953, 6; 26 June 1953, 6.

[74] *Daily Express*, 25 June 1953, 4.

[75] *Sunday Express*, 30 Aug. 1953, 4.

[76] *Daily Mirror*, 11–13 Nov. 1953.

and a detestation of hypocrisy: 'We give plain meanings in plain words so that we all can understand them.' On sexual matters, the paper declared that it was aiming to reflect the 'much healthier' and 'much franker' attitude to sex that had developed over recent years among young people. It suggested that complaints about this coverage were made only by an older generation who did not share this outlook. 'An attitude which seems perfectly normal to young people still shocks the elderly. And many critics are old fogies—well-meaning, no doubt, yet out of touch with modern trends and tastes.'[77] 'We're a cheeky, daring, gay newspaper', the series concluded defiantly, 'But we're blowed if we are a dirty newspaper.'

Once again, Cudlipp demonstrated his skill in linking sexual explicitness with democracy, modernity, and youthful idealism, rather than with commercialism or prurience. It was the paper's duty, he claimed, to satisfy the healthy, 'perfectly normal' curiosity of the younger generation, and that included honesty about the criminal and transgressive aspects of sexuality. The series impressed Fleet Street observers. One of the columnists in the trade paper *World's Press News* celebrated the articles as 'the best things the *Mirror* has done for a long time. . . . There were flaws and omissions in its arguments, but the arguments were beautifully put.'[78] Variations on these arguments enabled popular newspapers to justify the increasing detail of their crime journalism and to stereotype critics as 'prudes' who were out of touch with the new realities of the post-war world.

These developments posed a problem for the *News of the World*. On the one hand, rival newspapers were becoming more explicit in their reporting of the most sensational court cases, thereby encroaching on its traditional territory; at the same time, papers like the *Mirror* and the *Pictorial* were also offering, in their entertaining and informative features on a variety of sexual issues, a more positive vision of sexuality, which made the *News of the World*'s relentless catalogue of routine sexual offences seem rather dated. The American journalist Thomas Matthews observed in 1957 that the *News of the World*, while still 'extremely sex-conscious, still clings to the outmoded, moralistic view of sex as something delightfully furtive and shocking'. The *Mirror* and the *Pictorial*, by contrast, shared the attitude of the 'rising generation' that 'takes sex at its declined but up-to-date value, as just a bit of good healthy fun'.[79] The sharp decline in the *News of the World*'s circulation in the 1950s confirmed that readers were finding the paper's formula less appealing. When Stafford Somerfield became editor in 1960 he recognized that fundamental editorial changes were necessary and that in this new era 'it was not enough to print straightforward court reports'. He told his staff that the paper's style had to be altered, the make-up brightened with 'bigger pictures and bigger type' and 'more up-to-date language' used.[80] He

[77] *Daily Mirror*, 12 Nov. 1953, 2.

[78] *World's Press News*, 20 Nov. 1953, 14.

[79] T. S. Matthews, *The Sugar Pill: An Essay on Newspapers* (London: Victor Gollancz, 1957), 153.

[80] Somerfield, *Banner Headlines*, 111.

spotted the public's growing appetite in the television age for celebrity journalism, and increased the resources devoted to securing features involving major stars: he signalled his intent with a high-profile serialization of the life story of Diana Dors (see Chapter 7). Crime reporting was still to be a central part of the paper, but Somerfield placed a new emphasis on investigation and winning scoops rather than simply relying on transcripts from the courtroom. Reporters became more intrusive in a bid to obtain the 'story behind the story', and large sums of money were spent on winning the testimony of key participants in the most sensational cases. These aggressive techniques increasingly brought the paper into conflict with the Press Council.

THE GROWTH OF CHEQUEBOOK JOURNALISM: THE PROFUMO AFFAIR AND THE MOORS MURDERS

There was a long tradition in Fleet Street of securing 'confessions' or life stories from the protagonists in notable court cases. The practice was common enough by 1926 for the barrister Sir Ellis Hume-Williams to complain about the press's 'modern, sickly mania for making a quasi-hero of a man who has committed an abominable murder'.[81] In 1949, the *News of the World* spent over £10,000 paying for the defence of the 'acid bath murderer' John Haigh in return for his life story.[82] When John Christie arrived at West London Police Court in 1953 for the preliminaries of his murder case, he was met by two sets of solicitors, one sent by the *Sunday Pictorial* and the other by the *Sunday Dispatch*: both papers were hoping to obtain an exclusive. The *Pictorial* was successful, thanks to the careful negotiations of Harry Procter.[83] But the activities of the *News of the World* in particular ensured that this 'chequebook journalism' became significantly more prominent—and competitive—in the 1960s.

The most notorious example of the rise of chequebook journalism was during the Profumo affair in 1963. The essence of this scandal was the denial and subsequent admission by John Profumo, the War Minister, that he had had an 'improper acquaintanceship' with the young model Christine Keeler—who, it emerged, had also had a relationship with the assistant naval attaché at the Soviet embassy, Captain Yevgeny Ivanov.[84] What enabled the press to keep the story in the headlines for so long, however, was the series of court cases involving Keeler, her friend Mandy Rice-Davies, and the osteopath Stephen Ward, who had brought Keeler and Profumo together. In March 1963, Keeler and Rice-Davies were witnesses in the trial of the West Indian Johnny Edgecombe, one

[81] 200 H. C. Debs, 5s, Judicial Proceedings (Regulation of Reports) Bill, 10 Dec. 1926, col. 2458.

[82] Bainbridge and Stockdill, *News of the World Story*, 145.

[83] H. Procter, *The Street of Disillusion* (London: Allan Wingate, 1958), 174–6.

[84] On the Profumo affair see A. Summers and S. Dorrill, *Honeytrap* (London: Coronet, 1988).

of Keeler's lovers, who was accused of shooting at her. In itself a minor case, the press was nevertheless able to make innuendoes about connections to important London figures; Keeler then added to the drama by fleeing to Spain and failing to appear at the Old Bailey. Soon after Profumo's admission and resignation in June 1963, Stephen Ward was charged with living off immoral earnings. Keeler and Rice-Davies were among the many witnesses in the sensational trial that followed, which received huge coverage in all of the popular papers. The press revelled in the stories of orgies and casual sex in wealthy London circles and titillated readers with details of two-way mirrors and outrageous party games.

The most striking aspect of the coverage, though, was the willingness of the press to buy up the stories of the protagonists, irrespective of their involvement in ongoing court cases. Obtaining exclusives seemed to outweigh the possible danger of interfering with the administration of justice or prejudicing juries. In April, *Daily Express* journalists managed to track down Keeler—at that stage a missing witness—in Madrid and paid her £2,000 to speak about her life and her friendship with Profumo.[85] After Profumo's resignation, Keeler's value rocketed, and it took the huge sum of £23,000 for the *News of the World* to secure a five-part serialization of the 'Confessions of Christine'.[86] Mandy Rice-Davies was also pursued vigorously by the press. During the Ward trial she admitted that she was 'under contract to several newspapers'; her deal with the *Express* apparently included an extra payment of £500 if she mentioned the name of Bill Astor, the owner of Cliveden, whom she claimed to have slept with.[87]

The aggressive pursuit of the protagonists in the Profumo affair heralded a new era in the press coverage of crime and scandal. In the competitive climate of the 1960s, with every newspaper reporting the salacious details of court cases and television cameras filming the protagonists, papers like the *News of the World* had to work harder to secure an advantage and maintain the loyalty of readers. As the culture of celebrity blossomed, and the public became accustomed to reading life stories and 'confessions' of Hollywood stars, there was an appetite for similar personal narratives from those involved in high profile court cases. There was, in fact, a striking convergence of crime and celebrity journalism in these years. Keeler's confessions exhibited clear parallels with those of Diana Dors three years earlier. There were comparable descriptions of difficult early sexual experiences with a subsequent progression to involvement in sexually liberated circles; both women were open about their sexual appetite and their rejection of conventional, demure models of femininity. The Keeler articles, like the Dors series, were liberally illustrated with titillating photographs (including several of Lewis Morley's famous shots showing Keeler posed nude astride a chair). The text was full of the clichés of erotic melodrama. Describing her encounter with

[85] Beaverbrook Papers, H/226, Beaverbrook to Robert Edwards, 8 April 1963; Edwards to Beaverbrook, 9 April 1963.

[86] Somerfield, *Banner Headlines*, 139–44.

[87] Greenslade, *Press Gang*, 187.

Ivanov, for example, Keeler enthused that he was her 'perfect specimen of a man': 'And he wanted me. He couldn't have stopped now, anyway. We crashed across the room . . . . He pinioned me in a corner by the door. I relaxed. Because he was just kissing me with all the power of a man in a frenzy of passion . . . . There was a little bed . . . . From that second I too threw all reserve to the winds.'[88]

The *News of the World*'s rivals tried to ensure that their readers did not miss out on Keeler stories. The *Sunday Mirror* squeezed all it could from earlier interviews they had conducted with her. Most notably, it had obtained a handwritten letter from Profumo to Keeler, beginning with the affectionate greeting 'Darling . . .', and it printed this in full on the front page. The following week the paper disclosed 'What Christine Keeler Told Us About That Nuclear Question'.[89] *The People*, meanwhile, unsparingly exposed what it called 'the ugly truth' of Keeler's life. She was a 'cold-blooded harlot', a 'shameless slut', who 'smoked marijuana' and 'loved orgies', and even boasted 'of picking up down-and-outs and taking one of the scruffiest of them to sleep with her'.[90] With little or no concern for Keeler herself, the popular press scrutinized every aspect of her life and served it up for consumption by an eager public. Keeler became the first in a line of notorious figures that would escape the confines of the traditional court report and be given the full celebrity treatment: the 'Great Train Robbers' and the Kray twins would soon follow.

For many critics, these confessions and life stories posed a far greater moral threat than standard court reporting. If it was objectionable for newspapers to mine legal proceedings for details of crime and immorality, these details were at least presented as part of a record of official judgement and punishment, with the court transparently and unambiguously declaring society's disapproval of criminal behaviour and scrutinizing the veracity of any statements made. Keeler's narrative in the *News of the World*, recounting her sexual liaisons and her adventures with London's demi-monde, lacked this clear moral grounding, and there was no way of knowing whether incidents she described had been exaggerated or fabricated. When her story was published Keeler had not, it is true, been convicted of any offence, but her evident involvement in prostitution was enough to condemn her in the eyes of moralists. Yet far from being punished for her promiscuity and immorality, critics complained, she was richly rewarded by a national newspaper. It was feared that this might 'encourage some young women to believe they could make handsome profits out of immorality'.[91] The purchase of Keeler's 'confessions' generated a furore, and was widely denounced by politicians and religious leaders. Lord Shawcross, who had recently chaired the second Royal Commission on the Press, gained considerable attention for his scathing attack

[88] *News of the World*, 16 June 1963, 4.

[89] *Sunday Mirror*, 9 June 1963, 1, 36; 16 June 1963, 1.

[90] *The People*, 4 Aug. 1963, 1, 10–11.

[91] This fear was voiced by, among others, Sir Linton Andrews in *World's Press News*, 15 Nov. 1963, 12.

on 'the publicising of pimps, prostitutes or perverts in highly-paid interviews or feature articles'.[92] Lord Peddie asked the government directly whether 'the increasing practice' of buying the life stories of 'persons of undesirable notoriety should be referred to the Press Council'. Viscount Hailsham, Lord President of the Council, replied that the government deplored 'the publication in the Press of memoirs which lend glamour to crime, or to vice . . . and cater for an unhealthy interest in them', and confirmed that it would welcome a ruling from the Press Council.[93]

The Press Council responded in September with the most damning adjudication it had delivered since its establishment ten years previously. It was careful to make a distinction between 'the reporting of news' and 'its elaboration in memoirs and other articles'. It accepted that the 'extensive reporting of court proceedings in the Ward case was justified as news of exceptional interest and public concern', although it argued that 'some intimate detail should have been omitted' and condemned the way the press had given 'excessive prominence to' and 'glamorised' people concerned in 'prostitution and vice'. What the Council primarily objected to, however, was the 'publication of personal stories and feature articles of an unsavoury nature where the public interest does not require it'. The *News of the World*'s publication of the details of Keeler's 'sordid life story' was censured as being 'particularly damaging to the morals of young people'. The Council concluded that the paper had exploited 'vice and sex for commercial reward' and thereby 'done a disservice both to public welfare and to the Press'.[94]

Yet without sanctions to discipline newspapers, the Press Council was unable to rein in popular newspapers determined to obtain a competitive advantage by securing these confessional accounts. Stafford Somerfield, the editor of the *News of the World*, flatly rejected the Press Council's criticism, arguing that a 'healthy society must surely demand exposure, however sordid, in the context of recent events . . . the public is entitled to know what is going on.' He claimed that only by speaking to Keeler could the facts of the affair be ascertained, and 'to provide the facts we had to pay'. Nothing the paper had published, he added, 'sought to disguise as virtue that which is vicious', and he concluded by appealing to the court of public opinion: 'A prodigious and mounting readership tacitly acknowledges the rightness of the course we have followed'.[95] Somerfield did not, however, explain why exposing 'what is going on' required the inclusion of nude photos of Keeler and breathless descriptions of her earlier life as a model and showgirl. Many of the press's high-minded justifications for their aggressive pursuit of this story, especially those appealing to the security angle, were clearly

[92] For example, *Daily Mirror*, 20 June 1963, 1.

[93] Press Council, *The Press and the People: Annual Report 1964* (London: Press Council, 1964), 21.

[94] Ibid., 19. [95] Ibid., 18.

disingenuous. At the same time, many journalists sincerely believed that they had a right to expose the immorality of sections of the London elite, and suspected the Press Council of trying to protect this elite.

The lack of contrition at the *News of the World* was matched elsewhere in Fleet Street, and the Press Council's severe judgement did little to prevent journalists continuing to pursue Keeler. Having opened up her life to the press, Keeler found that she could not subsequently reclaim her privacy. In 1964, for example, the *Daily Sketch* published her telephone number, and she was deluged with abusive calls.[96] The following year, a number of newspapers refused her requests not to print her new name and address after her marriage; in fact, once they had discovered her whereabouts, photographers and reporters 'laid siege' to her house.[97] In 1969, Keeler gave up trying to escape the media attention and serialized another version of her story in the *News of the World*. Once again the Press Council censured the paper for 'an exploitation of sex and vice for commercial purposes'; once again Stafford Somerfield was unrepentant.[98] The whole Keeler saga left the Press Council appearing weak and ineffective.

The significance of the Profumo affair will be explored further in Chapter 7, but its legacy in terms of court coverage was an intensification of the competition for the personal stories of protagonists in major cases. Newspapers fed, and responded to, the public appetite for intimate 'revelations' and eye-witness testimony. This focus on the personal and the particular not only made it increasingly difficult to report crime with a due sense of perspective, the often unscrupulous pursuit of 'scoops' sometimes became a serious threat to the administration of justice. This threat became evident during the trial of Ian Brady and Myra Hindley for the 'Moors Murders' in April and May 1966. The nature of the case, involving the brutal murder of three children, ensured huge press attention, and the unusual participation of a woman in the crime—apparently betraying her 'feminine' instincts to protect the young—only added to the interest. Before the hearing started both the *News of the World* and the *People* declared it to be nothing less than 'the trial of the century'.[99] The evidence heard in court was so gruesome, however, that some popular newspapers sensed a mood of public revulsion and wrote about the case very cautiously (indeed, some of the journalists covering the case admitted suffering nightmares afterwards).[100] The *People* found that 'the horrifying nature of the allegations produces a kind of vocal numbness when anybody tries to raise the subject', and described local people avoiding newspapers with coverage of the court proceedings. It went on to halt its coverage of the case completely.[101] The *Express* and the *Mirror* provided readers with day-by-day reports of the trial, but some of the evidence—for example, the tape recording

[96] Press Council, *Annual Report 1965*, 97–8.
[97] Press Council, *Annual Report 1966*, 95–6.
[98] Press Council, *Annual Report 1970*, 70–2.
[99] *News of the World*, 17 April 1966, 1; *The People*, 17 April 1966, 12.
[100] Greenslade, *Press Gang*, 232.
[101] *The People*, 24 April 1966, 12.

of Lesley Ann Downey's murder—was described only briefly, and both papers included leading articles emphasizing the care they had taken in editing this material.[102]

The *News of the World*, on the other hand, was fully committed to its coverage because it had prepared for a sensational scoop by placing under contract one of the main prosecution witnesses, David Smith, the 18-year-old who had gone to the police after helping Brady dispose of one of the bodies. *News of the World* reporters looked after Smith and his wife, Maureen, for some months before the trial, paying hotel costs, sending them on holiday to France, and giving them small sums of money when required. After the trial Smith was promised £1000 for revelations about his experiences with Brady and Hindley.[103] But with its determination to obtain this exclusive, the *News of the World* put the 'trial of the century' in jeopardy.

These careful preparations dramatically unravelled when they were discovered by the defence counsel and exposed in court. When Smith agreed during his cross-examination that he had a financial incentive in the conviction of Brady and Hindley, there was uproar. The judge, Mr Justice Fenton Atkinson, observed that there 'there seems to be a gross interference with the course of justice', and the Attorney-General, Sir Elwyn Jones immediately promised an investigation.[104] Questions were subsequently raised in both Houses of Parliament. Fortunately for the *News of World*, Mr Justice Atkinson eventually decided that the substance of Smith's testimony had not been altered by the 'extraordinary arrangement' he had made with the paper. After 'careful consideration' the Attorney-General concurred, and did not recommend prosecution of the paper for contempt of court. Nevertheless, he told the Commons that the practice of paying witnesses gave rise to 'serious problems in relation to the administration of justice', and announced that the Government would examine the issue with a view to tightening the law.[105] In private, the Attorney-General and the Prime Minister, Harold Wilson, made clear to Lord Devlin, the Chairman of the Press Council, that they hoped that the press 'would put its own house in order' so as to make legislation unnecessary.[106] Devlin recognized the need for firm action from the Press Council, especially as *News of the World*'s contract with David Smith openly flouted the 1963 adjudication against chequebook journalism made in the wake of the Keeler affair. 'I think that the *News of the World* is the only newspaper which blatantly disregards what I believe is now the prevailing morality in Fleet Street', Devlin told the Attorney-General, and proposed a 'declaration of principle' to which the national press would be expected to subscribe. This was to be the Council's first formal statement on professional standards for the industry

[102] *Daily Express*, 7 May 1966, 10; *Daily Mirror*, 29 April 1966, 1.

[103] Greenslade, *Press Gang*, 232.

[104] Ibid; *Daily Mirror*, 23 April 1966, 7.

[105] *The Times*, 12 May 1966, 17.

[106] NA, Prem 13/1067, Sir Elwyn Jones to Harold Wilson, 13 May 1966.

and, Devlin noted when he submitted a draft to the government, it was 'regarded in Fleet Street as rather a revolutionary thing to have done'.[107]

The declaration of principle, issued on 27 November 1966, stated that no payment should be made by a newspaper 'to any person known or reasonably expected to be a witness in criminal proceedings already begun'; nor should newspapers question witnesses about their evidence until after the trial. A third clause stated that 'no payment should be made for feature articles to persons engaged in crime or other notorious misbehaviour where the public interest does not warrant it.'[108] Devlin expected little dissent from the first two rules, although he expected that 'some will jib—certainly the *News of the World* will—about the wording of the third'. This third rule was, he admitted to Elwyn Jones, 'a bit of a bonus anyway', a continuation of the efforts begun in 1963 to clamp down on what the Press Council regarded as the glamorization of vice.[109] The Attorney-General told the Prime Minister that the declaration went 'quite a way' to meeting the anxieties expressed about press practices, and that he was prepared to 'see how the new code of conduct works in practice'.[110]

It was, however, very optimistic to believe that voluntary regulation would stamp out the excesses of chequebook journalism. Many in Fleet Street, it is true, did accept the need for greater care to ensure that newspapers did not interfere with the administration of justice, if only because debacles like the Moors Murders trial were hugely damaging to the reputation of journalism. On the other hand, the Press Council was not generally held in high esteem, and editors and journalists were all too aware that it had no power to enforce its rules. As Devlin predicted, moreover, there was open resistance from the *News of the World*. After welcoming the first two points of the declaration, the paper criticized the Council for moving beyond the specific issue of payments while legal proceedings were ongoing. The third rule was 'another step on the road to censorship': 'The public interest demands that matters which are criminal, vicious and unsavoury should be exposed and not concealed. The greater the evil, the greater the need for exposure.'[111]

So while the declaration was enough to remove the issue from the public agenda in the short term, subsequent events confirmed that when a major story broke, fiercely competitive journalists would bend and break the voluntary code of conduct to obtain a scoop for their newspapers. Witnesses were still approached and inducements offered for their information. Nor were these practices confined to the popular press. During the 1978 trial of Jeremy Thorpe, the former Liberal Party leader, for conspiracy to murder a male model who was allegedly blackmailing him over a homosexual relationship, the *Sunday Telegraph*

107 NA, Prem 13/1067, Lord Devlin to Sir Elwyn Jones, 27 Oct. 1966.
108 *The Times*, 28 Nov. 1966, 9.
109 NA, Prem 13/1067, Lord Devlin to Sir Elwyn Jones, 27 Oct. 1966.
110 NA, Prem 13/1067, Sir Elwyn Jones to Harold Wilson, 22 Nov. 1966.
111 *News of the World*, 27 Nov. 1966, 10.

was found to have agreed a contract with the main prosecution witness, Peter Bessell, to serialize his story. The agreement stated that Bessell would receive £50,000 in the event of a conviction, and only half that amount for a shorter series of articles if Thorpe was found to be innocent: Bessell therefore appeared to have a clear incentive to help secure a guilty verdict. Just as in the Moors Murder trial, when this deal was exposed by the defence, there was a public outcry. The *Sunday Telegraph* pulled out of the contract, and was severely censured by the Press Council.[112]

There was a similar journalistic frenzy after the arrest of Peter Sutcliffe, the so-called 'Yorkshire Ripper', in January 1981. Four papers named Sutcliffe before he had been charged, and a string of witnesses were offered money for their stories. *People* journalists located Sutcliffe's best friend, Trevor Birdsall, and took him to a remote hotel outside Oldham; the police were only able to interview him after going through the paper. The *Daily Star* paid £26,500 to Sutcliffe's brothers, and a further £4,000 to the woman found with Sutcliffe when he was arrested. The *Mail* paid £5,000 to Sutcliffe's father and three of his daughters. Most controversially of all, there was a fierce battle for the story of Sutcliffe's wife, Sonia, although she resisted the various offers made to her. A lengthy report, eventually published by the Press Council in 1983, censured no fewer than seven newspapers for breaking its 1966 declaration of principle.[113] The Sutcliffe case starkly exposed the failures of voluntary regulation, and prompted calls for the Press Council to be replaced or radically reformed.[114]

Crime journalism in the second half of the century became preoccupied with the pursuit of intimate details, 'revelations', and 'confessions'. In the competitive environment of Fleet Street, this inevitably led to a heavy reliance on the chequebook and a frequent disregard for the sort of professional standards that the Press Council hoped to inculcate in the industry. Neither a clarification of the legal framework (the 1981 Contempt of Court Act) nor a change of regulatory regime (the replacement of the Press Council by the Press Complaints Commission in 1991) served to curb this tendency—as the reporting of the Soham murder case in 2004 indicated. The journalistic obsession with personalities encouraged public anxieties to be channelled into a hatred of the 'monsters' who had committed crimes, at the expense of any sense of perspective on the wider issues. And in the most high profile cases, the stories continued long after conviction. A survey of the press in 1985 found no fewer than 151 stories about the Moors Murderers, and a further 34 involving the

[112] S. Freeman and B. Penrose, *Rinkagate: The Rise and Fall of Jeremy Thorpe* (London: Bloomsbury, 1997).

[113] Greenslade, *Press Gang*, 435–41; G. Robertson, *People Against the Press: An Enquiry into the Press Council* (London: Quartet Books, 1983) 34, 92–8; Press Council, *Press Conduct in the Sutcliffe Case* (London: Press Council, 1983); Roger Ratcliffe, 'Cash for Questions', *Guardian*, 8 May 2006, *MediaGuardian*, 1–2.

[114] For example, Robertson, *People Against the Press.*

Yorkshire Ripper.[115] This sort of emotive coverage in the popular press was one of the reasons that public support for the death penalty remained so high after its abolition by parliament in 1969.

RAPE COVERAGE

Another area in which the press were accused of undermining the administration of justice was in the reporting of rape and sexual assault. It was widely accepted that the press had a responsibility to cover such cases sensitively and, unless there were special circumstances, to maintain the anonymity of the victim. The Press Council set out its policy in 1955 by criticizing the *Hull Daily Mail* for unnecessary explicitness in describing the rape of a 15-year-old girl. The council did not dispute that rape cases should be reported—'and in some instances reported at length'—but asserted that the 'duty to report the general outline of a case does not entail a duty to repeat its abhorrent elements'.[116] In 1966, meanwhile, the editor of *The Times* apologized to the Press Council for printing the names and addresses of three rape victims: the council agreed with the husband of one of the victims that no public interest was served by identifying them, and noted that other national dailies had not done so.[117] But the restraint generally exercised by the press was threatened in the 1970s as rape moved up the public agenda, driven on the one hand by rising concern about violent crime, and on the other by pressure from the resurgent women's movement.[118] In the mid-1970s, several popular papers dramatically increased their coverage of rape cases. A survey conducted by the sociologists Keith Soothill and Sylvia Walby found that while the *Daily Mirror* reported only one rape case in 1951, and five in 1961, in 1978 it reported no fewer than 26. The *Sun*'s total for 1978 was even higher at 32 cases, a three-fold increase on 1971. The *News of the World*, the only paper with a long tradition in covering rape cases—it had reported 22 in 1951—reported 72 in 1978, more than one a week.[119] Rape became a major news story.

This reporting of rape cases also became considerably more explicit than in previous decades. Journalists provided details not of the assaults, but also of the sexual histories of the victims as they emerged under cross-examination. Feminists complained that the press was cynically using these cases to titillate male readers, and that such intrusive coverage would discourage women from reporting rape to the police. An Advisory Group appointed by the Home Secretary in June 1975 and chaired by Justice Rose Heilbron agreed that disclosure of the victim's name

[115] Soothill and Walby, *Sex Crime*, 87.
[116] Press Council, Annual Report 1955, 18.
[117] Press Council, Annual Report 1966, 49.
[118] Hall et al., *Policing the Crisis*, ch. 9; A. Coote and B. Campbell, *Sweet Freedom: The Struggle for Women's Liberation* (London: Pan, 1982), 43–5.
[119] Soothill and Walby, *Sex Crime*, 18.

caused great distress and might stop women going to the authorities.[120] Indeed, evidence of the negative effects of media interest could be found in some of the press's own reports. In January 1976, for example, the *News of the World* covered a case in which a mother waited a day before reporting her daughter's rape to the police. 'With all the publicity about girls who had been raped and named' she had needed a night to think whether it was worth her daughter going through the ordeal.[121]

Fleet Street was nevertheless reluctant to modify its styles of reporting. In the *Daily Mirror*, Marje Proops had declared her support for guaranteeing anonymity to rape victims in June 1974, but other journalists were less convinced.[122] When Labour backbencher Robin Corbett brought his Sexual Offences (Amendment) Bill before the Commons in February 1976, the *Sun* admitted its scepticism of the provision to guarantee anonymity to rape victims, and suggested that it 'would usher in an era of secret accusers'. It was unfair for the victim to claim anonymity when the defendant was named, and there was, the paper insisted, 'a very real possibility of trumped-up charges being brought by hundreds of vindictive women who feel they have old scores to settle'.[123] Women, it seemed, could not be trusted with the privilege of anonymity. Corbett's Bill, which also included provisions to prevent the victim's sexual history being explored in court unnecessarily, did become law, but its effects on press reporting were relatively limited. Although newspapers no long named victims, identifying details were often still included, and because barristers continued to find ways to introduce questions about women's sexual past, this material also found its way into reports.[124] More broadly, feminists continued to be disturbed by the sensationalism of rape coverage, and the underlying journalistic assumptions that some victims may have 'asked for it' by behaving 'inappropriately'. The first *Women's Media Action Bulletin*, issued by the feminist network the Alliance for Fair Images and Representation in the Media in Summer 1979, listed among its main objections 'The treatment of violence against women as being acceptable and enjoyable, for example reporting rape in a way intended to titillate'.[125] The following year a group of thirty feminists occupied the offices of the *Sun* to protest at precisely this form of journalism.[126] But few feminists believed that their complaints provoked any serious reassessment in newspaper offices.

Editors and journalists consistently shrugged off accusations that their reporting of rape cases was insensitive or cynical. They did, however, sometimes ally with the women's movement to criticize the judiciary's handling of rape cases. One such example occurred in June 1977 when the Appeal Court reduced the sentence of a guardsman convicted of sexual assault from three years to three

120 Soothill and Walby, *Sex Crime*, 6–9

121 *News of the World*, 18 Jan. 1976, 11.

122 *Daily Mirror*, 18 June 1974, 4–5.

123 *The Sun*, 13 Feb. 1976, 2.

124 Soothill and Walby, *Sex Crime*, 4–5.

125 *Women's Media Action Bulletin*, No. 1, June 1979, 7.

126 Coote and Campbell, *Sweet Freedom*, 204.

months, suspended: one judge suggested that the guardsman had allowed his 'enthusiasm for sex to overcome his normal behaviour', while another argued that the victim would have been less severely injured had she submitted to rape.[127] The press was united in its condemnation of the judges—arguably, indeed, to the extent of contempt of court. The *Daily Express* described the decision as 'stupefying' and gave space to the feminist journalist Anna Coote to challenge the 'myths that enrage every woman' about rape—namely that 'A man can't help himself', 'Women don't really mind being forced to have sex' and 'Some women are fair game'.[128] The *Mail* despaired that the Court of Appeal demonstrated 'no glimmer of understanding of the lifelong mental anguish suffered by the victim of a violent sexual assault' and suggested that, far from sharing the 'increased sensitivity to the rights of women', it seemed 'to be strolling back in the general direction of the Middle Ages'.[129] The victim herself waived her right to anonymity and approached the *Sunday Mirror* to tell her story—without payment—so that the public could appreciate the nature of her ordeal. The *Mirror* also decided to publish the Appeal Court judgement in full, despite 'the harrowing and sickening details of the crime': this included explicit descriptions of the assailant putting his hand inside the victim's vagina, leading to severe bruising and a swollen vulva. The paper warned its readers that they must decide for themselves whether or not to read it, but hoped that those that did would be able to see why the *Mirror* believed that 'remedies must be applied to make the judges' ruling the last one of its kind'. In particular, the paper highlighted the fact that there were only two women among the 72 High Court judges—and none on the Court of Appeal. 'If even one of the judges in this case had been a woman', the paper insisted, it would have been unimaginable that such a legal 'outrage' would have been allowed.[130]

At times, therefore, feminists could find powerful support in the press for their campaign to change attitudes to rape. Popular newspapers tended to support heavy sentencing for all form of violent crime, and the women's movement could mobilize these sympathies against examples of court leniency. Yet the press remained interested above all in the 'sex fiend', the unknown rapist preying on unsuspecting women. It was far harder for feminists to draw attention to violence and abuse that took place in the home. For newspapers that idealized the family, domestic violence was not an appealing subject, and it was generally addressed on an individual basis in 'problem columns' rather than in major feature articles.

Court reporting exposed many of the contradictions in the popular press's attempts to package sex while remaining 'family newspapers'. Ostentatiously in

[127] C. Haste, *Rules of Desire: Sex in Britain, World War 1 to the Present* (London: Pimlico, 1994), 241.

[128] *Daily Express*, 21 June 1977, 10; 23 June 1977, 10.

[129] *Daily Mail*, 23 June 1977, 6.

[130] *Sunday Mirror*, 26 June 1977, 1–2.

favour of family values, and unstinting in defence of law and order, popular journalism was nevertheless so fascinated by examples of sexual transgression that reporters frequently upset the authorities with their ferocious pursuit of crime stories. Sex criminals were denounced as 'monsters' and 'fiends' at the same time as witnesses were paid to reveal more about them. Headlines advertised accounts of shocking deeds which soon degenerated into euphemism and evasion. Yet editors were unwilling to address these contradictions publicly or to consider what the popularity of such reports revealed about their readers. Instead the press was determined to maintain its 'common sense', black and white approach to sex, drawing clear distinctions between a 'normal' law-abiding majority and the 'deviant' minority who ended up in court. And as the next chapter demonstrates, it was the simplicity of the press's morality that gave it a platform to launch crusades on issues such as prostitution and homosexuality.

5

Moral Crusades: Prostitution and Homosexuality

The police station and the courtroom provided an endless supply of human interest stories, and they both remained central to popular journalism throughout the period. But journalists were not content merely to record the proceedings of the legal system: they also assumed the roles of detective and of judge themselves, independently exploring practices, people, or places they regarded as 'social problems'. W. T. Stead's exposure of child prostitution, in a series for the *Pall Mall Gazette* in 1885 entitled 'The Maiden Tribute of Modern Babylon', provided the classic example of this type of crusading journalism. Although Stead himself was jailed for his efforts, he successfully turned the spotlight of publicity onto the issue. The subsequent passage of a Criminal Law Amendment Act, raising the age of consent to 16 and introducing new measures against brothels, seemed to demonstrate the power of the press to stimulate political and legal action.[1]

Stead's campaign was a notable illustration of what the sociologists Jock Young and Stanley Cohen later memorably described as a 'moral panic'.[2] Stead identified and investigated a threat to societal values, presented it in a stylized fashion, amplified its dangers, and manned the 'moral barricades' demanding that the authorities act.[3] The episode entered Fleet Street mythology and encouraged many future editors and journalists to launch crusades on sexual issues. Sunday newspapers, in particular, developed a taste for such campaigns against 'vice'. Some of these campaigns provoked a conspicuous reaction from the police and Parliament, others did not; but they all helped to shape public opinion, by supporting particular versions of sexual morality, defining the boundaries of acceptable sexual expression, and consolidating stereotypes of 'deviants'.

[1] J. Walkowitz, *City of Dreadful Delight: Narratives of Sexual Danger in Late-Victorian London* (London: Virago, 1992), chs. 3 and 4; R. Schults, *Crusader in Babylon: W. T. Stead and the Pall Mall Gazette* (Lincoln: University of Nebraska Press, 1972).

[2] J. Young, 'The Role of the Police as Amplifiers of Deviancy, Negotiators of Reality and Translators of Fantasy', in S. Cohen (ed.), *Images of Deviance* (Harmondsworth: Penguin, 1971); S. Cohen, *Folk Devils and Moral Panics: The Creation of the Mods and Rockers* (St Albans: Paladin, 1973). For a survey of the 'moral panic' literature since the 1970s, see C. Critcher, *Moral Panics and the Media* (Buckingham: Open University Press, 2003).

[3] This description of a moral panic is taken from Cohen, *Folk Devils and Moral Panics*, 9.

Newspapers used the displays of moral indignation to try to unite a community of 'decent' readers against sexual transgression, and they were often very successful in stirring up hostility to individuals seen to be breaking these codes of behaviour.

This chapter explores two subjects that were the focus of prominent press crusades, namely prostitution and homosexuality. The similarities and differences in treatment of these two controversial issues provide interesting insights into the changing sensitivities of the press and the public. The Stead crusade in 1885 established prostitution as a legitimate topic of newspaper enquiry, and journalists reported on the menaces of 'white slavery' and the urban vice trade throughout the twentieth century. There were obvious fluctuations in the extent and nature of this press coverage—concern was particularly intense in the 1950s—but prostitution remained in the headlines across the period, repeatedly and routinely condemned by leader-writers and columnists.

The coverage of homosexuality, by contrast, was marked by notable discontinuities. In the first half of the twentieth century, popular newspaper editors tended to regard homosexuality as a distasteful topic that was unsuitable for a family audience. Journalists had learned how to produce melodramatic narratives about abduction and trafficking for the mass market, but it was more difficult to find appropriate language with which to write about homosexuality. As a result, most popular papers—with the exception of the *News of the World*—confined their coverage of the subject to the occasional court report. When homosexuality finally emerged as a subject of sustained press discussion in the 1950s, however, it proved far more contentious than prostitution. The Wolfenden proposals to decriminalize adult homosexuality split Fleet Street and provoked acrimonious debate; divisions remained apparent as the political climate shifted in favour of reform in the 1960s. The papers that supported decriminalization continued to portray homosexuality as 'unnatural' and objectionable, and regarded the gay rights movement with suspicion, although there were some signs of change in the tone of coverage in the 1970s, with increasingly clear distinctions made between homosexuality and paedophilia. Indeed by the end of the period, the paedophile had become the prime target for the crusading editor and the investigative journalist: here was a threat that could unite all parents.

Historians and sociologists have examined in some detail the role of the press in maintaining hostility to, and suspicion of, gay men and women.[4] This is a

[4] For example, F. Pearce, 'The British Press and the "Placing" of Male Homosexuality', in S. Cohen and J. Young (eds.), *The Manufacture of News: Social Problems, Deviance and the Mass Media* (revised edn., London: Constable, 1981), 303–16; S. Jeffery-Poulter, *Peers, Queers and Commons: The Struggle for Gay Law Reform from 1950 to the Present* (London: Routledge, 1991); P. Higgins, *Heterosexual Dictatorship: Male Homosexuality in Postwar Britain* (London: Fourth Estate, 1996), especially ch. 13; C. Waters, 'Disorders of the Mind, Disorders of the Body Social: Peter Wildeblood and the Making of the Modern Homosexual', in B. Conekin, F. Mort, and C. Waters (eds.), *Moments of Modernity: Reconstructing Britain 1945–1964* (London: Rivers Oram Press, 1999); M. Houlbrook, *Queer London: Perils and Pleasures in the Sexual Metropolis* (Chicago: University of Chicago Press, 2005). Rather less has been written about the portrayal of lesbianism,

very impressive body of work but it tends to be stronger on the continuities of the coverage than the gradual shifts of opinion in Fleet Street, or the differences between papers. It is evident that prejudice against homosexuals was firmly entrenched in the popular press and had by no means disappeared by the end of the period; nevertheless, it is important to understand the extent to which arguments in favour of 'toleration' and 'understanding', inadequate as they often were, gained ground in some papers.

THE PRESS AND THE MYTHOLOGY OF 'WHITE SLAVERY'

Prostitution became a subject of public debate in the final third of the nineteenth century largely as a result of feminist campaigns against the Contagious Diseases Acts (which forced prostitutes in areas around military garrisons to submit to tests for, and compulsory treatment of, venereal diseases).[5] Although some politicians accepted prostitution as a necessary evil—seeing the prostitute as 'the most efficient guardian of virtue'[6]—few were prepared to defend the practice openly, and it was vociferously condemned by religious leaders, women's organizations, and social commentators as an affront to public decency, a threat to the institution of marriage, and a danger to public health. 'Family newspapers' generally adopted an uncontroversial stance in support of this moral consensus until W. T. Stead's 'Maiden Tribute' series of 1885 propelled the issue up the press's agenda. Stead's melodramatic account of the abduction and exploitation of innocent young girls by sinister aristocratic villains had a dramatic effect on contemporary opinion, and heavily influenced later reporters.[7] In subsequent decades the press played an important role in developing the mythology of 'white slavery', although increasingly 'foreign' gangs, rather than aristocratic villains, were held to be responsible. Newspaper reports of the seizure and deception of English women, and their transportation to brothels abroad by 'alien', often Jewish, traders caused considerable concern in the years before the First World War, and helped campaigners to secure parliamentary support for the Criminal Law Amendment Act of 1912, which increased the penalties for procuration. Some observers were very sceptical about these stories of abduction. The feminist campaigner Teresa Billington-Grieg could find no one to authenticate them,

but see A. Oram, *Her Husband Was a Woman! Women's Gender-Crossing and Twentieth Century British Popular Culture* (London: Routledge, 2007).

5 J. Walkowitz, *Prostitution and Victorian Society* (Cambridge: Cambridge University Press, 1980); L. Bland, *Banishing the Beast: English Feminism and Sexual Morality 1885–1914* (London: Penguin, 1995), ch. 3.

6 W. Lecky, *History of European Morals* (1869), cited in J. Lewis, *Women in England 1870–1950* (Brighton: Harvester, 1984) 130.

7 Walkowitz, *City of Dreadful Delight*, chs. 3 and 4.

and concluded that they were nothing more than the result of 'a campaign of sedulously calculated sexual hysterics'. She remained in the minority, however, and the 'white slavers' continued to loom large in popular culture.[8]

During the inter-war period most indicators pointed to a decline in prostitution, and the issue lost some of its prominence in public debate.[9] Nevertheless, the press continued to find the subject a fruitful source of melodramatic narratives, and the spectre of 'white slavery' retained a prominent place in the journalistic imagination. The routine court reports of the Sunday newspapers suggested that the realities of prostitution were mundane, involving small-scale operations run by impecunious men and women desperate to escape poverty. In 1928, for example, *The People* described, under the euphemistic headline 'Not A Nice House', the trial of a man from Brixton accused of running a brothel: the defence pleaded that he 'had been ill and out of work for some time, and that he had a mortgage on the house', forcing him to allow it to be used 'for improper purposes'.[10] This was a typical, unglamorous, story. On the front page the following week, however, the paper printed a far more dramatic headline: 'Beautiful Girls in Bondage—Vast White Slave Plot Discovered'. A report from Delhi announced that a 'vast organisation engaged in kidnapping young beautiful girls and selling them to houses of ill-fame in India has been discovered', and that a 'similar organisation carrying on a trade in the beautiful girls of Kashmir was recently discovered'.[11] The tentacles of the white slavers stretched throughout the empire, it seemed; the repetition of the adjective 'beautiful' to describe the victims conveyed the impression of pure and virtuous girls being defiled by evil traffickers. As usual with such reports, few concrete details were provided. It was evident, though, that conservative papers like the *People* were more comfortable focusing on the deeds of foreign gangs than on the social conditions in Britain that drove people into prostitution. Such priorities were again clear four months later when the *People* did not cover the publication of the report of the Street Offences Committee, set up to examine the laws concerning prostitution. Wider debates about the nature and policing of prostitution were ignored in favour of melodrama and human interest.

By repeatedly emphasizing the responsibility of foreigners for much of the 'vice' in Britain, journalists suggested that a fundamentally moral nation was being corrupted by unwanted influences from abroad. Praising police action against disreputable night clubs and gambling dens in London in 1928, for example, the *Daily Mail* highlighted the 'Scores of Aliens on the Run' and observed that whenever such places were investigated 'there is usually an unwanted alien behind the operations. These aliens take the biggest share of the haul and

[8] Bland, *Banishing the Beast*, 297–303.

[9] M. Pugh, *'We Danced All Night': A Social History of Britain Between the Wars* (London: Bodley Head, 2008), 160.

[10] *The People*, 19 Aug. 1928, 2.

[11] *The People*, 26 Aug. 1928, 1.

run the least risk.'[12] The solution to this problem, argued the *Mail*, was to tighten immigration controls: 'We hope the authorities will not rest content with ejecting these unwelcome guests, but will also take steps to prevent them coming back. . . . We do not want these people here, where they are a nuisance and a danger to our peace.'[13]

Britons were also advised to be wary when travelling abroad, because foreigners could not be trusted to adhere to British standards of behaviour. The Sunday papers produced numerous accounts of women being deceived and left in compromising situations in international cities. In 1929, the *News of the World* described how women from a London dancing troupe, invited to perform in Belgium, had been tricked by 'a little Greek agent' (who himself was acting for a 'negro impresario'), and sent to 'a disorderly house of the worst type' in Luxembourg. According to the paper one of the dancers was told to 'make herself "particularly nice" to a certain gentleman' but refused with the words 'I am English'. The reports constructed a clear racial typology in which the virtuous and resolute English women eventually escaped from the clutches of a weak European middle-man and an immoral and vicious black criminal.[14] The implication of such reports was that nations and peoples which could not guarantee the safety and moral security of travelling women were less civilized than Britain.

Despite the frequent references to sinister foreign gangs, suggestions of organized 'white slavery' in Britain usually failed to survive serious scrutiny. In 1931, police in Newcastle were forced to deny reports that a 'great white slave traffic organisation' was operating on Tyneside and luring girls to London in large numbers with false offers of employment; the authorities had not, in fact, received a single complaint. Some of these stories circulated because journalists were prepared to give credence to rumours spread by alarmist local vigilance associations. In this Newcastle case, alongside the denial from the police, the *Mail* printed the claims of a local activist that he knew of 'many' instances of girls getting into 'awful situations'. 'We are having so many of these girls stranded in London,' he declared, 'that it is becoming a great danger'.[15] Even when there was no reliable evidence and firm denials from the police, speculation about 'white slavery' might not be entirely quashed. The National Vigilance Association was more level-headed than many local associations about 'periodical scare stories' and dismissed the majority of the reports of abduction and trafficking. 'Such cases simply do not occur', the association insisted: 'They generally turn out to be what somebody has told someone else or, alternatively, a girl running away from her home for purely private reasons'.[16] Whatever their provenance, though, journalists often found these stories too tempting to pass up. If any young girl

[12] *Daily Mail*, 17 Dec. 1928, 11. [13] *Daily Mail*, 18 Dec. 1928, 10.

[14] *News of the World*, 10 Mar. 1929, 5; also 17, 24 Feb. 1929, 1; 3 Mar. 1929, 4.

[15] *Daily Mail*, 16 Nov. 1931, 7; 18 Nov. 1931, 18.

[16] R. Porter and L. Hall, *The Facts of Life: The Creation of Sexual Knowledge in Britain, 1650–1950* (New Haven: Yale University Press, 1995), 264.

was potentially in danger of being seduced or coerced into prostitution, a limited social problem was transformed into an urgent national threat of concern to all newspaper readers. Such a threat could also be used to demand vigorous action against the 'criminals' and 'aliens' involved. 'White slavery' stories persisted because they were perfectly suited to the agenda of the popular press.

In the first half of the twentieth century the press devoted more space to prostitution and 'white slavery' than most other sexual offences, despite evidence suggesting that these practices were becoming less prevalent. The strong feelings that this coverage stirred up among readers were illustrated by Mass-Observation's 'Little Kinsey' survey of 1949. The survey found that 'The mention of prostitution aroused more indignation and disgust amongst the people we interviewed than any other single aspect of sex . . . alone amongst all the subjects we discussed with people in this investigation, prostitution has a majority against it in every group separately surveyed'. But investigators believed that some of this 'moralistic disapproval' was based on a 'misapprehension'. 'Sunday newspaper publicity given to the subject perhaps leads to exaggerated ideas of its extent. Certainly our survey suggests that prostitution, in its usual sense, plays a slighter part in our national life than is often imagined'. There was, furthermore, 'often a feeling of temporariness about attitudes to prostitution, signs that once the interviewer disappears round the corner the matter will be dismissed from mind'.[17] The combination of 'disgust' and 'temporariness' was typical of media-generated moral panic. The cumulative power of numerous newspaper articles could rouse passionate reactions about a subject on which most people had relatively little personal knowledge—but these feelings faded more quickly than those relating to issues which were more a part of everyday life, such as infidelity and promiscuity. Mass-Observation noted that 'reactions to extra-marital relations generally seem much sturdier and more lasting, and contain more indications of realistic, active opposition'.[18] On such matters readers were in a better position to form their own opinions without the help of newspapers. The survey thus demonstrated both the power of the press to shape opinions on sexual issues, and some of its limitations.

INVESTIGATION AND EXPOSURE: THE PROSTITUTION PANIC OF THE 1950S

Mass-Observation's survey was taken just as the press coverage of prostitution was starting to shift. Uncorroborated stories of 'white slavers', abduction, and

[17] Mass-Observation, 'Little Kinsey' survey 1949, reprinted in L. Stanley, *Sex Surveyed, 1949–1994: From Mass-Observation's 'Little Kinsey' to The National Survey and the Hite Reports* (London: Taylor & Francis, 1995), 143, 148, 150.

[18] Ibid., 150.

international trafficking became less common in the post-war period as reporters produced rather more detailed and realistic accounts of the ways in which gangs operated the trade in London. The press contributed to the growing concern about the visibility of prostitution in the capital, especially with the city on show to the world for the Olympics of 1948, the Festival of Britain in 1951, and the Coronation of 1953.[19] The most dramatic intervention came with Duncan Webb's exposure of the Messina gang in the *People* in September 1950. The criminal activities of the Messinas, five brothers from Malta who had managed to carve themselves a lucrative slice of London's prostitution trade, had been well known to politicians, police, and the press for some years. Back in January 1947, the *Sunday Pictorial*'s 'Vice in the Capital' series had described the brutal control a group of 'Maltese brothers' exercised over their women, but lamented that 'the police have been unable to pin a single thing on [them]'.[20] In 1950, however, under the bold front-page headline 'Arrest These Four Men', Duncan Webb declared that he had uncovered enough evidence to enable the police to act against the 'emperors of an empire of vice in London's West End' (**Illustration 5.1**).[21] His three-month investigation had produced proof of prostitution occurring at a number of premises owned, rented, or leased by the Messinas, and the *People*'s readers were given a detailed summary of the dossier that he was sending to the police, illustrated by photographs of the protagonists.

The *People*'s Messina articles were far more substantial than the vast majority of the popular press's pieces on prostitution in the first half of the century, but significant thematic continuities were apparent. The underlying story was, as so often in the past, that Britain was being corrupted by unwelcome foreign influences—even if the brothers, as Maltese subjects, held British nationality.[22] Webb noted that many of the prostitutes had 'come from the Continent to carry on their disgusting business', resulting in 'a state of affairs that would disgrace one of the licentious ports of the Middle East'. It was 'almost incredible', he complained, that vice on this scale existed at the heart of Empire.[23] In an account of the investigation three years later, Webb made this theme more explicit. After his initial enquiries had not uncovered any reliable evidence, he described, rather melodramatically, his vow that he would rather resign and pursue the investigation on his own than 'allow to continue this absolute subjugation of British morality to an alien corruption'. He told his editor that the paper 'owed it to the British people' to challenge the 'almost overwhelming influence this collection of filth had achieved over our English way of life'.[24]

[19] F. Mort, 'Mapping Sexual London: The Wolfenden Committee on Homosexual Offences and Prostitution: 1954–7', *New Formations*, no. 37 (1999), 92–113.

[20] *Sunday Pictorial*, 26 Jan. 1947, 6–7.

[21] *The People*, 3 Sept. 1950, 1.

[22] The validity of this British nationality became the subject of further investigations, eventually finding that only two of the five brothers had qualified legitimately: D. Webb, *Crime is my Business* (London: Frederick Muller, 1953), 192.

[23] *The People*, 3 Sept. 1950, 1–2.

[24] Webb, *Crime is my Business*, 133.

I want Cadburys!

THE PEOPLE

OVER 4,500,000 SALE

2d

ballito

ARREST THESE FOUR MEN

They are the emperors of a vice empire in the heart of London

- Today 'The People' has found out the facts about a vice ring in the heart of London that is a national scandal.
- This is an unsavoury story but we believe it is our duty to the public to reveal it so that swift action can be taken.

THE MESSINA GANG EXPOSED

By Duncan Webb

YESTERDAY I made the final entry in a dossier that uncovers the activities of a vice gang operating in the West End of London on a scale that will appal every decent man and woman.

Today I offer Scotland Yard evidence from my dossier that should enable them to arrest four men who are battening on women of the streets and profiting from their shameful trade.

FOUR DESPICABLE BROTHERS

"Lives of shame"

"I watched"

Turn to Page 2

THEIRS WAS AN ODD MARRIAGE

RED TROOPS HALTED IN 'BULGE,' ROUTED IN SOUTH

AFTER two days of furious fighting on a 50-mile front, the Communists in Korea have failed to achieve a decisive break-through.

Heavy casualties

Pole on the run 'fled British spy school' SAYS MOSCOW

MORE RAIN

ATTLEE HITS BACK AT CHURCHILL

Good Morning People!

'No' to busmen

THE TRAIN MISSED IT!

Thought reading

You'll feel better when you have a

GUINNESS

Illustration 5.1. **'Arrest These Four Men'**, *The People*, 3 Sept. 1950, 1. Duncan Webb's exposure of the Messina brothers marked the start of a new era of press investigations into prostitution.

The 'Arrest These Four Men' article was the most daring journalistic exposure of the sex trade since Stead, and the paper challenged the Messinas to sue for libel if they could defend themselves. Webb's snooping resulted in him being attacked three times, but he stubbornly continued his enquiries, enabling the *People* to feature the campaign against the Messinas on its front page for no fewer than eight consecutive weeks.[25] As each week went by, however, the paper's exaltation over its success in forcing the gang to flee from its usual haunts gradually shifted to frustration that the revelations had not led to arrests and prosecutions. A month after the original article, Webb reported that Messina prostitutes were operating once more, and that they were still only receiving small fines from the police. He demanded that a much harder line be taken: 'The public is entitled to ask when the courts are going to send these women to prison and when police intend to take steps to close down the premises from which they operate—and to arrest the four Messina brothers who run this vile gang.'[26] By the middle of October, questions were being asked in the House of Commons about the lack of police action and the *People* was attacking the Home Secretary, Chuter Ede, for his 'philosophical outlook' on this issue. 'If Mr Ede believes that the people are as tolerant as he is, he should glance through the hundreds of indignant readers' letters that have reached *The People*. They represent a rising tide of public opinion that will not be quietened by anything short of full-scale warfare against the masters of London's vice empire.'[27] The paper claimed to speak for the public in demanding tougher measures and firmer action, and, in a tactic that became increasingly familiar in Fleet Street crime coverage, contrasted the common sense of ordinary readers with the 'high-falutin' lectures' offered by politicians. Having presented the situation in such simplistic terms, the *People*'s logic appeared compelling. The police had to work within the framework of existing laws, however, and did not have the resources to launch 'full-scale warfare' against the gangs. When the articles were published, moreover, the brothers initially evaded police action by fleeing to Europe. But the family was eventually brought to justice: Alfredo and Attilio were convicted for living on immoral earnings in 1951, Eugenio and Carmelo were convicted in Belgium in 1956, and further charges were brought against the gang in 1958 and 1959.

The *People*'s investigation of the Messina gang tapped into a genuine concern about the brazenness of soliciting in London, and it was widely admired in Fleet Street. Hugh Cudlipp regarded it as the 'most courageous exposure of its kind' he had seen in a British newspaper, and the *Mirror* took the unusual step of publicly praising its rival.[28] At the *Express*, Max Aitken told his father,

[25] *The People*, 10 Sept.–22 Oct. 1950, 1.

[26] *The People*, 8 Oct. 1950, 1; 1 Oct. 1950, 1.

[27] *The People*, 22 Oct. 1950, 1.

[28] H. Cudlipp, *At Your Peril* (London: Weidenfeld & Nicolson, 1962), 293; *Daily Mirror*, 12 Nov. 1953, 2.

Lord Beaverbrook, that 'The exposure of the Messina gang has been good stuff for them [the *People*]. The exposures carried a crusading element well mixed up with sex.'[29] Duncan Webb pursued his enquiries for the *People* for several years, and other newspapers were inspired to investigate the sex trade themselves. The cumulative impact of these reports was to portray prostitution as a serious problem that the police were failing to contain, and they made a significant contribution to the Conservative government's decision to set up the Wolfenden committee to find solutions. In his memorandum to the Cabinet in February 1954 justifying the establishment of a committee, the Home Secretary, David Maxwell-Fyfe, observed that the 'activities of prostitutes soliciting in the streets of London have attracted much attention and there have been demands in Parliament, in the press and from leaders of the Churches for more effective measures to check these evils'. He admitted, in words that could have been taken straight from a newspaper editorial, that 'there can be no dispute that conditions in the streets in certain parts of London are now deplorable. They are probably without parallel in the capital cities of other civilised countries.'[30] In April, the Cabinet agreed to establish an inter-departmental committee to examine both prostitution and homosexuality, in the expectation that it would recommend increased powers to tackle public soliciting.

As the Wolfenden committee considered the evidence, the press continued relentlessly to expose the prevalence of prostitution in London. The *Sunday Pictorial*'s star investigator Harry Procter spent weeks uncovering details of thirty-seven separate 'call-girl' networks, leading to numerous arrests and convictions; in the *Empire News* the former Scotland Yard detective Robert Fabian railed against 'the dung-heap mountain of vice that is our capital city' and listed the 'black spots' that needed to be cleaned up; the *Daily Mirror* ran two campaigns on 'the shocking city', describing prostitution in the West End and then in Stepney.[31] The press was combining to create a 'moral panic' about prostitution using formulaic crusades relying on easy moral dichotomies. The women involved in the trade rarely received any sympathy or understanding. It was assumed that in the modern welfare state, women were no longer driven to prostitution by desperate poverty, but were 'abnormal' individuals who enjoyed the money or the lifestyle. Even the liberal *News Chronicle* accepted that 'most prostitutes today are hardened professionals not driven to it by want, but choosing it for gain'.[32] Hugh Cudlipp told his staff not to give the impression that prostitution was in

[29] House of Lords Record Office, Beaverbrook Papers, H/153, Max Aitken to Beaverbrook, 5 Feb. 1952.

[30] NA, CAB 129/66, C (54) 60 Sexual Offences—Memo by the Sec. of State for the Home Department and Minister for Welsh Affairs, 17? Feb. 1954.

[31] H. Procter, *The Street of Disillusion* (London: Allan Wingate, 1958), 203–6; *Empire News*, 15 July 1956; *Daily Mirror*, 16 July 1957, 9.

[32] *News Chronicle*, 27 Nov. 1958, 4.

any sense alluring or exciting, and discouraged the inclusion of photographs of prostitutes: 'These girls are trollops, not glamorous creatures'.[33]

Editors and journalists were so confident about the rectitude and value of their investigations that most did not pause to reflect on the methods they used or the consequences of exposure. Newspaper publicity by itself did not solve the 'problem'. 'Little Pat', one of the prostitutes identified in Procter's articles on the London sex trade, simply moved to the South Coast and capitalized on her notoriety by charging higher fees: she actually used the *Pictorial* report to advertise her services.[34] Some journalists became so eager for dramatic stories that they cut corners and made basic mistakes. In July 1956, the *People* printed the results of another Duncan Webb investigation, exposing a brothel-keeper under the headline 'Arrest This Beast'. But Webb had not taken the elementary precaution of checking whether the 'beast' in question was already subject to judicial proceedings, and when it emerged that he had been arrested almost a month earlier, the paper found itself in contempt of court. The *People* was fined £1,000, with Webb and Harry Ainsworth, the editor, fined £500 each. The trial raised a number of questions about the reporting methods used at the paper, and the judge, Lord Goddard, poured scorn on Webb's journalism: his article was 'sheer humbug . . . written in a highly sensational manner . . . with a view to increasing circulation and with no other object'.[35] But such public criticism did nothing to temper Fleet Street's enthusiasm for its crusade, and it continued unabated.

By September 1957, when the Wolfenden committee's report recommended increasing the penalties for street soliciting, the press had created a climate of opinion in favour of tougher action. While there was considerable disagreement in Fleet Street about the committee's proposals on the regulation of homosexuality, its stance on prostitution was widely applauded. 'The Wolfenden Report is the answer to the nauseating parade of vice in the streets,' declared the *Daily Mirror*: 'If the Government accept the Report—and act on it quickly—the streets will be cleaned up . . . . Tarts will no longer cling to every lamp-post.'[36] Newspaper opinion polls demonstrated strong public support. A Gallup survey conducted for the *News Chronicle* revealed that eight out of ten people agreed that prostitutes soliciting in public places should be subject to heavier penalties, although as many as a third also believed that licensed brothels might also have a role in improving the situation.[37] Polls in the *Mirror* and its Scottish sister paper the *Record* suggested even higher levels of approval for more punitive measures.[38] Another Gallup survey in The *News Chronicle* the following year confirmed the stability of public opinion: 67 per cent agreed that persistent prostitutes should

33 Procter, *Street of Disillusion*, 206. 34 Ibid.

35 Beaverbrook Papers, H/187, Pickering to Beaverbrook, 4 Oct. 1956; Pickering to Beaverbrook, 11 Oct. 1956.

36 *Daily Mirror*, 5 Sept. 1957, 1. 37 *News Chronicle*, 10 Sept. 1957, 1.

38 *Daily Mirror*, 12 Sept. 1957, 7; *Daily Record*, 11 Sept. 1957, 16.

be sent to prison, and 87 per cent agreed that 'men living on the earnings of prostitutes should be given heavier sentences'.[39]

Some liberal papers like the *News Chronicle*, as well as a number of women's organizations, did challenge aspects of the report and argued that punitive measures would merely drive the trade underground and lead to the establishment of 'call-girl' networks.[40] But such objections were drowned out by the chorus of approval. The strong backing from the press and the public enabled the Conservative government to push the Street Offences Bill through Parliament very swiftly in the early months of 1959. As well as significantly increasing penalties for prostitutes and pimps, the Act allowed women to be convicted of soliciting on the uncorroborated testimony of a single police officer. The clamour for tough new laws that had increased in intensity throughout the 1950s was finally satisfied.

PROSTITUTION IN 'PERMISSIVE BRITAIN'

The 1959 Street Offences Act was successful in its narrow aim of reducing the visibility of prostitution. Convictions for soliciting declined from almost 17,000 to 1,100 in 1962, and for a time press interest in the issue decreased too.[41] There were periodic investigations into the various ways in which prostitutes evaded the new laws,[42] and the Profumo scandal drew attention to the presence of 'courtesans' in elevated social circles, but in the early 1960s other subjects, such as abortion, contraception, and homosexuality received more publicity. In the second half of the 1960s, however, the papers that had called for the 1959 legislation became increasingly vociferous in their complaints that the problem had indeed simply been driven underground. In 1966, for example, the *News of the World* conducted a major investigation into 'London's Vice Madams', and argued that the 'national embarrassment' of street soliciting had been 'replaced by a growing cancer below the surface of society'.[43] On the tenth anniversary of the Street Offences Act, the Josephine Butler Society (formerly the Association for Social and Moral Hygiene) asked the *People* to examine whether the law was 'not only unfair in its discrimination against certain women, but has not reduced the danger to young girls being drawn into prostitution'.[44] A five-week study concluded that the Act had had a 'boomerang effect' and now tended to 'encourage vice rather than suppress it' because 'loose women, evil men and social cynics have found ways and means of exploiting the situation . . . . Ten years of

[39] *News Chronicle*, 17 Dec. 1958, 7.

[40] *News Chronicle*, 5 Sept. 1957, 4; 27 Nov. 1958, 4; 19 Dec. 1958, 4.

[41] C. Haste, *Rules of Desire. Sex In Britain: World War I to the Present* (London: Pimlico, 1992), 174.

[42] For example, *News of the World*, 24 Jan. 1960, 2.

[43] *News of the World*, 20 Nov. 1966, 10–11.

[44] *The People*, 5 Oct. 1969, 7.

an Act to protect public morality has achieved nothing.'[45] The consensus of the late 1950s had unravelled.

The rhetoric of 'loose women and evil men' underlined the moral continuities with the past, but there were some new preoccupations in these reports. One was the impact of immigration in creating new sources of demand for prostitution. 'Foreigners' had long been accused of playing a leading role in the organization of 'vice', but now attention turned to the way in which men from settled immigrant communities were becoming clients. The *People* argued that in Bradford this demand had produced 'a completely new kind of prostitute . . . the girl who calls by appointment to satisfy the demands of up to a dozen sex-starved Pakistanis sharing the same home'. With scarcely concealed alarm, the paper declared that 'Our investigators were able to discover only white girls operating this service'. There was a long history of hostility to inter-racial sex (see Chapter 4), and it remained a very sensitive subject in many communities. The author of the article did not have to voice his concerns explicitly to convey his message to readers, for his heated language betrayed his anxiety: he insisted that this was nothing less than an 'emergency' which the city ought to address 'quickly before it gets out of hand'.[46] Servicing 'sex-starved Pakistanis' was portrayed as the ultimate degradation for a white woman, a degradation all the more unbearable because it had been inadvertently prompted by 'the vigilance of Bradford police in clearing girls off the streets'.[47] Here was the clearest example of the 'boomerang effect' of the Street Offences Act.

The discussion of patterns of demand in Bradford was part of a gradual increase in interest in the role of male clients in sustaining prostitution. The press had traditionally concentrated on the women soliciting on the streets, and the pimps and 'madams' organizing the trade; women's organizations had been largely unsuccessful in encouraging journalists to portray the men purchasing sex as being a central part of the problem. The legacy of the sexual double standard was powerful, and many journalists believed that the male 'need' to visit prostitutes required little explanation. With the women's movement starting to display a new vigour in the late 1960s, however, the *People* paid greater attention to the feminist perspective. 'Sexual equality is today accepted in most spheres of human activity', argued the paper, 'but in matters of prostitution and immorality, it is not'. While the Street Offences Act increased penalties for prostitutes and those living off their earnings, 'it made no practical provision for dealing with others who encourage, support and exploit them'. In particular, the paper identified the 'growing menace' of the 'kerb-crawler' as demonstrating the need for firmer action against male clients. Kerb-crawling was described as 'one of the main influences in the corruption of young girls', and the *People* called for new laws to clamp down on the practice.[48] A delegate at the National Council of

[45] *The People*, 2 Nov. 1969, 3. [46] *The People*, 5 Oct. 1969, 8.
[47] Ibid. [48] *The People*, 12 Oct. 1969, 7; 2 Nov. 1969, 3.

Women's annual conference actually used the *People* articles as evidence in her speech decrying the Street Offences Act as 'one of the most glaring examples of discrimination against women in the law'.[49] Nevertheless, the extent of this shift should not be exaggerated. Many assumptions about male sexuality continued to be under-explored, and it remained more common for journalists to investigate why women became prostitutes than why men used them.

By the 1970s, journalists were also far more explicit in their descriptions of prostitutes and what they were offering than they had been twenty years previously. In the sexualized culture of 'permissive Britain' traditional euphemisms no longer seemed appropriate—but the consequence was that Cudlipp's reservations about 'glamorising' prostitutes were increasingly disregarded. A *News of the World* report on a 'Mayfair playpen' in 1973 provides a good example of the new style. Having been invited into the brothel by 'a tall brunette wearing a tight sweater and black slacks', the journalist was told that 'the charge was £6 to make love to her', and asked if he 'would like any extras'. He was then entertained by two other women, Sheila and Patina, before he made his 'excuse and left'. 'Sheila stripped to her red brassiere . . . . Patina then proceeded to simulate the love act with her on the double bed, continuously asking me to join them.' In another room was a specialist in bondage, who undressed 'to reveal a light red bra and matching briefs' and 'proudly pulled back curtains, revealing a wooden cross fitted with chains and shackles'.[50] The conventional moral condemnations of 'vice', 'sin', and 'immorality' remained in place, but the lubricious descriptions of the women made it harder than ever to disguise that the intention of these reports were to titillate readers. Trevor Kempson and Tina Dalgliesh perfected this form of revelatory investigation for the *News of the World* in the 1970s and 1980s, enabling readers to gain vicarious access to the most expensive clubs, escort agencies, and brothels. Dalgliesh went so far as to obtain a position at a Playboy Club as a 'bunny girl' to ascertain whether sex was being offered; Kempson, meanwhile, was the first to expose the notorious madam Linda St Clair.[51] These features, along with the celebrity confessions, increasingly replaced the court report as the paper's staple.

Editors and journalists ultimately refused to address the inconsistencies of their coverage of prostitution. On the one hand, newspapers admitted that sex would always be bought and sold, and that it was unrealistic for governments to attempt to eradicate the practice altogether. 'Prostitution is an age-old profession,' accepted the *People* in 1969. 'Nobody's ever going to stamp it out.'[52] On the other hand, editors seemed compelled to send out reporters to investigate the trade, bring it to public attention, denounce it, and demand vigorous action

[49] *The People*, 2 Nov. 1969, 3.

[50] *News of the World*, 29 April 1973, 1, 3.

[51] C. Bainbridge and R. Stockdill, *The News of the World Story: 150 Years of the World's Bestselling Newspaper* (London: HarperCollins, 1993), 242–52.

[52] *The People*, 5 Oct. 1969, 1. See also, *News of the World*, 23 Nov. 1958 [cutting from Lesbian and Gay Newsmedia Archive, Middlesex University]; *Daily Mirror*, 18 Dec. 1958, 2.

from the government. It was a very easy way of manufacturing a moral crusade spiced with details of illicit transactions and sexual transgression. Some of these investigations did have genuine journalistic merit, such as Webb's exposure of the Messina gang: these brothers had, after all, outwitted the police for several years. The majority, however, were routine reports which followed up obvious leads and produced little that was surprising or informative. Looking back over his career in 1976, Hugh Cudlipp described how the *Pictorial* had 'exposed vice' in Soho and in provincial cities in the years after the Second World War: yet this, he mused, had not been done 'successfully or with any permanence. Vice is still being exposed in 1976 when the vice is more vicious.'[53] Here, surely, was a recognition of the futility of the Fleet Street cycle of inquiry and moral indignation on the issue of prostitution. When the press focused on the subject, as it did in 1885, in 1912, and in the 1950s, it could certainly generate considerable pressure on the government and parliament to act; yet each time, the action taken was later deemed insufficient, and further measures demanded. It had been accepted in 1959 that the Street Offences Act would clear the streets at the expense of driving prostitutes underground; ten years later, when prostitution predictably flourished underground, this was regarded as a major problem. In each case, the punitive legislation hit hardest on the women on the streets, and their customers rarely received equal condemnation. In the 1960s, newspapers did start to turn attention to the demand for prostitution, as well as the supply, but it was difficult for them to break away from the well-established narratives of 'loose women' and 'evil' pimps; and with the focus firmly on human interest—and the titillation that offered—the wider issues were all too often left unexplored.

INTER-WAR RETICENCE ABOUT HOMOSEXUALITY

Despite its reputation as an 'unnameable' vice, homosexuality was never entirely absent from the pages of the press before 1918. The historian Harry Cocks has demonstrated that newspapers reported trials for homosexual offences throughout the nineteenth century, albeit in a euphemistic style and without describing the detail of the evidence. They created 'a form of discourse which simultaneously referred to homosexual desire, and tried to cover all traces of its existence with circumlocution and evasion'.[54] Certain trials, like those of the flamboyant cross-dressers Ernest Boulton and Frederick Park in 1870–71, or of Oscar Wilde in 1895, received considerable press attention.[55] The Wilde trial, in particular, did

[53] Cudlipp, *Walking on Water*, 181.

[54] H. Cocks, *Nameless Offences: Homosexual Desire in the Nineteenth Century* (London: I. B. Tauris, 2003), 78.

[55] C. Upchurch, 'Forgetting the Unthinkable: Cross-Dressers and British Society in the Case of Queen vs. Boulton and Others', *Gender and History*, 12/1 (2000), 127–57; A. Sinfield, *The*

much to establish the stereotype of the homosexual as an effeminate, decadent, aesthete. Nevertheless, it was only the authority of the court room that legitimated the discussion of homosexuality, and therefore this discussion remained focused on particular scandalous individuals and cases: in the first half of the twentieth century mainstream newspapers and magazines were very reluctant to delve more deeply into the subject. As the historian Matt Houlbrook has observed, 'it was exceptionally rare for any newspaper to investigate queer London independently between the end of the First World War and the early 1950s. . . . Unless engaged with the apparatus of the law, queer lives remained hidden from readers.'[56] As lesbianism was not a criminal offence, it received even less attention. In contrast to prostitution, then, homosexuality did not become the object of wider press crusades, and debate was generally closed down quickly.

Reports of court cases involving homosexual offences were more likely to be found in the *News of the World* than anywhere else. Patrick Higgins has estimated that the paper covered some thirty prosecutions a year in the early 1930s, an average of one a fortnight.[57] Other popular Sundays, such as the *People*, also included some routine cases, but they were far less common in the dailies. Sunday newspapers tended to select trials featuring authority figures, such as teachers, clergymen, army officers, scout masters, or employers; the working-class readership was thereby offered the opportunity to enjoy the disgrace of 'respectable' members of society—and encouraged the belief that homosexuality was an elite vice. Journalists were, however, slow to adopt the sexological and psychoanalytic language that was increasingly being used in medical and legal circles.[58] Headlines announced 'grave' or 'serious' charges, but after a description of the background events the reports dryly announced that 'indecent' or 'improper' offences had been committed. These gaps were to some extent filled by focusing on supposedly revealing circumstantial evidence: references to the 'effeminacy' of defendants were the most common way of emphasizing that these were 'unnatural' activities. Reporters played on, and knowingly reinforced, the widespread attitude that any sort of unusual or experimental sex was 'dirty'. The implication was that readers did not need to know the specifics of the case, this was just one of a wide range of sordid types of behaviour.

Only the most sensational trials involving 'unnatural' sexualities attracted the attention of the daily papers. In most of these cases, judges issued pleas for restraint in the coverage, and while reporters certainly did not downplay

Wilde Century: Effeminacy, Oscar Wilde and the Queer Moment (London: Cassell, 1994); H. David, *On Queer Street: A Social History of British Homosexuality 1895–1995* (London: HarperCollins, 1997), ch. 1.

56 Houlbrook, *Queer London*, 222.

57 Higgins, *Heterosexual Dictatorship*, 281.

58 See, for example, C. Waters, 'Havelock Ellis, Sigmund Freud and the State: Discourses of Homosexual Identity in Interwar Britain', in L. Bland and L. Doan (eds.), *Sexology in Culture: Labelling Bodies and Desires* (Cambridge: Polity Press, 1998); L. Doan, ' "Acts of Female Indecency": Sexology's Intervention in Legislating Lesbianism' in Bland and Doan (eds.), *Sexology in Culture.*

the drama and human interest of the proceedings, they remained very cautious when handling evidence relating to sexual practices. In May 1918, for example, Maud Allan, a dancer, sued the Independent MP Noel Pemberton-Billing for libel, after his publication, *The Vigilante*, printed an article entitled 'The Cult of the Clitoris' which suggested that Allan was a lesbian. Both the daily and Sunday papers devoted a considerable amount of space to the ensuing trial, which degenerated into an examination of Allan's character. While the press revelled in descriptions of colourful episodes in Allan's past, they were coy about the discussions of modern sexological literature that featured heavily in the cross-examinations. The popular papers refused to include the words 'clitoris' or 'lesbian'; the *News of the World* was alone in referring to 'homosexualists'. As the historian Lucy Bland has observed, 'the newspapers generally wrote darkly of unspecified "sexual perversions", "a certain vice", or the favoured term "moral pervert"'.[59] Plenty of people would have been able to decipher the coded language of these reports, but it seems that many readers were bemused. Lady Diana Manners, at the time working at Guy's Hospital in London, found the trial a topic of much conversation among the nurses around her, but could see that they were 'totally ignorant of any significations. They have a dim vision of Sodom and Gomorrah, which is built for them by the word "vice". But even that is hazy.'[60] The journalist Hannen Swaffer agreed that 'the public do not understand' the accusations in such cases 'because, in detail, they are never printed . . . . London wonders and asks questions, only to be told vague things.'[61] As will be seen below, Mass-Observation's surveys certainly testified to a widespread confusion and lack of knowledge about homosexuality.

This evasiveness about sexuality was also a marked feature of the reporting of the cross-dressing cases that captured the public imagination in the inter-war period.[62] These were consistently presented in terms of deception and gender transgression, and reporters were reluctant to explore potential sexual motivations or consider sexological explanations. In 1929, for example, Valerie Arkell-Smith became a *cause celebre* when it was discovered that she had passed herself off as 'Colonel Barker' and lived as the husband of another woman, Elfrida Haward, for four years. The Barker case was, the *Daily Sketch* reporter John Cannell recalled in his memoirs, 'one of the few stories that have really astonished Fleet Street', and the press attention was so intense that Arkell-Smith counsel's complained that the defendant's life had been 'practically made impossible'.[63] In an attempt to

[59] L. Bland, 'Trial by Sexology? Maud Allan, Salome and the "Cult of the Clitoris" Case', in Bland and Doan, *Sexology in Culture*, 194.

[60] Ibid., 194–5.

[61] *The People*, 23 Nov. 1924, 8.

[62] Oram, *Her Husband Was a Woman!* chs. 1–3.

[63] J. Cannell, *When Fleet Street Calls: Being the Experiences of a London Journalist* (London: Jarrolds, 1932), 204. See also J. Vernon, '"For Some Queer Reason": The Trials and Tribulations of Colonel Barker's Masquerade in Interwar Britain', *Signs*, 26/1 (2000), 37–62.

avoid 'anything prurient' being stated in court, the judge asked for the evidence about Barker and Haward's physical relationship to be provided in writing rather than orally, and although reporters naturally raised questions, they were far more interested in narrating the dramatic tale of the elaborate masquerade than in exploring any sexual dimension.[64] Despite coming so soon after the controversy over Radclyffe Hall's lesbian novel, *The Well of Loneliness* (discussed below), there was no explicit mention of lesbianism, and Arkell-Smith was not condemned as a 'deviant': in fact the press displayed an obvious admiration of her exploits. For the *News of the World*, this was a 'masterpiece of sex impersonation', an 'audacious change of identity' carried out with 'almost unparalleled daring'.[65] This case suggests that the argument of some historians that a 'distinct phobia of lesbians emerged in this period', with single women living 'in fear of being labelled sexually deviant', is a considerable overstatement. The press was reluctant to make this claim of Arkell-Smith, let alone about other women.[66]

There was a similar pattern with cases of male cross-dressing. Two years after the Barker trial, a male transvestite named Austin Hull was exposed as having lived as 'Norma Jackson' and marrying a man named George Burrows. Hull was charged with inducing another to commit 'gross indecency'.[67] While intrigued by the incident, the daily press was selective about what it reported, and directed attention away from the homosexual offences. The *Daily Mail*, for example, produced a short piece under the headline 'Masquerade As A Woman', which stated only that Hull had been 'indicted for an offence' as a result of posing as a woman for six months and deceiving 'many people'.[68] Readers of the *News of the World* might have had a better idea of the true nature of the charge—the paper referred to the possibility of 'acts of impropriety' and reported psychiatric evidence that Hull was 'not a moral pervert, but an invert'—but like the *Mail*, the human drama was provided by the issue of whether the defendant should appear in male or female clothing.[69] Similarly, Matt Houlbrook has noted that in the trial of 'Lady Austin's Camp Boys', men arrested in drag at a ballroom in Holland Park Avenue in February 1933, 'respectable' daily papers focused on gender transgression and maintained a 'discreet and decorous silence' about the details of the case. Once again it was the *News of the World* that disrupted these silences, simply by reporting the cross-examinations in greater detail.[70] The *Justice of the Peace and Local Government Review* was prompted to

64 *Daily Express*, 25 April 1929, 3.

65 *News of the World*, 10 Mar. 1929, 9.

66 D. Beddoe, *Back to Home and Duty: Women between the Wars 1918–1939* (London: Pandora, 1989), 4. See also S. Jeffreys, *The Spinster and her Enemies: Feminism and Sexuality 1880–1930* (London: Pandora, 1985), chs. 8 and 9; and C. Law, *Suffrage and Power: The Women's Movement 1918–28* (London: I.B. Tauris, 1997), 206–7.

67 A. McLaren, *The Trials of Masculinity: Policing Sexual Boundaries* (Chicago: University of Chicago Press, 1997), 214.

68 *Daily Mail*, 16 Nov. 1931, 5.

69 *News of the World*, 15 Nov. 1931, 3.

70 M. Houlbrook, '"Lady Austin's Camp Boys": Constituting the Queer Subject in 1930s London', *Gender and History*, 14/1 (2002), 32.

clarify the legal position in two editorials at the end of the 1930s because 'the shyness of the press about mentioning the real charge in these cases', namely soliciting or other homosexual offences, had created the misconception among magistrates that cross-dressing itself was illegal.[71] If magistrates were confused by press reporting, it is likely that ordinary readers would have been even more baffled.

There were a few occasions when same-sex desire escaped the court pages and entered the editorial and opinion columns, suitably disguised in euphemistic language. In 1924, for example, Hannen Swaffer, wrote an article in the *People* expressing his anxiety that 'abnormality' and an 'unhealthiness of outlook' was becoming common in artistic circles and creating a 'smear across London'. 'This frank parade of decadence is more general today', he argued, 'than it has ever been in England since the Restoration Period'. These 'strange people' were interested in ballet and 'attracted by everything written by, or about, the author of "The Ballad of Reading Gaol" . . . . You cannot, in a newspaper intended for general reading, put it more clearly than that.' Swaffer's article showed how firmly the stereotype of the aesthetic, effeminate, upper-class homosexual had solidified since Oscar Wilde's trial. It also demonstrated the contradictions that typified much writing about homosexuality. On the one hand, homosexuals supposedly offered a blatant defiance of traditional morality, a 'frank parade of decadence'; on the other, it was their secretiveness and elusiveness that created the greatest danger to society: 'Every night in London, there are parties to which devotees of this cult are the only people invited . . . this school of suggestiveness and innuendo is a more dangerous thing [than open immorality], because you cannot track it down. You do not know where it starts and where it ends.' Swaffer offered his words as a 'warning', in the belief that 'Publicity is the cure for many of the evils from which the State suffers'.[72]

The novelist Leonora Eyles followed up the subject in the next issue, writing about 'Women Friendships that People Talk About'. Close female 'friendships' were very common 'among artists, theatrical and society people' and in boarding schools, she revealed, noting that a psychoanalyst had explained the 'sudden orgy of decadence in both sexes' as an outcome of the Great War.[73] But these articles failed to generate the wider interest their authors sought. The circumlocutions and stilted expressions showed how difficult it was to write about homosexuality in a popular medium, and both pieces were too vague and insubstantial to form the basis of a moral crusade. Swaffer later admitted that he had been 'reproved' for writing the piece, for Fleet Street at this stage preferred to ignore the issue.[74] Similar attacks occasionally appeared in other popular publications—in June

71 Vernon, "For Some Queer Reason", 44–5.

72 *The People*, 23 Nov. 1924, 8; Oram, *Her Husband Was A Woman!*, 58.

73 *The People*, 30 Nov. 1924, 8.

74 *World's Press News*, 6 Nov. 1953, 4.

1925, for example, the weekly magazine *John Bull* highlighted the 'Painted Boy Menace' in London—but these were not usually picked up by newspapers.[75]

Far more successful in generating a reaction, because more focused on a specific target, was James Douglas's diatribe in the *Sunday Express* against Radclyffe Hall's novel, *The Well of Loneliness*, which described the life of a masculine lesbian, Stephen Gordon. Hall's book had already been favourably reviewed by a number of other papers when it came to the attention of Douglas, who had conducted a crusade against 'sex novels' for many years. In an article that was trumpeted on the *Express*'s advertising hoardings around the country, Douglas declared that *The Well of Loneliness* was 'A Book That Must Be Suppressed' because it addressed issues of 'sexual inversion and perversion' that were unsuitable for all but a specialist audience. 'Its theme is utterly inadmissible in the novel, because the novel is read by people of all ages . . . many things are discussed in scientific text-books that cannot be decently discussed in a work of fiction offered to the general reader'.[76] Douglas accused Hall of abandoning the unwritten rules that policed 'appropriate content' for the general reader—and which were, supposedly, followed by 'family newspapers'—by being too explicit about lesbian sexuality. The real problem, of course, was that Hall's treatment of lesbianism was more sympathetic than any found in the press; the novel was, after all, almost as euphemistic as the press in its descriptions of physical relationships, and some readers did not appreciate the full significance of these descriptions.[77] For Douglas, the book was an 'insidious piece of special pleading designed to display perverted decadence as a martyrdom inflicted upon these outcasts by a cruel society'. His main concern was that children should be protected from these 'specious fallacies and sophistries'. 'I would rather give a healthy boy or a healthy girl a phial of prussic acid than this novel. Poison kills the body, but moral poison kills the soul.' Like so many other journalists, he portrayed his crusade against this 'pestilence' as a patriotic defence of a pure nation: 'I know that the battle has been lost in France and Germany, but it has not yet been lost in England, and I do not believe that it will be lost.'[78]

Douglas's tirade is one of the most infamous pieces of twentieth-century popular journalism, and it produced immediate results: three days later the book was withdrawn by the publisher, Jonathan Cape, on the advice of the Home Secretary. In October, copies of the novel were seized and successfully prosecuted for obscenity. The case inevitably stirred up considerable concern in literary circles.[79] Nevertheless, to assess its impact on a wider audience, it is important to examine how it was covered in the rest of the popular press. It is rarely noted, for example, that the *Sunday Express* was not the only paper to

[75] Houlbrook, *Queer London*, 224–6.

[76] *Sunday Express*, 19 Aug. 1928, 10.

[77] J. Rose, *The Intellectual Life of the British Working Classes* (New Haven: Yale University Press, 2001), 210.

[78] *Sunday Express*, 19 Aug. 1928, 10.

[79] For a detailed account of these events, see D. Souhami, *The Trials of Radclyffe Hall* (London: Virago, 1999), chs. 20–5.

denounce the *The Well of Loneliness* on 19 August. The *People*—which had a higher circulation than the *Sunday Express*—reported that Scotland Yard had an interest in a 'secret book' which 'treats with astounding frankness a revolting aspect of modern life'. Despite acknowledging the 'brilliance of the writing' and admitting that the book's discussion of its subject was not 'blatant', the paper argued that 'nothing could justify its publication': 'The book, unless action is taken, will inevitably get into the hands of unscrupulous persons who will exploit its sexual aspects for their own ends.'[80] The significant difference between the articles in *The People* and the *Express* was that the former did not mention the name of the book or the author. Such openness, it declared, would increase the 'moral danger' posed by the work (it only named the novel the following week, after it had been suppressed). The *People* thus inadvertently highlighted James Douglas's hypocrisy. By fulminating against *The Well of Loneliness* in such extravagant terms in a popular newspaper, Douglas gave the book far more publicity than it had previously achieved. As *Time and Tide* observed, 'nothing is better calculated to direct public attention to the condemned work than these shrill Press denunciations'.[81] Inevitably the novel became a news story. The *Express* and the *Sketch* pursued the question of its suppression; a review in the *Daily News* denied its obscenity but criticized the way it presented 'as a martyr a woman in the grip of a vice', the *Daily Herald* bravely leapt to Hall's defence and lambasted ill-informed 'stunt journalism'.[82]

This controversy gave an unusual level of exposure to the subject of female same-sex desire, but it is important not to exaggerate the extent or explicitness of the coverage in the popular press. This was by no means the start of an open and frank debate on lesbianism: most papers showed no enthusiasm for prolonging the discussion even though the legal proceedings involving the book dragged on until December. Indeed, neither of the market-leading papers featured the novel prominently. The *News of the World* ignored the initial furore entirely, and provided relatively unsensational reports when the book went before court in November and December; likewise the *Daily Mail* restricted itself to factual descriptions of the legal developments.[83] All of the popular papers remained euphemistic in their reporting, generally referring to the novel's protagonist as exhibiting a form of 'sex perversion', 'inversion', or 'abnormality', but providing few further details. Nor was the case used as the launching point for a wider crusade against lesbianism. As the historian Alison Oram has shown, the idea of female homosexuality as a specific practice 'was muted in press reporting before the Second World War'.[84]

80 *The People*, 19 Aug. 1928, 2.

81 *Time and Tide*, 24 Aug. 1928, 791.

82 *Daily News*, 23 Aug. 1928, 4; *Daily Herald*, 20 Aug. 1928, 4; 21 Aug. 1928, 1; 24 Aug. 1928, 1, 4.

83 *News of the World*, 18 Nov. 1928, 3; 16 Dec. 1928, 8; *Daily Mail*, 24 Aug. 1928, 3; 17 Nov. 1928, 18; 15 Dec. 1928, 18.

84 Oram, *Her Husband was a Woman!*, 154.

In the first half of the century, then, the popular press condemned homosexuality unreservedly while limiting discussion and providing very little information about it. The hostility of journalists was fed by ignorance and fear. Very few had any detailed knowledge of sexological or psychological literature, and they mixed traditional moral rhetoric about an 'unnatural' and 'disgusting' vice with a sprinkling of poorly-understood scientific terms such as 'perversion' and 'inversion'. The words 'homosexual' and 'lesbian' were used only very rarely. A search of the *Daily Mirror* online archive reveals only two uses of 'homosexual', two of 'homosexuality', and three of 'lesbian' between 1903 and 1950.[85] There were some potent stereotypes—such as that gay men were 'effeminate'—but little consistency about whether homosexuality was an 'innate' or 'acquired' trait, or about how easy it was for 'normal' individuals to be 'corrupted'. Matt Houlbrook has demonstrated that understandings of 'queerness' remained fluid until the 1940s, and that men could have sex with other men while considering themselves to be 'normal'.[86] The confused and imprecise writing in the press must have contributed to this fluidity. Shrouded warnings about 'unnatural' sex were not enough to shape clear ideas about homosexuality or to generate a well-defined binary opposition between heterosexuality and homosexuality. Survey evidence and oral histories suggest that the press's combination of hostility and ignorance was widely shared. Mass-Observation considered homosexuality too sensitive to include in their main 'Little Kinsey' investigation of 1949, but their pilot research found that while 'popular feeling against it is very strong', about a third of respondents 'did not understand what homosexuality was', and comments that 'it never occurred to me' were common. The survey concluded that the 'isolationist manner' of homosexual groups made 'extensive ignorance of their existence at least a possibility'.[87]

'INTO THE TWILIGHT WORLD': INVESTIGATING HOMOSEXUALITY IN THE 1950S

It was only in the 1950s, as the popular press significantly extended and deepened its coverage of sexual issues, that this pattern started to alter significantly. A new generation of journalists responded to, and reinforced, a changing climate of opinion in which sexual knowledge was seen both as an essential part of citizenship in a modern welfare state, and also a prerequisite for ensuring marital stability after the turmoil of wartime. Whereas earlier sexology had been viewed

[85] *Daily Mirror* Digital Archive, accessed through Arcitext, http://www.arcitext.com/arcitext/index.html.

[86] Houlbrook, *Queer London*.

[87] Stanley, *Sex Surveyed*, 199–200.

with considerable caution, the press now became more open to, and interested in, scientific and psychological research into sexuality. In particular, reporting on the work of Professor Alfred Kinsey in America emboldened the press to address a wider range of sexual behaviour. As with prostitution, moreover, a steadily rising trend of arrests suggested to some that homosexuality was becoming more prevalent. Against this backdrop, homosexuality for the first time became a subject of sustained discussion and investigation in the popular press. But this more open debate did little to encourage toleration or understanding, at least initially. Whether using traditional moral rhetoric, or using more recent knowledge about 'deviance' and psychological 'maladjustment', journalists overlooked the humane implications of Kinsey's research and maintained their traditional hostility to homosexuality. Crucial distinctions between relationships involving consenting adults, and those involving adults and children, were repeatedly ignored. In the process, the press whipped up a moral panic and urged tough action against the homosexual 'menace'.

The *Sunday Pictorial*'s three-part series 'Evil Men', printed in May–June 1952, demonstrated these new tendencies clearly.[88] The self-declared intention of this series was to end the 'stupid, dangerous conspiracy of silence' that surrounded the subject of homosexuality: this was, the paper announced dramatically, the one remaining 'taboo' in an 'enlightened age' when 'most social evils are frankly discussed'.[89] Douglas Warth, the author of the articles, argued that this silence, far from protecting the innocent, had 'enabled the evil to spread'. Whereas most parents warned their children against prostitutes, 'few recognise the corrupting dangers of the evil men who, in increasing numbers, pervert youngsters to their unnatural ways'. Most people thought that 'mincing, effeminate young men who call themselves "queers"' were 'freaks and rarities', but they underestimated the prevalence of homosexuals who were not 'obviously effeminate'. 'Before the war, police reports assert, there were over a million known homosexuals in Britain. And both numbers and percentage have grown steeply since then.'[90]

Despite the taboo-smashing rhetoric, these warnings were similar to those given in Hannen Swaffer's piece almost three decades before. The difference was that Warth proceeded to discuss the issue in much greater depth, referring to medical and psychiatric research to flesh out his own investigations. This scientific evidence did add some complexity to traditional stereotypes. The clinical work of Dr Carl Lambert, a London psychiatrist, was used to confirm that homosexuals were not restricted to artistic circles but were to be found even in the 'most virile professions'; another specialist was quoted as saying that 'we all have some homosexual tendencies'. Ultimately, though, the medical

[88] This series has been widely discussed: for example, Pearce, 'The British Press and the "Placing" of Male Homosexuality', 306–8; Jeffery-Poulter, *Peers, Queers and Commons*, 11–12; Higgins, *Heterosexual Dictatorship*, 283–92; Waters, 'Disorders of the Mind.

[89] *Sunday Pictorial*, 11 May 1952, 1; 18 May 1952, 3.

[90] *Sunday Pictorial*, 25 May 1952, 6.

and psychological findings were used selectively and remained subordinate to the moralizing agenda. Warth admitted that there were a number of doctors who claimed that 'the problem could best be solved by making homosexuality legal between consenting adults', but he declared that this would be 'intolerable' and 'ineffective' because the danger of 'perverts' corrupting young people would remain: 'If homosexuality were tolerated here Britain would rapidly become decadent.' Rather than promoting acceptance and toleration, 'science' was employed in a simplistic fashion to apportion blame. Poor parenting, for example, was identified as one of the main factors in encouraging homosexuality. Clifford Allen, a government psychiatrist, was quoted as stating that 'Homosexuality is caused by identification with (or moulding oneself on) the mother', which could be caused by over-protectiveness on the part of the mother, or inattentiveness on the part of the father. Even more dangerously, science and psychology raised the seductive prospect that the 'problem' of homosexuality could be solved. Warth argued that instead of relying on prisons, the government should establish a new type of clinic, like Broadmoor, to which homosexual men should be sent 'until they are cured'. Doctors and psychiatrists would welcome the idea, he argued, because there was still 'a great deal to be learned about the delicately balanced endocrine glands which determine whether or not a man could take to these unpleasant activities'. If a patient did not respond to treatment, 'at least society would know that he was not at large spreading his poison and the misery that accompanies it'.[91] Science and psychology, in short, were used to put a modern, superficially 'progressive', spin on an old agenda of demonizing homosexuals.

The reaction to the 'Evil Men' series reaffirmed that the subject of homosexuality remained highly controversial. After reading the first article, the *Pictorial*'s Financial Director, James Cooke, burst into Hugh Cudlipp's office in 'a state of unprecedented anger' demanding that the series be stopped: he announced that he had cancelled his family's own subscription to the paper.[92] At a meeting of shareholders further disgust was expressed.[93] There were protests from the *Pictorial*'s circulation representatives around the country, and as the paper later admitted, a number of readers followed the Financial Director in cancelling their orders.[94] Given this response, it was not surprising that other editors did not accept the *Pictorial*'s invitation to enter the debate. Nevertheless, Cudlipp's prediction that homosexuality would become a topic of increasing importance was soon proved correct. The following year the arrests of a series of public figures for homosexual offences—including the Labour MP W. T. Field, the author Rupert Craft-Cooke, the Hampshire aristocrat Lord

[91] Ibid.; *Sunday Pictorial*, 1 June 1952, 12; 8 June 1952, 12.

[92] R. Edwards, *Newspapermen: Hugh Cudlipp, Cecil Harmsworth King and the Glory Days of Fleet Street* (London: Secker and Warburg, 2003), 247.

[93] Beaverbrook Papers, H/157, Frederick Ellis to E. J. Robertson, 9 June 1952.

[94] *Daily Mirror*, 11 Nov. 1953, 2.

Montagu of Beaulieu, and the actor Sir John Gielgud—provoked several warnings from judges about the extent of the 'problem' and forced the issue up the press's agenda.

It was, in particular, the arrest of John Gielgud in late October 1953 that opened the floodgates to a wave of newspaper comment. The *Sunday Express*'s columnist John Gordon was the first to plunge in. Gordon, an uncompromising Scotsman who had recently given up the editorship of the *Sunday Express* after twenty-five years, criticized the lenience shown to Gielgud (he was fined £10 for importuning in a public lavatory) and argued that it was 'utterly wrong that men who corrupt and befoul other men should strut in the public eye, enjoying adulation and applause, however great their genius'. More broadly he argued that behind the 'protective veil' of press reticence, a 'rot has flourished . . . until it is now a widespread disease. It has penetrated every phase of life. It infects politics, literature, the stage, the Church, and the youth movements.' He had little interest in pursuing the medical route that Warth had signposted, preferring 'sharp and severe punishment', and concerted action to ensure that homosexual men remained 'social lepers'.[95] Gordon was anxious about writing such a bold article without obtaining Beaverbrook's consent, but was pleased to find that it brought an 'exceptional response' from *Sunday Express* readers. Most correspondents agreed with his argument, although some did call for a more sympathetic policy.[96]

Around Fleet Street, editors suddenly felt the importance of clarifying the stance of their newspapers. The *News of the World* declared that 'the grip of this particular form of vice is ever tightening' and urged that the 'searchlight of public opinion' be used to 'reveal the extent of the evil in our midst'.[97] The *Daily Mirror* agreed that action was necessary and that the problem could no longer be ignored.[98] The *Sunday Times* was more measured, calling for a committee of enquiry, while the *New Statesman* and the *Spectator* spoke out in favour of decriminalization.[99] Unlike previous years, the popular press finally combined to give the issue of homosexuality momentum and propel it firmly onto the news agenda. The result was that, according to Patrick Higgins's calculations, the press covered more cases involving homosexual offences in 1954 than any year before or since.[100] The press excitement reached its peak with the sensational trial of Lord Montagu and the *Daily Mail* journalist Peter Wildeblood in March 1954, which became the most prominent case of its kind since the Wilde trials in 1895. By shifting their editorial policy in this way, the popular press made homosexuality so much more visible that it generated a sense of moral crisis. Gay men certainly felt the change in the climate: 'We thought we were all going to be

[95] *Sunday Express*, 25 Oct. 1953, 6.

[96] Beaverbrook Papers, H/165, John Gordon to Beaverbrook, 5 Jan. 1954; *Sunday Express*, 1 Nov. 1953, 3.

[97] *News of the World*, 1 Nov. 1953, 6.

[98] *Daily Mirror*, 6 Nov. 1953, 2.

[99] *Sunday Times*, 1, 8 Nov. 1954.

[100] Higgins, *Heterosexual Dictatorship*, 214.

arrested and there was going to be a big swoop', recalled one. 'The newspapers were full of it. I got so frightened I burnt all my love letters.'[101]

Many politicians, journalists, and doctors became alarmed at the way in which the press was demonizing and dehumanizing homosexuals. The *Observer* accused popular papers of speaking 'in the rabble-rousing tone of the witch-hunt', and a number of doctors and psychologists wrote letters and pamphlets in an attempt to calm the moral panic and expose some of the inaccuracies in the coverage.[102] Maxwell-Fyfe, the Home Secretary, was unsympathetic to the case for legal reform, but was keen to defuse the sense of crisis generated by the press. In February 1954 he proposed to the Cabinet that it should establish a committee to investigate homosexuality as well as prostitution, one of his central arguments being that a 'dispassionate survey by a competent and unprejudiced body might be of value in educating public opinion, which at present is ill-informed and apt to be misled by sensational articles in the press'. Maxwell-Fyfe had identified the press as a key part of the problem, and hoped to overcome it by encouraging responsible voices to speak directly to the public. There was, he admitted, a risk that such a committee might make 'embarrassing recommendations for altering the law', but this was a gamble worth taking so that the government could be seen to be dealing with the situation.[103] Ironically, then, the popular press's vociferous demands for action played a major part in bringing what many journalists wanted least of all: a committee that would eventually recommend the decriminalization of homosexuality.

Others were less concerned about educating the public than suppressing the coverage of homosexuality and returning to the previous culture of evasion. In February 1954, the Labour MP George Craddock called for a committee to investigate the potential danger to public morale caused by the 'gross and unnecessary details' supplied by the press in their reporting of homosexuality.[104] Winston Churchill, the Prime Minister, agreed that the matter could be resolved by restricting the press coverage. He suggested that the Cabinet should encourage an amenable backbencher to introduce a bill to prevent the publication of detailed information of criminal prosecutions for homosexual offences, just as the 1926 Regulation of Reports Act had curtailed the reporting of divorce cases.[105] A memorandum drawn up to consider this course of action accepted that sensational reports were 'injurious to public morals', could perhaps encourage 'imitation', and gave rise to 'exaggerated ideas of the prevalence of homosexual vice'; indeed it admitted that the 'restriction of Press reports would tend to allay public anxiety'. The opposing arguments were, however, even more persuasive.

[101] 'John Alcock', quoted in Jeffery-Poulter, *Peers, Queers, And Commons*, 23–4.

[102] Higgins, *Heterosexual Dictatorship*, 273; Waters, 'Disorders of the Mind', 140.

[103] National Archives CAB 129/66, C (54) 60 Sexual Offences—Memo by the Sec. of State for the Home Department and Minister for Welsh Affairs, 17 Feb. 1954.

[104] Ibid., 139.

[105] NA, CAB 128/27, C.C. (54) 20 Conclusions of Cabinet Meeting 17 Mar. 1954.

Prohibiting the coverage of criminal, as opposed to civil cases, was a serious encroachment on the principles of open justice and freedom of the press; it would also be difficult to justify the selection of homosexual offences, rather than any other type of crime.[106]

The Cabinet agreed that restricting newspaper coverage was not a realistic solution in the more permissive post-war climate, and agreed to Maxwell-Fyfe's proposal of a committee of enquiry. This was soon established under the chairmanship of John Wolfenden, the vice-chancellor of Reading University. Similar battles were replayed at the recently established Press Council, which addressed 'public protests' about the coverage of homosexuality in its first annual report. The Council rejected these complaints, arguing that reports of prosecutions of homosexual offences performed a 'useful public service'. Indeed, it echoed the words of the *News of the World* when it argued that 'if a great evil is rife in our midst, the facts should be made known in order that a search for the right means of reform should be encouraged'.[107] The Cabinet and the Press Council both recognized that the subject of homosexuality had become established on the press agenda and could not now be removed.

The popular press's interest in homosexuality was given added momentum by the uneasy atmosphere engendered by the Cold War. Political and sexual non-conformity have always been connected in the minds of suspicious patriots, and in these years many gay men were removed from positions in the United States federal government.[108] Although such persecution was not so prevalent in Britain, the Burgess and Maclean scandal ensured that homosexuality was associated with treachery and untrustworthiness. Guy Burgess and Donald MacLean hit the headlines when they abandoned their Foreign Office posts and defected to the Soviet Union in 1951, but initially there was little reference to their unconventional sexual habits. Revelations about their sexuality gradually came to be seen as providing an explanation both for their deceit and for their ability to remain undetected for so long. In September 1955, the *Sunday Pictorial* declared on its front page that the 'sordid secret of homosexuality' was 'one of the keys to the whole scandal of the Missing Diplomats', and criticized the government for attempting to 'hoodwink' the public by evading this angle in its statements on the case:

> The wretched squalid truth about Burgess and MacLean is that they were sex perverts. They were protected during most of their careers by men who knew or ought to have known about their homosexual tendencies. There has for years existed inside the Foreign

[106] NA, CAB 129/67, C (54) 121 Restrictions on Reporting of Proceedings for Homosexual Offences—Memo by the Sec. of State for the Home Department, 1 April 1954.

[107] Press Council *Press and the People: The First Annual Report* (London: Press Council, 1954), 9.

[108] D. Johnson, *The Lavender Scare: The Cold War Persecution of Gays and Lesbians in the Federal Government* (Chicago: University of Chicago Press, 2004).

Office service a chain or clique of perverted men . . . . Homosexuals—men who indulge in 'unnatural' love for one another—are known to be bad security risks. They are easily won over as traitors. Foreign agents seek them out as spies. [109]

The spy scandal enabled the press to portray homosexual men not only as a moral threat, but also as a threat to the safety of the nation at a time of international tension. Their sexual preferences laid them open to blackmail by foreign agents; many commentators implied that they were in any case inherently unreliable. The popular press enthusiastically fed fears about conspiracies engineered by this supposed 'clique of perverted men' at the heart of the establishment, with the *Pictorial* and the *Daily Mail* leading the chase to discover who had tipped off Burgess and Maclean and given them time to flee the country before they were exposed. At the *Express*, Arthur Christiansen told Beaverbrook that he had uncovered information identifying a 'notorious homosexual' on the Foreign Office Selection Board.[110] In March 1956, the *People* printed the most detailed account yet of Burgess's life, a set of five articles written anonymously by someone claiming to be his 'closest friend'.[111] Burgess was described as a 'sex maniac' who consorted with, and then exploited, those who 'shared his abnormal tastes': 'he was in a position to blackmail some of them—including men in influential positions—to get information for his Russian masters'.[112] The author argued that the morally corrupt elite had prevented this treacherous behaviour from being uncovered. 'Men like Burgess are only able to escape detection because they have friends in high places who practise the same terrible vices.'[113] The author of the series was eventually revealed as Goronwy Rees, who at the time was serving on the Wolfenden Committee. In the resulting scandal he was forced to resign from the Committee and from his position as principal of the University College of Wales, Aberystwyth.[114]

This cycle of exposure, finger-pointing, and demonization was reprised in 1962 when William John Vassall, a low-ranking clerk at the Admiralty, was uncovered as a Soviet spy. In his trial it emerged that the KGB had lured Vassall into having sex with a male agent, and used the resulting photographs to blackmail him into passing on secrets. The press gave extensive coverage to the sensational revelations, with the *Sunday Pictorial* paying Vassall £5,000 for his story, much to the consternation of many politicians.[115] Journalists once again raised the question of corruption at the heart of the Admiralty: 'Why was he never vetted effectively? Why was he allowed to have access to secrets when he was a

[109] *Sunday Pictorial*, 25 Sept. 1955, 1.

[110] Beaverbrook Papers, H/177, Christiansen to Beaverbrook, 10 Nov. 1955.

[111] *The People*, 11 Mar.–8 April 1956.

[112] *The People*, 18 Mar. 1956, 3.

[113] *The People*, 11 Mar. 1956, 3.

[114] Higgins, *Heterosexual Dictatorship*, 82–6; Mort, 'Mapping Sexual London'.

[115] *Sunday Pictorial*, 28 Oct.–11 Nov. 1962; R. Greenslade, *Press Gang: How Newspapers Make Profits from Propaganda* (London: Macmillan, 2003), 175–6.

known homosexual and lived well above his £15-a-week salary?', asked the *Daily Mail* the day after his conviction.[116] The *Express,* the *Mirror*, and the *Herald* suggested that there had been a warning of a spy in the Admiralty more than a year earlier, while the *Pictorial* reported that the scandal had prompted Scotland Yard detectives to draw up a list of 'homosexuals who hold top government jobs'.[117] The press implied that officials had either been negligent, or were protecting Vassall because he was part of a sinister network of homosexuals. The spotlight on Vassall's superiors in the Admiralty, Thomas Galbraith and Lord Carrington, became so intense that Galbraith resigned and the Macmillan government was forced to set up a tribunal of investigation under Lord Radcliffe. In the Commons, Macmillan condemned the press's 'suspicion and innuendo', lamenting that 'Fleet Street has generated an atmosphere around the Vassall case worthy of Titus Oates or Senator McCarthy'.[118] The tribunal, eventually published in April 1963, completely exonerated Galbraith and Carrington, and was severely critical of the press speculation, much of which it found to be entirely untrue. Two journalists who refused to reveal the source of their information were found guilty of contempt and imprisoned.

The popular press remained defiant in the face of this official censure, convinced that its coverage had highlighted important failings by the security services in dealing with 'a practising homosexual' who was 'of weak mental grasp'.[119] The *Daily Mail* dismissed the Radcliffe report as 'one of the great white-washing documents of our age', and, while regretting that newspapers 'made mistakes and drew false assumptions', maintained that they were 'right to pursue inquiries'. The press had been 'wrong in detail' but 'not in instinct'.[120] The tribunal's conclusion that the Admiralty and the Foreign Office could not be expected to identify homosexual members of staff was widely ridiculed by journalists who had spent much time characterizing Vassall as highly effeminate. It became the pretext for a vicious article in the *Sunday Mirror* headlined 'How To Spot A Potential Homo'. Lionel Crane, the article's author, offered 'a short course on how to pick a pervert', claiming that such men fell into two groups: the 'obvious' and the 'concealed'. The former, effeminate, individuals 'could be spotted by a One-Eyed Jack on a foggy day in Blackwall Tunnel'. Concealed homosexuals were obviously more difficult to identify, but after discussions with a psychiatrist, Crane described eight types of men that would be on his 'suspect list'. These types included the middle-aged man with 'an unnaturally strong affection for his mother'; the man with 'a consuming interest in youth'; the 'fussy dresser', the 'over-clean man', and the 'man who is adored by older women'. 'Most of us have an in-built instinct about possible, or probable, or latent homosexuals',

[116] *Daily Mail*, 23 Oct. 1962, 1.

[117] *Daily Mail*, 26 April 1963, 8; *Sunday Pictorial*, 28 Oct. 1962, 1.

[118] J. Lawton, *1963: Five Hundred Days* (London: Hodder and Stoughton, 1992), 7.

[119] *Daily Mail*, 26 April 1963, 1. [120] Ibid.

Crane argued, but it was important to 'sharpen this instinct'.[121] The piece so appalled the members of the Homosexual Law Reform Society (HLRS) that its executive committee wrote to the *Mirror*'s chairman, Cecil King, asking whether the 'reactionary and ill-informed' article represented a departure from his paper's generally progressive line. The committee received no reply.[122] It was one more demonstration of the way in which the Cold War climate left those who did not conform to society's norms at risk of exposure and persecution.

THE POPULAR PRESS, THE WOLFENDEN REPORT, AND THE CAMPAIGN FOR DECRIMINALIZATION

By the mid-1950s, the popular press had become much more forceful on the subject of homosexuality. Rather than being a 'distasteful' issue best avoided where possible, it had been redefined as a topic of pressing social concern which required government 'action'. In the place of the rather vague references to 'unnatural' vice, a more solid distinction between the 'normal' and 'homosexual' individual was emerging, supported by the findings of modern psychiatry. This heightened interest was confirmed by the extensive coverage that the Wolfenden Report received on its publication in September 1957. The members of the committee were startled by this publicity, Wolfenden later admitting that the press 'gave it more column-inches than any of us had dreamt of'.[123] The report did little to erode the basic prejudices that most editors and journalists held about homosexuality—as the coverage of the Vassall affair would demonstrate—but it was very important in starting to shift attitudes about the role of the law in dealing with issues of sexual morality. Publications for an educated readership, such as the *New Statesman* and the *Observer*, had supported the decriminalization of adult homosexuality for some years, and it was not a surprise when *The Times* and the *Manchester Guardian* backed the Wolfenden proposals. Popular newspapers, on the other hand, had been almost universally hostile to legal reform. Now, in September 1957, some mass-circulation newspapers, most notably the *Daily Mirror*, were also converted to decriminalization.

Most scholars have not fully recognized the significance of the *Mirror*'s support for Wolfenden, because they have concentrated instead on the anti-homosexual prejudice of the paper's editorial director, Hugh Cudlipp, the man responsible for commissioning the 'Evil Men' series for the *Sunday Pictorial* five years earlier. Patrick Higgins, for example, has described the *Mirror*'s response to the Wolfenden Report as 'difficult to gauge', noting that Cudlipp 'concentrated

[121] *Sunday Mirror*, 28 April 1963, 7.

[122] A. Grey, *Quest for Justice* (London: Sinclair-Stevenson, 1992), 82.

[123] J. Wolfenden, *Turning Points* (1976), cited in Jeffery-Poulter, *Peers, Queers and Commons*, 30.

on prostitution'.[124] The *Mirror* did initially focus on prostitution, but when, a week later, the Labour MP J. P. Mallalieu accused the paper of 'playing safe', it stated explicitly that it supported the recommendations on homosexuality. This was a bold decision, because it had been conducting a survey of its readers to discover their attitude to decriminalization, and found that after more than 11,000 responses, 52.5 per cent disagreed with the proposal. It declared bluntly that 'This newspaper believes these readers are wrong'.[125] Nor was this a temporary position. When the House of Commons finally got the opportunity to debate the report in November 1958, the *Mirror* accused both the government and the Labour party of being 'frightened by public opinion' into refusing to endorse decriminalization: 'The *Mirror* deplores this timorous behaviour. There are times when it is the duty of politicians to act in advance of public opinion. And the duty of responsible newspapers to support this lead.'[126] It is important not to exaggerate the extent of this shift in attitude. Homosexuality was still regarded as 'an odious offence' which should not be encouraged—the paper merely accepted Wolfenden's argument that 'it should not be the function of the law to punish a personal moral sin'.[127] Nevertheless, this was still a notable advance from the position of 'Evil Men' series articles five years earlier, particularly in the willingness to separate consenting adult homosexuality from the abuse of children: up to this point, the paper had routinely conflated the two. It was a significant boost to the cause of legal reform that Britain's most popular paper, read by a third of the nation's adults, was on its side. The *Mirror* went on to make an important contribution to convincing sceptical readers of the merits of decriminalization in the decade after 1957.

The significance of the *Mirror*'s stance is perhaps best illustrated by the reaction of some of its rivals to the Wolfenden proposals. The *Daily Express* dismissed the report as 'cumbersome nonsense' that should be torn up, while John Gordon used his column in the *Sunday Express* to condemn it as a 'Pansies' Charter'.[128] The *News of the World* rejected the distinction between a sin and a crime, and argued that the moment the state 'condoned' such behaviour, 'an entirely new outlook would result' that could lead 'to the most dreadful corruption and pollution'. Despite Wolfenden's assertion that homosexuality was not a disease, the paper called for 'chain of clinics . . . where the condition can be cured or curbed'. (The paper did, however, give space to committee member William Wells to defend the report.)[129] The *Daily Herald*, like the Labour party, was non-committal, urging the government to act swiftly against prostitution, while taking time to consider the more difficult issues relating to homosexuality: 'Homosexual

124 Higgins, *Heterosexual Dictatorship*, 283, 117.
125 *Daily Mirror*, 12 Sept. 1957, 2, 7.
126 *Daily Mirror*, 26 Nov. 1958, 2.
127 Ibid.
128 *Daily Express*, 5 Sept. 1957, 6; *Sunday Express*, 8 Sept. 1957, cited in Jeffery-Poulter, *Peers, Queers and Commons*, 33.
129 *News of the World*, 8 Sept. 1957, 6, 7.

vice—or weakness—is so abhorrent to normal minds that public opinion will be slow to accept such a change.'[130] The *Herald* asked its readers to complete a lengthy questionnaire on the subject, but found that many responses were confused or illogical. 'A large number of people are totally or partially ignorant of the whole problem of homosexuality', the paper concluded, '[they] approach the question with emotion so deep that it sweeps away all cool thought'. The readers who could 'put emotions aside', however, generally supported the report.[131]

In Scotland, the *Daily Record* was far more cautious about the report than its English sister paper, the *Mirror*, because it recognized that prejudice against homosexuals was even more firmly entrenched there than in England and Wales. The *Record* conducted exactly the same poll of readers as the *Mirror* and found that 85, rather than 52.5, per cent opposed decriminalization.[132] Most Scottish papers warmly applauded the dissenting minority report produced by James Adair, the former Procurator-General for Glasgow, which rejected any reform of the law on homosexuality.[133]

The *News Chronicle* was one of the few popular papers to join the *Mirror* in supporting the Wolfenden proposals, although it too recognized that reform was unpopular.[134] It commissioned a survey from Gallup, which found that 47 per cent opposed decriminalization, compared with 38 per cent in favour.[135] Another Gallup poll for the paper in December 1958, when it was clear that the government was not going to alter the homosexuality laws, found that 48 per cent were in favour of the status quo, with 25 per cent supporting decriminalization.[136]

The evidence of these opinion polls, and the vehement opposition of large sections of the popular press, helped to persuade an already unsympathetic Conservative government that reform could be avoided. The Cabinet concluded in November 1957 that 'public opinion was divided and strong views were held; and there was not a sufficient measure of public support for the Committee's recommendations to justify the Government introducing legislation to give effect to them'.[137] The Home Secretary, Rab Butler, announced the government's decision to the Commons a year later by stating that 'there was at present a very large section of the population who strongly repudiated homosexual conduct and whose moral sense would be offended by an alteration of the law.'[138] This appeal to the 'moral sense' of the public became the central strategy of the popular papers opposed to decriminalization. They attempted to portray reformers as an unrepresentative liberal clique attempting to foist supposedly 'advanced' metropolitan views on a

130 *Daily Herald*, 5 Sept. 1957, 4.
131 *Daily Herald*, 12 Sept. 1957, 4.
132 *Daily Record*, 11 Sept. 1957, 16.
133 R. Davidson and G. Davis, '"A Field for Private Members": The Wolfenden Committee and Scottish Homosexual Law Reform, 1950–67', *Twentieth Century British History*, 15/2 (2004), 174–201.
134 *News Chronicle*, 5 Sept. 1957, 4.
135 *News Chronicle*, 10 Sept. 1957, 1.
136 *News Chronicle*, 17 Dec. 1958, 7.
137 NA, CAB/128/31, C.C. 82 (57) 28 Nov. 1957.
138 *The Times*, 27 Nov. 1958, 4.

resistant nation. The *Daily Express* applauded Butler for not being deceived by 'a false agitation, covering socially disastrous proposals with specious arguments':

> Ordinary people have been bewildered and horrified at the persisting propaganda in favour of this change in the law. Eminent persons, including bishops of the established Anglican Church have been drawn into it! Does a wide body of opinion favour this change? It does not. But a subtle, industrious lobby has been at work giving a false picture.[139]

The *Daily Mail* concurred that decriminalization was 'still regarded askance by the great mass of the British public, and, in our opinion, rightly so. The mere fact that the law would regard as a private sin what has hitherto been an abominable crime would, of necessity, tend to weaken still more the moral sanction of the law as a whole.'[140] This strategy was well judged, because politicians who were prepared to consider reform were often held back by their anxiety about the public reaction. When considering a draft of the Labour Party's policy document *Signposts* in 1961, Harold Wilson protested about the endorsement of the Wolfenden proposals, arguing that it would cost the party 'six million votes'. Hugh Gaitskell, the party leader, agreed that such a vote-losing policy should be dropped, and it was duly removed from the document.[141] Wilson remained cautious about the reform throughout the 1960s, insisting that it be passed as a private members' bill rather than a government bill.

The Wolfenden Report exposed the divisions in Fleet Street both about the nature of homosexuality and about the proper relationship between morality and the law, and during the 1960s these differences became more apparent as attitudes began to shift. Opposition to decriminalization gradually weakened as a number of commentators became increasingly concerned about the practical consequences of imposing punitive laws. Amongst the prejudice and stereotyping that marked the coverage of the Vassall affair, for example, there were signs that growing numbers of journalists were coming to recognize the counter-productiveness of a law that trapped blameless homosexual men and forced them into desperate measures to protect their reputation. In the *Daily Mail* Peter Black denied that homosexual men were more inclined to treachery than heterosexual men, but 'the law as it stands gives the Communists a lever against them'. He argued that this punitive law did not reflect the 'innocently compassionate' views of the majority of the public, which 'accepts that homosexuality is an unlucky condition and is vaguely and humorously sorry for homosexuals'.[142] The *Daily Herald* likewise demanded that government 'scrap this law that breeds blackmail'.[143]

139 *Daily Express*, 28 Nov. 1958, cutting from Lesbian and Gay Newsmedia Archive.

140 *Daily Mail*, 24 Nov. 1958, cutting from Lesbian and Gay Newsmedia Archive.

141 P. Thompson, 'Labour's "Gannex Conscience"? Politics and Popular Attitudes in the "Permissive Society"', in R. Coopey, S. Fielding, and N. Tiratsoo (eds.), *The Wilson Governments 1964–1970* (London: Pinter Publishers, 1993), 139.

142 *Daily Mail*, 30 Apr. 1963, 8.

143 *Daily Herald*, 25 Oct. 1962, cited in Jeffery-Poulter, *Peers, Queers and Commons*, 62.

The unsatisfactory state of the law was highlighted in July 1964 when the Director of Public Prosecutions (DPP), Norman Skelhorn, announced that he wanted to be consulted about any prosecution of consenting adult homosexuals so that he could impose uniformity on widely differing policing practices around the country. His announcement came days after the *Sunday Mirror*'s dramatic accusation that an unnamed peer (later revealed as Lord Boothby) was homosexual. The accusation was later withdrawn, with the *Mirror* paying Boothby the considerable sum of £40,000 in damages (see Chapter 7). These controversies prompted further reconsiderations of the law, and led to the *Daily Telegraph* finally dropping its long-held opposition to decriminalization. The paper argued that 'there can no longer be any doubt that the moral corruption which follows from the attempt to punish homosexual vice between consenting adults is greater than that which would follow from the abolition of the law. It should be abolished.'[144]

This debate about the practical workings of the law did not necessarily entail a significant change in attitude to homosexuality itself. Nevertheless, in the 1960s popular newspapers did start to open their columns to those pressing for a more fundamental reconsideration of the treatment of homosexual men. In 1962, Bernard Levin, writing in the *Daily Mail*, lambasted the censoriousness and prudery that characterized the 'Puritans' of British society:

> The obscene and brutish clamour against homosexuals is a perfect example of the Puritan repelled by someone finding natural what he finds unnatural (in so far as it is not, anyway, a reflection of the clamourer's own buried doubts of his own masculinity); the desire to punish such people is to a great extent a wish to hurt or destroy something that the punisher cannot himself enjoy.[145]

Levin, one of the most famous columnists in Fleet Street, was an influential supporter of reform in a paper not known for its progressive attitudes. He periodically returned to the subject, praising, for example, the 'wisdom, courage and humanity' of the House of Lords when it recorded the first parliamentary vote in favour of decriminalization in May 1965.[146]

Levin was by no means the only liberal voice in the popular press. By the mid-1960s the HLRS found it easier to find journalists sympathetic to their cause. One notable example was Anne Sharpley, who approached the HLRS in 1964 seeking accurate information so that she could explore the subject of homosexuality in a less sensational fashion than was usual in the popular newspapers. Anthony Grey, one of the leading figures in the HLRS, believed that Sharpley's articles were 'a lasting influential turning-point in making sensible discussion of homosexuality easier'.[147] Her four-part series was noteworthy for

[144] *Daily Telegraph*, 20 July 1964, cited in H. M. Hyde, *The Other Love: An Historical and Contemporary Survey of Homosexuality in Britain* (London: Heinemann, 1970), 257.

[145] *Daily Mail*, 25 Oct. 1962, 14.

[146] *Daily Mail*, 26 May 1965, cited in Jeffery-Poulter, *Peers, Queers and Commons*, 72.

[147] Grey, *Quest for Justice*, 82.

its non-judgemental approach, its inclusion of interviews with homosexual men, and its early use of the term 'gay' as a 'light, unwounding' descriptive term.[148] Sharpley made clear that gay men were 'not going to change, vanish overnight, nor will they ever regard imprisonment as anything but an injustice'; she also underlined that they were no more likely to molest children than heterosexual men.[149] As the public learned more about the reality of homosexuality, she was confident they would support legal reform. After all, she concluded, homosexual men and women were not so different from everyone else: crimes 'we have laid in the past so eagerly at their door—promiscuity, child molesting, insincerity, brutality, depravity-can equally well be laid at ours. And so too, happily, can loyalty, appreciation of beauty, progress and order. And love.'[150]

Sharpley's articles represented the high-point of 1960s liberal popular journalism about homosexuality, and encouraged other female journalists, such as Monica Furlong and Marje Proops, to use the HLRS as a source of information. In the *Daily Mail*, Furlong denounced the 'wilful blindness, the almost laughable ignorance with which the subject of homosexuality has become surrounded' and called for 'a huge campaign to spread enlightenment and intelligent understanding'.[151] She argued that reform of the law was a necessary first step for this intelligent understanding: 'So long as the law remains harsh and uncomprehending it is easier for private citizens to hide behind their prejudices and fears.' She was particularly incensed by attempts to use aversion therapy to 'cure' gay men. 'That brainwashing as a treatment can be seriously entertained suggests how unhealthy and unbalanced our thinking on this whole subject has become.'[152] In the *Mirror*, meanwhile, Marje Proops was a vocal advocate of decriminalization who gave Leo Abse advice when he was drafting his homosexual law reform bills. Her position on this issue meant that she had to endure some unpleasant letters from homophobic readers, with one writing that 'You must be a lesbian yourself to want to make life easier for queers'.[153] Lord Arran, the sponsor of the Sexual Offences Bill in the Lords, also used his column in the *Evening Standard* to support the cause. And in addition to these regular columnists, sympathetic journalists were sometimes given the opportunity to place freelance pieces on the subject. In July 1964, for example, C. H. Rolph, an editor at the *New Statesman* and a leading figure in the HLRS, was invited by the *News of the World* to write on the subject of 'Homosexuals and the Law'. Rolph articulated the standard liberal arguments that dominated the reform movement at the time. While welcoming the recent guidance issued by the DPP, he warned that only legal reform would end the blackmail, corruption, and social stigma suffered by homosexual men. Without such reform, he argued, 'Jobs will still be lost, families

[148] *Evening Standard*, 20 July 1964, 7.
[149] Ibid.; *Evening Standard*, 21 July 1964, 7.
[150] *Evening Standard*, 23 July 1964, 8.
[151] *Daily Mail*, 21 Oct. 1964, 8.
[152] Ibid.
[153] A. Patmore, *Marje: The Guilt and the Gingerbread: The Authorized Biography* (London: Warner, 1993), 230.

broken up, men driven to suicide by the social consequences of a condition as blameless in itself as left handedness, colour blindness or stammering'.[154]

Prejudice and hostility against homosexual men certainly did not disappear from the popular press in the 1960s. The week after Rolph's article, for example, the *News of the World* published an investigation of the 'creeping menace of homosexuality in Britain today' which rehashed the well-worn idea that there was a 'vast "queer" brotherhood with tentacles reaching around the globe', and which reserved jobs in certain professions for gay men.[155] Even the more sympathetic writers only offered 'toleration' and 'pity' for homosexual men rather than genuine understanding or acceptance. Nevertheless, the atmosphere of moral panic that had been stoked up by the sensationalist articles of the early 1950s had largely dissipated, and most journalists recognized the problems involved in using the law to punish gay men. Even more importantly, assumptions associating homosexuality with the 'corruption' of children were increasingly challenged, and there was a growing acceptance that adult homosexuality need not be proscribed in order to protect the young. Proponents of decriminalization frequently mentioned the press when arguing in Parliament that their proposals had the support of a wide body of opinion,[156] and now that popular newspapers were gradually joining the elite papers on the side of reform, parliamentary opponents of decriminalization appeared increasingly isolated and old-fashioned. When Abse's Sexual Offences Bill reached its final stages in July 1967, the *Daily Express* was alone among the London popular dailies in voicing its disapproval. The paper maintained that the legislation had been sought only by 'a small minority', and that it would result in 'unnatural practices' becoming 'more easily indulged'. 'Parliament only brings discredit on itself,' the paper concluded, 'when it separates itself so decisively from the moral sense of the people.'[157] The *News of the World* also made clear its dislike of the Act.[158] The most vociferous opposition was restricted to Scotland, however, where most papers expressed their relief that the measure did not apply north of the border.[159] More in tune with the Fleet Street consensus were the *Daily Mirror*, who welcomed the 'Social Revolution', and Anne Scott-James in the *Daily Mail*, who ridiculed the objections of obstructive MPs and declared that it 'would have been a case for weeping' had the bill not passed.[160]

Yet if most popular newspapers were prepared to accept the legal toleration of an 'unfortunate' minority, they found it much harder to come to terms with

[154] *News of the World*, 19 July 1964, 11. [155] *News of the World*, 26 July 1964, 8.

[156] For example, Kenneth Robinson when introducing his reform bill in the House of Commons in June 1960: *The Times*, 30 June 1960, 5.

[157] *Daily Express*, 12 July 1967, 6.

[158] *News of the World*, 27 July 1967, cited in Jeffery-Poulter, *Peers, Queers and Commons*, 80–1.

[159] Davidson and Davis, "A Field for Private Members".

[160] *Daily Mirror*, 5 July 1967, 7; *Daily Mail*, 6 July 1967, 6.

that minority asserting itself and claiming rights and pleasures on its own behalf. When the Sexual Offences Act was finally passed, Lord Arran warned gay men that 'Any form of ostentatious behaviour, now or in the future, any form of public flaunting, would be utterly distasteful and would, I believe, make the sponsors of this Bill regret that they have done what they have done'.[161] Most journalists approved of his sentiments, and the Sunday papers, in particular, complained vociferously when they uncovered evidence of such 'public flaunting'. In March 1968, for example, the *People* exposed what it regarded as 'distasteful' behaviour in the Hope and Anchor pub in Leeds. Journalist Dennis Cassidy described finding men 'Dancing cheek-to-cheek . . . . Kissing passionately . . . . Holding hands, petting and embracing unashamedly in the packed room . . . . One 19-year-old youth pulled down his trousers and began to roll down his underpants while dancing with another boy.' Cassidy demanded that the police 'put a stop to the odd-goings-on there' which could, he claimed, have an 'adverse effect on curious, impressionable youngsters'. He was unable to produce any complaints about the pub from local people, however: he had only found it after being tipped of by a student newspaper.[162] Similar attacks were made on men 'cavorting in bushes' on Hampstead Heath.[163]

Yet many young gay men were not prepared to defer to politicians and the press and submissively accept their place on the margins of heterosexual society. After 1967, the gay subculture expanded significantly, and the formation of the Gay Liberation Front (GLF) in November 1970 marked a new phase in the campaign for legal reform and social change. The GLF did not want gay men and women merely to assimilate quietly into society, but to be open and unapologetic about their sexuality: the emphasis was on 'coming out', on both an individual and a collective basis. As one leading activist wrote in *Oz* magazine in January 1971, 'We are gay, and we are proud of it. We want to turn all gay people on to the fact, not that "gay is all right" or "gay is permissible", but that gay is good.'[164] Such opinions were a profound challenge to the many editors and journalists who, even while accepting decriminalization, remained hostile to homosexuality itself. The GLF initially received little press coverage, but when it became more prominent its demands were frequently criticized by the press. The campaign to reduce the gay age of consent also drew many sceptical and hostile comments from popular newspapers.[165]

The age of consent was particularly sensitive because one of the principal motivations for the demonization of homosexuals had traditionally been the association of homosexuality with a sexual interest in children and young boys.

161 House of Lords, 21 July 1967, cited in Jeffery-Poulter, *Peers, Queers and Commons*, 90.

162 *Sunday People*, 24 Mar. 1968, 6.

163 J. Weeks, *Coming Out: Homosexual Politics in Britain from The Nineteenth Century to The Present* (London: Quartet Books, 1990), 163; Hyde, *Other Love*, 278–80.

164 J. Green, *All Dressed Up: The Sixties and The Counterculture* (London: Pimlico, 1999), 390.

165 Jeffery-Poulter, *Peers, Queers and Commons*, chs. 5–6.

The popular press had helped to consolidate this association, not only by repeatedly asserting that homosexuals were dangerous because they corrupted youth, but also by reporting sexual offences involving adults in a similar style to those involving adults and children. It had been one of the main aims of a generation of gay writers and activists to remove these prejudices.[166] Those supporting legal reform in the 1960s were careful to emphasize that they wanted to decriminalize only adult homosexual relationships, and their caution on this point was shown by the reluctant acceptance of twenty-one as the age of consent, and stiff penalties for offences with minors. One indication that the old associations were slowly losing their potency was that by the mid-1970s, the popular press started to mark out paedophiles as a separate category of people who posed a threat to society. The rhetoric that had been used in the 1950s against homosexual men was now directed at paedophiles. In May 1975, for example, a front-page report in the *Sunday People* denounced the leaders of a paedophile self-help organization as 'The Vilest Men in Britain':

> These are faces of three leaders of a society whose aim will horrify every parent in the country. They are members of PAL—the Paedophile Action for Liberation. Paedophile means literally: 'Lover of children.' But these vile men do not talk of normal love of a child. They mean sex with a child.[167]

The report generated an immediate reaction. While MPs demanded action and petitions were drawn up, individuals mentioned in the article were attacked, and bricks were thrown through the window of the PAL headquarters.[168] The Press Council rejected complaints that the report was irresponsible, concluding that the language used, although strong, did not 'go beyond what is acceptable in a free society in such a case'.[169]

Two years later, the *Daily Mirror* identified a similar organization, the Paedophile Information Exchange, as a menace to society, and highlighted the growing commercial exploitation of child pornography.[170] Marje Proops sought to inject some moderation into the coverage, arguing that treatment should be 'readily available' for those who suffered from the 'dreadful sickness' of paedophilia, and that punitive action should be directed at the pornographers.[171] Most journalists ignored such distinctions and denounced both sets of men as 'perverts'. Margaret Thatcher picked up on the *Mirror*'s crusade and pledged to press for action from the government, leading the normally loyal Labour paper to give favourable coverage to the Conservative leader.[172] Here was an early example

[166] Peter Wildeblood, for example, argued in 1955 that it was 'very important' that a distinction was made between 'homosexuality' and 'pederasty': P. Wildeblood *Against The Law* (London: 1955), 12.

[167] *Sunday People*, 25 May 1975, 1, 20–1; Press Council, *Annual Report 1976*, 92–5.

[168] *Sunday People*, 1 June 1975, 2.

[169] Press Council, *Annual Report 1976*, 95.

[170] *Daily Mirror*, 5 Sept. 1977, 1, 14–15.

[171] Ibid.

[172] *Daily Mirror*, 5 Sept. 1977, 1; 6 Sept. 1977, 5.

of the way that Thatcher would be able to outmanoeuvre the Labour party on moral issues. More broadly, these press panics about paedophilia marked the start of a crusade that would continue intermittently for the next three decades. As society gradually accepted a range of sexualities, the paedophile remained distinct as the epitome of sexual 'perversion', an unquestioned enemy against which columnists and editorialists could fulminate. Prominent sexual attacks on children almost invariably prompted a wave of articles calling for firmer action from the police.

THE COVERAGE OF LESBIANISM AFTER 1945

In contrast to male homosexuality, lesbianism did not become a subject of intense debate in the post-war press. It was identified more explicitly as a specific sexual practice after 1945, but without the focus provided by the controversy about policing and law reform, discussion was irregular and unstructured.[173] The Sunday papers occasionally tried to whip up concern. A *Sunday Pictorial* article in December 1958 claimed, for example, that 'more Lesbians are seducing girls than homosexuals are seducing boys' and provided a dramatic account of such a seduction.[174] In November 1962 the same paper wrote suggestively about the 'shocking behaviour' of some female soldiers at a Women's Royal Army Corps barracks.[175] Nevertheless, most journalists simply did not believe that lesbians possessed the same potential to corrupt society as gay men, and the issue was slow to rise up the press agenda. With coverage so sketchy, confusion and ignorance about lesbianism remained long after the subject of male homosexuality had been opened up for discussion. When the *Daily Herald* asked in its questionnaire on the Wolfenden Report whether male and female homosexuals should be treated differently, for example, 8 per cent of female, and 6 per cent of male, respondents replied that they did not understand the question.[176] One journalist noted in 1962 that while the widespread public discussion of male homosexuality had begun 'to put parents on their guard against the emotional traps which turn boys into inverts', such possibilities 'hardly ever occur to the parents of most girls'.[177]

The discussion of lesbianism gradually became more common in the 1960s, encouraged partly by the formation of lesbian organizations such as the Minorities Research Group (which published a magazine, *Arena Three*) and KENRIC.[178] Some lesbians were alarmed at the attention these organizations received. Two

[173] Oram, *Her Husband was a Woman!*, ch. 6.
[174] *Sunday Pictorial*, 7 Dec. 1958, 8–9.
[175] *Sunday Pictorial*, 11 Nov. 1962, 19.
[176] *Daily Herald*, 12 Sept. 1957, 4.
[177] D. Rowe, 'A Quick Look At Lesbians', *The Twentieth Century*, Winter 1962–3, cited in A. Oram and A. Turnbull, *The Lesbian History Sourcebook* (London: Routledge, 2001), 218.
[178] E. Hamer, *Britannia's Glory: A History of Twentieth-Century Lesbians* (London: Cassell, 1996), 179.

women wrote to *Arena Three* in June 1965 after 'reading with alarm yet another article in the Sunday Press concerning the activities of MRG':

We think that too much publicity about your club's activities in the popular press is making it very difficult for two women to live together unnoticed, without being viewed with suspicion. My friend and I have lived together now for four years, during which time we have worked with normal people, who thought nothing unnatural about two women living together. Since these articles have been appearing in the Sunday press and on TV we have noticed an increasing (but Morbid) interest in our relationship with each other.[179]

The editors of *Arena Three* were themselves frustrated that while the press was starting to address the subject of lesbianism, many newspapers, including the *News of the World*, refused to accept advertisements for their magazine. A complaint of unfair discrimination to the Press Council was, however, not upheld.[180]

The release in 1969 of the controversial film *The Killing of Sister George*, which portrayed the lesbian relationships of three women, prompted a further flurry of articles. One of the most detailed was written by Marje Proops for the *Daily Mirror*. Despite having discussed male homosexuality frequently, she admitted that she found it difficult to address a subject which she believed remained 'taboo' outside 'small, sophisticated, knowing circles': 'I, like most other heterosexual women, prefer not to think about lesbianism.'[181] A psychiatrist confirmed to Proops that 'a large number of women . . . know nothing about it. They actually don't know what the word means, they don't know it goes on.' Proops described her own reaction to the film as 'mixed disgust and disquietude', and she obviously had few doubts that lesbians were psychologically abnormal. She was prepared to concede, however, that they posed little danger: 'They rarely seduce other women, almost never seduce little girls', and it was 'extremely unlikely' that lesbianism would become a 'vicious cult'. Confident that most women were 'level-headed and sensible' enough to resist any temptations to lesbianism, she suggested to her readers that they 'pity, rather than condemn, our less normal sisters'.[182] This article drew a number of critical responses, with several readers contrasting her sympathetic approach to male homosexuality with her manifest uneasiness about lesbianism. The reaction helped to shift her attitude. Two years later she was rather more open-minded when discussing a 'sad gay girl', and called for a 'deeper understanding' of lesbianism.[183]

In the 1970s, lesbianism became entangled with the broader controversy surrounding the women's liberation movement. Many of the female members of gay rights organizations had quickly become disillusioned with the male domination they experienced, and found women's liberation organizations a more conducive environment.[184] Unfortunately, the presence of prominent

[179] *Arena Three*, 2/6, June 1965, 11, cited in Oram and Turnbull, *Lesbian History Sourcebook*, 257.
[180] Press Council, *Annual Report 1971*, 50–2; Hamer, *Britannia's Glory*, 171, 195.
[181] *Daily Mirror*, 1 April 1969, 11. [182] Ibid.
[183] Patmore, *Marje*, 187. [184] Hamer, *Britannia's Glory*, ch. 10.

lesbians in the movement fuelled hostile press stereotypes. Feminists had long been forced to endure innuendos about their sexuality, and this tendency resurfaced in the press in the 1970s. It was a standard device of cartoonists to portray feminists as bespectacled and ugly (**see illustration 6.3**), implying that the root of their frustration was their inability to find a man. Journalists leapt on the statements of the minority of radical feminists advocating 'political lesbianism' as a means of achieving complete independence from men to characterize the movement as being populated by sexually deviant 'man-haters', and therefore of little relevance to ordinary heterosexual women.[185] The small number of openly lesbian women in the public eye had to face this hostility. When Maureen Colquhoun, the Labour MP for Northampton North, was outed in 1976, she was severely mocked by several journalists.[186] Jean Rook, the self-proclaimed 'First Lady of Fleet Street', wrote such a blistering attack on her in the *Daily Express* that a group of what Rook described as 'hefty, hairy-legged lesbian ladies' stormed into the *Express* office to protest. The editor, Derek Jameson, defused the situation by promising to print an open letter from Colquhoun in response, but Rook was unrepentant, describing the letter as an 'embarrassment' and continuing to use her columns to criticize gay rights activists of both sexes.[187] If popular newspapers never generated a moral panic around lesbianism, then, they did reinforce negative stereotypes about women who failed to conform to the expectations of heterosexuality.

The coverage of prostitution and homosexuality underlines how entrenched was the popular press's moralism. High profile crusades against 'vice' allowed newspapers both to burnish their credentials as defenders of 'family values', and to distract attention away from their own critics. The female prostitute was a slightly more ambivalent figure than the homosexual man. She held a certain illicit allure to papers which themselves were involved in the commercial exploitation of heterosexual sex, and which displayed titillating pictures of models and actresses with such prominence. But by treating sex so openly as a financial transaction, the prostitute and her customer stripped away the romance and sentiment which still surrounded it in popular culture and which newspapers, despite their occasional flippancy and cynicism, sought to preserve. Prostitution was therefore routinely condemned, and any suggestions of legalization dismissed out of hand, even if journalists were pragmatic enough to realize that because it was, in their favourite cliché, 'the world's oldest profession', it was unlikely to be eradicated. Yet newspapers seemed unable to follow their own logic, and allow the practice its covert existence. Of the sexual vices, it was the easiest

185 M. Collins, *Modern Love: An Intimate History of Men and Women in Twentieth Century Britain* (London: Atlantic Books, 2003), 186–92.

186 Hamer, *Britannia's Glory*, 199.

187 J. Rook, *Rook Eye's View* (London: Express Books, 1979), 131–3.

for newspapers to 'investigate' and 'expose'—after all, prostitutes needed to be visible enough to attract punters—and editors, especially of Sunday papers, could not for long resist the temptation to do so. The 'shocked' journalists undertaking these investigations invariably called for 'tougher' action from the government and the police. If such demands generated substantial public support in the 1950s, after the stiff penalties imposed in the 1959 Sexual Offences Act it was not entirely clear how much 'tougher' the authorities could be without infringing on civil liberties. Still the press continued to highlight the prevalence of prostitution, and demand 'action'.

In the first half of the twentieth century, newspapers' discussions of homosexuality remained so vague and evasive that sexological categories did not become firmly established and sexual identities retained considerable fluidity. Only in the early 1950s, when the press generated a moral panic about the prevalence of 'unnatural' offences, did well-defined oppositions between 'heterosexuality' and 'homosexuality' start to emerge. Fears about a furtive, conspiratorial network that had the potential to expand through the corruption of children encouraged the government to establish the Wolfenden committee to settle public anxiety. Once the committee had reported, attitudes to the regulation of homosexuality did gradually shift and the popular press actually played a significant role in fostering a climate of reform. In the 1970s, moreover, some of the hostility to 'abnormal' sexuality began to be focused on the 'paedophile'. But negative stereotypes about gay men and women remained very hard to shift and continued to shape popular journalism. The AIDS crisis of the 1980s revealed how far gay men were from acceptance, with the reporting of the *Sun*, the *Mail*, and the *Express*, in particular, portraying the disease as a 'gay plague'.[188] It would take far longer than David Maxwell-Fyfe predicted in 1954 for the press's misconceptions and prejudices to be swept away.

[188] R. Davenport-Hines, *Sex, Death and Punishment: Attitudes to Sex and Sexuality in Britain since the Renaissance* (London: Fontana, 1991), chs. 1, 9.

6

Titillation: The Evolution of the Newspaper Pin-up

In August 1953, a Miss Dacia Holmes from Nottingham wrote to the editor of the *Sunday Chronicle* to complain at the paper's recent tendency to include prominent photographs of 'undressed' young women. The *Chronicle*'s deputy editor, John Jarrett, was unusually unguarded in his letter of response. He expressed regret that Miss Holmes was unhappy, but claimed that the policy was dictated by the commercial pressures facing the paper:

> With costs as high as they are, it is essential that we increase circulation. I do assure you that nothing else in the paper is changing in any way that would upset you, but it is found that a picture of a pretty girl does achieve the effect necessary, and we would rather do it this way than, like some of our contemporaries, fill pages with semi-licentious stories.[1]

Holmes was unimpressed by Jarrett's reply. 'Either the morals of the country have reached a new "low", or most Sunday papers would like this to be so,' she told the editor of the *Sunday Express*, and pledged her allegiance to the one popular Sunday paper 'which does not resort to "sex" stories and "cheap" photographs to increase circulation'.[2]

Pictures of 'pretty girls' had been a central feature of the popular press for at least fifty years when Dacia Holmes protested to the *Chronicle*. Ever since the technology to reproduce half-tone photographs in newspapers was perfected at the end of the nineteenth century, editors had assumed that male and female readers alike would appreciate pictures of attractive women as 'brightening up' the news columns. Daily picture papers (the *Mirror* became a picture paper in 1904, the *Daily Sketch* was established as its rival in 1908) brought news photography to a mass audience, and were soon being mocked for their penchant for shots of 'bathing belles'. As photography began to be integrated into the make-up of all newspapers during the inter-war period, pictures of glamorous socialites and leading actresses became common. But it was only with the reinvention of the *Mirror* and the *Sunday Pictorial* in the mid-1930s that more overtly sexualized

[1] House of Lords Record Office, Beaverbrook Papers, H/164, John Jarrett, *Sunday Chronicle*, to Dacia Holmes, 19 Aug. 1953; Dacia Holmes to *Sunday Express*, 23 Aug. 1953.

[2] Ibid.

pin-up shots began to be regular features in the daily press; and it was in the 1950s that the pin-up spread throughout the spectrum of the press, thereby provoking the protests of Miss Holmes and many like-minded critics. Voluptuous films stars such as Marilyn Monroe, Brigitte Bardot, and Jayne Mansfield were presented explicitly as 'sex symbols', and even unsensational mid-market papers such as the *Sunday Chronicle* felt the need to compete with 'cheesecake' pictures. This tendency was compounded by the increasing sexualization of the display advertising in newspaper columns. With the relaunch of the *Sun* in 1969, the newspaper pin-up was updated for the permissive age and toplessness became the norm. The 'page three girl', a regular feature in the *Sun* from 1970, was so heavily publicized, and such a central part of the paper's appeal, that it became a defining symbol of British popular journalism. When a new popular paper, the *Daily Star*, launched in 1978, it was little surprise that topless pin-ups—'Starbirds'—were to be one of its chief selling features.

As the historian Joanne Meyerowitz has noted with reference to the United States, the proliferation of sexual representations of women is 'among the most significant developments' in the history of popular culture, but the manner in which the 'exposed female body' became the 'primary public symbol of eroticism' has been strangely under-explored by historians.[3] In Britain, popular newspapers played a crucial role in circulating and legitimizing these sexualized images. The ubiquity of newspapers made their photographs very difficult to avoid, all the more so when their life was extended by literally being pinned-up in male-dominated work environments. Editors, like John Jarrett in his letter to Holmes, reassured readers that pictures of 'pretty girls' were harmless, far less morally damaging than explicit language and 'semi-licentious' stories. Fleet Street tried to defuse criticism by maintaining, and rigorously policing, a 'common-sense' distinction between pin-ups and 'pornography'. The press presented the former as no more than healthy fun, if a little 'cheeky', in the vein of the seaside postcard; they condemned the latter as sordid and morally corrupting. Popular newspapers asserted their moral credentials by crusading against 'genuine' pornography, while dismissing those who criticized pin-ups as 'prudish' and 'Victorian'. The effectiveness of this defence left many of those who disliked the images feeling marginalized—at least until the popularization of a feminist language of opposition in the 1970s. Feminists sought to recast the terms of the debate, focusing on the way these photographs objectified women for the male gaze, rather than on any potential moral damage they might cause. For all the influence of their arguments, however, feminists were not able to dislodge the pin-up culture from the heart of popular journalism. Not only were pin-ups seen as essential circulation props, they had become central to the editorial identity of many popular papers.

[3] J. Meyerowitz, 'Women, Cheesecake, and Borderline Material: Responses to Girlie Pictures in the Mid-Twentieth-Century US', *Journal of Women's History*, 8/3 (1996), 9.

These pin-ups, and the debates surrounding them, reveal much about contemporary attitudes to public sexual display. Picture editors were very sensitive to what was acceptable to a family audience, and prevented the publication of anything they deemed too provocative or explicit—anything, in particular, which might alienate too many female readers. In the middle decades of the century, cleavage and exposed legs were common sights, but nipples and uncovered bottoms were generally considered inappropriate (unless they belonged to 'less civilized' non-white women, pictured in a colonial context, and subject to different standards of sexual propriety). By the 1970s these prohibitions were no longer deemed necessary, and breasts were fully uncovered, but the display of pubic hair remained very rare. These conventions served to eroticize breasts above all: they became the main signifier of sex in the public domain. The scrutiny of the female body encouraged by this pin-up culture inevitably had profound effects on women's body image and consolidated ideas of sexual difference. Male pin-ups did became more common—the *Sun* experimented for a time with a 'page 7 fella'—but men tended to be presented differently from women, and this 'beefcake' never achieved the editorial centrality of 'cheesecake'.

THE INTRODUCTION OF PHOTOGRAPHY INTO POPULAR NEWSPAPERS

By the mid-nineteenth century, illustrations were coming to have a central place in popular print culture. Victorian periodicals such as *Punch, Illustrated London News*, and the *Penny Illustrated Paper* updated the venerable tradition of wood-cut pictures for the machine age.[4] By contrast, national daily and Sunday newspapers remained visually austere, with dense columns of type relieved only by brief headlines and the occasional small sketch. Advertising was still primarily text-based, consisting largely of private classified advertisements, financial prospectuses, and announcements from public authorities.[5]

In the final decade of the nineteenth century, however, two significant developments heralded major changes in the appearance of newspapers. Technological improvements enabled the *Daily Graphic* in 1891 to print the first half-tone newspaper photograph (of George Lambert, a Liberal parliamentary candidate).[6]

[4] C. Kent, 'Matt Morgan and Transatlantic Illustrated Journalism, 1850–1890', in J. Wiener and M. Hampton (eds.), *Anglo-American Media Interactions, 1850–2000* (Basingstoke: Palgrave Macmillan, 2007).

[5] L. Brown, *Victorian News and Newspapers* (Oxford: Clarendon Press, 1985), 16–23.

[6] Eric Cheadle, 'Picture Editing', in W. W. Hadley (ed.), *The Kemsley Manual of Journalism* (London: Cassell, 1950), 79, 81; D. Griffiths, *The Encyclopedia of the British Press, 1422–1992* (London: Macmillan, 1992), 286. Rapid rotary printing of half-tone photographs was pioneered by Arkus Sapt for the *Daily Mirror*—H. Cudlipp, *Publish and Be Damned! The Astonishing Story of the Daily Mirror* (London: Andrew Dakers, 1953), 13; B. Hagerty, *Read All About It! 100 Sensational Years of the Daily Mirror* (Lydney, Glos.: First Stone, 2003), 14.

It would be more than a decade before the *Daily Mirror* pioneered rapid rotary printing of half-tone photographs, thereby making possible their inclusion in cheap mass circulation papers, but the *Graphic*'s breakthrough immediately increased interest in the visual dimension of the newspaper. At the same time the growth of the domestic consumer economy, with the expansion of the retail sector and the emergence of the department store, generated new demands for branded advertising. As newspapers began to reach a mass audience, the value of using them to carry eye-catching publicity for consumer products became increasingly apparent. The *Daily Mail* was the leader in this field. Soon after its spectacularly successful launch in 1896 the *Mail* was devoting substantial amounts of space to display advertising, which used bold typefaces and illustrations to attract the attention of readers and consolidate brand identity. By the end of the decade the advertising on the *Mail*'s front page was using display type, and illustrations followed a couple of years later.[7] These front-page illustrations made a striking visual contrast with the classified advertising of elite dailies such as *The Times*. Over the next century, press photography and illustrated advertising ensured that the visual dimension of the popular newspaper became as important as the textual one.

Both developments served to make images of the female body very prominent in popular newspapers. Retailers of women's fashions soon became one of the most important advertisers in the popular press, and most of the advertisements they placed featured sketches of women wearing the latest clothes. Any sketches that were even vaguely revealing could stir up anxiety, as the *Mail* discovered when it attempted to cater for the underwear and corset market. Wareham Smith, the *Mail*'s first advertising manager, recalled the 'howl of execration' that was provoked when the paper printed an illustrated advertisement of a woman in 'combinations': letters of protest 'poured in' complaining that the morals of young men might be 'contaminated'. Northcliffe insisted that such 'vulgar' advertisements be dropped, but Smith pointed out the retailers could not 'illustrate combinations properly without putting a women's body inside them', and underlined the substantial amounts of revenue involved.[8] After an appropriate delay, the *Mail* resumed illustrated lingerie advertising, and it gradually became an established feature of newspaper columns. Advertisers' use of images of women would continue to provoke controversy in years ahead. Even in 1962, Beaverbrook was concerned about public objections to an advertisement for a 'Glamourline' brassiere: he hoped, rather optimistically, that the manufacturer 'would get rid of their glamorous figure and put an old woman instead'.[9]

The introduction of photography ensured that women became more visible in the editorial content as well. The gendered imbalance of power in Victorian and Edwardian society meant that men inevitably dominated the news columns,

[7] W. Smith, *Spilt Ink* (London: Ernest Benn, 1932), 28–36.

[8] Smith, *Spilt Ink*, 42.

[9] Beaverbrook Papers, H/224, Beaverbrook to Blackburn, undated, Aug. 1962.

but picture editors soon came to the conclusion that photographs of attractive women did not need to be justified by conventional news values. The veneration of female beauty was deeply entrenched in Western culture, and male editors assumed that pictures of pretty women would appeal to both male and female readers. If these women were 'in the news' then so much the better, but if not they would still brighten the columns. Indeed, Northcliffe believed that an admiration of the female form was a prerequisite for a good journalist: 'I have no use for a man who cannot appreciate a pretty ankle,' he informed his news editor.[10] He reminded his staff of the value of featuring eye-catching women so frequently that by 1920 he was 'almost weary of repeating this'. In one bulletin, for example, he emphasized the way in which a dull leader page had been 'greatly relieved' by the *Mail* picture editor's 'happy thought of putting there a picture of Mary Pickford'; on another occasion, when such initiative had not been demonstrated, he grumbled that 'a few attractive ladies would make the paper look better'.[11]

Northcliffe often encouraged the *Mail* to follow the example of the *Daily Mirror*, which was well known for featuring the 'attractive ladies' he admired.[12] After failing as a paper aimed exclusively at women, Northcliffe had taken advantage of the technical innovations in the reproduction of photographs to relaunch the *Mirror*—for a period renamed the *Daily Illustrated Mirror*—as a picture paper for a mixed readership in January 1904. The interest in the female body was evident from the very first issue. The front page was dominated by a sketch of the Parisian actress Madeleine Carlier, who, tantalizingly, had just won a court case after breaching her contract by refusing to wear an 'immodest dress'.[13] Inside, readers were presented with a line drawing of Marguerite Corneille, a 'charming little music hall artiste', a photograph of Annie Oxley, who had recently won a beauty competition in Leeds, and a photograph of 'Tod Sloan's Pretty Sister'.[14] Such images—sketches became less common as the practice of press photography developed—were designed to convey female beauty and glamour, and were not overtly sexualized. The editorial desire for respectability and acceptance from a mixed-sex middle-class audience ensured that there was no attempt to push at the boundaries of decency. The captions, describing the 'lovely', 'delightful', and 'charming' subjects, reflected this concern with grace and good taste.

Similar qualities were sought in the candidates for the beauty contests that soon became a regular, and popular, feature of the *Mirror*, providing the paper with a regular supply of appealing photographs. In 1908, the paper claimed that 15,000 women had submitted pictures for its competition to find 'the most beautiful woman in the world'; each received a certificate of merit.[15] The *Mirror* tried to

10 T. Clarke, *My Northcliffe Diary* (London: Victor Gollancz, 1931), 246.
11 Northcliffe Bulletins, 6 Aug. 1920; 13 May 1919; 5 Aug. 1920.
12 Northcliffe Bulletins, 1 Aug. 1920; 5 Aug. 1920.
13 *Daily Illustrated Mirror*, 26 Jan. 1904, 1.
14 Ibid., 4, 5, 9.
15 Hagerty, *Read All About It!*, 17, 20.

disguise the repetitiveness of this type of feature by running a variety of themed competitions. In 1918, for example, it offered '£1, 000 For Lovely War Workers', while in 1924 it unveiled a swimmer from Plymouth as the winner of its 'Sports Beauty' contest.[16] The paper proudly proclaimed that the latter winner made 'a worthy addition to the growing list of hitherto unknown beauties revealed by the *Daily Mirror* beauty contests'.[17] Other papers followed the *Mirror*'s lead, and by the 1950s beauty competitions were very common features in both daily and Sunday papers. As well as organizing their own contests, newspapers sponsored and covered local, national, and international competitions. (For a time, indeed, the *News of the World* sponsored the Miss World contest.)[18] The press played a very important role in the popularization and institutionalization of the beauty competition, making a significant contribution to the tendency to rate and rank the female body.

If the beauty contest was one reliable source of photos, the beach was another. After the First World War, as women abandoned fussy Victorian beachwear for closer fitting one-piece bathing costumes, photographers were sent out to capture the latest fashions. The results peppered the pages of the popular press in the summer months. January Mortimer, a regular *Mail* columnist, claimed in 1920 that 'the simple and charming pictures of girls bathing and dancing on the seashore which appear almost daily in the newspapers' indicated a growing cultural acceptance of the beauty of the 'human form divine'.[19] Northcliffe was keenly aware of the interest in these pictures: a 'well-known public man' told him in June 1920 that he had felt it necessary 'to drop the *Daily Mail* in order to get the *Daily Mirror* bathing pictures'.[20] For some, indeed, these photographs set a benchmark for what could be decently displayed to a mainstream audience. When the dramatist Oscar Asche was censured by some theatre critics for the overt sensuality of the Bacchanalian scenes in his play *Cairo*, he retorted that the performance was no more provocative than the contents of popular newspapers: 'The criticism savours of hypocrisy when you find published, in the very Press which criticises, pictures of men and women dancing and romping in the sea in nothing but a wet, clinging bathing costume. Isn't that just as strong an "appeal to the sensual"?'[21] The predictable presence of this type of photograph, which did not satisfy any serious news values, marked out the popular papers from more upmarket rivals in a very visible way. As Political and Economic Planning remarked in 1938, 'a popular newspaper, indeed, might almost be defined as one which features a photograph of the first bathing belles of the season on Easter Tuesday morning'.[22]

[16] *Daily Mirror*, 4 Nov. 1918, 2; 11 Aug. 1924, 1, 2. [17] *Daily Mirror*, 11 Aug. 1924, 2.

[18] C. Bainbridge and R. Stockdill, *The News of the World Story: 150 Years of the World's Bestselling Newspaper* (London: HarperCollins, 1993), 172.

[19] *Daily Mail*, 27 July 1920, 6. [20] Northcliffe Bulletins, 23 July 1920.

[21] *Daily Mirror*, 18 Oct. 1921, 3; *Daily Express*, 18 Oct. 1921, 7.

[22] Political and Economic Planning, *Report on the British Press* (London: PEP, 1938), 155.

Newspapers competing in the mass circulation market struggled if they were not visually appealing. The *Daily Herald*, conscious of its duty to counter the propaganda and sensationalism of the right-wing press, tried hard to produce a relatively sober and serious paper, but as its rivals surged ahead it was gradually forced to compromise. The regular photo page it introduced in February 1926, was, the paper's historian Hew Richards has noted, 'closer to popular press style than the news pages', and a 'mix of something newsy, something sporty and at least one pretty girl became the norm'.[23] When the paper was relaunched by Odhams Press in 1930, the *Herald*'s similarity to its competitors became even more striking. Staff were soon complaining that any socialism had to be included 'on the back of a bathing beauty'.[24] The relaunch was hugely successful in terms of circulation, but some long-standing readers lamented the editorial sacrifices that had been made. One female reader complained to Walter Citrine, the General Secretary of the TUC, in 1933 of the

> now regular supply of pictures of half-naked women and girls, some of which are nothing short of indecent, and obviously chosen for their daring character . . . . Are all these nudity photos from day to day in the *Daily Herald* an accurate reflection of the *Daily Herald* directors' view of women's work in the world? Many women readers are getting disgusted with the *Daily Herald*'s contemptuous attitude towards women, but are ashamed to sign a protest.[25]

Citrine's reply, if there was one, is not recorded, but in a private letter the previous year he admitted that if it was to survive, the *Herald* would have to pander to the expectations generated by rivals: 'unfortunately today circulation depends upon newspapers making a popular appeal by methods that sometimes seem to us, who are not actually engaged in the newspapers business, trivial and childish'.[26] By the 1930s, pictures of attractive women seemed to be a necessary element of a popular newspaper.

THE INTRODUCTION OF THE PIN-UP

As photography became a standard feature of the daily and Sunday press in the late 1920s and early 1930s, integrated throughout newspapers as they abandoned linear make-up for the modern 'jigsaw' composition, picture papers like the *Mirror* and the *Sketch* began to lose their distinctive appeal. By 1934, the *Mirror*'s circulation lagged far behind that of the *Express*, the *Herald*, and the *Mail*,

23 H. Richards, *The Bloody Circus: The Daily Herald and the Left* (London: Pluto Press, 1997), 92.

24 F. Williams, *Dangerous Estate: The Anatomy of Newspapers* (London: Longmans Green, 1958), 198.

25 Modern Records Centre, University of Warwick, TUC Archive, MSS. 292/790.3/1 Complaints 1930–33, 'A Woman Worker' to Walter Citrine, 5 June 1933.

26 Ibid., Citrine to Watson, 26 May 1932.

and it was left with a dwindling readership largely made up of metropolitan, middle-class women. The reinvention of the *Mirror* and its sister paper, the *Sunday Pictorial*, as populist tabloids for a mixed-sex working-class readership involved new policies on the use of photography, and nowhere was this more evident than in the depiction of the female body. Photographs were increasingly designed to titillate male readers: they became more overtly sexualized, more flesh was exposed, and curves were more obviously emphasized.[27] The *Jane* cartoon strip, which had been launched in December 1932 as a satire on a guileless 'bright young thing', was transformed into a saucy feature in which the protagonist and her female companions repeatedly lost their clothes. Editors tested the limits of acceptability. The *Mirror* and the *Pictorial* printed a number of photographs of bare-breasted black women, in exotic imperial locations, until the *Pictorial* dared to publish in April 1938 what seems to have been the first photograph in a mainstream national paper of a topless white woman.[28] This nude shot was a relatively tasteful picture of a 'spring nymph' reaching up to the blossom of an apple tree, but the model's exposed nipples were visible in the dappled sunlight. For Hugh Cudlipp, the *Pictorial*'s recently-appointed editor, it sent out a clear signal that the paper was editorially repositioning itself: as he recalled later, it was 'one way of denoting to the readers that the old-fashioned Sunday sedative was positively under new management'.[29]

Topless pictures—except in the *Jane* cartoon—did not become the norm for another three decades, but the *Mirror* and the *Pictorial* ushered in a new era of popular journalism by making sexualized pin-ups a central element in their appeal. It soon became conventional wisdom in Fleet Street that pin-ups offered one of the quickest and most effective ways of attracting young male working-class readers, but the corollary of this was that they became a symbol of the populist and down-market. Such associations were not a problem for the *Mirror* and *Pictorial*, which portrayed themselves as 'vulgar but honest'—but they were for more 'respectable' papers like the *Mail* and the *Express*, which, in Northcliffe's formulation, aimed to be 'popular not vulgar'.[30]

The battle over respectability was fought by the *Mirror* and the *Pictorial* on the one hand, and its main rivals in the picture paper market, the *Daily Sketch* and its sister paper the *Sunday Graphic*, on the other. Lord Kemsley, the owner of the *Sketch* and *Graphic*, believed that the *Mirror* was damaging its reputation by straying into dangerously immoral territory, and that his own papers could

[27] See also M. Gabor, *The Pin-Up: A Modest History* (London: Pan, 1973), 106.

[28] *Daily Mirror*, 8 Nov. 1935, 19; 11 Nov. 1935, 9. *Sunday Pictorial*, 20 Feb. 1938, 20; 17 April 1938, 19. See H. Cudlipp, *At Your Peril* (London: Weidenfeld & Nicolson, 1962), 47–8; H. Cudlipp, 'Exclusive: The First Nude in Fleet Street', *British Journalism Review*, 5/3 (1994), 17–19.

[29] Cudlipp, *At Your Peril*, 47.

[30] Cardiff University, Bute Library, Cudlipp Papers, HC/2/2, Hugh Cudlipp to Cecil King, 27 May 1960; Northcliffe Bulletins, 22 May 1921.

capitalize by emphasizing their virtue. In 1937, he spoke publicly of the need for the press to maintain 'the highest standards of decency', and the *Sketch* launched a 'Clean and Clever' publicity campaign, declaring that it would provide 'All the News and Pictures Fit to Print'—and nothing unsuitable for a family audience.[31] In June 1938—two months after the nude in the *Pictorial*—the *Sketch* took the highly unusual step of taking out a full-page advertisement in a number of national and regional dailies to demonstrate the support its campaign against the 'degradation' of journalism had attracted from 'leaders of religious thought'.[32] The advertisement provided approving quotations from no fewer than sixteen clergymen and church representatives, including the Bishops of London and Manchester. None mentioned the *Mirror* or the *Pictorial* explicitly, but it was not difficult to read between the lines. The Reverend Bernard Grimley, for example, praised the *Sketch*'s guarantee 'not to use the sensational, ribald and pornographic pictures which are making their appearance elsewhere'. 'Dirt pays', he admitted, 'but only for a time, and amongst the least reputable part of the populace'.[33] The Bishop of Stafford, meanwhile, observed that 'for many years' he had taken a daily picture paper but had 'felt obliged to cease doing so'; he had now switched to the 'clean, wholesome and interesting' *Sketch*.[34] The *Sketch* gambled that the *Mirror* had crossed the boundary of acceptability, and that when the difference between the papers was highlighted to the public, there would be many disillusioned readers like the Bishop of Stafford ready to change their allegiance.

The gamble failed. The circulation of both the *Mirror* and the *Pictorial* continued to rise significantly, and their rates of growth were much faster than the *Sketch* and the *Graphic*. The *Mirror* may well have lost some conservative readers, and some of its female audience, but many others were enticed by the promise of bare flesh. A Mass-Observation survey of reading habits in December 1938 suggested that the contrasting editorial approaches were polarizing the market around attitudes to sexual content. One male respondent admitted, for example, that the presence of daring 'sex photos' was one of his main reasons for taking the *Mirror*: 'I dislike the *Sketch*. It is not modern. I don't only want "All the news and pictures fit to print". I want the other side as well.'[35] A female *Sketch* reader, on the other hand, believed the *Daily Mirror* to be 'the dirtiest little rag ever printed as a "daily" in this country', containing as it did 'many photos of half-naked females' in its 'nefarious pages'. She preferred the *Sketch* because it 'caters for the woman', and thereby highlighted the risk that some female readers might object to the *Mirror*'s new direction.[36] Overall, though, the *Mirror* welcomed the public controversy. It regarded the accusations of 'pornography'

[31] *Daily Sketch*, 1 June 1938, 2, 29.

[32] *Daily Sketch*, 23 June 1938, 2. For an example of the advertisement, see *Daily Telegraph*, 23 June 1938, 21.

[33] *Daily Telegraph*, 23 June 1938, 21.

[34] Ibid.

[35] M-O File Report A11, 'Motives and Methods of Newspaper Reading', Dec. 1938, 36.

[36] Ibid.

and 'sensationalism' as useful advertising, and was confident that it had not gone far enough to justify the *Sketch*'s wilder rhetoric and alienate substantial swathes of the family audience.

Looking back in 1953, Hugh Cudlipp recalled with glee that 'Lord Kemsley discovered to his chagrin that he had wasted his money on running a first-class publicity campaign for the rival newspaper'.[37] This was more than the gloating of the victor, for others in Fleet Street regarded the 'Clean and Clever' campaign as disastrously ill-judged. Writing in the same year, Beaverbrook warned *Express* director E. J. Robertson that 'as a general proposition' it was dangerous 'to attack the pornographic newspapers' because 'it only adds to their importance': 'You remember once upon a time the *Sketch* tried it, and strengthened the *Daily Mirror* in the most extraordinary way'.[38] The triumph of the *Mirror* over the *Sketch* confirmed that there was, by the late 1930s, a substantial public appetite for unapologetically entertaining and titillating forms of sexual content. The reinvented *Mirror* appeared to many to be 'modern' and in tune with the times, unlike the moralistic and outdated *Sketch*.

The paper rationing imposed soon after the outbreak of the Second World War seriously restricted the use of the pin-up in the *Mirror* and the *Pictorial*, but both papers tried to satisfy demand whenever possible. A particularly effective use of space was the *Jane* cartoon, the 'daily aphrodisiac' that developed into a national institution in these years.[39] Drawn by Norman Pett, the strip had become increasingly risqué in the late 1930s, but it was only in the early summer of 1942, at a difficult moment in the war, that Jane began brazenly to expose her breasts.[40] She became very popular among servicemen, and adorned the walls of many barracks: when Mass-Observation carried out a survey of favourite pin-ups in a service club in 1944, Jane came third in a list of twelve. The research found that 'Nearly everyone recognized Jane', with one private suggesting that 'many of us follow her adventures with more interest than, for instance, the war against Japan'.[41] Nor was this interest confined to the lower ranks. The Labour peer Lord Winster declared, with pardonable exaggeration, that 'at the Admiralty during the war no admiral ever settled down to his day's work until he had looked to see if the young lady's clothes were on or off that morning'.[42] For young boys the strip also offered an illicit thrill: Bernard Levin, 11 years old at the outbreak of the war, remembered Jane fondly as the 'last word in naughtiness'.[43] But she was popular among women as well as men, with

37 Cudlipp, *Publish and Be Damned!*, 118.

38 Beaverbrook Papers, H/164 Beaverbrook to Robertson, 28 Aug. 1953.

39 The phrase is Cudlipp's: *Publish and Be Damned!*, 191.

40 Daily Mirror Newspapers, *Jane at War* (London: Wolfe, 1976); A. Saunders, *Jane: A Pin-up at War* (Barnsley: Leo Cooper, 2004).

41 M-O File Report 2156, 'What is a Pin-Up Girl?', Sept. 1944.

42 *Daily Mirror*, 23 Mar. 1954, 2–3.

43 R. Allen and J. Frost, *Daily Mirror* (Cambridge: Stephens, 1981), 77.

some 90 per cent of all *Mirror* readers following her adventures.[44] Jane became as potent an emblem of the *Mirror* as the 'page three girl' later became for the *Sun*. When *Mirror* journalist Harry Procter joined the RAF, he was nicknamed 'the Jane-Man'—that was what the paper meant to his colleagues.[45] Cheeky, saucy, but not indecent or gratuitously explicit, the strip captured the tone of the paper very well.

Jane, and the other wartime pin-up photographs and cartoons in the popular press, were routinely justified at the time and subsequently as playing an important part in maintaining the 'morale' of hard-pressed servicemen. 'Jane peeled a week ago. The British 36th Division immediately gained six miles and the British attacked in the Arakan', joked the US servicemen's paper *Round-Up* after Jane was shown nude for the first time.[46] Lord Winster was grateful to the *Mirror* that 'During periods of bad news the Editor kept up morale by keeping her clothes off'.[47] 'Sally', a 'leggy blonde' drawn for the *News of the World* by Arthur Ferrier, was likewise remembered as helping to 'keep up the forces' morale'.[48] Hollywood studios and American popular magazines performed a similar service for the American army by sending pin-ups to soldiers overseas.[49] And if commercial publications were not available, substitutes were often found. When Hugh Cudlipp was posted to Suez with the army in 1942, he took it upon himself to put together aboard ship a two-page daily paper, the *Ocean News*. Having stumbled across 'a mass of old travel brochures', he and his colleagues 'cut out the coloured pictures of beautiful cruising girls' and pasted them onto the pages.[50]

The presentation of pin-ups as a harmless source of pleasure for men defending the country played a significant role in increasing their general acceptability in society. Moral or feminist disquiet was made to seem inappropriate: surely it was petty and prudish to complain about such images if they contributed to the war effort—and were there not more important things to worry about? Joanne Meyerowitz has observed that 'By the 1940s, the American public generally hailed the "pin-up girls" not as prostitutes but as patriots who boosted the morale of soldiers', and the same was true in Britain.[51] This was symbolically captured in the *Jane* strip celebrating victory in May 1945, in which jubilant soldiers aggressively, if good-naturedly, divested Jane of her clothes, leaving her barely covered in a Union Flag. Jane's nudity was a reward for the (male) nation; access to the female body was one of the spoils of war (**Illustration 6.1**).[52]

44 Cudlipp, *Publish and Be Damned!*, 76.
45 H. Procter, *The Street of Disillusion* (London: Allan Wingate, 1958), 74.
46 Daily Mirror Newspapers, *Jane at War*, back cover.
47 *Daily Mirror*, 23 Mar. 1954, 2–3.
48 Bainbridge and Stockdill, *News of the World Story*, 180.
49 Meyerowitz, 'Women, Cheesecake and Borderline Material', 12.
50 H. Cudlipp, *Walking on Water* (London: Bodley Head, 1976), 148–9.
51 Meyerowitz, 'Women, Cheesecake and Borderline Material', 12.
52 *Daily Mirror*, 8 May 1945, 7.

Illustration 6.1. *Jane*, *Daily Mirror*, 8 May 1945, 7. The V.E. day episode of the *Daily Mirror*'s Jane cartoon, one of the most popular pin-ups during the war; Jane's nudity is a reward for the male nation.

THE TRIUMPH OF THE PIN-UP IN THE 1950S

During the 1950s, the pin-up culture flourished in the popular press. The spectacular success of the *Mirror*, which had become market leader in 1949, encouraged rivals to imitate it as intense competition returned to Fleet Street. Substantial rises in operating and labour costs squeezed newspaper finances and a worrying new threat emerged in the form of television. In such circumstances opportunities to entice readers could not be lightly passed up. Suitable material also became more readily available to picture editors. After the acceptance of the wartime pin-up, film stars were marketed more explicitly than ever before as 'sex symbols': glamorous figures such as Marilyn Monroe, Jayne Mansfield, Sophia Loren, and Brigitte Bardot obtained a global celebrity and were endlessly photographed and interviewed. Countless other models and actresses sought to emulate these icons and provided a steady supply of attractive images. Pin-up techniques were also used more insistently in advertising. For Richard Hoggart, writing in 1957, the pin-up had become 'the most striking feature of mid-twentieth century mass art'. Previously confined to 'servicemen's billets and the cabs of lorries,' now, he lamented, 'we are all assaulted by them . . . . We are a democracy whose working-people are exchanging their birth-right for a mass of pin-ups.'[53]

The spread of the pin-up was traced almost obsessively in the private correspondence of the Express group as anxious editors and directors assessed whether their papers could maintain their popularity without increasing sexual content. There was a shared assumption that sexy images were very effective in improving sales. When the *Mirror*'s circulation threatened to overtake the *Express*'s in 1948, E. J. Robertson lamented to Beaverbrook that 'If the *Mirror* does take the lead it will not be on its merits as a newspaper but because of Jane and their other comic strips which appeal to the adolescents'—adding that the *Mirror* had been in 'extra demand' the previous day because 'Jane was presented in the nude'.[54] These concerns intensified in the early 1950s as more and more of the *Express*'s rivals introduced titillating pictures. Assessing the *Daily Herald*'s new look in January 1952, *Daily Express* editor Arthur Christiansen told Beaverbrook that the paper was 'an all-out copy of the *Daily Mirror* on the larger sheet' with 'Bosomy women' included on page three.[55] When the *Daily Sketch* was relaunched the following year, the paper seemed to have stayed faithful to its traditional policy of 'cleanliness'—Max Aitken told his father that it was just 'an expensive edition of the *Daily Mirror*, but with no tits and no strips'.[56] Within a few weeks,

53 R. Hoggart, *The Uses of Literacy* (first pub. 1957; London: Penguin, 1962), 213–14.

54 Beaverbrook Papers, H/131, Robertson to Beaverbrook, 19 Oct. 1948.

55 Beaverbrook Papers, H/155, Christiansen to Beaverbrook, 3 Jan. 1952.

56 Beaverbrook Papers, H/160, Max Aitken to Beaverbrook, 7 Jan. 1953.

however, Christiansen found that it was 'going in for a little cheesecake', and drew Beaverbrook's attention to a 'picture of a naked actress in a bubble bath'.[57] 'This tendency is becoming quite pronounced' he wrote after another fortnight.[58] Beaverbrook himself was struck by an illustrated story about nude bathing on the front page of the *Daily Mail*.[59]

Exposed flesh was even more common in the Sunday market as papers tried to keep up with the *Pictorial*. Max Aitken sent his father, who was out of England, examples so he could see for himself. The *Sunday Dispatch* is 'carrying plenty of "cheese-cake"', he wrote in January 1953. 'I enclose their front page, you will see Ava Gardner well displayed . . . . It is tending very much towards the *Empire News* who also have gone in lately for a considerable number of naked pictures, such as the one I enclose of an actress Diana Dors.'[60] By August 1953, as we have seen, the paper was receiving evidence that the *Sunday Chronicle* felt the need to display 'pretty girls' to attract readers.[61] While Beaverbrook was alive, however, the Express group refused to follow suit. At the heart of its policy was what it considered to be a crucial moral distinction between appealing studies of female beauty, suitable for all, and sexually provocative 'cheesecake', which it believed to be inappropriate for its family audience. 'We should be looking out for attractive pictures of women', wrote Christiansen, 'not bosomy, leggy, sexy pictures, but pictures that are pleasing without being blatant'.[62]

The *Mirror*'s editorial team watched the opposition just as closely, similarly assuming that rivals would increase their sexual content in the intensifying competition for readers. Hugh Cudlipp warned Cecil King in December 1952 that the imminent relaunch of the *Sketch* was a 'pressing problem': 'We should not be fooled by their statements that they are going to remain "clean and clever" and not rival the *Mirror*.'[63] They regarded the *Express*'s policy as nothing more than old-fashioned prudery, and were prepared vigorously to defend the *Mirror*'s inclusion of pin-ups. They claimed that the *Mirror* was merely reflecting modern attitudes to sexual display. 'It's no good the aged tut-tutting over the tastes of the younger generation', the paper declared in a lengthy statement of policy in 1953, asserting that it would make 'No apology for pretty girls in bikinis!' After all, the *Mirror* was only showing what could be seen at the seafront or in the cinema: 'So long as pretty girls dress the way they do on the public beaches or in the public films (which are censored), that is they way they will appear in the public newspapers.' It mocked critics who wanted 'Jane upholstered like a sofa and concealed in a crinoline', and suggested that complaints were motivated by

57 Beaverbrook Papers, H/162, Christiansen to Beaverbrook, 29 Jan. 1953.
58 Ibid., Christiansen to Beaverbrook, 12 Feb. 1953.
59 Ibid., Christiansen to Beaverbrook, 10 Mar. 1953.
60 Beaverbrook Papers, H/160, Max Aitken to Beaverbrook, 7 Jan. 1953.
61 See footnote 1.
62 Beaverbrook Papers, H/192 Arthur Christiansen to Max Aitken, 14 June 1957.
63 Cudlipp Papers, H.C. 2/2, Cudlipp to Cecil King, 29 Dec. 1952.

age and envy: 'What's disgusting about a pretty girl—if you aren't faded and jealous?'[64]

The *Mirror* also saw pin-ups as sweeteners that made serious news more palatable for male readers. Cudlipp described the basic editorial principle he had followed since redesigning the *Pictorial* in the 1930s as being 'to leave the reader gasping for breath, and then, leading him gently by the hand, to whisper in his ear: "Just a moment, friend. Before you take another look at that luscious Swedish blonde in the swimming pool on page 16, there's a piece on page 27 by the Foreign Editor of the *New York Times* analysing the sources of Hitler's power." '[65] This strategy may well have worked on some readers, although many others probably were satisfied by a second glance at the pin-ups. Arthur Seaton, the protagonist in Alan Sillitoe's bestselling novel of 1958, *Saturday Night, Sunday Morning*, represented the class of young men who looked for visual titillation above all else: 'He picked up the *Daily Mirror* and, seeing no good-looking women on the front page, turned to the middle. A nice bathing-suit, anyway.' That was enough for Arthur before he threw the paper down.[66]

Although much of the public debate about pin-ups revolved around moral issues and the danger of corrupting young people, many women were more concerned that these images were fostering unrealistic expectations of female beauty. These anxieties were being voiced well before they were pushed up the public agenda by the reinvigorated feminist movement in the 1970s. There is evidence that a significant number of women in earlier decades were left feeling inadequate by the glamour shots that were becoming so prevalent in popular culture. 'There is far, far too much unhappiness and misery caused in Britain by "perfect" girls, "perfect" figures of seaside queens, "perfect" legs', protested a correspondent to the *Sunday Express* in 1949. It was wrong, she added, to give so much publicity to women who were mostly 'empty-headed shells', fit merely for the 'curio-case'.[67] Some wives felt that the exposure to a constant stream of toned bodies encouraged husbands to become intolerant of imperfections. A thirty-five-year-old housewife from Barnsley lamented to Geoffrey Gorer that her husband no longer appreciated her: 'After gazing at some Venus-like figure in the Sunday paper my husband will insist on telling me I am getting fat, forgetting of course that I am nearing middle age and have had a family.'[68] In 1955, the Cardiff Divorce Court heard that a husband had lost his temper and beaten his wife after she complained about him 'studying a newspaper pin-up picture of a girl "not very fully clad in a swimsuit" ', and asked 'why he was looking at the picture when he had a good-looking wife beside him?'[69] The

[64] *Daily Mirror*, 13 Nov. 1953, 2. [65] Cudlipp, *At Your Peril*, 51.

[66] A. Sillitoe, *Saturday Night and Sunday Morning* (first pub. 1958; London: Grafton Books, 1990), 52.

[67] *Sunday Express*, 31 July 1949, 3.

[68] G. Gorer, *Exploring English Character* (London: Cresset Press, 1955), 134.

[69] *News of the World*, 4 Dec. 1955, 2.

husband ogling attractive women was a staple character of the seaside postcard and the humorous cartoon, but this comedy masked the lack of confidence many women felt in a culture that scrutinized and rated the female body with such enthusiasm.

It was the media's obsession with breasts that caused the greatest disquiet. Marje Proops felt obliged to speak out in September 1957 when a twenty-seven-year-old mother of two wrote to her that she was 'so self-conscious and unhappy' because she was 'only 33 inches round the bust'. This working-class mother's despair was such that she was considering spending £100 on a breast enlargement operation. 'Every day', Proops revealed, 'letters arrive in this office, and every day thousands of girls and women all over this country stare at themselves despairingly in looking-glasses because their bust measurement is, they think, too small'.[70] The 'Cult of the Big Bosom'—which she dated from 'the day Lana Turner was labelled Sweater Girl'[71]—had 'reached idiotic proportions'. Proops argued that it was 'time we revolted against tape-measure dictatorship', and while she did not develop an explicitly feminist analysis, she agreed with her correspondent that male thoughtlessness was a major factor: 'maybe if more men took a critical look at themselves now and then, they would be less free with their taunts about women'.[72] Four days later Proops wrote a second article about the 'amazing stack of letters' she had received in response to her comments: 'Never have I had such overwhelming support . . . from women of every age, shape and size. And from men too, believe it or not.'[73]

The following week, when film star Jayne Mansfield arrived in London flaunting her curvaceous figure, the *Daily Mirror* propelled the issue onto the front page. 'Has The Bust Had It?' asked the headline, as the paper considered whether the 'celebrity bosom' had become over-exposed (**Illustration 6.2**):

> London has become the bust-ling, bust-y rendezvous of the world. Famous beauties, with their even more famous busts fly in (or out) almost every day. 38 inches of Sophia Loren (the well-known bosom from Rome). 42 inches of Sabrina (the notable bosom from Blackpool). 38 inches of Marilyn Monroe (the distinguished bosom from Beverly Hills). And 36 1/2 inches of Diana Dors (the celebrated bosom from Bray). Ladies and Gentlemen—have we had it?[74]

The article provided another opportunity for readers to vent their frustration. 'All this talk about the bust's future is most belittling to types like me who were not endowed with good figures' complained one woman.[75] After reading hundreds of letters the reporter Donald Zec concluded that while readers had 'nothing against

[70] *Daily Mirror*, 13 Sept. 1957, 10?

[71] Lana Turner's appearance in a tight-fitting top in the 1937 film *They Won't Forget* earned her the nickname the 'Sweater Girl'.

[72] *Daily Mirror*, 13 Sept. 1957, 11.

[73] *Daily Mirror*, 17 Sept. 1957, 19.

[74] *Daily Mirror*, 26 Sept. 1957, 1, 8–9.

[75] *Daily Mirror*, 28 Sept. 1957, 7.

Daily Mirror THURS SEPT 26 1957

2d FORWARD WITH THE PEOPLE

No. 16,730

PAGE ONE QUESTION

HAS THE BUST HAD IT?

HERE it is again—the Celebrity Bosom. Yesterday Miss Jayne Mansfield, that bronzed and strapping Hollywood film star, bobbed across the tarmac at London Airport and coyly announced:

"I am 41 . . . 18 . . . and 35½. I'm tanned all over—every little inch of me."

Then she said how happy she was to be in Britain.

The Bust came first.

PAUSE NOW—for a question from the Daily Mirror [Vital statistics: 24 pages . . . read by 13,000,000 every day . . . price at present, 2d.]

HAS THE BUST HAD IT? CAN YOU STILL WIN FRIENDS AND INFLUENCE PEOPLE WITH A TAPE MEASURE? HAS INFLATION GONE TOO FAR?

We don't, of course, mean FINALLY. We do not advocate a bust-less world.

But we're just wondering.

London Airport has become the bustling, bust-y rendezvous of the world.

Famous beauties, with their even more famous busts fly in (or out) almost every day.

38 inches of SOPHIA LOREN (the well-known bosom from Rome).

40 inches of SABRINA (the notable bosom from Birmingham).

38 inches of MARILYN MONROE (the distinguished bosom from Beverly Hills).

And 36½ inches of DIANA DORS (the celebrated bosom from Bray).

Ladies and gentlemen—HAVE WE HAD IT?

What do you think! [illegible] better turn to Donald Zec (AND JAYNE MANSFIELD!) on the Centre Pages today.

Illustration 6.2. 'Has The Bust Had It?', *Daily Mirror*, 26 Sept. 1957, 1. This 1957 *Daily Mirror* article asked readers whether they have become tired of the over-exposed 'celebrity bosom'.

an attractive figure, displayed with taste', the 'outsize, over-exposed "Celebrity Bosom" HAS had it as far as most of you are concerned'.[76]

These gentle critiques of the pin-up culture helped to reassure female readers that their perspectives had not been forgotten, but ultimately they could do little to alter the customs of the boisterously male newsrooms, where the necessity of titillating readers remained an article of faith. Jack Nener, the *Mirror* editor between 1953 and 1961, agreed with Cudlipp that serious news needed to be lightened with glamour: he once demanded from his picture editor 'some tits to go with the rail strike'.[77] Journalists continued to write unself-consciously about the 'vital statistics' of the 'blondes' and 'beauties' that featured in the columns. Picture captions assumed the knowing complicity of male readers: 'Tear your eyes away from the picture for a second, chaps, and we'll tell you her name.'[78] Cartoons based their saucy humour on an imagined world of busty young maidens, overweight, overwrought wives and humourless, flat-chested spinsters. The continuing commitment to the pin-up was clearly demonstrated when Gerald Fairlie was sent to Ireland in 1961 to investigate the poor sales of the *News of the World*'s recently relaunched Irish edition. Fairlie concluded that the editors had been so conscious of previous problems with censors—the paper had been banned in the 1930s—that it 'leant over far too far backwards in trying not to offend'. Curious buyers, attracted by the *News of the World*'s reputation, had felt 'not merely disappointed, but cheated by the absence of pretty girls in bathing suits, and the occasional sensational story'. Fairlie insisted that remedial action be taken at once, and he made plain the priority:

> We must have bright pictures of pretty girls, freely sprinkled about the paper, and wherever possible on the top half of the front page (because Irish people are apt to buy their paper on what the eye catches sight of on the stalls). Censorship has been considerably relaxed in the last two years, particularly in pictures. . . . Objection could—and would—come to pictures featuring breasts or stressing posed bare legs. But a lovely female figure is perfectly all right as such, provided it is not too provocatively posed. In fact, lovely female forms are a necessity for our circulation. I stress this is a MUST.[79]

Fairlie's advice was taken, and *News of the World* started to include more daring content in its Irish edition. Some nude shots acceptable in Britain remained unsuitable for the Catholic market, however, and for some years the paper retained an artist in its Manchester office to paint underwear onto the more explicit pictures before they went on sale in Ireland.[80]

[76] *Daily Mirror*, 1 Oct. 1957, 11.

[77] R. Greenslade, *Press Gang: How Newspapers Make Profits from Propaganda* (London: Macmillan, 2003), 59.

[78] *Daily Mirror*, 12 Sept. 1957, 9.

[79] *News of the World* Archive, CIR/7/1, Report on the Irish Edition, 10 Sept. 1961. See also Bainbridge and Stockdill, *News of the World Story*, 212–14.

[80] Bainbridge and Stockdill, *News of the World Story*, 213.

THE PIN-UP IN 'PERMISSIVE BRITAIN'

The relaxation of the censorship regime in the 1960s enabled the much wider circulation of sexualized images in popular culture. Exposed flesh and simulated sex became much more common on television and cinema screens, and, after 1968, in theatres.[81] A new wave of glossy pornographic magazines emerged to complement the expanding urban sex industry, and the 'underground' and counter-cultural publications that flourished in the second half of the decade, such as *Oz* and *IT*, used explicit pictures to challenge the norms of respectable society.[82] In this context, the cheesecake of the popular press not only seemed less of a threat—moral campaigners such as Mary Whitehouse focused their attention on the policies of the BBC and the BBFC—it even came to seem rather dated, a throwback to the pre-permissive age. For most of the decade, however, there was relatively little enthusiasm in Fleet Street for introducing more explicit pictures. The *Daily Mirror* was comfortably market leader, its circulation rising to the unprecedented figure of 5.25 million copies a day in 1967: it had no need to stir up unnecessary controversy, and in any case Hugh Cudlipp and Cecil King were trying to build up its more serious content and attract middle-class readers. There was, moreover, a widespread belief at this time that popular newspapers would have to move gradually upmarket as the public became better educated.[83] Sunday papers were under greater pressure, and spiced up their photography a little more energetically, but in general they continued to rely on titillating investigations and serializations. It would take a daring outsider, seeking dramatic circulation increases for his relaunched paper, fundamentally to redraw the rules of the pin-up game.

The preoccupation of most picture editors in the 1960s was to illustrate the changing mores of what they perceived to be an increasingly 'permissive society'. They documented the shifts in clothing styles with endless shots of models posing in skimpy bikinis and brief mini-skirts; recorded the easing of media regulation with suggestive stills from controversial films and television programmes; and traced the changes in urban entertainment with tantalizing peaks at crowded strip-bars and nightclubs. Such pictures titillated readers while ostensibly providing news. But the insistent focus on the provocative, and on the fashions and activities of a young metropolitan elite, significantly exaggerated

[81] A. Aldgate, *Censorship and the Permissive Society: British Cinema and Theatre 1955–1965* (Oxford: Oxford University Press, 1995); A. Aldgate and J. Robertson, *Censorship in Theatre and Cinema* (Edinburgh: Edinburgh University Press, 2005), ch. 7; J. Green, *All Dressed Up: The Sixties and the Counterculture* (London: Pimlico, 1999), ch. 6.

[82] M. Collins, 'The Pornography of Permissiveness: Men's Sexuality and Women's Emancipation in Mid-Twentieth Century Britain', *History Workshop*, 47 (1999), 99–120; N. Fountain, *Underground: The London Alternative Press 1966–74* (London: Routledge, 1988).

[83] Cudlipp, *At Your Peril*, 369.

the spread of 'permissiveness', and often served to polarize opinion (see also Chapter 4).

A striking example of this process was the extensive coverage of the 'topless dress craze' in the summer of 1964, prompted by the arrest for indecency in Chicago of an American bather wearing a topless swimsuit designed by Rudi Gemreich.[84] The British press produced a flood of stories—which were often just vehicles for suitably titillating photographs—about women appearing in public similarly (un)dressed. 'It had to happen sooner or later,' reported the *News of the World* at the beginning of July: 'After all the controversy about topless dresses, a housewife wore one in a London high street yesterday. The place was Tottenham and it was the town's most memorable Saturday since the Spurs won the Cup.'[85] The paper just happened to have a photographer on the spot, and it felt compelled to print his picture—although not without the justification that it was doing so 'because it is news', and because it sought the opinions of readers on the new fashion. It emerged the following week that 75 per cent of readers were not in favour, but that did not stop the stories or the photos.[86] When two sisters appeared topless at a London film premiere on 22 July, the news was splashed across several front pages.[87] By 27 July, the *Mail* found that thirteen separate topless incidents had been reported by the press.[88] Many, as the paper underlined, had been manufactured, and featured models seeking publicity or posing for payment, but this did not prevent the press presenting the 'craze' as a sign of wider trends in society.[89] The *Mail* itself provided a front-page interview with French designer Reuben Torres who championed 'the virtues of baring the bosom'; the *Daily Herald*'s fashion editor reported on how the 'fashion climate' was rapidly changing in favour of more revealing clothing, while the *Express* highlighted the fact that there had been no complaints from viewers after a 'pretty redhead appeared in a topless dress during a news and current affairs programme on Anglia Television'.[90] The story eventually died down, but not before readers were given the impression that nudity would soon become socially acceptable.

Yet as popular newspapers reported on a world of shifting standards of sexual display, their own brand of visual titillation seemed to be stuck in the routines of the past. The *Mirror* retired the *Jane* cartoon in 1959 because it was becoming 'old hat'—but then replaced it with a similar strip featuring Jane's daughter. The constraints on pin-up photography—that nipples and bottoms should not be exposed—generally remained in place and models recycled familiar poses. Caption-writers continued to evoke a world in which readers' lives would be brightened by a glimpse of glamour. 'Doesn't She Make You Feel Better?' asked

[84] M. Thesander, *The Feminine Ideal* (London: Reaktion Books, 1997), 187.
[85] *News of the World*, 5 July 1964, 11.
[86] *News of the World*, 12 July 1964, 6.
[87] *Daily Express, Daily Herald, Daily Mail*, 23 July 1964, 1.
[88] *Daily Mail*, 27 July 1964, 8.
[89] Ibid.
[90] *Daily Mail*, 27 July 1964, 1, 8.

a headline in the (pre-Murdoch) *Sun* in 1964 above a photograph of young woman in a bikini: 'Her name's Jeannie Key and she's a student. But that's not important. What really matters is that she makes a glorious picture—a picture that makes everyone feel better.'[91] Presenting a photo of a model in a short dress, the *Mirror* patriotically declared in 1967 that 'The best single reason for not going abroad for your holidays this year is simply that all the best girls are right here in Britain.... Look out for them in the *Mirror*.'[92] It is not surprising that when the *People* surveyed the changes in censorship policy in 1968—the 'astonishing revolution' that had made the previously unacceptable 'commonplace'—it admitted that the one medium that 'has been almost out in the cold has been the much-maligned popular press'.[93]

It is in this context that Rupert Murdoch and Larry Lamb believed that there was a gap in the market for an aggressively populist tabloid with more sexually explicit imagery. It was apparent very soon after its relaunch in November 1969 that the *Sun* would feature a more raunchy style of photography. In particular, exposed nipples gradually became the norm rather than the exception. The paper signalled its intent in the second issue with a centre spread including two topless shots of the Swedish model Uschi Obermeier.[94] Semi-nudity soon became common, although it was a full year before a topless pin-up was displayed on page three, when the anniversary edition featured a 'birthday suit girl'.[95] On that day the paper cheerfully mocked its detractors:

> From time to time some self-appointed critic stamps his tiny foot and declares that *The Sun* is obsessed with sex. It is not *The Sun*, but the critics, who are obsessed. *The Sun*, like most of its readers, likes pretty girls. And if they're as pretty as today's Birthday Suit girl, 20-year-old Stephanie Rahn of Munich, who cares whether they're dressed or not?[96]

There was also celebrity endorsement from popular disc jockey Jimmy Young: 'Congratulations! What better way to start the day than gazing at the super *Sun* dollies.'[97] The paper unapologetically flaunted this aspect of its appeal—'*The Sun* is always best for nudes' was a frequently used tagline[98]—and the editorial team was confident that the associated controversy would only be beneficial, just as it had been for the *Mirror* and the *Pictorial* in the 1930s. 'The more the critics jumped up and down, the more popular the feature became', remembered Lamb in 1989.[99] By the mid-1970s the 'page three girl' had become a regular, institutionalized feature that was central to the paper's brand identity. It also

91 The *Sun*, 17 Sept. 1964, 10. 92 *Daily Mirror*, 3 July 1967, 3.
93 The *People*, 31 Mar. 1968, 14–15. 94 The *Sun*, 18 Nov. 1969, 18, 23.
95 The *Sun*, 17 Nov. 1970, 3. 96 The *Sun*, 17 Nov. 1970, 3. 97 Ibid.
98 R. Loncraine, 'Bosom of the Nation: Page Three in the 1970s and 1980s', in M. Gorji (ed.), *Rude Britannia* (Abingdon: Routledge, 2007), 98.
99 L. Lamb, *Sunrise: The Remarkable Rise of the Best-Selling Soaraway Sun* (London: Papermac, 1989), 115.

became a lucrative marketing opportunity as page three calendars and playing cards rapidly sold out.[100]

The *Sun* consistently argued that it was doing no more than responding to changes in contemporary culture—'The Permissive Society is a fact, not an opinion. We have reflected the fact where others have preferred to turn blind eyes.'[101] It portrayed itself as a fun, cheeky, freewheeling publication in tune with the spirit of the time, 'Britain's brightest, most irreverent, most unpredictable paper'.[102] As Patricia Holland and Rebecca Loncraine have argued, in the climate of the late 1960s and early 1970s, public nudity could plausibly be presented as a refreshing, even faintly radical, challenge to the stuffiness of respectable society. In this sense, the 'page three girl' could be seen as an 'image of defiant liberation'. Nudity was also becoming more common in the elite press, regularly to be found in fashion features, news photography, and in advertising.[103] When the *Sunday Times* attacked the *Sun* for 'baring their 17th nipple in nine days', Lamb pointed out that the *Sunday Times* had in fact displayed no fewer than 22 in its previous nine issues, and consoled *Sun* readers that although they were 'still fractionally under-privileged', the situation was 'not irretrievable'.[104] In such circumstances it was not difficult to characterize critics as old-fashioned prudes.

The *Sun*'s rivals were taken by surprise by the new paper's dramatic success and were forced to reconsider their approach. The *Mirror* was the paper most immediately threatened and it responded by cautiously increasing the explicitness of its photography. Pin-ups became more provocative, nipples were occasionally exposed, and in a photograph depicting a scene from Kenneth Tynan's controversial theatre production *Oh! Calcutta!*, pubic hair was even visible.[105] Yet this shift in policy was not pursued with any conviction. There was significant internal resistance, led by Marje Proops, to the inclusion of page three-style topless pin-ups, with the result that the more explicit shots had to be justified by some form of news value.[106] Under new editor Mike Molloy in 1975, topless pin-ups were regularly included, but before long the policy was altered once again and the paper settled on what Lamb felt was a hypocritical practice of printing 'naughty pin-up pictures—suspenders, wet t-shirts, phallic symbols, the lot', but without exposing nipples.[107]

The *Express* and the *Mail* preferred not to compete with the *Sun* in this field, and preserved their traditional distinction between the attractive and the gratuitous. Interviewed by the Longford Committee investigating pornography in 1971,

[100] Ibid. [101] The *Sun*, 17 Nov. 1970, 2. [102] Ibid, 1.

[103] Loncraine, 'Bosom of the Nation'; P. Holland, 'The Politics of the Smile: "Soft News" and the Sexualisation of the Popular Press', in C. Carter, G. Branston, and S. Allan (eds.), *News, Gender and Power* (London: Routledge, 1998), 23.

[104] Lamb, *Sunrise*, 185. [105] *Daily Mirror*, 28 July 1970, 3.

[106] P. Chippindale and C. Horrie, *Stick it up your Punter! The Uncut Story of the Sun Newspaper* (London: Simon and Schuster, 1999), 46.

[107] Lamb, *Sunrise*, 115.

Express proprietor Sir Max Aitken declared that he 'saw no objection to pictures of pretty girls in the *Express*, but if the *Express* ever printed pictures of nudes or even bare breasts, he would be inundated with protests from readers'.[108] *Mail* owner Vere Harmsworth agreed that '*Daily Mail* readers would also dislike such material'.[109] In the Sunday market there was a noticeable liberalization among the more populist titles, and nudity became fairly common in the *News of the World* and the *Sunday Mirror* in particular. But no paper elevated the topless pin-up to such a central place in its editorial content as did the *Sun*. And as the *Sun*'s circulation rose relentlessly, it was the 'page three girl' that became the symbol of the new era in popular journalism—diverting attention Lamb complained, from the 'very many other ways' in which the paper was 'breaking new ground'.[110]

THE FEMINIST CHALLENGE

The irony was that the 'page three girl' was becoming entrenched just as the resurgent feminist movement was drawing public attention to the consequences of the objectification of women in popular culture. The protests outside the Miss America contest in Atlantic City in 1968—in which campaigners dumped constricting underwear in a 'freedom trashcan', giving rise to the myth of 'bra-burning'—gained worldwide publicity and placed the issue firmly on the public agenda.[111] The feminist disruption of the televized Miss World contest in London in November 1970 came in the very week that the *Sun* had printed its very first 'page three girl'. Just as the moral anxieties about pin-ups seemed to be receding in the permissive age, these images were accused of a different type of offence: perpetuating damaging gender stereotypes. Women had been complaining about pin-ups for years, but now they were imbued with a fresh confidence that their feelings were shared, and offered a new intellectual framework within which to understand their feelings and formulate their complaints.

Popular newspapers ridiculed suggestions that they were demeaning women by pointing to the millions of female readers they entertained every day. They also tried to justify their content using quasi-feminist arguments, claiming that more explicit photographs served to celebrate the female body at a time when women's sexual pleasure had become as highly valued as men's.[112] This had a certain credibility at a time when Germaine Greer was declaring that the 'recent emphasis on the nipple, which was absent from the breast of popular pornography, is in women's favour, for the nipple is expressive and responsive'.[113]

108 Longford Committee, *Pornography: The Longford Report* (London: Coronet, 1972), 325.
109 Ibid. 110 Lamb, *Sunrise*, 110. 111 Thesander, *Feminine Ideal*, 185.
112 Holland, 'The Politics of the Smile', 23.
113 G. Greer, *The Female Eunuch* (London: Paladin, 1971), 34.

In March 1971, the *Sunday Mirror* produced a three-part adaptation of Greer's *Female Eunuch*, and one of the accompanying photographs indeed attempted to portray nakedness as a sign of feminist consciousness. Alongside a woman dolled up in hair curlers, lipstick, and a bra, another woman stood unclothed and unadorned, her breasts defiantly exposed: 'What a farce, this ritual we go through just to please men' read the headline.[114] Whether or not male readers leafing through the *Mirror*'s pages appreciated the intent behind the photograph is impossible to tell, but the text did contain a powerful statement of why sex often 'leaves women cold'. The previous week, moreover, Greer had been given space to attack the representation of woman found in 'advertisements and in glossy magazines'. 'This "ideal" woman is always young, her body hairless, her flesh buoyant and she never appears to have a sexual organ,' she argued. 'Women are now so brainwashed that they are never content with their own bodies.'[115] The *Sunday Mirror* did not reflect on its own contribution to this process, but it did at least give readers a chance to assess the arguments for themselves.

Popular papers also tried to demonstrate an egalitarian spirit by providing an increasing number of male pin-ups for female readers. As Rebecca Loncraine has demonstrated, in the early 1970s 'photographs of naked or scantily clad men' were regularly featured alongside pictures of topless women.[116] Captions conducted a knowing dialogue with female readers. In January 1973, for example, the *Sun* printed a large photo of 'dishy Roger Moore' bearing his chest for 'two young ladies to feast their eyes on':

> The girls—calling themselves only Jane and Myra—wrote to us this week to say how much they've warmed to *The Sun* in the past year. And as a special favour they asked for a pin-up picture of 007 star Roger, who they'd just love to meet in the flesh.[117]

The *Mirror* commemorated the Sex Discrimination and Equal Pay Acts becoming law in December 1975 with a front-page pin-up of 'hunky' singer Malcolm Roberts, and the headline 'Girls, it's your turn now'.[118] When a female reader complained that the picture of Roberts was 'in no way equal to the girl on Page Five as she was virtually naked and he had his trousers on', and demanded instead 'a (nearly) nude every day', the *Mirror* responded with a more revealing image of actor Patrick Mower in briefs.[119] Such content matched the increasing emphasis on female sexual pleasure that was evident in problem columns and feature articles.

The reality was, however, that sexist attitudes remained firmly entrenched in male-dominated newsrooms. There was never anything approaching equality in the portrayal of female and male bodies in photographs and cartoons—indeed the fashion for male pin-ups soon faded. While the *Sun*'s shots of women became

114 *Sunday Mirror*, 21 Mar. 1971, 11.
115 *Sunday Mirror*, 14 Mar. 1971, 10.
116 Loncraine, 'Bosom of the Nation', 102.
117 The *Sun*, 11 Jan. 1973, 14–15.
118 *Daily Mirror*, 29 Dec. 1975, 1.
119 *Daily Mirror*, 31 Dec. 1975, 12.

more explicit in the 1980s, increasingly using the props of soft-pornography, images of men become more conservative as new editor Kelvin Mackenzie feared that the 'Page Seven fella' might attract unwanted gay readers.[120] It was widely assumed in Fleet Street that women were not stimulated by visual images in the same way as men. More fundamentally, though, men's bodies were never scrutinized and rated in the same way as women's. The newspaper coverage of the 1970 Miss World competition exemplified the attitudes that the feminist campaigners were protesting about. As contestants arrived in London, the *Sun* lamented that 'we're in for a long, hard winter' because the 'lovely Miss World girls' had abandoned the mini-skirt for the 'midi' and thereby confirmed the trend for less revealing fashions.[121] The paper rejected accusations that the contest was a 'cattle market' by declaring that 'If you can't stand the cheesecake, stay out of the market.'[122] Meanwhile the *Daily Mirror* previewed the contest as if it was a horse race: 'You couldn't ask for a field of shapelier fillies than those coming under starter's orders tonight for the grand Miss World stakes.' The paper produced a 'form guide' that included a picture and the 'vital statistics' of each contestant.[123]

The feminist protest itself, in which the host Bob Hope was ambushed with smoke and flour-bombs, was reported, if at all, with little sympathy. The *Mail* dismissed the campaigners as 'yelling harpies' and asked what was 'degrading about celebrating the beauty of the human body?' A mocking cartoon portrayed a frumpy, bespectacled woman wearing a sash with 'Miss Women's Liberation Movement 1970' as a male spectator yelled 'Moo'.[124] A *Sunday Express* cartoon was similarly derisive, depicting an ageing, unattractive woman telling her young and shapely female companion that 'I'm all for Women's Liberation. I'm sick and tired of being nothing more than a sex symbol' (**Illustration 6.3**).[125] Perhaps even more revealing, though, was the fact that several papers devoted more space to a controversy over the choice of the winner of the Miss World competition than to the feminist intervention.[126]

Throughout the 1970s feminists campaigned against the ways in which the press objectified the female body and presented women as if they were sexually available for the men. An 'Alliance for Fair Images and Representation in the Media' was established and delegations were sent to the Advertising Standards Authority in an attempt to stimulate action against derogatory advertising. But while some of the language and perspectives of feminism did become visible in the press, Fleet Street's long-standing belief in the value of pin-up photography in circulation terms could not be shaken. When the *Daily Star* was launched to compete with the *Sun* in 1978, it was accepted the paper would try to at least match the *Sun*'s 'page three girl'. 'No newspaper in history lost sales by

[120] Loncraine, 'Bosom of the Nation', 102.
[121] The *Sun*, 5 Nov. 1970, 3.
[122] The *Sun*, 18 Nov. 1970, 2.
[123] *Daily Mirror*, 20 Nov. 1970, 14–15.
[124] *Daily Mirror*, 21 Nov. 1970, 1.
[125] *Sunday Express*, 22 Nov. 1970.
[126] The *Sun*, 23–4 Nov. 1970.

Illustration 6.3. 'Sunday Extra', *Sunday Express*, 22 Nov. 1970. This *Sunday Express* cartoon, printed shortly after the disruption of the Miss World contest in 1970, was a typical example of the tendency to portray feminists as unattractive and embittered.

projecting beautiful birds', the *Star*'s editor, Derek Jameson, told his staff, and he introduced the first full-colour topless pin-ups, the 'Starbirds'.[127] The thousands of letters written by women to Clare Short between 1986 and 1988 when she sought support for legislation to ban 'sexually provocative' photographs in the press testified to widespread unease at these pictures, while polls by *Woman* magazine and the *Star* newspaper found a clear majority of women opposed to 'Page Three'.[128] By 1988, even the originator of 'Page Three', *Sun* editor Larry Lamb, was expressing some regrets about its introduction:

I have come to the conclusion, over the years, that there is an element of sexploitation involved . . . [and] I do not like to feel that I was in any way responsible for the current

[127] Chippindale and Horrie, *Stick it up your Punter*, 83.

[128] Clare Short, *Dear Clare . . . . . . This is what Women Feel about Page 3,* letters edited and selected by K. Tunks and D. Hutchinson (London: Radius, 1991). *Woman*, 30 Aug. 1986, 44–5; *Star*, 31 July 1987, 2–3.

fiercely competitive situation in which the girls in some of our national newspapers get younger and younger and more and more top-heavy and less and less like the girl next door.[129]

But popular newspaper editor continue to follow Lamb's actions rather than his words; they have remained as convinced as John Jarrett in 1953 that a 'picture of a pretty girl does achieve the effect necessary'.

The pin-up was a feature in which the tension between commercial ambition and moral respectability played out in a very visible way. However disguised, it was, fundamentally, erotic entertainment for heterosexual men that could not be justified according to any ordinary scale of news values. Day after day, whatever the headlines, smiling models posed in their familiar stances; readers became so accustomed to their presence that few stopped to think about the ways in which they often jarred with surrounding news reports or with the papers' vocal defences of family morality. But the editors who successfully employed pin-ups knew their target audience very well and recognized the limits of explicitness that they could not cross. The *Mirror* in the 1930s, and the *Sun* in the 1970s, pushed back the boundaries and offended some, but they correctly calculated that not only would most of their market see these pictures as racy rather than indecent, many young male readers would be attracted by the titillation on offer. Moralists and, later, feminists, were able to persuade significant minorities that these pictures were damaging or demeaning, but they found it difficult to escape the charge that they were humourless prudes who should concentrate on 'real' pornography. As a result, the exposed female form continued to circulate throughout mainstream popular culture as the primary symbol of sexual pleasure, and the idea that women's bodies should be available for public scrutiny and consumption was powerfully reinforced.

[129] Lamb, *Sunrise*, 110.

7

Gossip and Scandal: Scrutinizing Public Figures

Popular journalism feeds off the basic human curiosity about other people. Always tell the news through people, Lord Northcliffe told his staff, 'because people are so much more interesting than things'.[1] He insisted that his papers provide 'Interviews, Descriptions of People and articles of the personal type'.[2] Reporters were always able to write about 'ordinary' individuals unexpectedly caught up in extraordinary events, but in order to ensure a steady supply of 'human interest' the press also cast its spotlight upon a regular cast of public figures—the royal family, aristocrats, socialites, politicians, actors and entertainers, sportsmen and women—whose stories could be developed and updated over months and years. Newspapers chronicled the lives of these noteworthy individuals, recorded their triumphs and disasters, and analysed their character traits—in the process providing the public with many of the satisfactions of reading popular fiction and many of the thrills of gossiping with friends. The rise of celebrity journalism provoked despair in commentators across the political spectrum. Newspapers were accused of peddling trivia and distracting readers from serious issues; of undermining the respect for privacy through constant intrusion and snooping; of promoting a shallow confessional culture which rewarded those with a gift for self-publicity. There was a widespread distaste at the cynical methods used to obtain the latest scoop. Despite the damage that was done to their reputation, however, Fleet Street continued to feed the appetite for celebrity journalism, convinced that it was one of the surest ways of building circulation.

This celebrity journalism had a significant impact on popular attitudes to sex and private life. Celebrities—especially royalty and cinema stars—were hugely influential in giving definition to notions of glamour and sex appeal. They set fashions in clothing, body-shape, and personal style; their intimate relationships informed ideas about love and romance. They were fantasy figures dreamt of,

1 Bodleian Library, Oxford, MS.Eng.hist d.303–5, Northcliffe Bulletins, 13 Nov. 1919; British Library, Northcliffe Papers, Add. MSS. 62234, Northcliffe to Alexander Kenealy, 'The Ten Commandments', undated.

2 Northcliffe Papers, Add. MSS. 62199, Memo to Marlowe 26 Dec. 1918.

and imitated by, millions of men and women around the country.[3] At the same time, the press coverage helped to set the boundaries between what was deemed 'public' and 'private'. Throughout the period, celebrity journalism routinely promised revelations about the 'real' person behind the public persona: 'intimate' details, personal 'secrets', 'private' photographs. But ideas about what sort of 'private' material was suitable for public consumption changed considerably, as did the aggressiveness with which reporters pursued stories that public figures wanted to keep quiet. In the first half of the century, the sexual proclivities and marital infidelities of prominent individuals were treated with considerable circumspection: a phone call to the editor or proprietor would usually be enough to suppress unwelcome stories. By the 1950s, however, a market was developing for confessional features in which celebrities would discuss their sexual exploits; with sexuality increasingly regarded as providing the key to individual identity, such information became highly valued. As commercial pressures increased and newspapers were forced to compete with television, journalists also became more ruthless in exposing personal and sexual indiscretions. The unravelling of the Profumo scandal in 1963 demonstrated the spectacular results that could be achieved. Editors came to recognize that uncovering similarly intimate or scandalous stories about public figures was one of the best ways for their papers to create an impact in the era of television.

The increasing intensity of the press's scrutiny was particularly obvious with regard to the royal family. No one had greater news value for the British popular press than the members of the royal family, but in the first half of the twentieth century reporters remained deferential and respectful to them. This deference was most famously demonstrated by the press's willingness to suppress news of Edward VIII's relationship with Wallis Simpson, a divorcee, until the last days of the abdication crisis. Fleet Street congratulated itself on its restraint, and contrasted the essential decency of British journalism with the brashness and intrusiveness of the American press. Only twenty years later, however, such complacency seemed out of place. During the 1950s, the *Mirror* and its competitors began to be more assertive in dealing with the Palace and challenged the culture of secrecy surrounding the monarchy. Arguing that the public should not be kept in the dark about the private affairs of the royal family, newspapers began to speculate and gossip about the Windsors' personal relationships. It was Princess Margaret, in particular, who faced the full glare of the press spotlight: the extensive coverage of her romance with Group-Captain Peter Townsend marked the true start of the 'royal soap opera' that would continue unabated for the rest of the century. Protests from the Palace and warnings from the Press Council did little to prevent the escalating competition for royal stories. By the 1970s,

[3] R. Dyer, *Stars* (London: BFI, 1979); Idem, *Heavenly Bodies: Film Stars and Society* (Basingstoke: Macmillan, 1987); C. Rojek, *Celebrity* (London: Reaktion, 2001); G. Turner, *Understanding Celebrity* (London: Sage, 2004).

the popular press were gleefully reporting the drawn-out collapse in Princess Margaret's marriage while desperately trying to find the latest news on Prince Charles's search for a bride. It was not difficult to predict the intense scrutiny that this bride would receive.

Yet no solutions could be found to the intrusiveness of the popular press. The issue of privacy legislation moved up the political agenda, and some commentators looked admiringly at countries such as France where public figures had substantial legal protection against the reporting of their public lives. Suitable legislation was very difficult to draw up, however, and in any case governments were very reluctant to challenge the jealously-guarded 'freedom of the press'. The Press Council lacked punitive sanctions and remained too weak to alter the culture of journalism. Ultimately it was the market reaction that mattered most when editors chose which stories to run and which to spike.

INTER-WAR SOCIETY JOURNALISM

'Gossip is the currency of speech; without it life would be dull and inexpressive.' For Ralph Blumenfeld, writing in 1933 shortly after his retirement as editor of the *Daily Express*, the gossip column was an essential element of popular journalism. The task of the 'Gossip Editor' was, as he described it, straightforward: 'to collect and present in brightly written paragraphs information about the characters and doings of persons who have achieved prominence'.[4] But associated with this apparently simple duty were many difficult decisions. Which 'prominent' people should be featured? What sort of material was suitable for the 'brightly written paragraphs'? What methods were appropriate in collecting the information? During the inter-war period, as newspaper gossip circulated more widely than ever before in papers such as the *Express*, the *Mail*, the *Mirror*, and the *Sketch*, each of the questions provoked considerable controversy.

In the 1920s, the upper classes remained at the top of the list of prominent people likely to feature in newspaper diary columns. Reporting on the activities of the court circle, the aristocracy, and the upper gentry—what Bagehot described as the 'theatrical show of society'[5]—had been a staple of British journalism for centuries, and despite the gradual weakening of the political and social power of landed families, they remained an object of press fascination well into the twentieth century.[6] Many commentators were struck by the remarkable persistence of this curiosity about the privileged and the wealthy. For Paul

4 R. Blumenfeld, *The Press in My Time* (London: Rich & Cowan, 1933), 93.

5 W. Bagehot, 'The English Constitution', cited in A. Smith, *Paper Voices: The Popular Press and Social Change 1935–65* (London: Chatto & Windus, 1975), 205.

6 On the declining political and social power of the aristocracy, see D. Cannadine, *The Decline and Fall of the British Aristocracy* (New Haven: Yale University Press, 1990).

Cohen-Portheim, a German writer describing his experiences of England in 1930, 'The interest which the whole nation takes in Society is astonishing. . . . Every newspaper tells you about their private lives, every illustrated paper is perpetually publishing photographs of them . . . . Their parties and their dresses, their weddings, christenings and funerals, their house and their travels are all described and depicted.'[7] Patrick Balfour, a society journalist himself, admitted three years later that the English press exhibited symptoms of 'lordolatry', shamelessly appealing to the snobbery of readers by making almost anything connected with the aristocracy into news. He believed that 'the idea of a lord' titillated middle-class readers in particular 'with a combination of awe and almost lascivious excitement'.[8] The novelist Aldous Huxley, meanwhile, was adamant that 'In no other country do so many newspapers devote so large a proportion of their space to a chronicle of the activities of the merely rich or the merely ennobled'. He was astonished that the middle classes were 'prepared to listen to the privileged class congratulating itself'.[9] Indeed, as Ross McKibbin has argued, Society as it was understood in the inter-war period had come to rely on the 'immense publicity' it received in popular newspapers: 'it could not exist without them'.[10]

Left-wing papers, notably the *Daily Herald* and *Reynolds News*, tried to puncture the glamour of Society by juxtaposing images of its ostentatious luxury with evidence of poverty and distress. Photographs from Ascot, printed in the *Herald* in 1925, emphasized that Society was 'flaunting its wealth, mostly unearned', while 'official figures were revealing the increasing suffering of the working class'.[11] Many of the 'highest in the land' were 'self-centred and self-indulgent', the paper claimed: 'No day passes without proof being given of the extent to which the canker of luxurious life, requiring vast sums of money to satisfy it, has eaten into that class'.[12] The bulk of the popular press, however, reported on Society with respect and admiration. Northcliffe firmly believed that most newspaper readers obtained vicarious enjoyment from stories about wealthy lifestyles and luxurious goods. He told his staff that 'Nine women out of ten would rather read about an evening dress costing a great deal of money—the sort of dress they will never in their lives have a chance of wearing—than about a simple frock such as they could afford'.[13] Social diaries and gossip columns flattered readers that they were part of a privileged circle privy to the latest developments in the world of the upper classes. Northcliffe insisted that these

[7] P. Cohen-Portheim, *England: The Unknown Isle* (1930), 112–13, cited in R. McKibbin, *Classes and Cultures* (Oxford: Oxford University Press, 1998), 34.

[8] P. Balfour, *Society Racket: A Critical Survey of Modern Social Life* (London: John Long Ltd., 1933), 22, 19, 24.

[9] R. Wilkes, *Scandal: A Scurrilous History of Gossip* (London: Atlantic Books, 2003), 3.

[10] McKibbin, *Classes and Cultures*, 23.

[11] *Daily Herald*, 17 June 1925.

[12] *Daily Herald*, 25 Mar. 1925, 4; 24 Mar. 1925, 4.

[13] H. Fyfe, *Northcliffe: An Intimate Biography* (London: G. Allen & Unwin, 1930), 93.

features were taken seriously: he was upset when the *Mirror*'s gossip column—'so important' to the paper—degenerated into 'trash', and reminded the editor of the *Mail* to ensure that the 'Social and women's side of Ascot' was 'well done'.[14] He believed that major Society stories had considerable news value. 'The most talked of item in this morning's news', he declared in May 1919, was the engagement of Lady Diane Manners, the famous society beauty, to Duff Cooper.[15]

In the competition to secure the latest information popular newspapers signed up columnists who were at ease moving in the circles they described. Patrick Balfour identified post-war diarists Hannen Swaffer, Charles Graves, Alan Parsons, and Percy Sewell as 'the first social columnists to know the world they wrote of', but in 1926 the *Sunday Express* topped them all by hiring Lord Castlerosse to produce the paper's 'Londoner's Log'.[16] Lady Eleanor Smith and Lord Donegall were soon added to the ranks of aristocratic columnists. More troubling to many in Society, however, was the developing practice of party guests selling snippets of gossip to the press. In November 1929, 'A London Hostess' wrote to *The Times* protesting about 'a new and dangerous tendency in our social life', namely the 'sneak-guests' who abused hospitality and made 'money out of their entertainment by contributing gossip to the newspapers afterwards about their fellow-guests, their host or hostess, and what was done and said when they were together'. This tendency, she claimed, had 'lately developed in certain quarters into a regular system of spying, followed by the publication of the most deplorable hints and insinuations'.[17]

The letter generated a heavy correspondence, with other socialites supporting the accusations of the 'London Hostess', and gossip columnists—including Lord Donegall—defending the honour of their profession.[18] One journalist suggested that it was now difficult to obtain a position on a London paper without both possessing 'a large circle of friends among the titled, political, or wealthy party-giving classes' and displaying a willingness to 'spy at these entertainments'.[19] *The Times* itself was convinced that the complaints were valid. An editorial agreed that the 'relaxation of old rules and principles' had drawn into Society men and women 'so eager to get their names into the social news that they stoop . . . to crude methods of bribery'. At the same time there had been 'an increase in gossip in general, and a disregard for old notions of privacy and privilege': it was no longer unusual for people 'to write in newspapers or publish in their reminiscences things they have heard under conditions which should have rendered them private'. This, the paper concluded, 'is the very soil in which the sneak-gossiper for the Press can thrive; and thrive he does'.[20] The propensity

14 Northcliffe Papers, Northcliffe to Roome, 20 June 1913; Northcliffe Bulletins 14 June 1921.

15 Northcliffe Papers, 2 May 1919.

16 Balfour, *Society Racket*, 92.

17 *The Times*, 25 Nov. 1929, 15.

18 *The Times*, 27 Nov. 1929, 15; 28 Nov. 1929, 15.

19 *The Times*, 27 Nov. 1929, 15.

20 *The Times*, 4 Dec. 1929, 15.

of insiders to sell stories about Society was confirmed, and brilliantly satirized, by Evelyn Waugh in his 1930 novel *Vile Bodies*.[21]

It is not surprising that the intensification of competition for social news, combined with the use of insiders to report on this enclosed world, provoked fears that the boundaries between public and private were shifting. Yet the extent to which inter-war gossip columnists were prepared to reveal sensitive personal information about the leaders of society should not be exaggerated. Most examples of broken confidences were relatively trivial, and the scathing criticism they provoked did not always match the gravity of the offence. One of the contributors to *The Times* correspondence believed, for example, that 'the almost incredible depths of caddishness and vulgarity to which certain people will descend' was illustrated by the revelation that he was privately critical of the publishers of his latest scholarly work.[22] Journalists remained very discreet about marital infidelities and sexual misdemeanours, particularly in comparison with brash American columnists such as Walter Winchell.[23] Northcliffe, Rothermere, and Beaverbrook all conducted numerous affairs themselves, and just as they expected these dalliances to remain private, so too they did not allow their papers to discuss the private relationships of public figures, even when they were common knowledge in Fleet Street circles. Beaverbrook insisted that the *Express*'s gossip column, 'Talk of London', should provide 'good clean wholesome news about People who matter': there was no question that it should include intrusive stories about sexual relationships, unless these details had entered the public arena in other ways, such as through divorce proceedings.[24] The result was that front-rank politicians—Lloyd-George is a good example—could keep mistresses confident that they would not be exposed even by their enemies in the press.[25]

It also remained relatively easy for well-connected individuals to prevent the publication of embarrassing stories. Patrick Balfour did not disguise the fact that 'if you ask a social columnist, politely, to keep his mouth shut it is quite on the cards that he will do so'. He advised readers that the 'safest way to prevent a story appearing in a newspaper' was simply to 'ring up the editor, tell him the story, and ask him not to print it'.[26] Fleet Street memoirs abound with anecdotes of favours being called in and stories being suppressed: of Riddell protecting

[21] E. Waugh, *Vile Bodies* (first pub. 1930; London: Penguin, 2000).

[22] *The Times*, 27 Nov. 1929, 15.

[23] The following nuggets of information were revealed in Walter Winchell's 'Your Broadway and Mine' column in the *New York Evening Graphic* on 18 June 1927: 'Professional "Gigolos" in Hollywood are wholesaling their services as escorts, quoting rates, $5 afternoons, and $10 evenings . . . . Agnes Ayres is suing S. Manuel Reachi for divorce. Marion Hayes is suing John for divorce because he drinks so much he coughs all night. Six bottles of gin, she says . . . . The Samuel Raphaelsons are divorcing. "Unknown Woman". . .'.

[24] House of Lords Record Office, Beaverbrook Papers, H/97, Beaverbrook to Robertson, 13 June 1932.

[25] J. Campbell, *If Love Were All . . .: The Story of Frances Stevenson and David Lloyd George* (London: Jonathan Cape, 2006).

[26] Balfour, *Society Racket*, 98, 97.

the 'important men' whose names were found in the records of a Westminster brothel, or Beaverbrook covering up for F. E. Smith (later Lord Birkenhead) when he was caught with a prostitute and gave a false name to the police.[27] Indeed, it was precisely this aspect of Fleet Street's culture that led Edward VIII's allies to believe that they could keep the King's relationship with Wallis Simpson out of the news.

Rather than spreading scandal, most gossip columns focused on recording notable events involving Society families—births, deaths, engagements, weddings, divorces, property transactions and such like—and describing the parties and entertainments of the Season. The minor snippets of private information that were included in such columns, and which so irritated many of the subjects, were usually designed principally to demonstrate the author's personal knowledge of this elevated world rather than damage reputations. Dragoman's description in the *Daily Express* of an 'informal party' thrown by Captain and Mrs Cunningham-Reid in December 1931 provides a flavour of the typical content:

> It started with a dinner party of a dozen or so; and ended with about sixty people dancing to the syncopated music of Jack London, a good-looking young negro who is an Olympic sprinter as well as a brilliant pianist. Plenty of good-looking women were to be seen there: Lady Brougham and Vaux, who looked lovely in a simple black lace dress, Lady Brecknock, and Miss Hilary Charles. An unusual diversion was the consuming, at 2am, of large quantities of peas and onions. Soon after this people began to leave.[28]

Such reports emphasized the wealth, beauty, and taste of the people they described. Here the entertainment was provided by a musician who was not only a 'brilliant pianist' but an Olympic sprinter. In the process the gossip columns glamorized privilege and helped to legitimize a hierarchical and profoundly unequal society.[29] While the Cunningham-Reid's guests were consuming their peas and onions, after all, many in Britain were struggling to come to terms with the consequences of the economic depression.

THE RISE OF THE FILM STAR

During the inter-war years, upper-class socialites found themselves increasingly outshone in the public imagination by a new breed of glamorous celebrity, the film star. By the 1930s, the cinema had assumed a central place in British popular culture, with around 18–19 million visits being made every week.[30] The industry was firmly based on the star system, and Hollywood studios spent considerable

[27] S. Somerfield, *Banner Headlines* (Shoreham-by-Sea: Scan Books, 1979), 64; J. Junor, *Memoirs: Listening for a Midnight Tram* (London: Chapmans, 1990), 62–3.

[28] *Daily Express*, 10 Dec. 1931, 19.

[29] McKibbin, *Classes and Cultures*, 419.

[30] Ibid., 419.

amounts of money publicizing their leading men and women.[31] The popular fascination with film stars was assiduously cultivated by the print media. A raft of magazines—including *Picturegoer* and *Picture Show*—emerged to cater for cinema fans, and popular newspapers were quick to establish regular film columns and reviews. Even more than the films themselves, the press were interested in the personalities. As the journalist and historian Robert Ensor noted in 1947, 'film-stars came to be for the popular Press nearly the most important persons living'.[32]

Film-stars became particularly important vehicles for the public discussion of sexuality. The pre-eminent attribute of the film-star was, after all, 'sex appeal' (a phrase coined in the early 1920s and which soon became ubiquitous).[33] Writing in the *Daily Mail* in 1930, Evelyn Waugh observed that most actresses 'concentrate above all things on "sex appeal"'. Although this made their films 'highly enjoyable'—Waugh admitted that he would 'wait in a queue of any length in order to see Miss Clara Bow or Miss Nancy Carroll or Miss Bebe Daniels'—it did mean that 'only one of an infinite series of emotions is aroused'.[34] But most journalists, less discriminating than Waugh, did not complain at the one-dimensionality of much cinema. They were happy to follow the agenda of the studios and helped to generate an aura of glamour and sexual allure around the performers rather than analyse the finer points of their acting ability. This applied to both male and female stars, although there were clear gender distinctions in the way they were presented. Leading men were described as being so extraordinarily charismatic and magnetic that they were able to entrance legions of female fans. Rudolph Valentino was the 'hero of the female population of five continents'; French actor Maurice Chevalier had 'stormed ten million feminine hearts', while John Gilbert, 'the screen's greatest lover', was the 'idol of twenty million women'.[35] So charming were these fantasy figures that ordinary men could barely hope to compete. Norah Alexander, the *Sunday Pictorial*'s film critic, claimed in 1942 that French star Charles Boyer—who had an 'undeniable hold over nine hundred and ninety-nine women out of every thousand'—had set 'new standards of love-making' and shown up the 'whole male sex' as 'inadequate, incompetent lovers'.[36] Good looks were an essential part of the appeal, but they were only one part of a broader set of desirable manly characteristics, alongside intelligence, honesty, toughness, good humour, and others: these men were not

[31] Dyer, *Stars*.

[32] R. C. K. Ensor, 'The Press', in E. Barker (ed.), *The Character of England* (Oxford: Clarendon Press, 1947), 419.

[33] J. Ayto, *Twentieth Century Words* (Oxford: Oxford University Press, 1999), 173; R. Graves and A. Hodge, *The Long Week-End: A Social History of Britain 1918–1939* (first pub. 1940; Harmondsworth: Penguin, 1971), 136.

[34] *Daily Mail*, 24 May 1930, 10.

[35] *Daily Mail*, 24 Aug. 1926, 10; *Daily Express*, 11 May 1931, 9; 21 Oct. 1931, 1.

[36] *Sunday Pictorial*, 18 Jan. 1942, 13.

defined by their appearance and physical attributes in quite the same way as their female equivalents.[37]

Male cinema-goers were assumed to be less emotional, and less prone to fan worship, than female ones: theirs was a more visual enjoyment that needed little elaboration. Considering the attractions of Ann Sheridan, the so-called 'Oomph girl' of Hollywood, Paul Holt approvingly quoted the definition that 'Oomph is a feminine desirability which can be observed with pleasure but cannot be discussed with respectability'.[38] Holt had previously weighed up Maureen O'Hara's chances of lasting success by assessing in turn her smile, eyes, profile, and face: an accompanying series of cropped photographs emphasized the intensity of this physical scrutiny.[39] The increasing preoccupation with the 'vital statistics' of female stars was another sign of the tendency to inspect, measure, and rate the female body.

The press reinforced the message of the cinema that 'sex appeal', especially for women, required the maintenance of physical appearance to more and more exacting standards.[40] Newspapers encouraged glamorous actresses to reveal their style 'secrets'—although the difficulties of achieving the 'screen look' without the Hollywood budget (and photographic trickery) were glossed over. The *Mirror* did not think it incongruous, for example, to invite Rudolph Valentino's lover and Hollywood femme fatale Pola Negri to advise the 'Girl Worker' on the 'Best Way Of Planning An Attractive Wardrobe' and how to 'Look Your Best During Business Hours'.[41] The *Daily Express* film book, meanwhile, provided 'film fashions', 'secrets of make-up' and 'some of the methods of slimming used by well-known players to meet the exacting demands of the camera'.[42] 'Looking your best' required educated consumption. Manufacturers of cosmetics and beauty treatments clamoured to sign up actresses to endorse their products, and these adverts became a staple of popular newspaper columns:

'After my nightly cleansing with Pond's Cold Cream,' says Miss Betty Balfour, the famous Cinema star, whose complexion is as fresh as the petals of a rose, 'the skin of my face, neck and hands seems so deliciously soft and refreshed . . .'

For The Most Beautiful Hair In The World—4 Out Of 5 Top Hollywood Stars Use Lustre-Crème Shampoo.[43]

By 1934, the Labour politician Ellen Wilkinson was blaming films for the fact that 'clever women are not fashionable any more':

Three times daily, every day of the week, some part of the public is unconsciously absorbing their standards. And the woman the public is being educated to approve of

[37] A. Bingham, *Gender, Modernity, and the Popular Press in Inter-War Britain* (Oxford: Oxford University Press, 2004), 226–7.

[38] *Daily Express*, 29 Aug. 1939, 15.

[39] *Daily Express*, 13 May 1939, 23.

[40] J. Stacey, *Stargazing: Hollywood Cinema and Female Spectatorship* (London: Routledge, 1994).

[41] *Daily Mirror*, 27 Feb. 1927, 4.

[42] *Daily Express*, 13 Nov. 1935, 3.

[43] *Daily Mirror*, 22 April 1926, 8; 17 Mar. 1954, 12.

is the blonde bombshell who is too old at twenty-five. These marvellous creatures of the screen, dressed as by Paris on a supposed typist's salary of £3 a week, are shown turning the head of the managing director. . . . Moral for the young women in the audience. . . . Why grind for degree or diploma? Why not spend the money on face creams and massage . . . higher profits, quicker returns?[44]

Wilkinson's fears would be frequently repeated in the years ahead, but commercial logic dictated that the press would continue to work with, rather than against, the cinema. Indeed, as the press's pin-up culture became further entrenched (see Chapter 6), the 'blonde bombshells' of the screen would be displayed even more prominently.

There was inevitably a huge amount of interest in the private lives of film celebrities. Hollywood studies recognized the publicity value in catering to this curiosity by providing carefully selected stories to the press, and the press gobbled them up enthusiastically. Rudolph Valentino's marriage in 1923 reached the front pages of the British press, and the romantic entanglements of Hollywood stars became increasingly visible in the following years.[45] The Royal Commission on the Press complained in 1949 that popular newspapers 'presented the matrimonial adventures of a film star as though they possessed the same intrinsic importance as events affecting the peace of the continent'.[46] More scandalous stories also entered the public domain, usually when legal proceedings were instituted. The manslaughter trial of American film comedian Roscoe 'Fatty' Arbuckle in 1921, and the death of young director Al Stein in the same year, received sensational coverage in the British press and helped to consolidate Hollywood's reputation for 'orgies' and heavy drinking.[47] A number of drug-related deaths led to the *People* expressing its concern in 1923 that 'incalculable harm' was being done to the reputation of the British film industry 'by the constant disclosures of the horrors perpetrated at Hollywood'.[48] As long as the authorities did not become involved, however, studios were able to protect the privacy of most stars relatively effectively, hiding the tempestuous affairs and sexual liaisons of leading stars. Some American columnists, notably Walter Winchell and Louella Parsons, provided relatively harmless gossip for their readers—'Not terribly vicious libels, just intimate details about the private lives of artists: who their latest lovers are; whom they go about with', observed the author Edgar Wallace in 1932. Yet for Wallace 'every line' of this gossip was 'libellous' by British standards—and he was grateful that the British press did not follow suit.[49] Although Hollywood actors were less sensitive targets than British politicians—or the royal family—Fleet

[44] *Daily Express*, 17 Jan. 1934, 10.

[45] *Daily Express*, 16. Mar 1923, 1; *Daily Mirror*, 16 Mar. 1923, 1.

[46] Royal Commission on the Press 1947–49, *Report* (London: HMSO, 1949), Cmd. 7700, 131.

[47] *Daily Mirror*, 1 Oct. 1921, 1; *Daily Express*, 11 Oct. 1921, 1; *Daily Mail*, 11 Oct. 1921, 7; *News of the World*, 16 Oct. 1921, 3.

[48] The *People*, 28 Jan. 1923, 6.

[49] *Daily Mail*, 8 Feb. 1932, 10.

Street for a long time remained cautious about trying to exploit the market for scandal.

ROYAL JOURNALISM: FROM EVASION TO INTRUSION

The only celebrities who consistently stimulated greater human interest than film stars were the royal family. The adulatory coverage that the monarchy received in the inter-war period was, however, a relatively recent development. George IV and William IV were often subjected to fierce satirical attacks by journalists and cartoonists; Queen Victoria's retirement from public life after the death of Prince Albert in 1861 provoked much adverse comment, and the rakish activities of her son, the Prince of Wales, drew the scorn of public moralists.[50] In the final quarter of the nineteenth century, the monarchy recovered its public esteem, partly due to the way it was presented as the focal point of Britain's expanding Empire.[51] Victoria's golden and diamond jubilees, and the coronations of Edward VII and George V, were celebrated with lavish rituals that emphasized the power and prestige of the Empire. The new popular daily press, intensely patriotic and imperialistic, played a very important part in bringing the magic of monarchy to a wider audience. Although keen to focus on the human details about the royal family, Fleet Street reporters were cautious about revealing anything that went beyond the anodyne. Edward's VII's colourful past was discreetly overlooked, for example, and he was presented as a dignified and statesman-like figure.[52] The *Daily Mirror*'s front-page photograph of Edward on his deathbed prompted controversy: this was, however, an official picture and its use had been authorized by Queen Alexandra, the King's widow. The accompanying report was reverential, observing the 'manliness and lofty dignity of King Edward's features'.[53]

George V, Edward's eminently respectable successor, had little appetite for the modern mass media: he was suspicious of the press and resisted for some years the opportunity to broadcast a radio message at Christmas. Yet as the head of the nation during the Great War, and the leader of public commemorations after 1918, he was treated with considerable respect and deference, and his staff worked diligently to maintain favourable publicity.[54] During the 1920s,

[50] D. Cannadine, 'The Context, Performance and Meaning of Ritual: The British Monarchy and the "Invention of Tradition", *c*.1820–1977', in E. Hobsbawm and T. Ranger (eds.), *The Invention of Tradition* (Cambridge: Cambridge University Press, 1983); R. Wilkes, *Scandal* ch.2.

[51] J. Plunkett, *Queen Victoria: First Media Monarch* (Oxford: Oxford University Press, 2003).

[52] To the popular newspapers he was 'Edward the Peacemaker': see, for example, *Daily Mirror*, 9 May 1910, 1; 16 May 1910, 1.

[53] *Daily Mirror*, 16 May 1910, 1; D. and E. Seymour (eds.), *A Century of News: A Journey Through History with the Daily Mirror* (London: Contender Books, 2003), 15–16.

[54] McKibbin, *Classes and Cultures*, 6–9; M. Pugh, *'We Danced All Night': A Social History of Britain Between the Wars* (London: Bodley Head, 2008), ch. 18.

though, the press found the King's sons more interesting and approachable. Prince Albert's marriage to Lady Elizabeth Bowes-Lyon was enthusiastically celebrated—'because all know that he is marrying for love, and because he has chosen a British bride', gushed the *Mail*[55]—as were the births of daughters Elizabeth and Margaret. They were presented as exemplifying a typically British domestic happiness and stability. But it was Edward, Prince of Wales, who attracted the bulk of the headlines. A handsome, charismatic individual, he possessed all the glamour of Hollywood stars and was similarly influential in setting fashions.[56] His numerous royal tours were reported in considerable detail and his photograph became a familiar sight in newspapers around the world—so familiar, in fact, that Beaverbrook felt obliged to remind the editor of the *Daily Express* that 'the Prince of Wales should not appear on the front page unless there is definite news of importance concerning him'.[57]

Amidst this extensive coverage Fleet Street was keen to remind readers of the relative restraint of royal journalism in Britain. When the Prince of Wales visited the United States in 1924, for example, the *People* printed a contribution from 'One who was with him' to outline the differences between his treatment by the American and the British press. The Prince had assumed that when

> American newspapers saw that he wanted a quiet holiday they would draw off their reporters, or, at any rate, understand that news of the Royal visitor's movements would be confined to discreet paragraphs like those in the British Court Circular, or the restrained half columns we are used to reading in the English newspapers wherever the Prince fills some public or semi-public duty.[58]

On the contrary, the Prince 'found with horror that he was expected to be as exposed and as affable to reporters as a well-boomed circus fat lady'; if he spoke to a reporter, moreover, 'One word of casual interest became a column of sensational revelations, so that the most intimate matters of the Prince's household were set forth with relish and detail, and marvellous elaboration for the delectation of a million homes'. The result was that the Prince was forced to keep his plans secret and try to slip away from the reporters tracking him.[59] British newspapers were happy to retail gossipy snippets—'The Rambler' told the *Mirror*'s readers, for example, that Prince teased his sister-in-law 'in a happy, brotherly fashion about her height'[60]—but they were unfailingly respectful in the language they used to discuss his private life, and usually refused to speculate about his personal relationships. Most significantly, his affairs with married women, such as Mrs Freya Dudley Ward, and from 1934, Mrs Wallis Simpson, were kept hidden from the public.

[55] *Daily Mail*, 26 April 1923, 6.
[56] P. Ziegler, *Edward VIII: The Official Biography* (London: Collins, 1990).
[57] Beaverbrook Papers, H/81 Beaverbrook to Baxter, 12 Dec. 1931.
[58] The *People*, 16 Nov. 1924, 8. [59] Ibid. [60] *Daily Mirror*, 22 April 1926, 9.

The deference of the British press to the royal family is most clearly demonstrated by its handling of the abdication crisis. This episode is a very familiar one, and does not need to be recounted in detail.[61] The relevant feature here is Fleet Street's willingness to maintain its silence about Edward's relationship with Wallis Simpson after his accession to the throne in January 1936, despite the considerable attention it was receiving in newspapers abroad, and especially in the United States. By the summer of 1936, growing numbers of clippings from foreign papers were circulating privately in Britain, and letters were written to London papers enquiring about the rumours, but they made no response.[62] The international frenzy intensified in August after photographs appeared of Mrs Simpson accompanying Edward on a Mediterranean cruise aboard the steam yacht *Nahlin*. One set of pictures appeared in the British press, but with no explanation of Simpson's significance.[63] In October, the King asked Lord Beaverbrook to use his influence to keep publicity of Mrs Simpson's divorce hearing to a minimum, with the result that only very small circulation publications such as *Cavalcade* and *News Review* offered any hints about the developing scandal.[64] The leading figures in Fleet Street were generally united on the need for reticence. Howell Gwynne, the widely-respected editor of the *Morning Post*, told his colleagues that 'in such a delicate matter as this, the Press should follow the Government and not dictate to it'; he also believed that silence was necessary because the 'sensational press' would be unable to handle the story 'with dignity and caution'. But writing to the Prime Minister, Stanley Baldwin, on 12 November, he feared that it was 'impossible to expect that this self-imposed silence will last very much longer', and warned that after months of rumours the press was 'undoubtedly getting very restive'.[65] In fact, Fleet Street's discipline was maintained until 2 December, when the Bishop of Bradford referred to the crisis in a speech: this was read by the press as the moment finally to bring the story into public arena. Nine days later Edward abdicated.

As Political and Economic Planning noted two years later, what was known in Fleet Street as the 'great silence' provided 'evidence of the falsehood of the common belief that there are London newspapers which will sacrifice anything for the sake of sensational news'.[66] The press felt it had a duty to protect the dignity of the monarchy by not circulating damaging rumours; perhaps more importantly, editors feared a major backlash from readers if they broke the

[61] See, for example, Ziegler, *Edward VIII*; S. Williams, *The People's King: The True Story of the Abdication* (London: Allen Lane, 2003); Pugh, *'We Danced All Night'*, ch. 18.

[62] National Archives, PREM 1/446, Constitutional Crisis—Attitude of the British Press [unsigned memo], Dec. 1936.

[63] Ibid.

[64] A. Chisholm and M. Davie, *Beaverbrook: A Life* (London: Hutchinson, 1992), 336–8.

[65] NA, PREM 1/446, H. A. Gwynne to Baldwin, 12 Nov. 1936.

[66] Political and Economic Planning, *Report on the British Press* (London: PEP, 1938), 260.

scandal, especially given Edward's popularity.[67] When news of the relationship finally emerged popular newspapers tried to make up for lost time, covering the constitutional crisis from every angle and offering detailed summaries of Wallis Simpson's life story. This was a fantastic human drama, involving a stark conflict between duty and love. Edward later wrote of the intensity of being at the centre of this media storm:

> Publicity was part of my heritage, and I was never so naïve as to suppose that my romance was a tender shoot to be protected from the prying curiosity of the Press. But what stared at me from the newspapers that were brought to my room on Thursday morning really shocked me. Could this be the King, or was I some common felon? The Press creates: the Press destroys.[68]

It was even worse, he recalled, for Simpson: 'The world can hold few worse shocks for a sensitive woman than to come without warning upon her own grossly magnified countenance upon the front page of a sensational newspaper.'[69] In fact, Edward received powerful press support from the *Express* and the *Mail*, as Beaverbrook and Rothermere used their papers to accuse Baldwin of unnecessarily forcing out a popular King. The *Mirror* was also initially sympathetic to Edward's position, before coming to accept the government's position. But the rest of the national press, and the majority of the provincial papers, shared Baldwin's view that Simpson would not make a suitable queen, and agreed that a morganatic marriage was not an appropriate solution to the crisis. Once Edward had made his decision to abdicate, though, the divisions in Fleet Street closed and the whole spectrum of the press patriotically rallied in support of King George VI. The *Express* admitted on 12 December that it 'would have preferred an alternative to abdication' but turned its attention to the new King: 'Nobody doubts that he will show the same high character and worth as his father. He is happy in the love of a wife and family. The British people will try to make him happy in the regard of a nation.'[70]

Newspapers emphasized that their decision to remain silent about Edward's relationship had been a responsible one taken with the national good in mind. The *Daily Mirror* told how it had withheld the story 'until it was clear that the problem could not be solved by diplomatic methods. This course we took with the welfare of the nation and the Empire at heart.'[71] The *People* likewise claimed that 'the freest Press in Europe voluntarily and deliberately refrained from discussing the King's private life until it was proved to be a matter of public consequence'.[72] *The Times* agreed that 'it was a true exercise of responsibility

[67] B. Pimlott, *The Queen: A Biography of Elizabeth II (*London: HarperCollins, 1996), 34.

[68] Edward, Duke of Windsor, *A King's Story, the Memoirs of the Duke of Windsor,* quoted in H. Cudlipp, *Publish and be Damned! The Sensational Story of the Daily Mirror* (London: Andrew Dakers, 1953), 92

[69] Ibid. [70] *Daily Express*, 11 Dec. 1936, 12. [71] *Daily Mirror*, 4 Dec. 1936, 12.

[72] *The People*, 6 Dec. 1936, 12.

to spare elaborate or sensational publicity for the King's private affairs before they had reached the threshold of decision'.[73] Several papers contrasted their own patriotic reticence with the reckless scandal-mongering of the American press. The *Mirror* condemned the American 'lies' which had 'poisoned' the minds of many readers around the world and vulgarized the King's relationship: 'Venomous gossip, twisted headlines, and base rumours have been America's biggest export for the past six months'. This 'cheap and crude' journalism gave 'no real indication of the nature of his Majesty's romance'.[74] *The Times* similarly celebrated the fact that the British press had 'wisely' ignored the 'campaign of publicity' in the US, and showed a 'common self-restraint', noting rather patronizingly that 'Americans are an essentially personal people, who are in the habit of assessing other countries by the character of their outstanding figures'.[75] The *Manchester Guardian* was grateful that the abdication had been achieved without the 'nauseating publicity and turmoil that surrounded the marital affairs of royalty under the third and fourth Georges. Yet had the example of the American press been followed, we should have had the same orgy of scandal in which our ancestors indulged.'[76]

The tone of the American coverage of the affair was certainly very different to that in Britain. Unlike the British press, American newspapers had no incentive to be restrained in their reporting of the story, so they speculated and exaggerated. Whereas the British press had cropped photographs to remove Mrs Simpson from the King's side, for example, one American publication actually doctored a photograph of the couple to create the impression that they were walking hand in hand.[77] American journalists were also more willing to discuss the personal lives of the protagonists in more detail than their British counterparts. When the *Express*'s American correspondent submitted a feature on Mrs Simpson, for example, Beaverbrook told him that parts of the article were too intimate and intrusive. 'You have been in the centre of this business in New York and you have seen a great deal in the papers there with very considerable latitude', he wrote:

> But in Britain . . . it would not be possible at present, or, indeed, at any time, to deal as freely with Mrs Simpson's life as in this dispatch of yours . . . you should restrain the personal note to the extent of following, for instance, the lines adopted by the most conservative newspaper that you can find on the American Continent.[78]

But amidst the self-congratulation on the triumph of British values—'No other country in the world could have accomplished so great a change with such simplicity and quiet dignity', boasted the *People*[79]—few stopped to

[73] *The Times*, 14 Dec. 1936, 15.
[74] *Daily Mirror*, 7 Dec. 1936, 12–13.
[75] *The Times*, 3 Dec. 1936, 15.
[76] *Manchester Guardian*, 12 Dec. 1936.
[77] *Daily Mirror*, 7 Dec. 1936, 12–13; Wilkes, *Scandal*, 236.
[78] Beaverbrook Papers, H/108, Beaverbrook to CVR Thompson, 5 Dec. 1936.
[79] *The People*, 13 Dec. 1936, 12.

consider whether British press would have shown any greater restraint than the American press had it been reporting on a foreign notable rather than a domestic royal.

Once the crisis had blown over, moreover, the certainty that the press's silence had been beneficial began to crumble. Evidence accumulated that the British public did not appreciate being kept in the dark about such a big story. Robert Graves and Alan Hodge argued in 1940 that 'the hush-hush over Mrs Simpson . . . had made many people realize for the first time that newspapers did not necessarily print the whole news', and the investigations of Mass-Observation seemed to confirm that opinion.[80] Mass-Observation founder Tom Harrisson, writing for the magazine *Horizon*, agreed that the press suffered a 'big knock' to its prestige 'when the Simpson crisis blew up and the public found major news had been withheld from them for months'.[81] A younger generation of journalists were also uncomfortable with the press's acquiescence to the Palace's agenda. Papers such as the *Mirror* and *Pictorial*, which during the Second World War became increasingly critical of the old-fashioned attitudes and hierarchies they believed were hindering the war effort and preventing social improvement, began to take a less deferential approach to the monarchy. In April 1942, for example, the *Pictorial* produced a story highlighting the unnecessary extravagance of the redecoration of the King's Mayfair flat: this was deemed a threat to public morale by the censor and suppressed.[82] The *Pictorial*'s post-war editor, Hugh Cudlipp, was determined not to join unthinkingly the 'fanfare of adulation which the British newspapers sounded whenever the name of Royalty was mentioned'.[83] 'It was more than light-hearted impudence,' Cudlipp later recalled, 'it was a reflection of the new healthy mood of questioning authority, especially the Establishment. The mood was no longer docile acceptance and silent reverence.'[84]

This 'new mood' was evident when rumours about Princess Elizabeth's romance with Philip Mountbatten circulated in the winter of 1946–47. The *Pictorial* responded by conducting a survey of readers on the question 'Should Our Future Queen Wed Philip?' Brushing aside denials from the Palace that an engagement was not imminent, the paper declared that the British people should have the opportunity to express their views, 'not after the event as was the case with another Royal crisis in 1936 but before it'.[85] The *Pictorial* employed a powerful rhetoric of popular democracy, suggesting that in the more equal society that it was

[80] Graves and Hodge, *The Long Week-end*, 428. Mass-Observation, File Report 1, Oct. 1939, 2.

[81] M-O, File Report 375 'The Popular Press?', by Tom Harrison, published *Horizon* Aug. 1940, 169.

[82] R. Edwards, *Newspapermen: Hugh Cudlipp, Cecil Harmsworth King and the Glory Days of Fleet Street* (London: Secker & Warburg, 2003), 165.

[83] H. Cudlipp, *At Your Peril* (London: Weidenfeld & Nicolson, 1962), 81.

[84] H. Cudlipp, *Walking on Water* (London: Bodley Head, 1976), 180.

[85] *Sunday Pictorial*, 5 Jan. 1947, 1.

fighting for, the Palace and the politicians would not be able to ignore the voice of the people. The paper declared that everyone who had voted had 'rendered a valuable service to our democratic system'.[86] In the end, 64 per cent of readers were in favour of the marriage if the couple were in love, but in many respects the result was less important than the fact that (a section of) the public had been given a chance to speak.[87] Others believed that canvassing opinion about such a private matter was an egregious impertinence. 'Many people are saying that the *Sunday Pictorial*'s intrusion into the Royal Family's affairs is a breach of good taste,' wrote Arthur Christiansen to Beaverbrook, 'but people often read things that are in bad taste'.[88] Edward Hulton, the proprietor of *Picture Post*, was one of those appalled by the exercise: 'The journalism of the *Sunday Pictorial* has reached a new low.... It is difficult to write with any restraint about this latest effort by this self-appointed voice of the people, which is as genuinely mischievous and politically harmful as it is in gross bad taste, and infinitely wounding to the feelings of all those concerned.'[89] The *Pictorial* itself was unapologetic, arguing that among the 'thousands and thousands' of letters it had received, only 234 people criticized its survey.[90]

Increasingly unwilling to wait for official announcements from the Palace, the press also began to compete more aggressively for royal exclusives. On 9 July 1947 the *Daily Mail*, relying on sources in Greece, announced the engagement of Princess Elizabeth and Philip Mountbatten. The story was initially denied by the Palace press office, before its accuracy was officially confirmed the following day.[91] The following March, the *People* reported on its front page that Elizabeth was expecting her first child in October, news that was officially verified only in June.[92] Speculative stories were encouraged by the continued secrecy surrounding the royal family. Commander Richard Colville, the Palace press officer from 1947 to 1968, and known in Fleet Street as the 'Abominable No-Man', regarded journalists with disdain: as Ben Pimlott has observed, he refused 'to treat even the most modest press request for personal information as legitimate'.[93] When Marion Crawford, the former governess at the Palace, published her recollections as *The Little Princesses* in 1950 (it was serialized in the United States in the *Ladies' Home Journal*, and subsequently in *Woman's Own* in Britain), Colville was mortified by the betrayal, despite the relatively innocuous content. Rather than recognize the benefits in feeding the demand for news with authorized stories, however, he only intensified his efforts to prevent information leaking out.[94]

Colville's strategy was a futile one when all the evidence in Fleet Street suggested that public interest in royalty was greater than ever at mid-century.

86 *Sunday Pictorial*, 19 Jan. 1947, 7.
87 *Sunday Pictorial*, 19 Jan. 1947, 1, 7.
88 Beaverbrook Papers, H/120, Arthur Christiansen to Beaverbrook, 17 Jan. 1947.
89 Cudlipp, *At Your Peril*, 150.
90 *Sunday Pictorial*, 19 Jan. 1947, 7.
91 *Daily Mail*, 9 July 1947, 1; 10 July 1947, 1.
92 The *People*, 21 Mar. 1948, 1; 6 June 1948, 1.
93 Pimlott, *The Queen*, 165.
94 Ibid.

The *Sunday Express*'s serialization of the Duke of Windsor's memoirs in the winter of 1947–8 was 'easily the best seller' it had ever had, attracting no fewer than 500,000 extra readers.[95] 'There is no possible doubt', *Express* Director E. J. Robertson told Beaverbrook in August 1951, 'that any feature dealing with Royalty, or near Royalty, these days will sell'.[96] The accession of the young Elizabeth to the throne after the death of George VI in February 1952 only increased interest amidst talk of a new 'Elizabethan Age'. The Coronation ceremony of June 1953 was the most significant media event the nation had ever witnessed: 20 million people crowded around television sets to watch the extensive BBC coverage, and newspapers achieved record circulations.[97] As competition intensified in Fleet Street during the 1950s, it was inevitable that there would be a scramble for royal stories.

The greater aggressiveness in royal journalism was most clearly demonstrated when rumours of Princess Margaret's romance with Group-Captain Peter Townsend, an equerry to the Queen, started to emerge. The relationship was first revealed to British readers by the *People* in June 1953, less than two weeks after the coronation. With echoes of 1936, the paper referred to 'scandalous rumours' being circulated abroad that 'the princess is in love with a divorced man and that she wishes to marry him'. The *People* feigned to believe that the rumours were 'utterly untrue' and demanded an official denial.[98] This time, however, the British press drove the story forward itself rather than simply waiting for events to unfold. Hugh Cudlipp, now editorial director at the *Mirror*, discussed policy with his colleagues and they agreed 'to try to avoid the childish secrecy which had concealed from the British public the romance between Edward VIII and Wallis Simpson until the decisive stage had been reached and the opinion of the populace, for or against, could not matter'.[99] From being a scandalous rumour, several papers quickly came to regard it as an attractive love story involving a popular princess and a dashing RAF officer who had served valiantly during the war. Commander Colville, as usual, refused to comment, but now the newspapers were prepared to fill the vacuum of information with their own speculation.

When Townsend was hastily appointed Air Attaché to the British embassy in Brussels, the press suggested that this was a clumsy attempt by the Palace to exile him and whipped up sympathy for the 'ace pilot' and 'war hero'.[100] There were reports that the Cabinet had voted to block the prospective marriage, much to the exasperation of the government, which considered issuing a statement

[95] Beaverbrook Papers, H/130 Robertson to Beaverbrook, 13 Jan. 1948; H/138 Gordon to Beaverbrook, 4 July 1950.

[96] Beaverbrook Papers, H/151 Robertson to Beaverbrook, 29 August 1951.

[97] A. Briggs, *The History of Broadcasting in the UK, Vol. IV: Sound and Vision* (Oxford: Oxford University Press, 1979), 457–73.

[98] *The People*, 14 June 1953, 1.

[99] Cudlipp, *At Your Peril*, 141.

[100] *Daily Mirror*, 3 July 1953, 1; *The People*, 12 July 1953, 1.

calling an end to the 'deplorable speculation and gossip'.[101] Following the earlier example of its sister paper, the *Mirror* decided to conduct a poll of readers so that 'the voice of the British people' could be heard. It declared that a 'true and deep affection is reported to exist' between the couple, but 'the Church's attitude on the re-marriage of divorced persons' provided a serious obstacle. The description of Townsend on the voting form made quite apparent the answer the *Mirror* was expecting: 'Group Captain Peter Townsend, 38 years old Battle of Britain pilot, was the innocent party in a divorce. He was given custody of his two children and his former wife has recently remarried. If Princess Margaret, now 22, so desires, should she be allowed to marry him? Yes—No?'[102] Four days later over 70,000 responses had been received, with more than 96 per cent in favour of the marriage.[103]

A relationship that the Palace had tried hard to frustrate and keep quiet now seemed to have the public seal of approval, and both the Palace and the Church were being presented as old-fashioned and out-of-touch for trying to prevent it. The *Mirror*'s poll provoked a storm of criticism, just as the *Pictorial*'s had in 1947. The *Mirror* was equally unrepentant, dismissing the 'pompous, self-appointed arbiters of "good taste"' who had accused the paper of the 'frightful crime of telling the public the things the public is entitled to know!'[104] Fleet Street, united in silence in 1936, was now seriously divided. The Press Council was just about to have its first meeting, and it wasted no time in condemning the poll as 'contrary to the best traditions of British journalism'.[105] *The Times* similarly made clear its disgust for scandalmongers involved in 'the cruel business of prying into private lives'.[106]

Critics kept on returning to the way the press was undermining the restraint and respect that traditionally governed the public sphere. In March 1955, Harold Macmillan described a further round of speculation in his diary as 'a horrible breach of good manners'.[107] The allegations of bad taste multiplied in August when, on the eve of the Princess's twenty-fifth birthday, the *Mirror* produced its infamous front-page headline, 'Come On Margaret! Please Make Up Your Mind!' (**Illustration 7.1**)[108] The Press Council intervened once again, resolving that 'Such coarse impertinence was an insult to the Princess and an offence against the decencies of British public life'.[109] But the *Mirror* protested that

[101] *Tribune*, 10 July 1953; *Daily Mirror*, 10 July 1953; National Archives, PREM 11/524 (Press Speculation about Princess Margaret), JRC, Note, 16 July 1953.

[102] *Daily Mirror*, 13 July 1953, 1.

[103] *Daily Mirror*, 17 July 1953, 1.

[104] *Daily Mirror*, 21 July 1953, 1.

[105] Press Council, *The Press and the People: First Annual Report* (London: Press Council, 1954), 22.

[106] *The Times*, 24 July 1953, 9.

[107] P. Catterall (ed.), *The Macmillan Diaries: The Cabinet Years 1950–1957* (London: Pan, 2004), 401; Cudlipp, *At Your Peril*, 143.

[108] *Daily Mirror*, 19 Aug. 1955, 1.

[109] Press Council, *Annual Report* 1956, 24.

Daily Mirror FRI AUG. 19 1955

1½d FORWARD WITH THE PEOPLE No. 16,077

• The Princess is 25 on Sunday.

• Will she wed? When will she announce her decision?

COME ON MARGARET!

FOR two years the world has buzzed with this question:

Will Princess Margaret marry 40-year-old Group Captain Peter Townsend?—OR Won't she?

Five months ago, Group Captain Townsend told the Daily Mirror: '. . . the word cannot come from me. You will appreciate it must come from other people . . .'

On Sunday the Princess will be 25. She could then, if she wished, notify Parliament direct of her desire to marry without first seeking the consent of her sister the Queen.

She could end the hubbub.

Will she please make up her mind?

Please make up your mind!

Illustration 7.1. **'Come On Margaret!'**, *Daily Mirror*, 19 Aug. 1955, 1. This headline, imploring Princess Margaret to make up her mind about whether to marry Peter Townsend, was denounced by the Press Council as an 'offence against the decencies of British public life'.

these 'decencies' and 'good manners' were elitist, class-bound concepts that were designed to silence the popular press: the 'vulgar frankness' of the *Mirror* was the natural idiom of the readers it was addressing.[110] Furthermore, it was exactly this snobbery that was responsible for the Palace's disapproval of Townsend. 'The young man concerned has committed two offences: he was born a member of the middle class and he divorced a wife who deserted him.' Rejecting him as an appropriate partner on those grounds 'strikes the overwhelming majority of the public as being a piece of archaic humbug'.[111] Pursuing this story, and championing the cause of a man 'outside the established slate of royal bridegrooms', was part of the *Mirror*'s ongoing crusade against the rigidities of British society. It also reflected the paper's underlying sentimentality. The public seemed to desire a happy ending to the royal romance, and the *Mirror* was impatient with those placing obstacles in the path of true love.

In contrast to 1936, the commercial rewards of covering the story now seemed to outweigh the damage done by public criticism. When Peter Townsend returned to Britain on 12 October 1955, the press went into a frenzy. Pleas from the Palace to respect Princess Margaret's privacy were completely ignored. When Margaret and Townsend spent a weekend at Allanbay Park in Berkshire, they were surrounded by photographers and reporters. Some papers chartered aircraft to monitor the house from above, and £1,000 was offered in an attempt to bribe a butler.[112] Between 12 October and 5 November, the Margaret-Townsend story was on the front page of the *Mirror* no fewer than sixteen times. Other papers followed the story almost as enthusiastically. One loyal *Daily Herald* reader, who had bought the paper since 1928, gave it up in disgust on 15 October when it devoted three of its eight pages, including the front page, to the romance, while covering the final day of the Labour Party Annual conference in a seven-inch, one column report on page six.[113] The pursuit increasingly overrode deference to the institutions of state. When the Palace refused to follow the press agenda by releasing a statement, it was fiercely lambasted: 'Never has the Royal Family been led into such stupidity', declared the *Mirror*.[114] In the aftermath of Margaret's eventual decision not to marry Townsend, the popular press channelled much of its consternation at the Church of England and its teachings on divorce. The *Express*, the *News Chronicle*, and the *Mirror* all produced editorials critical of Church policy; 'The serious upshot of the whole affair in Parliament and the country is a demand for disestablishment' argued

[110] *Daily Mirror*, 27 Aug. 1955, 1. Cudlipp later admitted that the headline, which he himself penned, had gone too far: B. Hagerty, *Read All About It! 100 Sensational Years of the Daily Mirror* (Lydney, Glos.: First Stone, 2003), 83.

[111] Ibid.

[112] T. Aronson, *Princess Margaret: A Biography* (London: Michael O'Mara, 1997), 142.

[113] *Daily Herald* Archives from TUC archive, Modern Record Centre, Warwick, MSS.292/790.3/5 Complaints 1956–63, H. T. Buckle to Chairman, TUC, 24 May 1957.

[114] *Daily Mirror*, 26 Oct. 1955, 1.

Kingsley Martin in the *New Statesman*.[115] The *Mirror* printed several angry letters in its correspondence columns. 'I am ashamed to be British. I vow I shall never set foot in a church again', wrote one reader. 'Throw out this Church which sanctifies arranged marriages but will not allow couples in love to marry', declared another.[116]

The coverage of Princess Margaret's relationship with Peter Townsend marked a watershed in royal journalism. In an increasingly competitive media environment—ITV launched shortly before the height of the Townsend speculation—newspapers were prepared to go to greater and greater lengths to satisfy what seemed to be an insatiable public demand for news about the royal family. (In October 1956, for example, the *Daily Sketch* printed a report about a private party for the Duke of Kent's twenty-first birthday which had been obtained by a female journalist smuggling herself in by hiding in the boot of a car.)[117] Beyond the hard-headed commercial realism there was also a genuine desire in some parts of Fleet Street to challenge what seemed to be an outdated and fundamentally undemocratic culture of secrecy surrounding the Palace. And while the Palace fought a rearguard action, in the absence of a privacy law or statutory controls on the press they could do little to stop newspapers becoming increasingly intrusive. Of course this was not the end of the deferential coverage of the monarchy, and the irreverent tone that had developed by the 1990s was still a long way off. Nevertheless, as Malcolm Muggeridge recognized in an article in the *New Statesman* in October 1955, there had been a decisive shift towards the monarchy as 'soap opera'.[118]

INTIMATE REVELATIONS: THE SEXUALIZATION OF CELEBRITY CULTURE

Despite the greater intrusiveness of royal journalism in the 1950s, there remained a discreet silence over the more intimate details of personal relationships. Such discretion became more and more unusual for those celebrities, and particularly Hollywood stars, who relied on 'sex appeal' for their success. As the boundaries between public and private shifted and the discussion of sex became more explicit, a market started to emerge for intimate revelations and confessions. This was a market that seemed attractive to Fleet Street executives coming to the conclusion that if popular newspapers were to survive in the television era, they would have to provide the sort of content not being transmitted on the small screen.

[115] Quoted in the *Daily Mirror*, 5 Nov. 1955, 2. See also F. Williams, 'Fleet Street Notebook', *New Statesman*, 5 Nov. 1955.

[116] *Daily Mirror*, 4 Nov. 1955, 6; 5 Nov. 1955, 2.

[117] *Daily Sketch*, 10 Oct. 1956; the reporter's actions were condemned by the Press Council in its 1957 report: Press Council, *Annual Report* 1957, 22.

[118] M. Muggeridge, 'Royal Soap Opera', *New Statesman*, 22 Oct. 1955, 499–500.

Emboldened by the success of gossip magazines such as *Confidential* across the Atlantic, editors in Britain started to invest large sums in acquiring sensational memoirs.[119]

The payment of £40,000 by Stuart Campbell of *The People* for Errol Flynn's memoirs in October 1959 heralded this era of the celebrity confessional. Serialized immediately after his death under the title 'My Wicked, Wicked, Life', the paper boasted that Flynn's story was the 'frankest confession ever made by a famous star' and claimed that no fewer than 37 other actors and actresses had instructed lawyers to try to prevent its publication. 'The worried 37—most of them women—know they have been involved with Flynn in scandalous escapades whose disclosure could ruin them.' (**Illustration 7.2**)[120] Running for over two months, articles described Flynn's sexual escapades, drinking, and drug-taking under headlines such as 'Twin Lovelies Ambushed Me At Night . . . . I Gave In' and 'Three Weeks Of Orgy—With Barrymore The Sex-Mad Drunk'.[121] 'My favourite occupation is still love, prolonged bouts of love', wrote Flynn, adding that it was 'impossible to count the women I have known, loved, been loved by, or just taken by'.[122] The memoir was hugely popular, increasing the *People*'s circulation by almost 200,000 copies and enabling it to overtake the *Pictorial* to become the second most popular Sunday.[123]

Stafford Somerfield, the newly-appointed editor of the most popular Sunday, the *News of the World*, was very conscious that his paper's traditional formula of court reports and crime appeared increasingly dated as the culture of celebrity intensified. On his first day as editor in 1959, Somerfield demanded a series of articles that would create a major impact and make readers' 'hair curl'.[124] The result was the purchase of the rights to Diana Dors's autobiography, *Swinging Dors* for £36,000.[125] Running for two months from January 1960, Dors's 'frank and full account of the men she loved and the wild life she has lived' was every bit as titillating as Flynn's memoirs.[126] She admitted that when she was younger she had been 'a naughty girl': 'There were no half measures at my parties . . . off came the sweaters, bras and panties. In fact it was a case of off with everything—except the lights . . . . Every night was party night.'[127] She revealed that—unknown to her—her home with her former husband Dennis Hamilton had hosted parties in which Hamilton and his friends had sex with young women while guests looked on through a two-way mirror; it had also been a venue for

[119] S. Bernstein, *Mr. Confidential: The Man, the Magazine & the Movieland Massacre* (New York: Walford Press, 2006).

[120] The *People*, 18 Oct. 1959, 1.

[121] The *People*, 15 Nov. 1959, 4; 22 Nov. 1959, 2–3.

[122] The *People*, 25 Oct. 1959, 2–3.

[123] Cudlipp, *At Your Peril*, 294–5.

[124] Somerfield, *Banner Headlines*, 111.

[125] *News of the World* Archive, EDF/61, 61/1 Christopher Shaw, Director of London International Press Ltd, to Acting Editor of NotW, 16 Jan. 1960; Somerfield, *Banner Headlines*, 111.

[126] *News of the World*, 17 Jan. 1960, 1.

[127] *News of the World*, 31 Jan. 1960, 4–5.

LAWYERS ALL OUT TO STOP
'My wicked, wicked life'

THE PEOPLE

THE PAPER THAT LOOKS AHEAD

37 FILM STARS NAMED IN ERROL FLYNN CONFESSION

ALL Hollywood is quaking at the disclosure that, shortly before his death, Errol Flynn wrote the frankest confession ever made by a famous star.

Almost every well-known actor and actress in Hollywood is mentioned in it. And 37 stars are understood to have instructed lawyers to try and get stories about them suppressed.

They're all in the book!

For Flynn left orders for his confession to be printed as a book. It is called "My Wicked, Wicked Life." And it lives up to its title.

'My wicked, wicked life'

We've got it and WE'LL PRINT IT!

"The People" will be the first newspaper in the world to print Errol Flynn's fantastic story.

We have secured the serial rights against open competition from nearly all Fleet Street. Not for years has there been such a fight for a manuscript among London newspapers.

Why? Because every Editor knows that "My Wicked, Wicked Life" is the most sensational confession ever written by a film star.

First long instalment of this latest "People" serial will begin NEXT SUNDAY.

Reds seize US envoy in Moscow street

Split on Labour policy: more outbursts

APPALLING

A 'GHOST SHIP' DRIFTS IN GALE

Union cash for Churchill college

WE'RE BROKE—BILLY GRAHAM

Five boys escape

George Gee dies on stage

If you like coffee you'll love 'CAMP'

Illustration 7.2. 'My wicked, wicked life', *The People*, 18 Oct. 1959, 1. The *People*'s serialization of Errol Flynn's memoirs in 1959 heralded a new era of press competition for celebrity 'confessions'.

'blue movies' starring 'couples I had called friends and who are still well known in the West End'.[128]

There was a thin veneer of morality coating the articles in an attempt to make them acceptable in a 'family newspaper'. Dors claimed that her 'wild life' was 'all behind' her: 'today I'm a happy wife. Soon I hope to become a devoted mother.'[129] She also held Hamilton responsible for the most raucous activities: 'My cheeks burn merely to recall the succession of stage-struck girls who were betrayed under my roof.'[130] At the same time, she made no apologies for her own actions and taunted her critics for the lack of fun in their lives.[131] Dors's memoirs—liberally illustrated with titillating photos of her—offered a provocative celebration of female sexual pleasure in a paper more accustomed to focus on the punishment of sexual transgression. The series was an immediate hit with readers, adding over 100,000 copies to a previously falling circulation.[132] In a desperate bid to prevent readers defecting for the Dors story, the *Sunday Pictorial* ran concurrently a series on the life of Dennis Hamilton, recounting in detail his voyeuristic use of mirrors and peep-holes.[133] In the spring of 1960 few working-class newspaper readers can have avoided discovering something about the sex lives of Dors and Hamilton.

This new tendency for celebrity confessions dismayed the Press Council, which in its meeting of March 1960 denounced the 'debased standard of articles' represented by the Flynn, Hamilton, and Dors memoirs. The Council declared that these features 'sank below the accepted standards of decency' and criticized the Dors and Hamilton articles, in particular, for containing 'material that was grossly lewd and salacious'.[134] Once again, however, the papers involved were unrepentant. Appearing on the television show 'The Editors', Somerfield remained defiant, arguing that the Dors memoirs were 'fascinating', had proved popular with readers, and were merely one part of a 'balanced' newspaper. In the face of tough questioning from the MPs Judith Hart and Jeremy Thorpe, he raised doubt about the need for the Press Council at all, and suggested that the obscenity laws were a sufficient safeguard of national morality.[135]

Despite the widespread criticism, then, such serializations proliferated. Within months the *News of the World* had bought Brigitte Bardot's life story and paid £15,000 for the rights to Jayne Mansfield's memoirs.[136] The Bardot articles illustrated the press's determination to maximize the sexual dimension of these

[128] *News of the World*, 24 Jan. 1960, 4–5; 7 Feb. 1960, 4–5.

[129] *News of the World*, 24 Jan. 1960, 1.

[130] Ibid, 4–5.

[131] *News of the World*, 14 Feb. 1960, 4–5.

[132] Somerfield, *Banner Headlines*, 115.

[133] *Sunday Pictorial*, 24 Jan.–21 Feb. 1960.

[134] Press Council, Annual Report 1960, 31–2.

[135] 'I wasn't dissatisfied with that night's work', he later recalled, 'as the publicity value was enormous.' Somerfield, *Banner Headlines*, 112–14.

[136] *News of the World* Archive, EDF/27; EDF/145/2 C.J. Lear, Features Editor, to Christopher Shaw, London International Press, 11 Nov. 1960.

celebrity features whatever the circumstances. The interviews Bardot gave for the series explained her growing hatred of being cast as a 'sex symbol'; indeed, she had become so depressed that she attempted suicide shortly after the *News of the World* had started publishing its articles. Undaunted, the paper pressed ahead with the series, unconcerned at the contradiction of displaying titillating pin-up shots underneath such headlines as 'The Tragedy of Being a Sex Symbol'.[137] Publicity posters were sent out to newsagents featuring a smiling Bardot displaying her generous cleavage: 'See more of me in the *News of the World*' promised the text.[138] In many respects these serializations prepared the way for the lurid coverage of the Profumo affair in 1963. But Hollywood stars were almost expected to lead 'wild' lives—the revelation that leading politicians were doing the same caused far more of a stir.

THE PROFUMO AFFAIR AND THE APPETITE FOR SCANDAL

It was one thing to serialize confessional memoirs, quite another to break a scandal that the protagonists sought to keep secret. For all the increasing intrusiveness of the press in the post-war period, Fleet Street remained reluctant to probe too deeply into the personal affairs of leading politicians. With the assistance of Beaverbrook and Lord Camrose, the proprietor of the *Daily Telegraph*, Winston Churchill was able to prevent news of the stroke he suffered in June 1953 from leaking out: he issued a statement announcing that doctors had prescribed rest without revealing the seriousness of his condition.[139] Marital infidelities conducted by high-profile public men—such as Lord Boothby's relationship with Dorothy Macmillan, and Hugh Gaitskell's with Anne Fleming—were kept discreetly out of the public eye.[140] Even when ministers and MPs had been forced to resign due to sexual 'improprieties'—such as Sir Paul Latham and Ian Harvey, found guilty of homosexual offences in 1942 and 1958 respectively—they were treated relatively gently by the press.[141]

The Profumo scandal is often taken to be a turning-point in this regard. As Lord Denning remarked in his report into the circumstances leading to Profumo's resignation, 'Public men are more vulnerable than they were before

[137] *News of the World*, 9 Oct. 1960, 4–5. [138] *News of the World* Archive EDF/27/35.

[139] M. Gilbert, *Winston S. Churchill, Vol. III, Never Despair 1945–65* (London: Heinemann, 1988), ch. 45; R. Cockett, *My Dear Max: The Letters of Brendan Bracken to Lord Beaverbrook, 1925–1958* (The Historian's London Press, 1990), 147.

[140] Pugh, '*We Danced All Night!*', 136–7; B. Brivati, *Hugh Gaitskell*, new edn.: (London: Politico's, 2006).

[141] P. Higgins, *Heterosexual Dictatorship: Male Homosexuality in Postwar Britain* (London: Fourth Estate, 1996), 247–8, 306–7.

[because] . . . scandalous information about well-known people has become a marketable commodity'.[142] And indeed, once Profumo had offered his resignation to the House of Commons on 5 June 1963, the press publicized and investigated the story far more extensively than might have been expected in earlier decades. Yet it should be remembered that news of Profumo's affair with Christine Keeler had been circulating in Fleet Street for several months without any paper acquiring the confidence to publicly challenge the War Minister.[143] The *Sunday Pictorial* had gathered the most substantial evidence. In January 1963, having fought off interest from the *News of the World*, it paid £1,000 for Keeler's story, and obtained a letter to her from Profumo (the 'Darling Christine' letter). After careful consideration, however, the paper decided that it was too risky to break the story. In June it finally published the letter along with an explanation of why it had not acted earlier:

> The Editor was not satisfied that this letter constituted evidence of any substantial nature. It was effusive but not conclusive. Publication of the letter might have ruined the public career of a Minister on 'evidence' from a young woman who clearly would not have produced the letter if Mr Profumo's interests were uppermost in her consideration. The existence of the letter was not disclosed to the public. Miss Christine Keeler's story was not published.[144]

The *News of the World* took the information it had to the Prime Minister's principal private secretary at the beginning of February 1963: the visit from the *News of the World* executive was—supposedly—the first that Macmillan had heard of the affair, but the paper agreed that it would not print the allegations.[145] The British libel law was heavily weighted in favour of the plaintiff, and like the *Pictorial*, the *News of the World* feared that it would not be able to defend its story adequately if Profumo took the case to court—a threat he made explicit in the House of Commons in March. 'Though most national newspapers possessed information which cast serious doubts on Mr Profumo's veracity', an editorial observed after Profumo's resignation, 'the risk of penal damages in the courts was such that nothing was published beyond the vaguest of innuendoes which were unintelligible to the general public'.[146]

The *Express* was the only paper that published a detailed interview with Keeler before the full story broke, having tracked her down in Spain in April 1963 when she should have been appearing in London as a witness in a shooting case. Beaverbrook was deeply concerned that the paper had gone too far, telling the editor, Bob Edwards, that he was 'shocked at the purchase of the memoirs of

[142] Quoted in Press Council, *Annual Report* 1964, 19–20.

[143] Lord Denning, *Lord Denning's Report* (London: HMSO, 1963) Cmd. 2152; A. Summers and S. Dorril, *Honeytrap* (London: Coronet, 1988).

[144] *Sunday Pictorial*, 9 June 1963, 1.

[145] *News of the World*, 23 June 1963, 1.

[146] *News of the World*, 9 June 1963, 10.

Christine for £2,000' and demanding to know whether Edwards was 'in on that racket?'[147] Edwards reassured the proprietor that it was an important story and that he had been 'extremely careful in handling the story to take out anything in the nature of hints and innuendoes against anybody else', adding that he didn't think 'anybody in Westminster or elsewhere regarded the story as a smear on anybody or even yellow journalism'.[148] The *Express* had caused a stir among those in the know a few weeks earlier by juxtaposing a speculative story about Profumo offering his resignation to Macmillan with the news that Keeler had gone missing from the shooting trial: in its evidence to the Denning tribunal the paper was adamant that this had been a coincidence.[149] Despite all the information in its possession, therefore, the national press steered a fairly cautious course over the Profumo allegations, leaving *Private Eye* and a handful of small circulation publications to fan the rumours.

After Profumo's resignation, however, many of the restraints finally snapped. Fleet Street was awash with gossip about sexual indiscretions in elevated circles. Reporters were dispatched to investigate the activities of Keeler, Stephen Ward, and their associates, in a bid to uncover further scandal. Readers were presented with a flurry of vague stories and unsubstantiated rumours about incriminating photographs taken at high-society orgies. The *News of the World*'s Peter Earle tracked down and interviewed Mariella Novotny, the host of one such party: 'She Knows The Man In The Mask' screamed a front-page headline, referring to one of the most sensitive photos.[150] A week later the *People*'s front-page was dominated by the news that three unnamed ministers had been caught up in Lord Denning's investigation of 'damaging rumours':

> He has been told that 'compromising pictures' exist of two of the ministers . . . . One of the pictures was in a set of photographs produced during a recent divorce case [the Argyll case]. Some people claim that a leading minister is recognisable in the photograph . . . the second picture . . . is alleged to show a member of the Government at the side of a swimming pool in a group that includes Christine Keeler. The third minister is also the subject of a rumour that connects him with the Christine Keeler set. Lord Denning has been told of an alleged meeting between the minister and a girl.[151]

The *Daily Mirror*, meanwhile, ran a headline reading 'Prince Philip And The Profumo Scandal—Rumour Is Utterly Unfounded', without specifying the rumour in question. (While rejecting a complaint about this story, the Press Council observed disapprovingly that its 'sensational treatment . . . was distasteful and did not accord with the newspaper's apparent attitude of being activated by the highest motives.')[152] Malcolm Muggeridge claimed that in his forty years in

147 Beaverbrook Papers, H/226, Beaverbrook to Edwards, 8 April 1963.

148 Beaverbrook Papers, H/226, Edwards to Beaverbrook, 9 April 1963.

149 *Daily Express*, 15 Mar. 1963, 1; Beaverbrook Papers, H/228 Blackburn to Beaverbrook, 12 July 1963.

150 *News of the World*, 30 June 1963, 1.

151 The *People*, 7 July 1963, 1.

152 Press Council, Annual Report 1964, 8.

journalism he had never experienced anything like the 'tidal wave of slanderous talk' that was coursing through Fleet Street.[153]

The spreading of such rumours to the public was unprecedented, and demonstrated the extent to which the press had been emboldened by Profumo's fall. The reports could be justified both by security concerns—the *People* quoted a Special Branch officer's warning that 'We know only too well now that the Russians jump at the chance of exploiting any moral weakness'[154]—and by the widespread perception that British elites had become morally corrupt. 'Last week the Upper Classes passed unquietly away', Muggeridge declared dramatically in the *Sunday Mirror*, arguing that the scandalous stories undermined not just the upper classes but the class system as a whole. Ultimately, though, the press did not go so far as to satisfy public curiosity by naming the high-profile individuals linked to the most sensational stories. Some journalists regretted that more of their material was not actually used. Alfred Draper, one of the *Express*'s leading reporters, later recalled that 'During the months of investigative journalism we built up an enormous dossier of stories which had all been thoroughly checked and owed nothing to gossip. But Lord Beaverbrook did not use any of it. Once the question of security was ruled out he lost interest'.[155] The irony was that by spreading unsubstantiated rumours the press was actually reducing the likelihood of the libel law being reformed, and therefore eventually being in a position to name names. As Lord Devlin, the chairman of the Press Council, observed in 1965, while many agreed that the libel laws were 'oppressive', they were regarded as 'a form of rough justice to be set against excesses which are within the law'.[156] As long as statutory regulation seemed unattainable, the libel laws were viewed as one of the few means of taming an unruly press.

The extent to which the press's post-Profumo boldness was still tempered by fears of legal challenge is illustrated by the Boothby scandal of 1964. On 12 July, the *Sunday Mirror* sensationally claimed that Sir John Simpson, the Metropolitan Commissioner, had ordered Scotland Yard to investigate an 'alleged homosexual relationship between a prominent peer and a leading thug in the London underworld'.[157] The unnamed peer was Lord Robert Boothby, the 'thug' was Ronnie Kray, and the *Mirror* was in possession of a photograph of the two together. This was exactly the sort of story that might have been suppressed in previous decades, but after the events of 1963, the *Mirror* editor Reginald Payne decided to run it (although without taking the precaution of checking with either of his superiors, Hugh Cudlipp and Cecil King). As Roy Greenslade has noted, the real issue was the Krays's racketeering, but the appetite for sexual scandal led

153 *Sunday Mirror*, 23 June 1963, 7.

154 The *People*, 7 July 1963, 1.

155 A. Draper, *Scoops and Swindles: Memoirs of a Fleet Street Journalist* (London: Buchan & Enright, 1988), 287.

156 Press Council, Annual Report 1965, 1.

157 *Sunday Mirror*, 12 July 1964, 1.

Payne to focus on that aspect.[158] The following week, the *Mirror* told readers that 'The Picture We Must Not Print' showed 'a well-known member of the House of Lords seated on a sofa with a gangster who leads the biggest protection racket London has ever known'.[159] In private, the government was seriously concerned: the Solicitor-General admitted that he didn't believe Boothby's explanations, and inconsistencies were found between his statements to the police and to the Home Secretary.[160] 'According to British press tradition, it can be taken as reasonably certain that there is a hardcore of truth in all of this', wrote one Home Office official. 'It can thus be assumed that Lord Boothby . . . will soon be the central figure of a scandal that will overshadow the Profumo affair'.[161] It later emerged that there may indeed have been a 'hardcore of truth', but when Boothby wrote a letter to *The Times* strenuously denying the rumours and threatening to sue the *Mirror*, the paper backed down. Cecil King, who had been trying to improve the *Mirror*'s reputation, quickly agreed to pay Boothby the huge sum of £40,000; Reginald Payne was sacked shortly afterwards.[162] Fleet Street could hardly have been given a clearer warning of the consequences of being unable to support scandalous accusations.

The press would have to wait ten years from Profumo's fall before it brought about the resignation of ministers as a direct result of their sexual indiscretions. In May 1973, Lord Lambton, the Minister for the RAF, resigned when he found that his liaisons with prostitutes were about to be exposed by the Sunday press. Earl Jellicoe, the Leader of the House of Lords, followed days later after admitting that he too had paid for sex. The *News of the World* had been investigating a 'vice ring' featuring prominent individuals for some months, and reported at the end of the April that the 'laws of libel and the need to protect our sources of information inhibit this newspaper from revealing all it knows on all these topics'.[163] The paper was then contacted by Norma Levy, one of the women that Lambton had visited, her husband Colin, and a friend, Peter Goodsell, who offered to sell incriminating photographs of Lambton.[164] With the assistance of Goodsell and the Levys, *News of the World* journalists took photos of Lambton in 'compromising situations', but after a dispute over payment, the Levys sold their pictures to the *People*. The resignations—before the Sundays could break the story—prompted a press frenzy as the dailies investigated the matter themselves. On the following Sunday, the *News of the*

158 R. Greenslade, *Press Gang: How Newspapers Make Profits from Propaganda* (London: Macmillan, 2003), 161.

159 *Sunday Mirror*, 19 July 1964, 1.

160 NA, PREM 11/4689, Note of meeting in Home Secretary's room, 21 July.

161 NA, PREM 11/4689, Geoffrey Otton to Sir Timothy Bligh, 31 July 1964.

162 *The Times*, 1 Aug. 1964; 6. Aug. 1964; R. R. James, *Bob Boothby: A Portrait* (London: Hodder & Stoughton, 1981), 414–21; Greenslade, *Press Gang*, 161.

163 *News of the World*, 29 April 1973, 4.

164 *News of the World*, 27 May 1973, 1.

World and the *People* produced their own extensive reports and published photographs of the 'love nest' used by Levy and Lambton. Both also printed Levy's allegations that further ministers were involved, despite admitting that there was 'no independent corroboration'.[165]

The feverish atmosphere of the Profumo affair appeared to be returning, although this time there was no cause to fear security breaches. The *People* justified its actions by arguing that 'Even in this permissive age "illicit" sex is widely condemned', albeit 'not as savagely as it used to be'. Although many people now 'claim to believe that sex is the private affair of the participants', the paper insisted that 'this tolerance doesn't extend to everyone. It stops short at men and women who are in authority.... Once you're in a position of trust, you can't act like one of the Likely Lads.'[166] But several commentators suggested that the press coverage of the affair had far exceeded what was necessary. Harold Evans, editor of the *Sunday Times*, condemned in particular the 'odious business of pornographic photography' and the circulation of unsubstantiated rumours.[167] The Press Council criticized the *News of the World* for handing over incriminating material to Levy and Goodsell—'persons of ill repute'—and reiterated its policy that the press should not pay persons engaged in crime or other notorious misbehaviour.[168] The lack of impact such warnings made is illustrated by the fact that many *News of the World* staff were more concerned that the paper had lost a scoop to the *People*: they believed that editor Lear was showing too much caution in breaking scandals.[169] The discretion that had once characterized Fleet Street was swiftly dying out.

By the 1970s, then, the scramble for celebrity scoops ensured that popular papers took more risks and spent more resources delving into the lives of public figures. There was fierce competition, in particular, for royal exclusives, which meant that Prince Charles's search for a bride, and the collapse of Princess Margaret's marriage, were discussed in endless detail. Politicians and commentators became more vociferous in their demands for privacy legislation or tighter regulation to curb the excesses of the press. In 1972, the Younger Committee on Privacy called on the Press Council to increase its lay representation and to codify its rulings so that it could take a tougher line on privacy questions. The Royal Commission on the Press in 1977 made similar recommendations.[170] Despite widespread political agreement that journalists were becoming too

165 Ibid; The *People*, 27 May 1973, 1.

166 The *People*, 27 May 1973, 10.

167 A. Smith (ed.), *The British Press Since the War* (Newton Abbot: David & Charles, 1974), 205.

168 Press Council, *Press Conduct in the Lambton Affair: A Report by the Press Council* (London: Press Council, 1974).

169 C. Bainbridge and R. Stockdill, *The News of the World Story: 150 Years of the World's Bestselling Newspaper* (London: HarperCollins, 1993), 238.

170 T. O'Malley and C. Soley, *Regulating the Press* (London: Pluto Press, 2000).

intrusive, and that the Press Council was ineffective, it proved impossible to reach a consensus on a solution that did not encroach too gravely on the hallowed 'freedom of the press'. There were genuine fears about prohibiting investigative journalism; perhaps more importantly, though, governments feared the press backlash that implementing privacy legislation would have provoked. While the debates about regulation and legislation rumbled on[171] the press was left to foster the celebrity culture, and the 'articles of a personal type' that Northcliffe demanded at the start of the century began to overwhelm all other sorts of news.

Over the course of the century, the press's coverage of public figures changed dramatically. In the increasingly competitive and less deferential media environment of the 1950s and 1960s, the inter-war discretion about personal relationships was gradually eroded. The greater willingness to discuss sexual behaviour inevitably heightened curiosity about the habits of the rich and famous. At the same time the growing belief that sexuality was the defining feature of the private self meant that interviews and memoirs were seen as being incomplete without some revelations about this aspect of the personality. Some film stars and entertainers exploited the lucrative new market in intimate 'confessions', but these developments were more problematic for politicians, officials, and members of the royal family who were widely expected to conform to the expectations of family morality. It was by no means impossible for those in the public eye to shield their private lives from journalists, especially with the expert advice of public relations consultants such as Max Clifford,[172] but it became significantly harder after the journalistic frenzy of the Profumo Affair. Yet this increasing intrusiveness carried dangers for the press. Although circulation figures demonstrated the public's appetite for celebrity gossip, many readers seemed to regard their consumption of this material as a guilty pleasure, and they did not necessarily have much respect for those who produced it. Lord Shawcross, the chairman of the Second Royal Commission on the Press, recognized this ambivalence in an article he wrote for the Press Council reflecting on the events of 1963. Considering why public 'ill-favour' towards newspapers existed despite huge circulations, he suggested that 'although as individuals we may not be averse to wallowing vicariously in stories of sexual perversion and promiscuity, although we enjoy the spark of malice and listen curiously to the tongue of

[171] Public outrage about intrusive journalism reached another high point in the late 1980s, provoking the famous warning from the Conservative MP David Mellor that the press had entered the 'last-chance saloon'. This crisis led in 1991 to the Press Council being replaced by the Press Complaints Commission (PCC), which monitored an industry code of conduct, but proposed legislation to curb journalistic intrusion was eventually dropped. After incorporating the European Convention on Human Rights into British law in 1998, the Labour government left it to the courts and PCC to find a balance between the freedom of expression and the right to privacy. On this, see A. Bingham, '"Drinking in the Last Chance Saloon": The British Press and the Crisis of Self-Regulation, 1989–1995', *Media History*, 13/1 (April 2007), 79–92.

[172] M. Clifford and A. Levin, *Read All About It* (London: Virgin Books, 2006).

scandal, we do not approve of those who, for profit, purvey these things.'[173] The popular press's ever more vigorous pursuit of the celebrity agenda in the final decades of the century was often at the expense of the trust that had allowed journalists to educate and inform, rather than merely entertain, their readers.

[173] Lord Shawcross, 'Curbs on the Rights of Disclosure', in *The Press and the People—The Tenth Annual Report of the Press Council* (London: Press Council, 1963), 10.

Conclusions

The popular press is one of the most distinctive elements of British culture. In no comparable Western country have mass market newspapers been as fiercely competitive or achieved quite the same influence and prominence as in Britain. Fleet Street's uniquely successful brand of popular journalism has provided millions of ordinary readers with one of their main windows onto the world, and has shaped the nation's political and social life in countless ways.

One of the most striking features of this journalism throughout the twentieth century was its preoccupation with sex. It was an article of faith in Fleet Street that sex was an unrivalled way of building circulation—but it was also recognized that, handled wrongly, it was liable to cause considerable offence. Popular newspapers consequently found it very difficult to keep sex in proportion. They hugely magnified many news stories with a sexual dimension, paying lavish attention, for example, to the transgressions recorded in the courtroom or revelations about celebrity romances. At other times they went out of their way to evade certain uncomfortable issues, such as homosexuality or venereal diseases. Sensational headlines and suggestive photographs were routinely used to tantalize readers, but reporters tended to drift into euphemism rather than provide graphic physical descriptions.

These inconsistencies ultimately stemmed from the difficulties of maintaining circulation in an intensely competitive media environment while preserving a commitment to being a 'family newspaper'. The modern popular press emerged in the late nineteenth century in an undemocratic, socially stratified nation in which political and cultural elites displayed marked hostility to the emerging 'mass society'. The proprietors and editors of popular newspapers could not avoid this elite condescension, but they quickly realized that if their publications were to gain social acceptance and win over lower middle-class and upper working-class readers, they would need to demonstrate their respectability. One of the most effective ways to achieve that in a society in which order and 'decency' were so highly valued, and obscenity so carefully policed, was to publicize a commitment to conventional morality and, in particular, to family values. Popular newspapers declared loudly that they were 'family publications' suitable for all. Where the elite press had tended to idealize its readers as men of affairs relaxing in London clubs, papers like the *Mail* and the *Express* targeted the reader at the ordinary family breakfast table, and included content for the housewife and the child.

If respectability and family morality were necessary defensive strategies, popular newspapers also had to find ways of making themselves attractive to potential readers. Faced with a population in which the majority had a low level of education, journalists could not aim too high. Newspapers could inform and instruct, but they also had to entertain and intrigue—to provide the 'human interest' that was believed to capture readers. One apparently infallible way of providing human interest was to play on the curiosity about sex. The combination of widespread sexual ignorance and a strict censorship regime ensured that sex provoked both fear and fascination. Newspapers developed ways of playing on these emotions while preserving their status as 'family newspapers'. As the century progressed and attitudes to sex shifted, popular newspapers were able to include a broader range of sexual content, but they remained faithful to the idea that this content was constrained by the nature of its audience.

Surveying the press's treatment of sex over the six decades since 1918, one inevitably finds huge variety both within and between newspapers. There was not a simple and smooth progress towards greater 'openness' about sex, nor is it easy to identify clear turning-points which apply across the whole market. It is possible, nevertheless, to divide the period loosely into three phases and discern some significant differences in the press's role in, and coverage of, British sexual culture.

In the first phase, broadly encompassing the inter-war period, the popular press reacted slowly and cautiously to the increasing prominence that sex achieved in public discourse after 1918. Important authors, such as Marie Stopes, were given space to articulate some of their ideas, and key moments of controversy, such as Lord Dawson's speech about birth control in 1921, were reported fully. But editors were reluctant to risk upsetting readers by discussing sexual matters in detail or taking a decisive line on questions of policy. They rejected the idea that the press had a responsibility to educate the public about sex and respected conventional notions of privacy. They maintained a strong faith in the decency of the British people and there was little overt discussion of sexual pleasure. The rarity of strong opinion meant that whenever crusading articles were printed—such as the *Sunday Express*'s vigorous attacks on birth control in 1921, and its condemnation of Radclyffe Hall's *The Well of Loneliness* in 1928—they created a real stir. In general, however, popular newspapers preferred to persist with the genres of journalism that they had perfected, such as titillating divorce reports, exposures of the horrors of 'white slavery', and gossipy stories about the turbulent love lives of cinema stars.

During the second phase, from the Second World War to the late 1960s, popular newspapers expanded their coverage of sex significantly, and developed what they portrayed as more modern approaches to it. Sex was presented as a source of entertainment, but also as a subject about which the public required up-to-date, scientific, information. The *Daily Mirror* and the *Sunday Pictorial*, relaunched in the mid-1930s to target the untapped sections of the working-class market, led the way in formulating this new style. While not abandoning 'family values', these papers gradually moved away from some of the more constricting notions of middle-class respectability and perfected a more 'vulgar', irreverent, authentically working-class voice. At first they focused squarely on titillation, with more overtly eroticized pin-ups and cartoons, and provocative feature content. But as the *Mirror* and the *Pictorial* developed a popular politics to match their populist content, they began to make more serious interventions on sexual issues. They used a democratic, progressive language to campaign for the spreading of sexual knowledge, and argued that newspapers themselves had a responsibility to educate the public, rather than merely calling on others to do so. The *Mirror*'s 1942 series on the dangers of venereal diseases marked an important breakthrough in this campaign, serving to demonstrate that the popular press could indeed play an important role in disseminating information about sexual welfare. The startling commercial success of the *Mirror*'s new brand of popular journalism ensured, moreover, that rivals started to imitate and adapt it, although papers like the *Daily* and *Sunday Express* remained faithful for many years to earlier definitions of the 'family publication'.

In the two decades after the Second World War, the popular press played a very significant role in opening up the public discussion of sex. Sex-related reporting became far more wide-ranging, extensive, and detailed. The enthusiasm with which Dr Kinsey's *Sexual Behaviour in the Human Female* was covered in 1953 was only the most conspicuous sign of the growing interest in various aspects of sexological and psychological research. Campaigning organizations found it easier to gain access to the news pages, and issues like contraception and abortion were explored more thoroughly. But newspapers were no longer content merely to report and record, they were increasingly determined to intervene in debates and shape British sexual culture. By producing educational articles, commissioning sex surveys, launching moral crusades and conducting investigations into 'vice', popular newspapers claimed to be combating ignorance and exposing threats to family values. They certainly destabilized the notion that sex was a private, intimate activity that should remain confidential. The greater inquisitiveness about the personal relationships of public figures was evident in the intense speculation about Princess Margaret's emotional life and the wave of celebrity confessions at the end of the decade.

The press tended to present this new approach to sex as a 'modern', 'enlightened' response to lingering 'Victorian' prudery, but editors were oblivious to the ways in which it was shaped by the prejudices and preconceptions of a relatively enclosed world of self-confident, metropolitan, heterosexual, middle-aged men. Although advice columnists helped to undermine some traditional gender assumptions by encouraging women to be informed about, and take pleasure in, sex, ideas about sexual difference were very resilient and continued to influence newspaper content. Nowhere was this clearer than in the photography, where the greater willingness to display images of the sexualized female body intensified the pressures on women to see themselves as sexual playthings and to conform to media ideals of attractiveness. The increasing interest in the early 1950s in tackling the 'social problem' of homosexuality also placed gay men under unwelcome scrutiny and led to them being demonized as corrupters of society. The *Daily Mirror* did become a powerful supporter of the Wolfenden proposals to decriminalize consenting sex between men, as did most other popular papers by the mid-1960s, but journalists consolidated the idea of a dichotomy between 'normal' and 'deviant' sexuality, and suspicion of gay men and women took a long time to fade from the pages of the press.

The popular journalism of the 1950s helped to prepare the way for the much broader sexualization of the media in the 1960s, and made a significant contribution to the climate of reform that produced liberalizing legislation during Wilson's Labour government. But as the rest of the media became more sexually explicit, the popular press's post-war editorial formula gradually lost its potency. During this third phase, from the late-1960s, the newspapers' standard claim that they were exploring sexual issues to challenge sexual ignorance started to lose its credibility, and their titillating content looked increasingly pale against the material provided elsewhere. At the same time the family values that the press had championed for so long seemed in danger of looking old-fashioned to younger readers.

It was Rupert Murdoch's *Sun* that successfully updated the formula for a more permissive and more consumerist age. The paper further expanded the amount of sexual content and increased the emphasis placed upon sexual pleasure, steadily moving away from what it regarded as an anachronistic attachment to educating the public. Titillating features became more brazen, with topless pin-ups, raunchy serials, and ever-more intrusive and speculative celebrity journalism. The information and advice that was provided assumed a basic sexual literacy and was directed to providing instruction in sexual technique and on how to become the 'perfect lover'. The commitment to family values was not dropped, though, but rather reworked into a critique of the excesses of 'permissiveness' and the unwarranted demands of 'radicals' and special interest groups. This morality developed a harder edge in the second half of the 1970s, leading the paper to support the new right Conservatism of Margaret Thatcher. At the same time, the preoccupation with sex increasingly seeped into conventional news reporting, leading to what Patricia Holland has called the 'sexualisation of public events', whereby reporting of the public sphere insistently focused on any sexual dimension, however tangential to the main story.[1]

By 1978, when the *Sun* overtook the *Mirror* to become Britain's best-selling daily newspaper, it was evident that this formula had triumphed commercially. Content analysis demonstrated that the *Sun* dedicated almost three times as much

[1] P. Holland, 'The Page Three Girl Speaks to Women, Too: A Sun-Sational Survey', *Screen*, 24/3 (1983), 87–8.

feature space to sex than its rival, and this was clearly one of the main causes of its spectacular circulation growth.[2] The 'page three girl', in particular, had become the defining symbol of modern popular journalism. Victor Matthews flattered the *Sun* by launching a brazen imitation in the form of the *Star*, and intensified the competition in sexual titillation. The Sunday papers, too, were learning from the *Sun*'s success. By the end of the 1970s the *News of the World* had ended its traditional reliance on court reporting in favour of pursuing celebrity revelations and undertaking investigations into various manifestations of 'permissiveness', such as the spread of 'wife-swapping' and escort agencies.[3] The process of the sexualization of the popular press was largely complete, and the journalism of subsequent decades was essentially variations on well-established themes.

In 1971, Hugh Cudlipp, who had done so much to transform the popular press's coverage of sex in the middle decades of the century, admitted to his former colleague Cecil King that the aggressive competition from the *Sun* had forced the *Mirror* to 'lower its standards'. But he wondered whether the usual techniques would continue to work in an era of greater sexual freedom: 'I am beginning to suspect that what titillates the middle-aged will not titillate the younger generation—who, after all, enjoy sex on draft.' He even speculated that an entirely new editorial approach would be devised: 'Somebody, maybe, will one day think up an idea more interesting than sex.'[4] Many years later, despite falling sales across the popular newspaper market, we are still waiting.

[2] Royal Commission on the Press, *An Analysis of Newspaper Content: A Report by Professor Denis McQuail* (London: HMSO, 1977), Cmd. 6810–4, 26.

[3] C. Bainbridge and R. Stockdill, *The News of the World Story: 150 Years of the World's Bestselling Newspaper* (London: HarperCollins, 1993), 242.

[4] Bute Library, University of Cardiff, Cudlipp Papers, HC 212 Hugh Cudlipp to Cecil King, 12 Oct. 1971.

Selected Bibliography

MANUSCRIPT SOURCES

Bodleian Library, Oxford

Daily Herald Papers, from archives of the Labour Party.
Lord Northcliffe's Bulletins to the *Daily Mail* 1915–22.
Mass-Observation File Reports.
Robert Ensor Papers.
Society of Women Journalists and Writers, correspondence and papers 1927–62.

British Library, London

Evelyn Wrench Papers.
Lord Northcliffe Papers.
Marie Stopes Papers.

British Library of Political and Economic Science, LSE, London

British Birth Control Papers.
Gerald Barry Papers.

Bute Library, University of Cardiff

Hugh Cudlipp Papers.

Christ Church, Oxford

Tom Driberg Papers.

House of Lords Record Office, London

Beaverbrook Papers (BBK C Series, 102–3; 196; 276; 282–7; H Series, 43–232; 256–9).

Modern Records Centre, Warwick

Daily Herald Papers, from TUC Archive.

National Archives, Kew

Cabinet: CAB 21, CAB 124, CAB 127, CAB 128, CAB 129.
General Register Office: RG 23.
Home Office: HO 45, HO 252, HO 272, HO 345.
Lord Chamberlain's Office: LCO 2.
Medical Research Council: FD 1.
Ministry of Health: MH 55, MH 102; HLG 7; BN 10/220.
Prime Minister's Office: PREM 1, PREM 4, PREM 8, PREM 11, PREM 13.

Treasury: T 161.
War Office: WO 219.

News International Archive, London

News of the World Papers.

Trinity College, Cambridge

Walter Layton Papers.

Wellcome Library, London

Abortion Law Reform Association Papers.
Family Planning Association Papers.
Marie Stopes Papers.

Women's Library, London

British Vigilance Association Papers.
Campaign Against Pornography Papers.
Miss Great Britain Papers.
Women's Media Action Group Papers.

PRINTED PRIMARY SOURCES

Newspapers

Daily Chronicle, Daily Express, Daily Herald, Daily Mail, Daily Mirror, Daily News, Daily Record, Daily Sketch, Daily Star, Daily Telegraph, Empire News, Evening Standard, Lloyd's Weekly News, Manchester Guardian, Morning Post, News Chronicle, News of the World, The Observer, The People, Reynolds News, The Sun, Sunday Chronicle, Sunday Dispatch, Sunday Express, Sunday Mirror, Sunday Pictorial, Sunday Times, The Times.

Press industry magazines and annuals

Newspaper Press Directory, Newspaper World, UK Press Gazette, World's Press News, The Writer.

Other magazines

The Adelphi, John Bull, New Society, New Statesman, Punch, Spectator, Woman and Home.

Parliamentary Papers

Committee on Homosexual Offences and Prostitution, *Report* (London: HMSO, 1957), Cmd. 247.

Hansard, *Parliamentary Debates*, Fifth Series.

Lord Denning, *Lord Denning's Report* (London: HMSO, 1963) Cmd. 2152.

Royal Commission on the Press 1947–49, *Minutes of Evidence* (London: HMSO, 1948).

Royal Commission on the Press 1947–9, *Report* (London: HMSO, 1949), Cmd. 7700.

Royal Commission on the Press 1961–62, *Report* (London: HMSO, 1962), Cmd. 1811.

Royal Commission on the Press 1974–77, *Final Report* (London: HMSO, 1977), Cmd 6810; *Attitudes to the Press*, Cmd. 6810–3; *Analysis of Newspaper Content*, Cmd. 6810–4.

Royal Commission on Venereal Diseases, *Final Report* (London: HMSO, 1916), Cmd. 8189.

Select Committee on the Matrimonial Causes (Regulation of Reports) Bill, *Minutes of Evidence*, P.P. (1923), VII.

Reports etc.

Longford Committee, *Pornography: The Longford Report* (London: Coronet, 1972).

Political and Economic Planning (PEP), *Report on the British Press* (London: PEP, 1938).

Press Council, *The Press and the People* (London: Press Council), Annual Reports 1954–1978.

Press Council, *Privacy, Press and Public* (London: Press Council, 1971).

Press Council, *Press Conduct and the Lambton Affair* (London: Press Council, 1974).

Trades Union Congress, *Images of Inequality: The Portrayal of Women in the Media and Advertising* (London: TUC, 1984).

Circulation surveys

Abrams, M., *The Newspaper Reading Public of Tomorrow* (London: Odhams Press, 1964).

—— *Education, Social Class and the Reading of Newspapers and Magazines* (London: IPA, 1965).

Coglan, W., *The Readership of Newspapers and Periodicals in GB, 1936* (London: ISBA, 1936).

Harrison, G. and F. Mitchell, *The Home Market: A Handbook of Statistics* (London: George Allen & Unwin, 1936).

—— —— and M. Abrams, *The Home Market*, revised edn. (London: George Allen & Unwin, 1939).

Hobson J., H. Henry and M. Abrams, *The Hulton Readership Survey* (London: Hulton Press, 1949).

Institute of Practitioners in Advertising, *National Readership Survey* (London: IPA, 1956; 1967).

Kimble, P., *Newspaper Reading in the Third Year of War* (London: George Allen & Unwin, 1942).

Lyall, H., *Press Circulations Analysed* (London: London Research Bureau, 1928).

Mass-Observation, *The Press and its Readers* (London: Arts and Technics Ltd., 1949).

Repford Ltd., *Investigated Press Circulations* (London: Repford Ltd., 1932).

Diaries and letters

Ball, S. (ed.), *The Headlam Diaries 1935–1951* (Cambridge: Cambridge University Press, 1999).

Catterall, P. (ed.), *The Macmillan Diaries: The Cabinet Years 1950–1957* (London: Pan, 2004).

Cockett, R. (ed.), *My Dear Max: The Letters of Brendan Bracken to Lord Beaverbrook, 1925–1958* (London: The Historian's Press, 1990).

Crowson, N. (ed.), *Fleet Street, Press Barons and Politics: The Journals of Collin Brooks, 1932–40* (London: Royal Historical Society, 1998).

King, C. *With Malice Toward None: A War Diary* (London: Sidgwick & Jackson, 1970).

Nicolson, N. (ed.), *Harold Nicolson, Diaries and Letters 1930–39* (London: Collins, 1966).

Young, K. (ed.), *The Diaries of Sir Robert Bruce Lockhart 1915–38* (London: Macmillan, 1973).

Memoirs, anthologies, handbooks, fiction

Angell, N., *After All: The Autobiography of Norman Angell* (London: Hamish Hamilton, 1951).

Balfour, P., *Society Racket: A Critical Survey of Modern Social Life* (London: John Long Ltd., 1933).

Berry, P. and Bishop, A. (eds.), *Testament of a Generation: The Journalism of Vera Brittain and Winifred Holtby* (London: Virago, 1985).

Blumenfeld, R. D., *The Press in my Time* (London: Rich & Cowan, 1933).

Braddock, A. P., *Applied Psychology for Advertisers* (London: Butterworth, 1933).

Braithwaite, B. and Walsh, N., *Home Sweet Home: The Best of Good Housekeeping 1922–39* (London: Leopard, 1995).

Brodzky V. et al. (eds.), *Fleet Street: The Inside Story of Journalism* (London: MacDonald & Co., 1966).

Cannell, J., *When Fleet Street Calls: Being the Experiences of a London Journalist* (London: Jarrolds, 1932).

Christiansen, A., *Headlines All my Life* (London: Heinemann, 1961).

Clarke, T., *My Northcliffe Diary* (London: Victor Gollancz, 1931).

——— *Northcliffe in History: An Intimate Study of Press Power* (London: Hutchinson, 1950).

Clifford, M. and Levin, A., *Read All About It* (London: Virgin Books, 2006).

Crawshay, M., *Journalism for Women* (London: Fleet Publications, 1932).

Cudlipp, H., *Publish and Be Damned! The Astonishing Story of the Daily Mirror* (London: Andrew Dakers, 1953).

——— *At Your Peril* (London: Weidenfeld & Nicolson, 1962).

——— *Walking on Water* (London: Bodley Head, 1976).

Cummings, A. J., *The Press and a Changing Civilisation* (London: John Lane, 1936).

Daily Mirror Newspapers, *Jane at War* (London: Wolfe, 1976).

Dark, S., *The Life of Sir Arthur Pearson* (London: Hodder & Stoughton, 1922).

Deane, P. (ed.), *History in our Hands: A Critical Anthology of Writings on Literature, Culture and Politics from the 1930s* (London: Leicester University Press, 1998).

Draper, A., *Scoops and Swindles: Memoirs of a Fleet Street Journalist* (London: Buchan & Enright, 1988).

Ervine, St John, *The Future of the Press* (London: World's Press News, 1933).
Fenn, H., *Thirty-Five Years in the Divorce Courts* (London: T. Werner Laurie, 1910).
Fyfe, H., *Northcliffe: An Intimate Biography* (London: G. Allen & Unwin, 1930).
—— *Sixty Years of Fleet Street* (London: W. H. Allen, 1949).
Gibbs, P., *Adventures in Journalism* (London: William Heinemann, 1923).
Gorer, G., *Exploring English Character* (London: Cresset Press, 1955).
Graves, R. and Hodge, A., *The Long Week-End: A Social History of Britain 1918–1939* (first pub. 1940; Harmondsworth: Penguin, 1971).
Greenly, A. J., *Psychology as a Sales Factor*, 2nd edn. (London: Pitman, 1929).
Hadley, W. W. (ed.), *The Kemsley Book of Journalism* (London: Cassell, 1950).
Haig, M., *Notes on the Way* (London: Macmillan, 1937).
Hall, R. (ed.), *Dear Dr Stopes: Sex in the 1920s* (Harmondsworth: Penguin, 1981).
Herd, H., *The Making of Modern Journalism* (London: G. Allen & Unwin, 1927).
Hopkinson, T. (ed.), *Picture Post 1938–50* (London: Penguin, 1970).
Jones, K., *Fleet Street and Downing Street* (London: Hutchinson, 1920).
Junor, J., *Memoirs: Listening for a Midnight Tram* (London: Chapmans, 1990).
King, C., *Strictly Personal: Some Memoirs of Cecil H. King* (London: Weidenfeld & Nicolson, 1969).
Lamb, L., *Sunrise: The Remarkable Rise of the Best-Selling Soaraway Sun* (London: Papermac, 1989).
Lansbury, G., *The Miracle of Fleet Street: The Story of the Daily Herald* (London: Labour Publishing, 1925).
Leavis, F. R., *Mass Civilisation and a Minority Culture* (Cambridge: Gordon Fraser, 1930).
Leavis, Q. D., *Fiction and the Reading Public* (first pub. 1932; London: Chatto & Windus, 1965).
Morison, S., *The English Newspaper 1622–1932* (Cambridge: Cambridge University Press, 1932).
Moseley, S., *Short Story Writing and Freelance Journalism* (London: Pitman, 1926).
Orwell, G., *The Road to Wigan Pier* (first pub. 1937; Harmondsworth: Penguin, 1978).
Orwell, S. and Angus, I. (eds.), *The Collected Essays, Journalism and Letters of George Orwell*, i: *1920–40* (Harmondsworth: Penguin, 1970).
Procter, H., *The Street of Disillusion* (London: Allan Wingate, 1958).
Proops, M., *Dear Marje . . .* (London: Book Club Associates, 1976).
Roberts, R., *The Classic Slum: Salford Life in the First Quarter of the Century* (Harmondsworth: Penguin, 1973).
Russell, G., *Advertisement Writing* (London: Ernest Benn, 1927).
Sillitoe, A., *Saturday Night and Sunday Morning* (first pub. 1958; London: Grafton Books, 1990).
Smith, W., *Spilt Ink* (London: Ernest Benn, 1932).
Somerfield, S., *Banner Headlines* (Shoreham-by-Sea: Scan Books, 1979).
Spender, D. (ed.), *Time and Tide Wait for No Man* (London: Pandora, 1984).
Stannard, R., *With the Dictators of Fleet Street* (London: Hutchinson, 1934).
Steed, H. W., *The Press* (Harmondsworth: Penguin, 1938).
Stott, M. (ed.), *Women Talking: An Anthology from the Guardian Women's Page 1922–35, 1957–71* (London: Pandora, 1987).

Waugh, E., *Vile Bodies* (first pub. 1930; London: Penguin, 2000).
—— *Scoop* (first pub. 1938; Harmondsworth: Penguin, 1967).
Webb, D., *Crime is my Business* (London: Frederick Muller, 1953).
Whitehouse, M., *Cleaning-Up TV: From Protest to Participation* (London: Blandford, 1967).
Wildeblood, P., *Against The Law* (first pub. 1955; Harmonsdsworth: Penguin, 1957).

SECONDARY LITERATURE

Addison, P., *The Road to 1945: British Politics and The Second World War* (London: Jonathan Cape, 1975).
Adorno, T. and Horkheimer, M., 'The Culture Industry: Enlightenment as Mass Deception', in id., *The Dialectic of Enlightenment*, trans. J. Cumming (London: Allan Lane, 1973).
Alberti, J., *Beyond Suffrage: Feminists in War and Peace, 1914–28* (Basingstoke: Macmillan, 1989).
Aldgate, A., *Censorship and the Permissive Society: British Cinema and Theatre 1955–1965* (Oxford: Oxford University Press, 1995).
—— and Robertson, J., *Censorship in Theatre and Cinema* (Edinburgh: Edinburgh University Press, 2005).
Alexander, S., 'Becoming a Woman in London in the 1920s and '30s', in ead., *Becoming a Woman and Other Essays* (New York: New York University Press, 1995).
Allen, R. and Frost, J., *Daily Mirror* (Cambridge: Stephens, 1981).
—— *Voice of Britain: The Inside Story of the Daily Express* (Cambridge: Stephens, 1983).
Anderson, B., *Imagined Communities: Reflections on the Origin and Spread of Nationalism*, (first pub. 1983; rev. edn. London: Verso, 1991).
Aronson, T., *Princess Margaret: A Biography* (London: Michael O'Mara, 1997).
Ayerst, D., *The Guardian: Biography of a Newspaper* (London: Collins, 1971).
Ayto, J., *Twentieth Century Words* (Oxford: Oxford University Press, 1999).
Bainbridge, C. and Stockdill, R., *The News of the World Story: 150 Years of the World's Bestselling Newspaper* (London: HarperCollins, 1993).
Baldick, C., *The Oxford English Literary History, Vol. 10, 1910–1940: The Modern Age* (Oxford: Oxford University Press, 2004).
Beers, L., 'Whose Opinion? Changing Attitudes Towards Opinion Polling in British Politics 1937–64', *Twentieth Century British History*, 17/2 (2006), 177–205.
Beetham, M., *A Magazine of her Own? Domesticity and Desire in the Woman's Magazine 1800–1914* (London: Routledge, 1996).
Benson, J., *The Rise of Consumer Society in Britain 1880–1990* (London: Longman, 1994).
Benjamin, I., *The Black Press in Britain* (Stoke: Trentham Books, 1995).
Bernstein, S., *Mr. Confidential: The Man, the Magazine & the Movieland Massacre* (New York: Walford Press, 2006).
Berridge, V., 'Popular Sunday Papers and Mid-Victorian Society', in G. Boyce, J. Curran, and P. Wingate (eds.), *Newspaper History from the Seventeenth Century to the Present Day* (London: Constable, 1978).

——*Health and Society in Britain since 1939* (Cambridge: Cambridge University Press, 1999).

Bingham, A., *Gender, Modernity, and the Popular Press in Inter-War Britain* (Oxford: Oxford University Press, 2004).

——'The British Popular Press and Venereal Disease during the Second World War', *Historical Journal*, 48/4 (2005), 1055–76.

——"Drinking in the Last Chance Saloon". The British Press and the Crisis of Self-Regulation, 1989–1995', *Media History*, 13/1 (April 2007), 79–92.

Bland, L., *Banishing the Beast: English Feminism and Sexual Morality 1885–1914* (London: Penguin, 1995).

——'White Women and Men of Colour: Miscegenation Fears in Britain after the Great War', *Gender and History*, 17/1 (2005), 29–61.

——and Doan, L. (eds.), *Sexology in Culture: Labelling Bodies and Desires* (Cambridge: Polity Press, 1998).

Boyce, G., Curran, J., and Wingate, P. (eds.), *Newspaper History from the Seventeenth Century to the Present Day* (London: Constable, 1978).

Brake, L., Bell, B., and Finkelstein, D. (eds.), *Nineteenth Century Media and the Construction of Identities* (Basingstoke: Palgrave, 2000).

Brendon, P., *The Life and Death of the Press Barons* (London: Secker & Warburg, 1982).

Briggs, A., *The History of Broadcasting in the UK, Vol. IV: Sound and Vision* (Oxford: Oxford University Press, 1979).

Brivati, B., *Hugh Gaitskell*, new edn. (London: Politico's, 2006).

Bromley, M. and O'Malley, T. (eds.), *A Journalism Reader* (London: Routledge, 1997).

Brooke, S., 'Gender and Working-Class Identity in Britain during the 1950s', *Journal of Social History*, 35 (2001), 773–95.

Brookes, B., *Abortion in England 1900–67* (London: Croom Helm, 1988).

Brown, C., *The Death of Christian Britain: Understanding Secularisation 1800–2000* (London: Routledge, 2001).

Brown, L., *Victorian News and Newspapers* (Oxford: Clarendon Press, 1985).

Butler, D. and Butler, G., *Twentieth-Century British Political Facts 1900–2000*, 8th edn. (Basingstoke: Macmillan, 2000).

Caine, B., *English Feminism 1780–1980* (Oxford: Oxford University Press, 1997).

Campbell, J., *If Love Were All. . . : The Story of Frances Stevenson and David Lloyd George* (London: Jonathan Cape, 2006).

Cannadine, D., 'The Context, Performance and Meaning of Ritual: The British Monarchy and the "Invention of Tradition", *c*.1820–1977' in E. Hobsbawm, and T. Ranger (eds.), *The Invention of Tradition* (Cambridge: Cambridge University Press, 1983).

——*The Decline and Fall of the British Aristocracy* (New Haven: Yale University Press, 1990).

Carey, J., *The Intellectuals and the Masses: Pride and Prejudice among the Literary Intelligensia 1880–1939* (London: Faber and Faber, 1992).

Carter, C., Branston, G., and Allan, S. (eds.), *News, Gender and Power* (London: Routledge, 1998).

Catterall, P., Seymour-Ure, C., and Smith, A. (eds.), *Northcliffe's Legacy: Aspects of the British Popular Press 1896–1996* (Basingstoke: Macmillan, 2000).

Chalaby, J. K., *The Invention of Journalism* (Basingstoke: Macmillan, 1998).

Chambers, D., Steiner L., and Fleming, C., *Women and Journalism* (London: Routledge, 2004).

Chibnall, S., *Law-and-Order News: An Analysis of Crime Reporting in the British Press* (London: Tavistock Publications, 1977).

Chippindale, P. and Horrie, C., *Stick it up your Punter: The Uncut Story of the Sun Newspaper* (London: Simon & Schuster, 1999).

Chisholm, A. and Davie, M., *Beaverbrook: A Life* (London: Hutchinson, 1992).

Cocks, H., *Nameless Offences: Homosexual Desire in the Nineteenth Century* (London: IB Tauris, 2003).

——— and Houlbrook, M. (eds.), *Advances in the Modern History of Sexuality* (Basingstoke: Palgrave Macmillan, 2006).

Cohen, S. (ed.), *Images of Deviance* (Harmondsworth: Penguin, 1971).

——— *Folk Devils and Moral Panics: The Creation of the Mods and Rockers* (St Albans: Paladin, 1973).

Collins, M., 'The Pornography of Permissiveness: Men's Sexuality and Women's Emancipation in Mid-Twentieth Century Britain', *History Workshop*, 47 (1999), 99–120.

——— *Modern Love: An Intimate History of Men and Women in Twentieth Century Britain* (London: Atlantic Books, 2003).

Conboy, M., *The Press and Popular Culture* (London: Sage, 2002).

——— *Tabloid Britain: Constructing a Community Through Language* (London: Routledge, 2006).

Conekin, B., Mort, F., and Waters, C. (eds.), *Moments of Modernity: Reconstructing Britain 1945–64* (London: Rivers Oram Press, 1999).

Cook, H., *The Long Sexual Revolution: English Women, Sex, and Contraception 1800–1975* (Oxford: Oxford University Press, 2004).

Coote, A. and Campbell, B., *Sweet Freedom, The Struggle for Women's Liberation* (London: Pan, 1982).

Craig, S., *Men, Masculinity and the Media* (Newbury Park, Calif.: Sage, 1992).

Crisell, A., *An Introductory History of British Broadcasting* (London: Routledge, 1997).

Critcher, C., *Moral Panics and the Media* (Buckingham: Open University Press, 2003).

Curran, J., 'The Impact of Advertising on the British Media', *Media, Culture and Society*, 3/1 (1981), 43–69.

——— Douglas, A. and Whannel, G., 'The Political Economy of the Human Interest Story', in A. Smith (ed.), *Newspapers and Democracy: International Essays on a Changing Medium* (Cambridge, Mass.: MIT Press, 1980).

——— and Scaton, J., *Power without Responsibility*, 5th edn. (London: Routledge, 1997).

——— Smith, A. and Wingate, P. (eds.), *Impacts and Influences: Essays on Media Power in the Twentieth Century* (London: Methuen, 1987).

Curtis Jr., L. P., *Jack the Ripper and the London Press* (New Haven: Yale University Press, 2001).

Daunton, M. and Reiger, B. (eds.), *Meanings of Modernity: Britain from the Late-Victorian Era to World War II* (Oxford: Berg, 2001).

Davenport-Hines, R., *Sex, Death and Punishment: Attitudes to Sex and Sexuality in Britain since the Renaissance* (London: Fontana, 1991).

Davey, C., 'Birth Control in Britain during the Interwar Years: Evidence from the Stopes Correspondence', *Journal of Family History*, 13/3 (1988).

David, H., *On Queer Street: A Social History of British Homosexuality 1895–1995* (London: HarperCollins, 1997).

Davidson R. and Davis, G., '"A Field for Private Members": The Wolfenden Committee and Scottish Homosexual Law Reform, 1950–67', *Twentieth Century British History*, 15/2 (2004), 174–201.

Davies, A., *Leisure, Gender and Poverty: Working-Class Culture in Salford and Manchester* (Buckingham: Open University Press, 1992).

Davies, K., Dickey, J., and Stratford, T. (eds.), *Out of Focus: Writings on Women and the Media* (London: Women's Press, 1987).

Doan, L., '"Acts of Female Indecency": Sexology's Intervention in Legislating Lesbianism', in L. Bland and L. Doan (eds.), *Sexology in Culture: Labelling Bodies and Desires* (Cambridge: Polity Press, 1998).

Dyer, G., *Advertising as Communication* (London: Methuen, 1982).

Dyer, R., *Stars* (London: BFI, 1979).

—— *Heavenly Bodies: Film Stars and Society* (Basingstoke: Macmillan, 1987).

Dyhouse, C., *Feminism and the Family in England 1880–1939* (Oxford: Basil Blackwell, 1989).

Edelman, M., *The Mirror: A Political History* (London: Hamish Hamilton, 1966).

Edwards, R., *Newspapermen: Hugh Cudlipp, Cecil Harmsworth King and the Glory Days of Fleet Street* (London: Secker & Warburg, 2003).

Emery, M., Emery, E., and Roberts, N., *The Press and America: An Interpretive History of the Mass Media*, 9th edn. (Boston: Allyn and Bacon, 2000).

Engel, M., *Tickle the Public: One Hundred Years of the Popular Press* (London: Indigo, 1997).

Ensor, R. C. K., 'The Press', in Sir Ernest Barker (ed.), *The Character of England* (Oxford: Clarendon Press, 1947).

Farrar, M., *News from the Front: War Correspondents on the Western Front* (Stroud: Sutton, 1998).

Ferguson, M., *Forever Feminine: Women's Magazines and the Cult of Femininity* (London: Heinemann, 1983).

Fink, J. and Holden, K., 'Pictures from the Margins of Marriage: Representations of Spinsters and Single Mothers in the Mid-Victorian Novel, Inter-War Hollywood Melodrama and British Film of the 1950s and 1960s', *Gender and History*, 11/2 (July 1999), 233–55.

Fisher, K., '"She was quite satisfied with the arrangements I made": Gender and Birth Control in Britain 1920–1950', *Past and Present*, 169 (2000), 161–93.

—— *Birth Control, Sex, and Marriage in Britain 1918–60* (Oxford: Oxford University Press, 2006).

—— and S. Szreter, '"They Prefer Withdrawal": The Choice of Birth Control in Britain, 1918–1950', *Journal of Interdisciplinary History*, 34/2 (2003), 263–91.

Foucault, M., *The Will to Knowledge: The History of Sexuality, Vol. 1*, trans. Robert Hurley (first pub. 1976; Harmondsworth: Penguin, 1990).

Fountain, N., *Underground: The London Alternative Press 1966–74* (London: Routledge, 1988).

Fowler, B., *The Alienated Reader: Women and Romantic Literature in the Twentieth Century* (Hemel Hempstead: Harvester Wheatsheaf, 1991).

Fowler, D., *The First Teenagers: The Life-Style of Young Wage-Earners in Inter-War Britain* (London: Woburn, 1995).

Fowler, R., *Language in the News: Discourse and Ideology in the Press* (London: Routledge, 1991).

Francis, M., 'The Domestication of the Male? Recent Research on Nineteenth and Twentieth-Century British Masculinity', *The Historical Journal*, 45/3 (2002), 637–52.

Fryer, P., *Staying Power: Black People in Britain since 1504* (London: Pluto, 1984).

Gabor, M., *The Pin-Up: A Modest History* (London: Pan, 1973),

Garnett, M. and Weight, R., *The A-Z Guide to Modern British History* (London: Jonathan Cape, 2003).

Gathorne-Hardy, J., *Alfred C. Kinsey: Sex The Measure of All Things—A Biography* (London: Pimlico, 1999).

Giddens, A., *The Transformation of Intimacy: Sexuality, Love and Eroticism in Modern Societies* (Cambridge: Polity Press, 1992).

Giles, J., *Women, Identity and Private Life in Britain 1900–50* (Basingstoke: Macmillan, 1995).

Gittins, D., *Fair Sex: Family Size and Structure, 1900–39* (London: Hutchinson, 1982).

Gledhill, C. and Swanson, G. (eds.), *Nationalising Femininity: Culture, Sexuality and Cinema in Britain in World War Two* (Manchester: Manchester University Press, 1996).

Goodman, N., *Wilson Jameson* (London: George Allen & Unwin, 1970).

Gordon, P. and Rosenberg, D., *Daily Racism: The Press and Black People in Britain* (London: Runnymede Trust, 1989).

Green, J., *All Dressed Up: The Sixties and the Counterculture* (London: Pimlico, 1999).

Greenfield, J. and Reid, C., 'Women's Magazines and the Commercial Orchestration of Femininity in the 1930s: Evidence from *Woman's Own*', *Media History*, 4/2 (Dec. 1998), 161–74.

—— O'Connell, S., and Reid, C., 'Fashioning Masculinity: *Men Only*, Consumption and the Development of Marketing in the 1930s', *Twentieth Century British History*, 10/4 (1999), 457–76.

Greenslade, R., *Press Gang: How Newspapers Make Profits from Propaganda* (London: Macmillan, 2003).

Greer, G., *The Female Eunuch* (London: Paladin, 1971).

Grey, A., *Quest for Justice* (London: Sinclair-Stevenson, 1992).

Griffiths, D. (ed.), *The Encyclopedia of the British Press 1422–1992* (London: Macmillan, 1992).

Gunter, B., *Media Sex: What Are The Issues?* (Mahwah: Lawrence Erlbaum Associates, 2002).

Habermas, J., *The Structural Transformation of the Public Sphere: An Inquiry into a Category of Bourgeois Society*, trans. T. Burger (Cambridge: Polity, 1989).

Hagerty, B., *Read All About It! 100 Sensational Years of the Daily Mirror* (Lydney, Glos.: First Stone, 2003).

Hall, L., *Sex, Gender and Social Change in Britain since 1880* (Basingstoke: Macmillan, 2000).

——'Birds, Bees and General Embarrassment: Sex Education in Britain, From Social Purity To Section 28', in R. Aldrich (ed.), *Public or Private Education? Lessons From History* (London: Woburn Press, 2004).

Hall, S., Critcher, C., Jefferson, T., Clarke, J., and Roberts, B., *Policing the Crisis: Mugging, the State, and Law and Order* (London: Macmillan, 1978).

Halsey, A. H. (ed.), *British Social Trends Since 1900* (Basingstoke: Macmillan, 1988).

Hamer, E., *Britannia's Glory: A History of Twentieth-Century Lesbians* (London: Cassell, 1996).

Hampshire, J. and Lewis, J., '"The Ravages of Permissiveness": Sex Education and the Permissive Society', *Twentieth Century British History*, 15/3 (2004), 290–312.

Hampton, M., *Visions of the Press in Britain, 1850–1950* (Urbana: University of Illinois Press, 2004).

Harrison, B., *Prudent Revolutionaries* (Oxford: Clarendon Press, 1987).

Haste, C., *Rules of Desire: Sex in Britain, World War 1 to the Present* (London: Pimlico, 1994).

Hawkins, G. and Zimring, F., *Pornography in a Free Society* (Cambridge: Cambridge University Press, 1991).

Higgins, P., *Heterosexual Dictatorship: Male Homosexuality in Postwar Britain* (London: Fourth Estate, 1996).

Hill, J., *Sex, Class and Realism: British Cinema, 1956–63* (London: BFI, 1986).

Hoggart, R., *The Uses of Literacy* (first pub. 1957; London: Penguin, 1962).

Holland, P., 'The Page Three Girl Speaks to Women, Too: A Sun-Sational Survey', *Screen*, 24/3 (1983), 84–102.

——'The Politics of the Smile: "Soft News" and the Sexualisation of the Popular Press', in C. Carter, G. Branston, and S. Allan (eds.), *News, Gender and Power* (London: Routledge, 1998).

Holmes, C., *John Bull's Island: Immigration and British Society 1881–1981* (Basingstoke: Macmillan, 1988).

Horwood, C., '"Girls Who Arouse Dangerous Passions": Women and Bathing 1900–39', *Women's History Review*, 9/4 (2000), 653–73.

Houlbrook, M., '"Lady Austin's Camp Boys": Constituting the Queer Subject in 1930s London', *Gender and History*, 14/1 (2002), 21–61.

——*Queer London: Perils and Pleasures in the Sexual Metropolis* (Chicago: University of Chicago Press, 2005).

Howes, K., *Broadcasting It: An Encyclopaedia of Homosexuality on Film, Radio and TV in the UK 1923–1993* (London: Cassells, 1993).

Hubback, D., *No Ordinary Press Baron: A life of Walter Layton* (London: Weidenfeld & Nicolson, 1985).

Hubble, N., *Mass Observation and Everyday Life: Culture, History and Theory* (Basingstoke: Palgrave Macmillan, 2006).

Humble, N., *The Feminine Middlebrow Novel 1920s to 1950s: Class, Domesticity, and Bohemianism* (Oxford: Oxford University Press, 2001).

Humphries, A., 'Coming Apart: The British Newspaper Press and the Divorce Court', in L. Brake, B. Bell, and D. Finkelstein (eds.), *Nineteenth-Century Media and the Construction of Identities* (Basingstoke: Macmillan, 2000).

Humphries, S., *A Secret World of Sex—Forbidden Fruit: The British Experience 1900–1950* (London: Sidgwick & Jackson, 1988).

—— and Gordon, P., *A Man's World: From Boyhood to Manhood 1900–60* (London: BBC Books, 1996).

Husband, C. (ed.), *White Media & Black Britain: A Critical Look at the Role of the Media In Race Relations Today* (London: Arrow, 1975).

Hyde, H. M., *The Other Love: An Historical and Contemporary Survey of Homosexuality in Britain* (London: Heinemann, 1970).

Hynes, S., *A War Imagined: The First World War and English Culture* (London: Bodley Head, 1990).

Jackson, K., *George Newnes and the New Journalism in Britain, 1880–1910: Culture and Profit* (Aldershot: Ashgate, 2001).

James, R. R., *Bob Boothby: A Portrait* (London: Hodder & Stoughton, 1981).

Jeffery, T. and McClelland, K., 'A World Fit to Live In: The *Daily Mail* and the Middle Classes 1918–39', in J. Curran, A. Smith, and P. Wingate (eds.), *Impacts and Influences: Essays on Media Power in the Twentieth Century* (London: Methuen, 1987).

Jeffery-Poulter, S., *Peers, Queers and Commons: The Struggle for Gay Law Reform from 1950 to the Present* (London: Routledge, 1991).

Jeffreys, S., *The Spinster and her Enemies: Feminism and Sexuality 1880–1930* (London: Pandora, 1985).

Johnson, C. and Turnock, R. (eds.), *ITV Cultures: Independent Television over Fifty Years* (Maidenhead: Open University Press, 2005).

Johnson, D., *The Lavender Scare: The Cold War Persecution of Gays and Lesbians in the Federal Government* (Chicago: University of Chicago Press, 2004).

Jones, A., *Powers of the Press: Newspapers, Power and the Public in Nineteenth Century England* (Aldershot: Scolar, 1996).

Kemp, S. and Squires, J. (eds.), *Feminisms* (Oxford: Oxford University Press, 1997).

Kent, 'Matt Morgan and Transatlantic Illustrated Journalism, 1850–1890', in J. Wiener and M. Hampton (eds.), *Anglo-American Media Interactions, 1850–2000* (Basingstoke Palgrave Macmillan, 2007).

Kent, R., *Agony: Problem Pages Through The Ages* (London: Star, 1987).

Kent, S. K., *Making Peace: The Reconstruction of Gender in Inter-War Britain* (Princeton: Princeton University Press, 1993).

—— *Gender and Power in Britain 1640–1990* (London: Routledge, 1999).

Kohn, M., *Dope Girls: The Birth of the British Drugs Underground* (London: Lawrence & Wishart, 1992).

Koss, S., *Fleet Street Radical: A. G. Gardiner and the Daily News* (London: Allen Lane, 1973).

—— *The Rise and Fall of the Political Press, Vol. 1, The Nineteenth Century* (London: Hamish Hamilton, 1981).

—— *The Rise and Fall of the Political Press, Vol. 2, The Twentieth Century* (London: Hamish Hamilton, 1984).

Langhamer, C., *Women's Leisure in England, 1920–1960* (Manchester: Manchester University Press, 2000).

Lawton, J., *1963: Five Hundred Days* (London: Hodder & Stoughton, 1992).

Lazarsfeld P. and Merton R., 'Mass Communication, Popular Taste and Organized Social Action', in L. Bryson (ed.), *The Communication of Ideas* (New York: Harper & Bros., 1948), reprinted in P. Marris and S. Thornham (eds.), *Media Studies: A Reader*, 2nd edn. (Edinburgh: Edinburgh University Press, 1999), 18–30.

Lee, A. J., *The Origins of the Popular Press in England 1855–1914* (London: Croom Helm, 1976).

LeMahieu, D., *A Culture for Democracy: Mass Communication and the Cultivated Mind in Britain between the Wars* (Oxford: Clarendon Press, 1988).

Levine, P., ' "Walking the Streets in a Way No Decent Woman Should": Women Police in World War 1', *Journal of Modern History*, 66/1 (1994), 34–79.

——*Prostitution, Race and Politics: Policing Venereal Disease in the British Empire* (New York: Routledge, 2003).

Lewis, J. (ed.), *Labour and Love: Women's Experience of Home and Family 1850–1940* (Oxford: Basil Blackwell, 1986).

——'Public Institution and Private Relationship: Marriage and Marriage Guidance, 1920–68', *Twentieth Century British History*, 1/3 (1990), 233–63.

Light, A., *Forever England: Femininity, Literature and Conservatism between the Wars* (London: Routledge, 1991).

Linton, D., *The Twentieth Century Newspaper Press in Britain: An Annotated Bibliography* (London: Mansell, 1994).

Loncraine, R., 'Bosom of the Nation: Page Three in the 1970s and 1980s', in M. Gorji (ed.), *Rude Britannia* (Abingdon: Routledge, 2007).

McAleer, J., *Popular Reading and Publishing in Britain, 1914–50* (Oxford: Clarendon Press, 1992).

——*Passion's Fortune: The Story of Mills and Boon* (Oxford: Oxford University Press, 1999).

McDonald, I., *The History of the Times, Volume V: Struggles in War and Peace 1939–66* (London: Times Books, 1984).

McDonnell, J., *Public Service Broadcasting: A Reader* (London: Routledge, 1991).

McGillivray, D., *Doing Rude Things: The History of the British Sex Film, 1957–81* (London: Sun Tavern Fields, 1992).

McKibbin, R., *Classes and Cultures: England 1918–1951* (Oxford: Oxford University Press, 1998).

McLaren, A., *The Trials of Manhood: Policing Sexual Boundaries 1870–1930* (Chicago: University of Chicago Press, 1997).

McNair, B., *Mediated Sex: Pornography and Postmodern Culture* (London: Arnold, 1996).

Mandler, P., 'The Problem with Cultural History', *Cultural and Social History*, 1/1 (2004), 94–117.

Marris, P. and Thornham, S. (eds.), *Media Studies: A Reader*, 2nd edn. (Edinburgh: Edinburgh University Press, 1999).

Mason, M., *The Making of Victorian Sexuality* (Oxford: Oxford University Press, 1994).

Matthews, J. J., '"They had such a lot of fun": The Women's League of Health and Beauty between the Wars', *History Workshop Journal*, 30 (1990), 22–54.

Matthews, T. S., *The Sugar Pill: An Essay on Newspapers* (London: Victor Gollancz, 1957).

Melman, B., *Women and the Popular Imagination in the Twenties: Flappers and Nymphs* (Basingstoke: Macmillan, 1988).

Meyerowitz, J., 'Women, Cheesecake, and Borderline Material: Responses to Girlie Pictures in the Mid-Twentieth-Century US', *Journal of Women's History*, 8/3 (1996), 9–35.

Millett, K., *Sexual Politics* (New York: Doubleday, 1970).

Minney, R. J., *Viscount Southwood* (London: Odhams Press, 1954).

Mort, F., 'Mapping Sexual London: The Wolfenden Committee on Homosexual Offences and Prostitution: 1954–7', *New Formations*, no. 37 (1999), 92–113.

—— *Dangerous Sexualities: Medico-Moral Politics in England Since 1830*, 2nd edn. (London: Routledge, 2000).

Nead, L., *The Female Nude: Art, Obscenity and Sexuality* (London: Routledge, 1992).

Negrine, R., *Politics and the Mass Media in Britain*, 2nd edn. (London: Routledge, 1994).

Newburn, T., *Permission and Regulation: Laws and Morals in Post-War Britain* (London: Routledge, 1992).

Nicholas, S., *The Echo of War: Home Front Propaganda and the Wartime BBC, 1939–45* (Manchester: Manchester University Press, 1996).

—— 'From John Bull to John Citizen: Images of National Identity and Citizenship on the Wartime BBC', in R. Weight and A. Beach (eds.), *The Right to Belong: Citizenship and National Identity in Britain 1930–1960* (London: I. B. Tauris, 1998).

O'Malley, T. and Soley, C., *Regulating the Press* (London: Pluto Press, 2000).

Oram, A., 'Repressed and Thwarted, or Bearer of the New World? The Spinster in Inter-War Feminist Discourses', *Women's History Review*, 1/3 (1992), 413–34.

—— *Her Husband Was a Woman! Women's Gender-Crossing and Twentieth Century British Popular Culture* (London: Routledge, 2007).

—— and Turnbull, A. (eds.), *The Lesbian History Sourcebook* (London: Routledge, 2001).

Panayi, P., *The Impact of Immigration: A Documentary History of the Effects and Experiences of Immigrants in Britain since 1945* (Manchester: Manchester University Press, 1999).

Patmore, A., *Marge: The Guilt and the Gingerbread: The Authorized Biography* (London: Warner, 1993).

Pearce, F., 'The British Press and the "Placing" of Male Homosexuality', in S. Cohen and J. Young (eds.), *The Manufacture of News: Social Problems, Deviance and the Mass Media* (rev. edn., London: Constable, 1981), 303–16.

Peiss, K., 'Making Up, Making Over: Cosmetics, Consumer Culture and Women's Identity', in V. de Grazia and E. Furlough, *The Sex of Things* (Berkeley: University of California Press, 1996).

Phillips M. and Phillips, T., *Windrush: The Irresistible Rise of Multi-Racial Britain* (London: HarperCollins, 1998).

Plunkett, J., *Queen Victoria: First Media Monarch* (Oxford: Oxford University Press, 2003).

Porter, R. and Hall, L., *The Facts of Life: The Creation of Sexual Knowledge in Britain 1650–1950* (New Haven: Yale University Press, 1995).

Pound, R. and Harmsworth, G., *Northcliffe* (London: Cassell, 1959).

Pronay, N. and Spring, D. (eds.), *Propaganda, Politics and Film, 1918–45* (London: Macmillan, 1982).

Pugh, M., *Women and the Women's Movement in Britain 1914–59* (Basingstoke, Macmillan, 1992).

—— 'The *Daily Mirror* and the Revival of Labour 1935–45', *Twentieth Century British History*, 9/3 (1998), 420–38.

—— *'We Danced All Night': A Social History of Britain Between the Wars* (London: Bodley Head, 2008).

Pumphrey, M., 'The Flapper, the Housewife and the Making of Modernity', *Cultural Studies*, 1/2 (1987), 179–94.

Purvis, J. (ed.), *Women's History in Britain, 1870–1945* (London: UCL Press, 1995).

Rapp, R. and Ross, E., 'The 1920s: Feminism, Consumerism, and Political Backlash in the United States', in J. Friedlander, B. Wiesen Cook, A. Kessler-Harris, and C. Smith-Rosenburg (eds.), *Women in Culture and Politics* (Bloomington: Indiana University Press, 1986), 52–61.

Reed, D., *The Popular Magazine in Britain and the United States 1880–1960* (London: The British Library, 1997).

Reinders, R., 'Racialism on the Left: E. D. Morel and the "Black Horror on the Rhine"', *International Review of Social History* 13 (1968), 1–28.

Reynolds, D., *Rich Relations: The American Occupation of Britain, 1942–45* (London: HarperCollins, 1996).

Richards, H., *The Bloody Circus: The Daily Herald and the Left* (London: Pluto Press, 1997).

Richards, J., *The Age of the Dream Palace: Cinema and Society in Britain 1930–1939* (London: Routledge & Kegan Paul, 1984).

Robb, G. and Erber, N. (eds.), *Disorder in the Court: Trials and Sexual Conflict at the Turn of the Century* (Basingstoke: Macmillan, 1999).

Roberts, E., *A Woman's Place: An Oral History of Working-Class Women 1890–1940* (Oxford: Blackwell, 1984).

Robertson, J., *The British Board of Film Censors: Film Censorship in Britain, 1896–1950* (Beckenham: Croom Helm, 1985).

Robertson, R., *People Against the Press: An Enquiry into the Press Council* (London: Quartet Books, 1983).

Rojek, C., *Celebrity* (London: Reaktion Books, 2001).

Roper, M. and Tosh, J., *Manful Assertions: Masculinities in Britain since 1800* (London: Routledge, 1991).

Rose, J., *The Intellectual Life of the British Working Classes* (New Haven: Yale University Press, 2001).

Rose, J., *Marie Stopes and the Sexual Revolution* (London: Faber and Faber, 1992).

Rose, S., 'Sex, Citizenship, and the Nation in World War II Britain', *American Historical Review*, 103/4 (1998), 1147–76.

—— *Which People's War? National Identity and Citizenship in Wartime Britain 1939–1945* (Oxford: Oxford University Press, 2003).

Rosen, M., *Popcorn Venus: Women, Movies and the American Dream* (New York: Coward, McCann, and Geoghegan, 1973).

Rowbotham, S., *A Century of Women: The History of Women in Britain and the United States* (London: Viking, 1997).

Saunders, A., *Jane: A Pin-up at War* (Barnsley: Leo Cooper, 2004).

Savage, G., 'Erotic Stories and Public Decency: Newspaper Reporting of Divorce Proceedings in England', *The Historical Journal*, 41/2 (1998), 511–28.

Schults, R., *Crusader in Babylon: W. T. Stead and the Pall Mall Gazette* (Lincoln: University of Nebraska Press, 1972).

Schwarz, B., 'Black Metropolis, White England' in M. Nava and A. O'Shea (eds.), *Modern Times: Reflections on A Century of English Modernity* (London: Routledge, 1996).

Scott, J. (ed.), *Feminism and History* (Oxford: Oxford University Press, 1996).

Seymour, D. and Seymour, E. (eds.), *A Century of News: A Journey Through History with the Daily Mirror* (London: Contender Books, 2003),

Seymour-Ure, C., 'The Press and the Party System between the Wars', in G. Peele and C. Cook (eds.), *The Politics Of Reappraisal* (London: Macmillan, 1975).

—— *The British Press and Broadcasting since 1945*, 2nd edn. (Oxford: Blackwell, 1996).

Shawcross, W., *Murdoch* (London: Simon and Schuster, 1993).

Short, C., *Dear Clare . . . . . . this is what women feel about Page 3*, letters edited and selected by K. Tunks and D. Hutchinson (London: Radius, 1991).

Sinfield, A., *The Wilde Century: Effeminacy, Oscar Wilde and the Queer Moment* (London: Cassell, 1994).

Slater E. and Woodside, M., *Patterns of Marriage: A Study of Marriage Relationships in the Urban Working Classes* (London: Cassell and Company Ltd., 1951).

Sloan, B., *'I Watched a Wild Hog Eat my Baby!' A Colorful History of Tabloids and Their Cultural Impact* (New York: Prometheus Books, 2001).

Smith, A. (ed.), *The British Press since the War* (Newton Abbot: David and Charles, 1974).

Smith, A. C. H., with Immirizi, E., and Blackwell, T., *Paper Voices: The Popular Press and Social Change 1935–65* (London: Chatto & Windus, 1975).

Soland, B., *Becoming Modern: Young Women and the Reconstruction of Womanhood in the 1920s* (Princeton: Princeton University Press, 2000).

Soloway, R., *Birth Control and the Population Question in England, 1877–1930* (Chapel Hill: University of California Press, 1982).

Soothill, K. and Walby, S., *Sex Crime in the News* (London: Routledge, 1991).

Souhami, D., *The Trials of Radclyffe Hall* (London: Virago, 1999).

Stacey, J., *Stargazing: Hollywood Cinema and Female Spectatorship* (London: Routledge, 1994).

Stanley, L., *Sex Surveyed, 1949–1994: From Mass Observation's 'Little Kinsey' to the National Survey and the Hite Reports* (London: Taylor & Francis, 1995).

Stephenson, H. and Bromley, M. (eds.), *Sex, Lies and Democracy: The Press and the Public* (London: Longman, 1998).

Stott, M., *Forgetting's No Excuse: The Autobiography of Mary Stott* (London: Faber, 1973).

Street, S., *British National Cinema* (London: Routledge, 1997).

Summerfield, P., *Reconstructing Women's Wartime Lives: Discourse and Subjectivity in Oral Histories of the Second World War* (Manchester: Manchester University Press, 1998).

Summers A. and Dorril, S., *Honeytrap* (London: Coronet, 1988).

Sutherland, J., *Offensive Literature: Decensorship in Britain 1960–1982* (London: Junction Books, 1982).

Szreter, S., *Fertility, Class and Gender 1860–1940* (Cambridge: Cambridge University Press, 1996).

—— 'Victorian Britain, 1837–1963: Towards a Social History of Sexuality', *Journal of Victorian Culture*, 1/1 (Spring 1996) 136–47.

Taylor, A. J. P., *Beaverbrook* (London: Hamilton, 1972).

Taylor, S. J., *The Great Outsiders: Northcliffe, Rothermere and The Daily Mail* (London: Weidenfeld & Nicolson, 1996).

—— *The Reluctant Press Lord: Esmond Rothermere and The Daily Mail* (London: Weidenfeld & Nicolson, 1998).

Thane, P., 'What Difference Did the Vote Make?', in A. Vickery (ed.), *Women, Privilege and Power: British Politics, 1750 to the Present* (Stanford: Stanford University Press, 2001).

—— 'Population Politics in Post-War British Culture', in C. Conekin, F. Mort, and C. Waters (eds.), *Moments of Modernity: Reconstructing Britain 1945–64* (London: Rivers Oram Press, 1999).

Thesander, M., *The Feminine Ideal* (London: Reaktion Books, 1997).

Thompson, J. Lee, *Northcliffe: Press Baron in Politics 1865–1922* (London: John Murray, 2000).

Thompson, P., 'Labour's "Gannex Conscience"? Politics and Popular Attitudes in the "Permissive Society"', in R. Coopey, S. Fielding, and N. Tiratsoo (eds.), *The Wilson Governments 1964–1970* (London: Pinter Publishers, 1993).

Tinkler, P., *Constructing Girlhood: Popular Magazines for Girls Growing Up in England 1920–1950* (London: Taylor & Francis, 1995).

Tosh, J., *A Man's Place: Masculinity and the Middle-Class Home in Victorian England* (New Haven: Yale University Press, 1999).

Travis, A., *Bound and Gagged: A Secret History of Obscenity in Britain* (London: Profile, 2000).

Tunstall, J., *The Media in Britain* (London: Constable, 1983).

—— *Newspaper Power: The New National Press in Britain* (Oxford: Clarendon Press, 1996).

Turner, G., *Understanding Celebrity* (London: Sage, 2004).

Upchurch, C., 'Forgetting the Unthinkable: Cross-Dressers and British Society in the Case of Queen vs. Boulton and Others', *Gender and History*, 12/1 (2000), 127–57.

Van Zoonen, L., *Feminist Media Studies* (London: Sage, 1994).

Vernon, J., '"For Some Queer Reason": The Trials and Tribulations of Colonel Barker's Masquerade in Interwar Britain', *Signs*, 26/1 (2000), 37–62.

Vicinus, M., 'Lesbian Perversity and Victorian Marriage: The 1864 Codrington Divorce Trial', *The Journal of British Studies*, 36/1 (1997), 70–98.

Wadsworth, A. P., 'Newspaper Circulations 1800–1954', *Transactions of the Manchester Statistical Society*, Session 1954–55 (1955).

Walkowitz, J., *Prostitution and Victorian Society* (Cambridge: Cambridge University Press, 1980).

—— *City of Dreadful Delight: Narratives of Sexual Danger In Late Victorian London* (Chicago: University of Chicago Press, 1992).

Walter, A. (ed.), *Come Together: The Years of Gay Liberation 1970–73* (London: Gay Men's Press, 1980).

Wandor, M., *Once A Feminist: Stories of a Generation* (London: Virago, 1990).

Waters, C., '"Dark Strangers" in our Midst: Discourse of Race and Nation in Britain, 1947–63', *Journal of British Studies*, 36 (1997), 207–38.

—— 'Havelock Ellis, Sigmund Freud and the State: Discourses of Homosexual Identity in Interwar Britain', in L. Bland and L. Doan (eds.), *Sexology in Culture: Labelling Bodies and Desires* (Cambridge: Polity Press, 1998).

—— 'Disorders of the Mind, Disorders of the Body Social: Peter Wildeblood and the Making of the Modern Homosexual', in B. Conekin, F. Mort, and C. Waters (eds.), *Moments of Modernity: Reconstructing Britain 1945–1964* (London: Rivers Oram Press, 1999).

Watson, J. and Hill, A., *Dictionary of Media and Communication Studies*, 5th edn. (London: Arnold, 2000).

Webster, W., *Englishness and Empire 1939–1965* (Oxford: Oxford University Press, 2005).

Weeks, J., *Sex, Politics and Society: The Regulation of Sexuality since 1800* (London: Longman, 1981).

—— *Coming Out: Homosexual Politics in Britain from the Nineteenth Century to the Present*, rev. edn. (London: Quartet Books, 1990).

Wellings, K., 'Help or Hype: An Analysis of Media Coverage of the 1983 "Pill Scare"', *British Journal of Family Planning*, 12 (1986), 92–8.

White, C., *Women's Magazines 1693–1968* (London: Michael Joseph, 1970).

Wiener. J. (ed.), *Papers For The Millions: The New Journalism in Britain, 1850s to 1914* (New York: Greenwood, 1988).

—— and M. Hampton (eds.), *Anglo-American Media Interactions, 1850–2000* (Basingstoke: Palgrave Macmillan, 2007).

Wilkes, R., *Scandal: A Scurrilous History of Gossip* (London: Atlantic Books, 2003).

Williams, F., *Dangerous Estate: The Anatomy of Newspapers* (first pub. 1957; London: Longmans, Green, 1958).

Williams, K., *British Writers and the Media 1930–45* (Basingstoke: Macmillan, 1996).

Williams, R., *The Long Revolution* (Harmondsworth: Penguin, 1965).

Williams, S., *The People's King: The True Story of the Abdication* (London: Allen Lane, 2003).

Wilmott, P. and Young, M., *Family and Kinship in East London* (first pub. 1957; Harmondsworth: Penguin, 1986).

Wilson, E., *Adorned in Dreams: Fashion and Modernity* (London: Virago, 1985).

Winship, J., *Inside Women's Magazines* (London: Pandora, 1987).

Wolf, N., *The Beauty Myth: How Images of Beauty Are Used Against Women* (London: Chatto & Windus, 1990).

Woollacott, A., 'Khaki Fever and its Control: Gender, Class, Age and Sexual Morality on the British Homefront in World War 1', *Journal of Contemporary History*, 29/2 (1994), 325–47.

Ziegler, P., *Edward VIII: The Official Biography* (London: Collins, 1990).

Zweiniger-Bargielowska, I. (ed.), *Women in Twentieth Century Britain* (Harlow: Longman, 2001).

Index